Con-cs   5⁰⁰

S0-ACD-616

HENRY JAMES

SELECTED LITERARY
CRITICISM

HENRY JAMES

SELECTED LITERARY CRITICISM

★

EDITED BY

MORRIS SHAPIRA

PREFACED WITH

A NOTE ON "JAMES AS CRITIC" BY

F. R. LEAVIS

CAMBRIDGE UNIVERSITY PRESS

CAMBRIDGE
LONDON NEW YORK NEW ROCHELLE
MELBOURNE SYDNEY

Published by the Press Syndicate of the University of Cambridge
The Pitt Building, Trumpington Street, Cambridge CB2 1RP
32 East 57th Street, New York, NY 10022, USA
296 Beaconsfield Parade, Middle Park, Melbourne 3206, Australia

Introduction © F. R. Leavis 1963
Introduction © Mrs Q. D. Leavis 1978

First published by Heinemann Educational Books Ltd 1963
This paperback edition first published by the
Cambridge University Press 1981

First printed in Great Britain by
Butler and Tanner Ltd, Frome and London
Reprinted in Great Britain at the
University Press, Cambridge

British Library Cataloguing in Publication Data
James, Henry
Selected literary criticism.
1. Literature, Modern – Addresses, essays, lectures
I. Shapira, Morris
809'.03'4   PN710   80–49685
ISBN 0 521 28365 5

To
Downing College
and the functioning of criticism
in the present time

CONTENTS

EDITOR'S NOTE

DR. LEAVIS' essay was originally a lecture delivered to under-graduates reading for the English Tripos. Because it is so much addressed to its original audience, he was reluctant to allow it to be printed as an introduction to a book intended for the general reader. The professional intention, however, gives a professional intensity and thoroughness to the de-academizing of the study—the reading—of criticism. It is an introduction to what is lively in James's criticism so it isn't parochial in its effect. I am very grateful to Dr. Leavis.

Dedicating somebody else's essays is impudence; I hope, though, that James would have forgiven my dedicating his to Downing College. The education that it has used its "immense academic privilege" to foster might have been inspired by the implied ideal of the London Note printed on Pages 176–179—the ideal implied by James's dismay at Oxford classicism. The dedication is an attempt to express the gratitude of all those who have had the privilege of an education so upsetting to one's desire for "prescribed lines" and that has given one so much to think about and test as experience grows and changes. It is grati-tude too for intellectual society in which there was the community of interest to provoke and sustain liveliness and radicalness of discussion. My own special gratitude is for the Research Fellowship that gave me the time to re-read all James's criticism in order to make this selection.

This volume is also a symbolic repayment of the generosity of the American Government which, under the provisions of the Smith-Mundt Act, allowed me to spend a year at Harvard University, doing the initial work for this book. The other thanks I must express are to Mr. Francis Moran for doing the proof reading and to Mr. John Newton, Mr. Geoffrey Strickland, Mr. Norman Henfrey, and Mr. H. A. Mason for their questioning the essays selected.

All the essays, except the one on *The Tempest*, have been included on the grounds that they represent James at his strongest. May I recom-mend to the reader who would like to explore further *French Poets and Novelists* and *Notes on Novelists* as well as the *Hawthorne* in the English Men of Letters Series. (It is reprinted by Edmund Wilson in his *The Shock of Recognition*.) In *French Poets and Novelists* the two essays on Balzac and the one on Mérimée are particularly worthwhile. And

ix

for the reader who would like to explore still further there are the mostly young essays collected by Mr. Albert Mordell in a paperback *Literary Reviews and Essays by Henry James*. The reader of some of those might well agree with James's contemporaries that the young James is much more strikingly intelligent, unconventional and right as a critic than as a writer of fiction.

James made four collections of his literary criticism

> *French Poets and Novelists* (*FP and N*) 1878
> *Partial Portraits* (*PP*) 1888
> *Essays in London and Elsewhere* (*E in L and E*) 1893
> *Notes on Novelists* (*N on N*) 1914

The essays in this book come from the following:

Mr. Walt Whitman: *The Nation* I (16 November, 1865), 625–626

Our Mutual Friend: *The Nation* I (21 November, 1865), 786–787

The Belton Estate: *The Nation* II (4 January, 1866), 21–22

Taine's English Literature: *Atlantic Monthly* XXIX (April 1872), 469–472

Swinburne's Essays: *The Nation* XXI (29 July, 1875), 73–74

Charles Baudelaire: *The Nation* XXII (27 April, 1876), 279–281. Reprinted in *FP and N*, 1878

Daniel Deronda: A Conversation: *Atlantic Monthly* XXXVIII (December 1876), 684–694. Reprinted in *PP*, 1888

The Art of Fiction: *Longman's Magazine* IV (September 1884), 502–521. Reprinted in *PP*, 1888

Emerson: *Macmillan's Magazine* LVII (December 1887), 86–98. Reprinted in *PP*, 1888

Guy de Maupassant: *Fortnightly Review* XLIX (March 1888), 364–386. Reprinted in *PP*, 1888

The Journal of the Brothers de Goncourt: *Fortnightly Review* L (October 1888), 501–520. Reprinted in *E in L and E*, 1893

Criticism: *New Review* IV (May 1891), 398–402. Reprinted in *E in L and E*, 1893

Gustave Flaubert: *Macmillan's Magazine* LXVII (March 1893), 332–343. Reprinted in *E in L and E*, 1893

George Sand: *Yellow Book* XII (January 1897) 15–38. Reprinted in *N on N*, 1914

London Notes: *Harper's Weekly* XLI (26 June, 1897) 639–640. Reprinted in *N on N*, 1914

London Notes: *Harper's Weekly* XLI (21 August, 1897) 834. Reprinted in *N on N*, 1914

The Future of the Novel: *The International Library of Famous Literature*, edited by Dr. Richard Garnett. 1899. Vol XIV. xi–xxii

Honoré de Balzac: *The Two Young Brides* by Honoré de Balzac 1902. v–xliii.
    Reprinted in *N on N*, 1914
Gustave Flaubert: *Madame Bovary* by Gustave Flaubert 1902. v–xliii. Re-
    printed in *N on N*, 1914
Emile Zola: *Atlantic Monthly* XCII (August 1903), 193–210. Reprinted in
    N on N, 1914
D' Annunzio: *Quarterly Review* CXCIX (April 1904), 383–419. Reprinted in
    N on N, 1914
The Tempest: *The Complete Works of William Shakespeare*, edited by Sidney
    Lee. Vol. XVI. ix–xxxii. 1907
The New Novel: *The Times Literary Supplement* No. 635 (19 March, 1914), 133–
                                        134
                        No. 637 (2 April, 1914), 157–
                                        158
    Reprinted, revised and enlarged in *N on N*, 1914

Where James revised or altered his essays on republication, I have
used the later version.

MORRIS SHAPIRA

THE effect, if not the prime office, of criticism is to make our absorption and our enjoyment of the things that feed the mind as aware of itself as possible, since that awareness quickens the mental demand, which thus in turn wanders further and further for pasture. This action on the part of the mind practically amounts to a reaching out for the reasons of its interests, as only by its so ascertaining them can the interest grow more various. This is the very education of our imaginative life; and thanks to it the general question of how to refine, and of why certain things refine more and most, on that happy consciousness becomes for us of the last importance. Then we cease to be only instinctive and at the mercy of chance, feeling that we can ourselves take a hand in our satisfaction and provide for it, making ourselves safe against dearth, and through the door opened by that perception criticism enters, if we but give it time, as a flood, the great flood of awareness; so maintaining its high tide unless through some lapse of our sense for it, some flat reversion to instinct alone, we block up the ingress and sit in stale and shrinking waters.

Henry James: "The New Novel, 1914"

IN every great novel, who is the hero all the time? Not any of the characters, but some unnamed and nameless flame behind them all.

D. H. Lawrence: "The Novel", *Reflections on the Death of a Porcupine, and other essays*

MANY of the books which now croud the world, may be justly suspected to be written for the sake of some invisible order of beings, for surely they are of no use to any of the corporeal inhabitants of the world. Of the productions of the last bounteous year, how many can be said to serve any purpose of use or pleasure? The only end of writing is to enable the readers better to enjoy life, or better to endure it.

Samuel Johnson: Review of *A Free Enquiry into the Nature and Origin of Evil*

JAMES AS CRITIC

F. R. LEAVIS

HENRY JAMES the critic has in recent years attained to something of classical standing. He even figures academically as prescribed reading for students of "English" who are to take papers on Literary Criticism. It doesn't of course follow that this acceptance carries with it any just recognition of his strength and his limitations—of the qualities that make him worth study. In fact, there is an irony attending his acceptance as a distinguished critic that corresponds to the irony attending his recognized status among the great novelists. It is a characteristic of the age when "English" has conquered Classics in the field of humane education, and an industry of specialized addiction on the part of academics to this and that modern author is acquiring an American aspect and scale in our universities, that the established "appreciation" of the favoured authors should not uncommonly be conventional—flagrantly conventional, and not at all conducive to optimism in genuine admirers of the given author.

Thus, when there is question of James as critic, it is generally assumed that the Prefaces give us him at his most impressive and valuable, and that in the volume of the collected Prefaces we have a major critical classic. Yet few have read any considerable proportion of that volume, and very few indeed of those who have made pertinacious attempts to read it have brought much of value away. For the fact is, not only that it requires a great effort, but that the effort is not repaying. Those academics who take seriously the suggestion that it is the "novelist's *vade-mecum*" [1] will indeed be drawing from it a new academicism, for that is what the attempt to establish a general interest and validity in it must yield. And one can only deplore any offer to deaden the under-graduate reading English with such a misdirection and such a *corvée*.

The preface the undergraduate might profitably be told to read, along with the novel itself, that to *Roderick Hudson*, is not commonly singled out for attention. Its examination of that strikingly promising early work is immediately intelligible and critically enlightening. The main point it makes explains—with a general critical profit for the reading of James—why the obvious weaknesses of the novel, the

---

[1] Henry James: Letters to W. D. Howells, 17 August, 1908.

impossibility of making the postulated artistic genius anything but a postulate and the too rapid disintegrative effect on Roderick of the *femme fatale*, don't prevent *Roderick Hudson's* being a distinguished success. "The centre of interest throughout *Roderick*," James tells us, "is in Rowland Mallet's consciousness, and the drama is the very drama of that consciousness." And we see how the novel does in fact justify that account. But the Prefaces in general belong essentially to that phase of the late James in which they were written. One must not expect to find out from James's discussion of it how one is to take an example of his more difficult and problematic works. Those who assume naïvely that they *are* getting light (and it seems to be a not uncommon illusion) are likely to come away with some notable misconception. Thus, because of such a misadventure on the part of an influential commentator,[1] there has been a notion current that *The Awkward Age* is a comedy, though anyone who reads comprehendingly what is there (and the work is one of those in which the difficulty of the late James is triumphantly vindicated) sees that—if we are to talk in these terms—it is a tragedy. James's analytic discussion serves a special technical preoccupation, one that had for him an absorbing intensity characteristic of that late phase (and consider the given retrospective occasion!); and the resultant abstraction, with its inadvertent emphasis, suggests the false account of the novel that has been taken up (people don't expect to understand a late work of James unless they know beforehand on authority what they are to find). Of course, readers of the novelist who study him closely because of a genuine response to what he has written may very well find some critical interest in the Prefaces. What should certainly be found is reason for reflecting on the way in which, in the late James, what began as a short story or *nouvelle* will end as a two-volume novel.

If the collection of the Prefaces ought not to be prescribed as a critical classic, James nevertheless has his place among the classical critics. Like all great original artists, he was distinguished by critical intelligence where his art was in question. Coming when he did, and writing for an English-speaking public, he was inevitably concerned to insist that the novelist's art was, as seriously as any, an *art*. Not that its standing as such was not, in one sense—the most important, firmly established: there had been Jane Austen, Dickens, Hawthorne, Charlotte Brontë, and George Eliot. What James, of course, had to contend for was a general full recognition among the educated that creative

---

[1] Percy Lubbock: *The Craft of Fiction*, p. 193.

talent—creative genius—was at least as likely to go into the novel as into any mode of art, and that for the critic and the "educated" reader to be innocent of their corresponding obligation was ignoble. The obligation was to be intelligent and to know that a novel might challenge all the intelligence and the most responsible judgment one could command. George Eliot had not waited to be assured that there would be a community capable of a perceptive response to the inventions of her genius, but towards the successors of George Eliot the public had none the less a duty. As James himself had, as time went on, his own poignant reason for knowing, the sense an artist has, or has not, that he may count on getting recognition from an intelligent public matters immensely to him—matters to him as an artist and a creative power.

James's distinctive position in criticism is given by these considerations: he, more than anyone else, was George Eliot's successor; he was an intimate of the Parisian literary world before he decided that he was irretrievably an Anglo-Saxon and must settle in England; the clear unignorable challenge for the novelist as artist, the vindicator of the artistic conscience in the art of fiction, was for him, inevitably, Flaubert, yet his decision that he was an "Anglo-Saxon" was that which he rested in. He knew France, creative France, intimately and affectionately: his Anglo-Saxonism was fully conscious and fully informed; it cannot be charged with provincialism. The representative document is his appraisal of Flaubert; sympathetic, grateful, admiring, full of piety, but inexorable in its limiting judgment. This indeed is a classical piece of criticism, one that can be prescribed for the close attention of the literary student. What we have here, in the attack, the close relevance, the essential economy, the combined trenchancy and suppleness, the sensitiveness and the penetration, is the critical intelligence of the creative writer, the practising novelist—an intelligence trained and refined in the *atelier*; but there is nothing technical or esoteric about the critique. All that could propose itself to the student as something to be carried away for his own use is what can be derived from an example of convincingly relevant intelligence: he can take the incitement to try and be himself as intelligent. But the way in which James arrives at and makes his major value-judgment—the limiting or reluctantly qualifying judgment that is the upshot of his critique—has a general and central significance for criticism, a clear general bearing.

What we come to here is the basic matter of criticism that lies at the bottom of James's handling of the theme of "morality". The point of putting the word in inverted commas is that it covers more than one issue, and, even in what may be called *loci classici* for the discussion of "art and morality", often, within one text, has a shifting force. It has more than one force, and (the student will perceive) some subtle transitions, in James's own reflections for which it provides the focus. In the commentary on Besant he is merely, or mainly, concerned to dismiss the idea that the novelist should be required to limit himself by the prohibitions and decorums of prudery, propriety and social convention. That his Anglo-Saxonism doesn't entail any lack of plainness, directness or completeness in this dismissal is put beyond question in his critique of Maupassant. But he has a criticism to make of this artist for whose un-Anglo-Saxon single-mindedness of devotion to art he is expressing an intense admiration. It is that Maupassant, militantly anti-sentimental vindicator of the right (or duty) of the novelist to render the whole of life as it presents itself to him, seems unaware of the part the moral sense actually plays in life. With the easy directness of a great Victorian Anglo-Saxon, James permits himself the gloss that Maupassant never, in his score of volumes, presents a gentleman.

But what basic to criticism is at issue under "art and morality" doesn't get fairly suggested—or not suggested with any felicity—by the question, however much point it may have in the given context, as to whether the novelist's presentment of life allows adequately for the part we know to be played in life by the "moral sense". James, of course, was well aware of this. The important thing about his criticism as he deals with Maupassant is the way (it is at once firm, responsible and subtle) in which, defining his essential value-judgments—or, to put it in other terms, intimating as a literary critic his sense of the human significance of Maupassant's art—he invokes "life".

He is insisting—and this, perhaps, is the important thing in the given context—that in respect of any art one takes seriously one *has* to make value-judgments, since a real response entails this; it entails forming an implicit critical sense of the human significance of the art in question, and the demand of intelligence is that one should bring one's sense to conscious definition. In Maupassant he was dealing with that reaction against "bourgeois" moralism (think of the prosecution of *Madame Bovary*) which denied any possible relevance of moral judgment to art. This meant the exaltation of art into something absolute, a self-justifying end in itself: *l'art pour l'art*. We don't, when Aestheticism is in question, think first of Maupassant, who was not addicted to Beauty; but he was (as James observes) the disciple of Flaubert, and for him too art was an absolute or ultimate: it was art for art's sake. You could say no more of a work than: "This is perfect; this is perfectly done." The critic could do no more than, within its own terms, point out the elements and structure of its perfection. It was irrelevant, supererogatory and presumptuous to ask questions about the value or significance (we need the words in association) of the perfectly done.

James discusses this implicit attitude of Maupassant. He points out. with his characteristic force of delicacy, that there is still the question of *interest*; the most resolute amoralism or anti-moralism doesn't eliminate that. He then asks of Maupassant: "Is *this* all there is in life? Does life reduce to this? Has it no more than this in the way of interest to offer?" He brings home to his reader, that is, that there is no eliminating and no escaping the appeal to life, however much one may suppose oneself to believe in the ultimateness or self-sufficiency of art.

It doesn't take a great deal of reflection to establish that "life" is a large word and doesn't admit of definition. But some of the most important words we have to use don't admit of definition. And this truth holds of literary criticism. Not only can we not, for instance, do without the word "life"; any attempt to think out a major critical issue entails using positively the shifts in force the word is bound to be incurring as it feels its way on and out and in towards its fulfilment. And it would hardly be questioned that there is point in saying that a critic who would be intelligent about the novel must be intelligent about life: no discussion of the novel by any other kind of critic is worth attention.

When one remarks that the strength of James's criticism of the novel is his being himself a novelist one may complete the observation by noting how, in his own criticism, it is on the supreme need for the *novelist*, the novelist as artist, to be intelligent about life that the accent falls; always implicitly, explicitly in key places. There is nothing technical, it is worth repeating, in his examination of Flaubert, where, in criticism, we have a clear example of the consummate professional taking the challenge. And when he comes to the judgment that the masterpiece, *Madame Bovary*, is qualified by a default of intelligence in the master, the default of intelligence in the artist as artist *is* a default of intelligence about life. James, when he comes out with the explicit judgment, is considering in the first place Flaubert's heroine, Emma Bovary—"Madame Bovary herself as a vessel of experience".[1] But the implicit effect of the whole approach is to bring the criticism against the Flaubertian exaltation of "Art", for the mode and spirit of James's

[1] From *Gustave Flaubert, 1902*; p. 221 in this selection.

critique, with its essential appeal to life, implicitly challenges the contradiction represented by the Aesthetic way of exalting "Art". An intensity of addiction to an Art that is set over against life, an addiction that offers to manifest itself creatively in the rejection of life (subsumed under *la platitude bourgoise*), must certainly be held to be a major default of intelligence. James doesn't actually say that, but his criticism, in its constant habit, conveys and enforces a refutation of Aestheticism as clear and basic as its dismissal of the opposite kind of fallacy. In many ways he expresses his charged sense that the creativity of art is the creativity of life—that the creative impulse *is* life, and could be nothing else.

Addressing himself *ad hominem* to Maupassant, he points out that the cynic-sensualist's art is confined for its creative purposes to a sadly limited range or interests, since it leaves so much of life out. James's criticism, of course, is concerned for something more than range and variety: he can't conceive an artist, or (it follows) a critic, who is not concerned for significance. "Significance", again, is a term that doesn't admit of close definition, and, again, the critic can't do without it. It points to the wholeness of a created work to that which makes it one—to the principle of life that determines its growth and organization. Observations regarding "significance" are intimately bound up with judgments regarding "value"; the two terms are in close attendance upon one another. Discussion of "significance" entails in the most challenging way the anti-Aesthetic reference to life ("Art and Life"—we use the antithesis, knowing that we are not judging it to be meaningless, or anything but useful, when we remind ourselves that art is a manifestation of life or it is nothing). The creative writer's concern to render life *is* a concern for significance, a preoccupation with expressing his sense of what most matters. The creative drive in his art *is* a drive to clarify and convey his perception of relative importances. The work that commands the reader's most deeply engaged, the critic's most serious, attention asks at a deep level: "What, at bottom, do men live *for*?" And in work that strikes us as great art we are aware of a potent normative suggestion: "*These* are the possibilities and inevitablenesses, and, in the face of them, *this* is the valid and the wise (or the sane) attitude." Lawrence, asked, towards the end, about the creative impulsion in his own work, said: "One writes out of one's moral sense; for the race, as it were." [1]

"Moral" too is a difficult word and a necessary one. Lawrence's use

[1] Edward Nehls (ed.): *D. H. Lawrence, a composite biography*, Vol. 2, p. 414.

of it here is special, but central and right. A great writer is a man
impelled by a deep irresistible sense of responsibility, and he appeals to
a deep sense of responsibility in us. A great work of art explores and
evokes the grounds and sanctions of our most important choices,
valuations and decisions—those decisions which are not acts of will, but
are so important that they seem to make themselves rather than to be
made by us. The tone (or *timbre*) of this kind of formulation is not,
indeed, characteristic of James: for criticism, and statements of the
grounds of criticism, in which (as in the utterance just quoted) the
word moral has "religious" in close attendance, the student will go to
Lawrence.[1] But James in his way bears the same testimony, exemplifies
the same truth. If not with the Laurentian astonishingness, the clair-
voyant, deep-striking and wide-ranging genius, he is, as critic, finely and
strongly central. For the student, his place in history adds to his value
as that. His intelligence about the need of his time alerted and quickened
by his Parisian initiation, he dealt firmly with Victorian moralism in the
way the time—the state of British and American culture—required.
On the other hand, strong in his un-British inwardness with France, he
yielded no ground to the opposed fallacies of Aestheticism, which had
so great an attraction for the would-be enlightened and unprovincial.
He had achieved a centrality that made him strong to deal with all
provincialisms. He expressed with a fine and irresistible sincerity his
sense of Flaubert's place in the history of the novel, and of the indebted-
ness to Flaubert that should be felt by all practitioners. But, making his
famous decision in favour of the country of George Eliot,[2] a decision
that was a mature conscious realization of what for him was fact and
necessity, he knew, while not the less committed to go on developing
his own post-Flaubertian conscience of the *atelier*, that he belonged, not
with Flaubert's associates and disciples, but with George Eliot, Hawthorne, Dickens and Jane Austen.[3]

[1] The epigraph by Lawrence suggests how different his timbre is from James's.
[2] "... my last layers of resistance to a long-encroaching weariness and satiety with
the French mind and its utterance has fallen from me like a garment. I have done
with 'em, forever, and am turning English all over. I desire only to feed on English life and the contact of English minds." Letter to William James, 29 July,
1876.
[3] The "post-Flaubertian" conscience of the *atelier* expresses itself in a way of
talking about "form" and "composition" that makes us a little uneasy sometimes
—more than a little when it goes with such a reference as we have here to Jane
Austen: "They all represent the pursuit of a style, of the ideally right one for its
relations, and would still be interesting if the style had not been achieved. *Madame
Bovary, Salammbô, Saint Antoine, L'Education* are so written and so composed
(though the last-named in a minor degree) that the more we look at them the

That the sophisticated "conscience of the *atelier*" had not tendency to make him less sensitively and supply responsive to great art in the creation of which the artistic conscience engaged had been of a different ethos from that characteristic of his own work—had been (let us say) wholly English in genesis and habit—his "Conversation" on *Daniel Deronda* may serve as a demonstration. Even if one registers a disagreement here or there, it is impossible to read this critique, with its quick and witty sensitiveness of intelligence, without some keen pleasure when one reflects that it was written as a contemporary review. The conversation form, which lends itself to the effect of ease and lightness and also permits a command of varied tone, belongs to the critical method with which James responds to the given challenge —one that he takes, it is clear, with a warm and growing admiration and a proper kind of humility. He uses the conversation, with its different voices, representing a diversity of approaches and possibilities of response, to convey a due sense of the complexity both of the work and the critical recognition it calls for.

Those who have read (and there are authorities—James suffers much from authorities—who assert it as a patent truth) that Balzac is pre-eminently the master from whom he descends should consider how he deals with *La Comédie humaine*. He admires immensely and wonderingly the portentous energy, industry and courage of its creator, and the degree of success he has achieved. What he admires is the antithesis of himself. He reflects with a kind of envy on the conditions of

---

more we find in them, under this head, a beauty of intention and of effect; the more they figure in the too often dreary desert of fictional prose a class by themselves and a little living oasis. So far as that desert is of the complexion of our own English speech it supplies with remarkably rarity this particular source of refreshment. So strikingly is that the case, so scant for the most part any dream of a scheme of beauty in these connections, that a critic betrayed at artless moments into a plea for composition may find himself as blankly met as if his plea were for trigonometry. He makes inevitably his reflections, which are numerous enough; one of them being that if we turn our back so squarely, so universally to this order of considerations it is because the novel is so preponderantly cultivated among us by women, in other words by a sex ever gracefully, comfortably, enviably unconscious (it would be too much to call them even suspicious) of the requirements of form. The case is at any rate sharply enough made for us, or against us, by the circumstance that women are held to have achieved on all our ground, in spite of this weakness and others, as great results as any. The judgment is undoubtedly founded: Jane Austen was instinctive and charming . . ." (p. 228).

That Jane Austen's art had made a deep and decisive impact on James is proved (if that were necessary) by *The Europeans*. His being able to refer to her in such a context as "instinctive" proves that he himself as critic can be insufficiently conscious. The passage might be noted by the student as a monitory *locus classicus* for the term "form".

an old civilization that made possible, in Balzac's attempt to "faire concurrence à l'état civil", his "solidity of specification", his effect of structure and density. The antithesis of the poverty that James, in a famous passage, notes as offered Hawthorne by the American scene[1]— that is what Balzac's France gave Balzac. But, without anything in the nature of envy, James is constating how different in *kind* Balzac's energy is from his own. For the upshot of James's critique is a drastic limiting or privative judgment, one that comes under the rubric of "significance".

The significance we look for in creative literature is a matter of the sense of life, the sense of the potentialities of human experience, it conveys. It may fairly be said that life in *La Comédie humaine*, life for the reader immersed in the "comedy", is populous, an immensely demonstrative energy, and insistently "actual", but that the "life" that provides the themes and materials for Henry James's art hardly makes its presence felt. For all its populousness, Balzac's world strikes James as dauntingly empty. He conveys this judgment while his explicit emphasis falls on mass, weight and extent; the effect of "solidity" or "reality" he acclaims is significantly qualified in the acclaiming. "A born son of Touraine, it must be said, he pictures his province, on every pretext and occasion, with filial passion and extraordinary breadth. The prime aspect in his scene all the while, it must be added, is the money aspect. The general money question so loads him up and weighs him down that he moves through the human comedy, from beginning to end, very much in the fashion of a camel, the ship of the desert, surmounted with a cargo. 'Things' for him are francs and centimes more than any others, and I give up as inscrutable, unfathomable, the nature, the peculiar avidity of his interest in them. It makes us wonder again and again what then is the use on Balzac's scale of the divine faculty. The imagination, as we all know, may be employed up to a certain point in inventing uses for money; but its office beyond that point is surely to make us forget that anything so odious exists. This is what Balzac never forgot; his universe goes on expressing itself for him, to its furthest reaches, on its finest sides, in the terms of the market. To say these things, however, is after all to come out where we want, to suggest his extraordinary scale and his terrible completeness. I am not sure that he does not see character too, see passion, motive, personality, as quite in the order of the 'things' we have spoken of. He makes them no less concrete and palpable. handles them no less directly and freely.

[1] Henry James: *Hawthorne* (English Men of Letters), pp. 42–43.

It is the whole business in fine—that grand total to which he proposed
to himself to do high justice—that gives him his place apart, makes him
among the novelists, the largest, weightiest presence. There are some
of his obsessions—that of the material, that of the financial, that of the
'social', that of the technical, political, civil—for which I feel myself
unable to judge him, judgment losing itself unexpectedly in a particular shade of pity. The way to judge him is to try to walk all round
him—on which we see how remarkably far we have to go." (P. 197.)

There would be no point in summarizing the criticism or (it is
hardly, the student will find, a separable thing) the way in which
James makes it. The student will find a good and relatively simple
illustration here of how James repays some attentive reading. A criticism of very much the same kind is brought against Arnold Bennett in
the late essay, "The New Novel". And again the student should note
the way in which the criticism is conveyed. James has his idiosyncrasy
of expression, but his essential method, his approach and movement in
criticism, can hardly be *imitated*. The learning that can be done by the
reader is only of the right kind.

But there is no need to particularize further. The reader, aware
enough of the distinction of James the critic to look with adverted
interest through a varied collection of his criticism, will do his own
exploring, picking-out and discriminating. For there *are*, of course,
discriminations to be made: its interest doesn't invariably, or often
wholly, lie in its convincing rightness and inevitableness. We turn up
with some eagerness his review of *Our Mutual Friend*, and comment,
perhaps, that he rightly judges it to be inferior and tired, and yet doesn't
do it justice. To dismiss Bradley Headstone and Eugene Wrayburn
in that way—is *that* right? Isn't there some subtle and convincing
psychology that is at the same time penetrating insight into the con-
ditioning civilization? Haven't we some strong Dickens in the water-
side parts? And so on. We note his brief sentence on Lawrence in "The
New Novel". And we may remind ourselves, observing how seriously
he there takes Hugh Walpole, the type Book Society novelist of the
time, that Walpole enjoyed great "social" advantages, and was cul-
tivating the old, lonely, recognition-starved James—in the same spirit
that later (*via hommage* to Virginia Woolf) won him the entry into
Bloomsbury and *The Criterion*.

Reading James on Whitman and Baudelaire, we comment that his
being an intelligent novelist didn't help him here. But we don't feel
superior—or oughtn't to: that is in and of the whole "lesson", the

total interest and profit of reading any representative collection of his criticism. Reading him on Baudelaire, for instance, though we may exclaim at his being able to rank Baudelaire below Gautier, we may find it salutary to explain to ourselves why it was natural, and almost inevitable, for him to do so. We might even, considering James's Baudelaire (whom he presents carefully), be led to ask whether in the post-Eliotic Baudelaire there doesn't perhaps tend also to be a deflection —of another kind.

F. R. LEAVIS

MR. WALT WHITMAN

1865

It has been a melancholy task to read this book;[1] and it is a still more melancholy one to write about it. Perhaps since the day of Mr. Tupper's *Philosophy* there has been no more difficult reading of the poetic sort. It exhibits the effort of an essentially prosaic mind to lift itself, by a prolonged muscular strain, into poetry. Like hundreds of other good patriots, during the last four years, Mr. Walt Whitman has imagined that a certain amount of violent sympathy with the great deeds and sufferings of our soldiers, and of admiration for our national energy, together with a ready command of picturesque language, are sufficient inspiration for a poet. If this were the case, we had been a nation of poets. The constant developments of the war moved us continually to strong feeling and to strong expression of it. But in those cases in which these expressions were written out and printed with all due regard to prosody, they failed to make poetry, as any one may see by consulting now in cold blood the back volumes of the *Rebellion Record*. *Of course* the city of Manhattan, as Mr. Whitman delights to call it, when regiments poured through it in the first months of the war, and its own sole god, to borrow the words of a real poet, ceased for a while to be the millionaire, was a noble spectacle, and a poetical statement to this effect is possible. *Of course* the tumult of a battle is grand, the results of a battle tragic, and the untimely deaths of young men a theme for elegies. But he is not a poet who merely reiterates these plain facts *ore rotundo*. He only sings them worthily who views them from a height. Every tragic event collects about it a number of persons who delight to dwell upon its superficial points— of minds which are bullied by the *accidents* of the affair. The temper of such minds seems to us to be the reverse of the poetic temper; for the poet, although he incidentally masters, grasps, and uses the superficial traits of his theme, is really a poet only in so far as he extracts its latent meaning and holds it up to common eyes. And yet from such minds most of our war-verses have come, and Mr. Whitman's utterances, much as the assertion may surprise his friends, are in this respect no exception to general fashion. They are an exception, however, in that

[1] *Drum-Taps*, by Walt Whitman. New York, 1865.

they openly pretend to be something better; and this it is that makes them melancholy reading. Mr. Whitman is very fond of blowing his own trumpet, and he has made very explicit claims for his book. "Shut not your doors," he exclaims at the outset—

> Shut not your doors to me, proud libraries,
> For that which was lacking among you all, yet needed most,
>   I bring;
> A book I have made for your dear sake, O soldiers,
> And for you, O soul of man, and you, love of comrades;
> The words of my book nothing, the life of it everything;
> A book separate, not link'd with the rest, nor felt by the intellect;
> But you will feel every word, O Libertad! arm'd Libertad!
> It shall pass by the intellect to swim the sea, the air,
> With joy with you, O soul of man.

These are great pretensions, but it seems to us that the following are even greater:

> From Paumanok starting, I fly like a bird,
> Around and around to soar, to sing the idea of all;
> To the north betaking myself, to sing there arctic songs,
> To Kanada, 'till I absorb Kanada in myself—to Michigan then ,
> To Wisconsin, Iowa, Minnesota, to sing their songs (they are
>   inimitable);
> Then to Ohio and Indiana, to sing theirs—to Missouri and Kansas
>   and Arkansas, to sing theirs,
> To Tennessee and Kentucky—to the Carolinas and Georgia, to
>   sing theirs,
> To Texas, and so along up towards California, to roam accepted
>   everywhere;
> To sing first (to the tap of the war-drum, if need be)
> The idea of all—of the western world, one and inseparable,
> And then the song of each member of these States.

Mr. Whitman's primary purpose is to celebrate the greatness of our armies; his secondary purpose is to celebrate the greatness of the city of New York. He pursues these objects through a hundred pages of matter which remind us irresistibly of the story of the college professor who, on a venturesome youth's bringing him a theme done in blank verse, reminded him that it was not customary in writing prose to begin each line with a capital. The frequent capitals are the only marks of verse in Mr. Whitman's writing. There is, fortunately, but one attempt at rhyme. We say fortunately, for if the inequality of Mr.

Whitman's lines were self-registering, as it would be in the case of an anticipated syllable at their close, the effect would be painful in the extreme. As the case stands, each line starts off by itself, in resolute independence of its companions, without a visible goal. But if Mr. Whitman does not write verse, he does not write ordinary prose. The reader has seen that liberty is "libertad". In like manner, comrade is "camerado"; Americans are "Americanos"; a pavement is a "trottoir", and Mr. Whitman himself is a "chansonnier". If there is one thing that Mr. Whitman is not, it is this, for Béranger was a *chansonnier*. To appreciate the force of our conjunction, the reader should compare his military lyrics with Mr. Whitman's declamations. Our author's novelty, however, is not in his words, but in the form of his writing. As we have said, it begins for all the world like verse and turns out to be arrant prose. It is more like Mr. Tupper's proverbs than anything we have met. But what if, in form, it *is* prose? it may be asked. Very good poetry has come out of prose before this. To this we would reply that it must first have gone into it. Prose, in order to be good poetry, must first be good prose. As a general principle, we know of no circumstance more likely to impugn a writer's earnestness than the adoption of an anomalous style. He must have something very original to say if none of the old vehicles will carry his thoughts. Of course he *may* be surprisingly original. Still, presumption is against him. If on examination the matter of his discourse proves very valuable, it justifies, or at any rate excuses, his literary innovation.

But if, on the other hand, it is of a common quality, with nothing new about it, but its manners, the public will judge the writer harshly. The most that can be said of Mr. Whitman's vaticinations is, that, cast in a fluent and familiar manner, the average substance of them might escape unchallenged. But we have seen that Mr. Whitman prides himself especially on the substance—the life—of his poetry. It may be rough, it may be grim, it may be clumsy—such we take to be the author's argument—but it is sincere, it is sublime, it appeals to the soul of man, it is the voice of a people. He tells us, in the lines quoted, that the words of his book are nothing. To our perception they are everything, and very little at that. A great deal of verse that is nothing but words has, during the war, been sympathetically sighed over and cut out of newspaper corners, because it has possessed a certain simple melody. But Mr. Whitman's verse, we are confident, would have failed even of this triumph, for the simple reason that no triumph, however small, is won but through the exercise of art, and that this

volume is an offence against art. It is not enough to be grim and
rough and careless; common sense is also necessary, for it is by common
sense that we are judged. There exists in even the commonest minds,
in literary matters, a certain precise instinct of conservatism, which is
very shrewd in detecting wanton eccentricities. To this instinct Mr.
Whitman's attitude seems monstrous. It is monstrous because it pretends to persuade the soul while it slights the intellect ; because it pretends to gratify the feelings while it outrages the taste. The point is
that it does this *on theory*, wilfully, consciously, arrogantly. It is the
little nursery game of "open your mouth and shut your eyes". Our
hearts are often touched through a compromise with the artistic sense,
but never in direct violation of it. Mr. Whitman sits down at the outset
and counts out the intelligence. This were indeed a wise precaution on
his part if the intelligence were only submissive! But when she is
deliberately insulted, she takes her revenge by simply standing erect
and open-eyed. This is assuredly the best she can do. And if she could
find a voice she would probably address Mr. Whitman as follows:
"You came to woo my sister, the human soul. Instead of giving me a
kick as you approach, you should either greet me courteously, or, at
least, steal in unobserved. But now you have me on your hands. Your
chances are poor. What the human heart desires above all is sincerity,
and you do not appear to me sincere. For a lover you talk entirely too
much about yourself. In one place you threaten to absorb Kanada.
In another you call upon the city of New York to incarnate you, as
you have incarnated it. In another you inform us that neither youth
pertains to you nor 'delicatesse', that you are awkward in the parlour,
that you do not dance, and that you have neither bearing, beauty,
knowledge, nor fortune. In another place, by an allusion to your
'little songs', you seem to identify yourself with the third person of the
Trinity. For a poet who claims to sing 'the idea of all', this is tolerably
egotistical. We look in vain, however, through your book for a single
idea. We find nothing but flashy imitations of ideas. We find a medley
of extravagances and commonplaces. We find art, measure, grace,
sense sneered at on every page, and nothing positive given us in their
stead. To be positive one must have something to say; to be positive
requires reason, labour, and art; and art requires, above all things, a
suppression of one's self, a subordination of one's self to an idea. This
will never do for you, whose plan is to adapt the scheme of the universe
to your own limitations. You cannot entertain and exhibit ideas; but,
as we have seen, you are prepared to incarnate them. It is for this

reason, doubtless, that when once you have planted yourself squarely before the public, and in view of the great service you have done to the ideal, have become, as you say, 'accepted everywhere', you can afford to deal exclusively in words. What would be bald nonsense and dreary platitudes in any one else becomes sublimity in you. But all this is a mistake. To become adopted as a national poet, it is not enough to discard everything in particular and to accept everything in general, to amass crudity upon crudity, to discharge the undigested contents of your blotting-book into the lap of the public. You must respect the public which you address; for it has taste, if you have not. It delights in the grand, the heroic, and the masculine; but it delights to see these conceptions cast into worthy form. It is indifferent to brute sublimity. It will never do for you to thrust your hands into your pockets and cry out that, as the research of form is an intolerable bore, the shortest and most economical way for the public to embrace its idols—for the nation to realize its genius—is in your own person. This democratic, liberty-loving, American populace, this stern and war-tried people, is a great civilizer. It is devoted to refinement. If it has sustained a monstrous war, and practised human nature's best in so many ways for the last five years, it is not to put up with spurious poetry afterwards. To sing aright our battles and our glories it is not enough to have served in a hospital (however praiseworthy the task in itself), to be aggressively careless, inelegant, and ignorant, and to be constantly pre-occupied with yourself. It is not enough to be rude, lugubrious, and grim. You must also be serious. You must forget yourself in your ideas. Your personal qualities—the vigour of your temperament, the manly independence of your nature, the tenderness of your heart— these facts are impertinent. You must be *possessed*, and you must strive to possess your possession. If in your striving you break into divine eloquence, then you are a poet. If the idea which possesses you is the idea of your country's greatness, then you are a national poet; and not otherwise."

2

OUR MUTUAL FRIEND[1]

1865

OUR MUTUAL FRIEND is, to our perception, the poorest of Mr. Dickens works. And it is poor with the poverty not of momentary embarrassment, but of permanent exhaustion. It is wanting in inspiration. For the last ten years it has seemed to us that Mr. Dickens has been unmistakably forcing himself. *Bleak House* was forced; *Little Dorrit* was laboured; the present work is dug out as with a spade and pickaxe. Of course—to anticipate the usual argument—who but Dickens could have written it? Who, indeed? Who else would have established a lady in business in a novel on the admirably solid basis of her always putting on gloves and tying a handkerchief round her head in moments of grief, and of her habitually addressing her family with "Peace! hold!" It is needless to say that Mrs. Reginald Wilfer is first and last the occasion of considerable true humour. When, after conducting her daughter to Mrs. Boffin's carriage, in sight of all the envious neighbours, she is described as enjoying her triumph during the next quarter of an hour by airing herself on the door-step "in a kind of splendidly serene trance", we laugh with as uncritical a laugh as could be desired of us. We pay the same tribute to her assertions, as she narrates the glories of the society she enjoyed at her father's table, that she has known as many as three copper-plate engravers exchanging the most exquisite sallies and retorts there at one time. But when to these we have added a dozen more happy examples of the humour which was exhaled from every line of Mr. Dickens's earlier writings, we shall have closed the list of the merits of the work before us. To say that the conduct of the story, with all its complications, betrays a long, practised hand, is to pay no compliment worthy the author. If this were, indeed, a compliment, we should be inclined to carry it further, and congratulate him on his success in what we should call the manufacture of fiction; for in so doing we should express a feeling that has attended us throughout the book. Seldom, we reflected, had we read a book so intensely *written*, so little seen, known, or felt.

In all Mr. Dickens's works the fantastic has been his great resource; and while his fancy was lively and vigorous it accomplished great

[1] *Our Mutual Friend*, by Charles Dickens. New York: Harper Brothers, 1865.

6

things. But the fantastic, when the fancy is dead, is a very poor business. The movement of Mr. Dickens's fancy in Mrs. Wilfer and Mr. Boffin and Lady Tippins, and the Lammles and Miss Wren, and even in Eugene Wrayburn, is, to our mind, a movement lifeless, forced, mechanical. It is the letter of his old humour without the spirit. It is hardly too much to say that every character here put before us is a mere bundle of eccentricities, animated by no principle of nature whatever. In former days there reigned in Mr. Dickens's extravagances a comparative consistency; they were exaggerated statements of types that really existed. We had, perhaps, never known a Newman Noggs nor a Pecksniff, nor a Micawber; but we had known persons of whom these figures were but the strictly logical consummation. But among the grotesque creatures who occupy the pages before us, there is not one whom we can refer to as an existing type. In all Mr. Dickens's stories, indeed, the reader has been called upon, and has willingly consented, to accept a certain number of figures or creatures of pure fancy, for this was the author's poetry. He was, moreover, always repaid for his concession by a peculiar beauty or power in these exceptional characters. But he is now expected to make the same concession with a very inadequate reward. What do we get in return for accepting Miss Jenny Wren as a possible person? This young lady is the type of a certain class of characters of which Mr. Dickens has made a speciality, and with which he has been accustomed to draw alternate smiles and tears, according as he pressed one spring or another. But this is very cheap merriment and very cheap pathos. Miss Jenny Wren is a poor little dwarf, afflicted, as she constantly reiterates, with a "bad back" and "queer legs", who makes doll's dresses, and is for ever pricking at those with whom she converses, in the air, with her needle, and assuring them that she knows their "tricks and their manners". Like all Mr. Dickens's pathetic characters, she is a little monster; she is deformed, unhealthy, unnatural; she belongs to the troop of hunchbacks, imbeciles, and precocious children who have carried on the sentimental business in all Mr. Dickens's novels; the little Nells, the Smikes, the Paul Dombeys.

Mr. Dickens goes as far out of the way for his wicked people as he does for his good ones. Rogue Riderhood, indeed, in the present story, is villainous with a sufficiently natural villainy; he belongs to that quarter of society in which the author is most at his ease. But was there ever such wickedness as that of the Lammles and Mr. Fledgeby? Not that people have not been as mischievous as they; but was any one ever mischievous in that singular fashion? Did a couple of elegant swindlers ever take such particular pains to be aggressively inhuman —for we can find no other word for the gratuitous distortions to which they are subjected. The word *humanity* strikes us as strangely discordant, in the midst of these pages; for, let us boldly declare it, there is no humanity here. Humanity is nearer home than the Boffins, and the Lammles, and the Wilfers, and the Veneerings. It is in what men have in common with each other, and not in what they have in distinction. The people just named have nothing in common with each other, except the fact that they have nothing in common with mankind at large. What a world were this world if the world of *Our Mutual Friend* were an honest reflection of it! But a community of eccentrics is impossible. Rules alone are consistent with each other; exceptions are inconsistent. Society is maintained by natural sense and natural feeling. We cannot conceive a society in which these principles are not in some manner represented. Where in these pages are the depositaries of that intelligence without which the movement of life would cease? Who represents nature? Accepting half of Mr. Dickens's persons as intentionally grotesque, where are those exemplars of sound humanity who should afford us the proper measure of their companions' variations? We ought not, in justice to the author, to seek them among his weaker—that is, his mere conventional—characters; in John Harmon, Lizzie Hexam, or Mortimer Lightwood; but we assuredly cannot find them among his stronger—that is, his artificial creations. Suppose we take Eugene Wrayburn and Bradley Headstone. They occupy a half-way position between the habitual probable of nature and the habitual impossible of Mr. Dickens. A large portion of the story rests upon the enmity borne by Headstone to Wrayburn, both being in love with the same woman. Wrayburn is a gentleman, and Headstone is one of the people. Wrayburn is well-bred, careless, elegant, sceptical, and idle: Headstone is a high-tempered, hard-working, ambitious young schoolmaster. There lay in the opposition of these two characters a very good story. But the prime requisite was that they should *be* characters: Mr. Dickens, according to his usual plan, has made them simply figures, and between them the story that was to be, the story that should have been, has evaporated. Wrayburn lounges about with his hands in his pockets, smoking a cigar, and talking nonsense. Headstone strides about, clenching his fists and biting his lips and grasping his stick. There is one scene in which Wrayburn chaffs the schoolmaster with easy insolence, while the latter writhes

impotently under his well-bred sarcasm. This scene is very clever, but
it is very insufficient. If the majority of readers were not so timid in
the use of words we should call it vulgar. By this we do not mean to
indicate the conventional impropriety of two gentlemen exchanging
lively personalities; we mean to emphasize the essentially small character of these personalities. In other words, the moment, dramatically,
is great, while the author's conception is weak. The friction of two
men, of two characters, of two passions, produces stronger sparks than
Wrayburn's boyish repartees and Headstone's melodramatic commonplaces. Such scenes as this are useful in fixing the limits of Mr.
Dickens's insight. Insight is, perhaps, too strong a word; for we are
convinced that it is one of the chief conditions of his genius not to see
beneath the surface of things. If we might hazard a definition of his
literary character, we should accordingly, call him the greatest of
superficial novelists. We are aware that this definition confines him
to an inferior rank in the department of letters which he adorns; but we
accept this consequence of our proposition. It were, in our opinion,
an offence against humanity to place Mr. Dickens among the greatest
novelists. For, to repeat what we have already intimated, he has
created nothing but figure. He has added nothing to our understanding
of human character. He is master of but two alternatives: he reconciles us to what is commonplace, and he reconciles us to what is odd.
The value of the former service is questionable; and the manner in
which Mr. Dickens performs it sometimes conveys a certain impression
of charlatanism. The value of the latter service is incontestable, and here
Mr. Dickens is an honest, an admirable artist. But what is the condition of the truly great novelist? For him there are no alternatives,
for him there are no oddities, for him there is nothing outside of
humanity. He cannot shirk it; it imposes itself upon him. For him
alone, therefore, there is a true and a false; for him alone is it possible
to be right, because it is possible to be wrong. Mr. Dickens is a great
observer and a great humorist, but he is nothing of a philosopher.
Some people may hereupon say, so much the better; we say, so much
the worse. For a novelist very soon has need of a little philosophy.
In treating of Micawber, and Boffin, and Pickwick, *et hoc genus omne*,
he can, indeed, dispense with it, for this—we say it with all deference—
is not serious writing. But when he comes to tell the story of a passion,
a story like that of Headstone and Wrayburn, he becomes a moralist
as well as an artist. He must know *man* as well as *men*, and to know
man is to be a philosopher. The writer who knows men alone, if he

has Mr. Dickens's humour and fancy, will give us figures and pictures for which we cannot be too grateful, for he will enlarge our knowledge of the world. But when he introduces men and women whose interest is preconceived to lie not in the poverty, the weakness, the drollery of their natures, but in their complete and unconscious subjection to ordinary and healthy human emotions, all his humour, all, his fancy, will avail him nothing if, out of the fullness of his sympathy, he is unable to prosecute those generalizations in which alone consists the real greatness of a work of art. This may sound like very subtle talk about a very simple matter; it is rather very simple talk about a very subtle matter. A story based upon those elementary passions in which alone we seek the true and final manifestation of character must be told in a spirit of intellectual superiority to those passions. That is, the author must understand what he is talking about. The perusal of a story so told is one of the most elevating experiences within the reach of the human mind. The perusal of a story which is not so told is infinitely depressing and unprofitable.

3

THE BELTON ESTATE

1866

HERE, in the natural order of events, is a new novel by Mr. Trollope. This time it is Miss Clara Amedroz who is agitated by conflicting thoughts. Like most of Mr. Trollope's recent heroines, she is no longer in the first blush of youth; and her story, like most of Mr. Trollope's recent stories, is that of a woman standing irresolute between a better lover and a worse. She first rejects the better for the worse, and then rejects the worse for the better. This latter movement is final, and Captain Aylmer, like Crosbie, in *The Small House at Allington*, has to put up with a red-nosed Lady Emily. The reader will surmise that we are not in *The Belton Estate* introduced to very new ground. The book is, nevertheless, to our mind, more readable than many of its predecessors. It is comparatively short, and has the advantage of being a single story, unencumbered by any subordinate or co-ordinate plot. The interest of Mr. Trollope's main narrative is usually so far from being intense that repeated interruption on behalf of the actors charged with the more strictly humorous business is often very near proving altogether fatal. To become involved in one of his love stories is very like sinking into a gentle slumber; and it is well known that when you are aroused from your slumber to see something which your well-meaning intruder considers very entertaining, it is a difficult matter to woo it back again. In the tale before us we slumber on gently to the end. There is no heroine but Miss Clara Amedroz, and no heroes but her two suitors. The lady loves amiss, but discovers it in time, and invests her affections more safely. Such, in strictness, is the substance of the tale; but it is filled out as Mr. Trollope alone knows how to fill out the primitive meagreness of his dramatic skeletons. The three persons whom we have mentioned are each a character in a way, and their sayings and doings, their comings and goings, are registered to the letter and timed to the minute. They write a number of letters, which are duly transcribed; they make frequent railway journeys by the down-train from London; they have cups of tea in their bedrooms; and they do, in short, in the novel very much as the reader is doing out of it. We do not make these remarks in a tone of complaint. Mr. Trollope has been long enough before the public to have enabled it to take his measure. We do not open his books with the expectation of being thrilled, or convinced, or deeply moved in any way, and, accordingly, when we find one to be as flat as a Dutch landscape, we remind ourselves that we have wittingly travelled into Holland, and that we have no right to abuse the scenery for being in character. We reflect, moreover, that there are a vast number of excellent Dutchmen for whom this low-lying horizon has infinite charms. If we are passionate and egotistical, we turn our back upon them for a nation of irreclaimable dullards; but if we are critical and disinterested, we endeavour to view the prospect from a Dutch stand-point.

Looking at *The Belton Estate*, then, from Mr. Trollope's own point of view, it is a very pleasing tale. It contains not a word against nature. It relates, with great knowledge, humour, and grace of style, the history of the affections of a charming young lady. No unlawful devices are resorted to in order to interest us. People and things are painted as they stand. Miss Clara Amedroz is charming—by the sweetness of her face and figure, the propriety of her manners, and the amiability of her disposition. Represented thus, without perversion or exaggeration, she engages our sympathy as one whom we can understand, from having known a hundred women exactly like her. Will Belton, the lover whom she finally accepts, is still more vividly natural. Even the critic, who judges the book strictly from a reader's stand-point, must admit that Mr. Trollope has drawn few better figures than this, or even (what is more to the purpose) that, as a representation, he is an approach to ideal excellence. The author understands him well in the life, and the reader understands him well in the book. As soon as he begins to talk we begin to know and to like him, as we know and like such men in the flesh after half an hour of their society. It is true that for many of us half an hour of their society is sufficient, and that here Will Belton is kept before us for days and weeks. No better reason for this is needed than the presumption that the author does not tire of such men so rapidly as we: men healthy, hearty, and shrewd, but men, as we take the liberty of declaring, utterly without mind. Mr. Trollope is simply unable to depict a *mind* in any liberal sense of the word. He tried it in John Grey in *Can You Forgive Her?* but most readers will agree that he failed to express very vividly this gentleman's scholarly intelligence. Will Belton is an enterprising young squire, with a head large enough for a hundred prejudices, but too small for a single opinion, and a heart competent—on the condition, however, as it seems to us, of considerable generous self-contraction on her part—to embrace Miss Amedroz.

The other lover, Captain Aylmer, is not as successful a figure as his rival, but he is yet a very fair likeness of a man who probably abounds in the ranks of that society from which Mr. Trollope recruits his characters, and who occurs, we venture to believe, in that society alone. Not that there are not in all walks of life weak and passionless men who allow their mothers to bully their affianced wives, and who are utterly incompetent to entertain the idea. But in no other society than that to which Captain Aylmer belongs do such frigidity and such stupidity stand so little in the way of social success. They seem in his case, indeed, to be a passport to it. His prospects depend upon his being respectable, and his being respectable depends, apparently, on his being contemptible. We do not suppose, however, that Mr. Trollope likes him any better than we. In fact, Mr. Trollope never fails to betray his antipathy for mean people and mean actions. And antipathetic to his tastes as is Captain Aylmer's nature, it is the more creditable to him that he has described it so coolly, critically, and temperately. Mr. Trollope is never guilty of an excess in any direction, and the vice of his villain is of so mild a quality that it is powerless to prejudice him against his even milder virtues. These seem to us insufficient to account for Clara's passion, for we are bound to believe that for her it was a passion. As far as the reader sees, Captain Aylmer has done nothing to excite it and everything to quench it, and, indeed, we are quite taken by surprise when, after her aunt's death, she answers his proposal with so emphatic an affirmative. It is a pleasant surprise, however, to find any of Mr. Trollope's people doing a thing contrary to common sense. Nothing can be better—always from the Dutch point of view—than the management of the reaction in both parties against their engagement; but to base the rupture of a marriage engagement upon an indisposition on the part of the gentleman's mother that the lady shall maintain an acquaintance of long standing with another lady whose past history is discovered to offer a certain little vantage-point for scandal, is, even from the Dutch point of view, an unwarrantable piece of puerility. But the shabbiness of grand society—and especially the secret meannesses, parsimonies, and cruelties of the exemplary British matron—have as great an attraction for Mr. Trollope as they had for Thackeray; and the account of Clara's visit to the home of her intended, the description of the magnificent bullying of Lady Aylmer, and the picture of Miss Aylmer—"as ignorant, weak,

and stupid a poor woman as you shall find anywhere in Europe"—
make a sketch almost as relentless as the satire of *Vanity Fair* or *The
Newcomes*. There are several other passages equally clever, notably the
chapter in which Belton delivers up Miss Amedroz to her lover's care
at the hotel in London; and in which, secure in his expression elsewhere of Belton's superiority to Aylmer, the author feels that he can
afford to make him still more delicately natural than he has made him
already by contrasting him, *pro tempore*, very disadvantageously with
his rival, and causing him to lose his temper and make a fool of himself.

Such praise as this we may freely bestow on the work before us,
because, qualified by the important stricture which we have kept in
reserve, we feel that it will not seem excessive. Our great objection to
The Belton Estate is that, as we read it, we seemed to be reading a work
written for children; a work below the apprehension of the average
man and woman, or, at the very most, on a level with it, and in no
particular above it. *The Belton Estate* is a *stupid* book; and in a much
deeper sense than that of being simply dull, for a dull book is always a
book that might have been lively. A dull book is a failure. Mr. Trollope's story is stupid and a success. It is essentially, organically, consistently stupid; stupid in direct proportion to its strength. It is without
a single idea. It is utterly incompetent to the primary functions of a
book, of whatever nature, namely—to suggest thought. In a certain
way, indeed, it suggests thought; but this is only on the ruins of its
own existence as a book. It acts as the occasion, not as the cause, of
thought. It indicates the manner in which a novel should *not*, on any
account, be written. That it should deal exclusively with dull, flat,
commonplace people was to be expected; and this need not be a
fault; but it deals with such people as one of themselves; and this is
what Lady Aylmer would call a "damning" fault. Mr. Trollope is a
good observer; but he is literally nothing else. He is apparently as
incapable of disengaging an idea as of drawing an inference. All his
incidents are, if we may so express it, *empirical*. He has seen and heard
every act and every speech that appears in his pages. That minds like
his should exist, and exist in plenty, is neither to be wondered at nor
to be deplored; but that such a mind as his should devote itself to
writing novels, and that these novels should be successful, appears to
us an extraordinary fact.

[4]

TAINE'S ENGLISH LITERATURE[1]

1872

WE hesitate to express perfect satisfaction at the appearance of an English version of M. Taine's massive essay.[1] On the one hand, the performance is no more than a proper compliment to a highly complimentary work; but, on the other, it involves so effective a violation of the spirit of that work and so rude a displacement of its stand-point, as to interfere with a just comprehension of it. M. Taine himself, however, stands sponsor in a short Preface, and the liberal reception of the two volumes seems to indicate that English readers are not sensible of having unduly lost by the transfer. The English version may fairly demand success on its own merits, being careful, exact, and spirited. It errs, we think, on the side of a too literal exactness, through which it frequently ceases to be idiomatic. "He tore from his vitals, . . ." for instance, "the idea which he had conceived", would render M. Taine's figure better than "he tore from his *entrails*". And it is surely in strong contradiction to the author's portrait of Lord Macaulay to translate his allusion to the great historian's *physionomie animée et pensante* by "an animated and pensive face". No one, we fancy, not even M. Taine, ever accused Lord Macaulay of being pensive.

M. Taine's work is a history of our literature only in a partial sense of the term. "Just as astronomy," he says, "is at bottom a problem in mechanics, and physiology a problem in chemistry, so history at bottom is a problem in psychology." His aim has been "to establish the psychology of a people". A happier title for his work, therefore, save for its amplitude, would be, "A Comparative Survey of the English Mind in the leading Works of its Literature". It is a picture of the English intellect, with literary examples and allusions in evidence, and not a record of works nor an accumulation of facts. To philological or biographical research it makes no claim. In this direction it is altogether incomplete. Various important works are unmentioned, common tradition as to facts is implicitly accepted, and dates, references, and minor detail conspicuous by their absence. The work is wholly critical and pictorial, and involves no larger information than

[1] *History of English Literature*, by H. A. Taine. Translated by H. Van Laun. New York: Holt and Williams, 1871.

the perusal of a vast body of common documents. Its purpose is to
discover in the strongest features of the strongest works the temper of
the race and time; which involves a considerable neglect not only of
works, but of features. But what is mainly to the point with the
English reader (as it is of course excessively obvious in the English
version) is that M. Taine writes from an avowedly foreign stand-point.
The unit of comparison is throughout assumed to be the French mind.
The author's undertaking strikes us, therefore, constantly as an *excursion*. It is not as if he and our English tongue were old friends, as if
through a taste early formed and long indulged he had gradually been
won to the pious project of paying his debt and embodying his impressions; but as if rather, on reaching his intellectual majority and
coming into a handsome property of doctrine and dogma, he had cast
about him for a field to conquer, a likely subject for experiment, and,
measuring the vast capacity of our English record of expression, he had
made a deliberate and immediate choice. We may fancy him declaring,
too, that he would do the thing handsomely; devote five or six years
to it, and spend five or six months in the country. He has performed
his task with a vigour proportionate to this sturdy resolve; but in the
nature of the case his treatment of the subject lacks that indefinable
quality of spiritual initiation which is the tardy consummate fruit of a
wasteful, purposeless, passionate sympathy. His opinions are prompted,
not by a sentiment, but by a design. He remains an interpreter of the
English mind to the mind of another race; and only remotely, therefore,—only by allowance and assistance,—an interpreter of the English
mind to itself. A greater fault than any of his special errors of judgment
is a certain reduced, contracted, and limited air in the whole field. He
has made his subject as definite as his method.

M. Taine is fairly well known by this time as a man with a method,
the apostle of a theory,—the theory that "vice and virtue are products,
like vitriol and sugar", and that art, literature, and conduct are the
result of forces which differ from those of the physical world only in
being less easily ascertainable. His three main factors—they have lately
been reiterated to satiety—are the race, the medium, and the time.
Between them they shape the phenomena of history. We have not the
purpose of discussing this doctrine; it opens up a dispute as ancient
as history itself,—the quarrel between the minds which cling to the
supernatural and the minds which dismiss it. M. Taine's originality is not in his holding of these principles, but in his lively disposition to apply them, or, rather, in the very temper and terms in

which he applies them. No real observer but perceives that a group of works is more or less the product of a "situation", and that as he himself is for ever conscious of the attrition of infinite waves of circumstance, so the cause to which, by genius as by "fate", he contributes, is a larger deposit in a more general current. Observers differ, first, as to whether there are elements in the deposit which cannot be found in the current; second, as to the variety and complexity of the elements: maintaining, on the one side, that fairly to enumerate them and establish their mutual relations the vision of science is as yet too dim; and, on the other, that a complete analysis is at last decently possible, and with it a complete explanation. M. Taine is an observer of the latter class; in his own sole person indeed he almost includes it. He pays in his Preface a handsome tribute to the great service rendered by Sainte-Beuve to the new criticism. Now Sainte-Beuve is, to our sense, the better apostle of the two. In purpose the least doctrinal of critics, it was by his very horror of dogmas, moulds, and formulas, that he so effectively contributed to the science of literary interpretation. The truly devout patience with which he kept his final conclusion in abeyance until after an exhaustive survey of the facts, after perpetual returns and ever-deferred farewells to them, is his living testimony to the importance of the facts. Just as he could never reconcile himself to saying his last word on book or author, so he never pretended to have devised a method which should be a key to truth. The truth for M. Taine lies stored up, as one may say, in great lumps and blocks, to be released and detached by a few lively hammer-blows; while for Sainte-Beuve it was a diffused and imponderable essence, as vague as the carbon in the air which nourishes vegetation, and, like it, to be disengaged by patient chemistry. His only method was fairly to dissolve his attention in the sea of circumstance surrounding the object of his study, and we cannot but think his frank provisional empiricism more truly scientific than M. Taine's premature philosophy. In fact, M. Taine plays fast and loose with his theory, and is mainly successful in so far as he is inconsequent to it. There is a constantly visible hiatus between his formula and his application of it. It serves as his badge and motto, but his best strokes are prompted by the independent personal impression. The larger conditions of his subject loom vaguely in the background, like a richly figured tapestry of good regulation pattern, gleaming here and there in the author's fitful glance, and serving a picturesque purpose decidedly more than a scientific one. This is especially noticeable in the early chapters of the present work, where the changes are rung to excess upon a note of rather slender strain,—the common "Gothic" properties of history and fiction,—Norse blood, gloomy climate, ferocious manners, considered as shaping forces. The same remark applies, we imagine, to the author's volumes on Italy, where a thin soil of historical evidence is often made to produce some most luxuriant flowers of deduction. The historical position is vague, light, and often insecure, and the author's passage from the general conditions to the particular case is apt to be a flying leap of fancy, which, though admirable writing, is rather imperfect science.

We of course lack space to discuss his work in its parts. His portrayal of authors and works is always an attempt to fix the leading or motive faculty, and through his neglect of familiar details and his amplification of the intellectual essence which is the object of his search, his figures often seem out of drawing to English eyes. He distorts the outline, confounds the light and shade, and alters the colouring. His judgments are sometimes very happy and sometimes very erroneous. He proposes some very wise amendments to critical tradition; in other cases he enforces the common verdict with admirable point and vigour. For Spenser, for instance, we doubt whether the case has ever been stated with a more sympathetic and penetrating eloquence. His errors and misjudgments arise partly from his being so thoroughly a stranger to what we may call the intellectual climate of our literature, and partly from his passionate desire to simplify his conception and reduce it to the limits, not merely of the distinctly knowable, but of the symmetrically and neatly presentable. The leading trait of his mind, and its great defect, is an inordinate haste to conclude, combined with a passion for a sort of largely pictorial and splendidly comprehensive expression. A glance at the list of his works will show how actively he has kept terms with each of these tendencies. He is, to our sense, far from being a man of perceptions; the bent of his genius seems to be to generate ideas and images on two distinct lines. For ourselves, on the whole, we prefer his images. These are immensely rich and vivid, and on this side the author is a great artist. His constant effort is to reconcile and harmonize these two groups, and make them illumine and vivify each other. Where he succeeds his success is admirable, and the reader feels that he has rarely seen a truth so completely presented. Where he fails the violence of his diction only serves to emphasize the inadequacy of his conception. M. Taine's great strength is to be found close to his eminent fallibility as a critic,—in his magnificent power of eloquent and vivid statement and presentation. His style is admirable; we know of none that is at once more splendid and more definite, that has at once more structure and more colour. Just as his natural preference is evidently for energy and vehemence in talent, his own movement is toward a sort of monstrous cumulative violence of expression; to clinch, to strike, to hit hard, to hit again, till the idea rings and resounds, to force colour *à l'outrance* and make proportion massive, is his notion of complete utterance. This is productive of many effects splendid in themselves, but it is fatal to truth in so far as truth resides in fine shades and degrees.

In this intense constructive glow, M. Taine quite forgets his subject and his starting-point; the impetus of his rhetoric, the effort to complete his picture and reach forward to the strongest word and the largest phrase, altogether absorbs him. For ourselves, we confess that, as we read, we cease to hold him at all rigidly to his premises, and content ourselves with simply enjoying the superb movement of his imagination, thankful when it lights his topic at all truly, and mainly conscious of its radiance as colour, heat, and force. Thus, while as a gallery of portraits the work demands constant revision and correction, as a sort of enormous *tableau vivant*, ingeniously and artificially combined, it is extremely rich and various. A phrase of very frequent occurrence with M. Taine, and very wholesome in its frequency, is *la grande invention*; his own tendency is to practise it. In effort and inclination however, he is nothing if not impartial; and there is something almost touching in the sympathetic breadth of his admiration for a tone of genius so foreign to French tradition as the great Scriptural inspiration of Bunyan and of Milton. To passionate vigour he always does justice. On the other hand, when he deals with a subject simply because it stands in his path, he is far less satisfactory. His estimate of Swift is a striking example of his tendency to overcharge his portrait and make a picture at all hazards. Swift was a bitter and incisive genius, but he had neither the volume nor the force implied in M. Taine's report of him. We might add a hundred instances of the fatally defective perception of "values", as the painters say, produced by the author's foreign stand-point. M. Taine expresses altogether the "Continental" view of Byron, between which and the English view there is much the same difference as between the estimate Byron courted and the estimate he feared. A hundred special points may be conceded; but few modern Englishmen are prepared to accept him, as a whole, as the consistently massive phenomenon described by M. Taine. Touching the later poets, the author is extremely incomplete and fallacious; he pretends,

indeed, merely to sketch general tendencies. On Wordsworth, however, he has some pertinent remarks from that protesting man-of-the-
world point of view to which the great frugal bard drives most Englishmen for desperate refuge, let alone an epigrammatic Frenchman. We
are tempted to say that a Frenchman who should have twisted himself
into a relish for Wordsworth would almost have forfeited our respect.
On Thackeray and Dickens he has two chapters of great suggestiveness
to those who know the authors, but on the whole of excessively contracted outline. Of course, one cannot pronounce upon important
literary figures, of whatever dimensions, without a certain work of
elimination; but a valid charge against M. Taine is that, whereas your
distinctly sensitive critic finds this process to be an effort, M. Taine
has the air of finding it a relief. A compromise is perfectly legitimate so
long as it is not offered as a synthesis.

With all abatements, and especially in spite of one most important
abatement, M. Taine's work remains a very admirable performance.
As a philosophical effort it is decidedly a failure; as the application of a
theory it is ineffective; but it is a great literary achievement. The
fruit of an extremely powerful, vivacious, and observant mind, it is
rich in suggestive sidelights and forcible aids to opinion. With a great
many errors of detail, as a broad expression of the general essence of
the English genius it seems to us equally eloquent and just. M. Taine
has felt this genius with an intensity and conceived it with a lucidity
which, in themselves, form a great intellectual feat. Even under this
head the work is not conclusive in the sense in which the author
tenders it, but it is largely and vividly contributive, and we shall wait
till we have done better ourselves before we judge it too harshly. It
is, in other words, very entertaining provisional criticism and very
perfect final art. It is, indeed, a more significant testimony to the
French genius than to the English, and bears more directly upon the
author's native literature than on our own. In its powerful, though
arbitrary, unity of composition, in its sustained aesthetic temper, its
brilliancy, variety, and symmetry, it is a really monumental accession
to a literature which, whatever its limitations in the reach of its ideas,
is a splendid series of masterly compositions.

5

SWINBURNE'S ESSAYS[1]

1875

MR. SWINBURNE has by this time impressed upon the general public a tolerably vivid image of his literary personality. His line is a definite one: his note is familiar, and we know what to expect from him. He was at pains, indeed, a year ago to quicken the apprehension of American readers by an effusion directed more or less explicitly to themselves. This piece of literature was brief, but it was very remarkable. Mr. Emerson had had occasion to speak of Mr. Swinburne with qualified admiration, and this circumstance, coming to Mr. Swinburne's ears, had prompted him to uncork on the spot the vials of his wrath. He addressed to a newspaper a letter of which it is but a colourless account to say that it embodied the very hysterics of gross vituperation. Mr. Swinburne has some extremely just remarks about Byron's unamenableness to quotation, his having to be taken in the gross. This is almost equally true of our author himself; he must be judged by all he has done, and we must allow, in our judgment, the weight he would obviously claim for it to his elaborate tribute to the genius of Mr. Emerson. His tone has two distinct notes—the note of measureless praise and the note of furious denunciation. Each is in need of a correction, but we confess that, with all its faults, we prefer the former. That Mr. Swinburne has a kindness for his more restrictive strain is, however, very obvious. He is over-ready to sound it, and he is not particular about his pretext. Some people, he says, for instance, affirm that a writer may have a very effective style and yet have nothing of value to express with it. Mr. Swinburne demands that they prove their assertion. "This flattering unction the very foolishest of malignants will hardly, in this case [that of Mr. D. G. Rossetti], be able to lay upon the corrosive sore which he calls his soul; the ulcer of ill-will must rot unrelieved by the rancid ointment of such fiction." In Mr. W. M. Rossetti's edition of Shelley there is in a certain line an interpolation of the word "autumn". "For the conception of this atrocity the editor is not responsible; for its adoption he is. A thousand years of purgatorial fire would be insufficient expiation for the criminal on whose

[1] *Essays and Studies*, by Algernon Charles Swinburne. London: Chatto & Windus, 1875.

deaf and desperate head must rest the original guilt of defacing the
text of Shelley with this most damnable corruption."

The essays before us are upon Victor Hugo, D. G. Rossetti, William
Morris, Matthew Arnold as a poet, Shelley, Byron, Coleridge, and John
Ford. To these are added two papers upon pictures—the drawings of
the old masters at Florence and the Royal Academy Exhibition of 1868.
Mr. Swinburne, in writing of poets, cannot fail to say a great many
felicitous things. His own insight into the poetic mystery is so deep,
his perception in matters of language so refined, his power of appreciation so large and active, his imagination, especially, so sympathetic
and flexible, that we constantly feel him to be one who has a valid
right to judge and pass sentence. The variety of his sympathies in
poetry is especially remarkable, and is in itself a pledge of criticism of a
liberal kind. Victor Hugo is his divinity—a divinity whom indeed, to
our sense, he effectually conceals and obliterates in the suffocating
fumes of his rhetoric. On the other hand, one of the best papers in the
volume is a disquisition on the poetry of Mr. Matthew Arnold, of
which his relish seems hardly less intense and for whom he states the
case with no less prodigious a redundancy of phrase. Matthew Arnold's
canons of style, we should have said, are a positive negation of those
of Mr. Swinburne's, and it is to the credit of the latter's breadth of
taste that he should have entered into an intellectual temperament
which is so little his own. The other articles contain similar examples
of his vivacity and energy of perception, and offer a number of happy
judgments and suggestive observations. His estimate of Byron as a
poet (not in the least as a man—on this point his utterances are consummately futile) is singularly discriminating; his measurement of
Shelley's lyric force is eloquently adequate; his closing words upon
John Ford are worth quoting as a specimen of strong apprehension
and solid statement. Mr. Swinburne is by no means always solid, and
this passage represents him at his best:

No poet is less forgettable than Ford; none fastens (as it were) the fangs
of his genius and his will more deeply in your memory. You cannot shake
hands with him and pass him by; you cannot fall in with him and out again
at pleasure; if he touch you once he takes you, and what he takes he keeps his
hold of; his work becomes part of your thought and parcel of your spiritual
furniture for ever; he signs himself upon you as with a seal of deliberate and
decisive power. His force is never the force of accident; the casual divinity
of beauty which falls, as though direct from heaven, upon stray lines and
phrases of some poets, falls never by any such heavenly chance on his; his

strength of impulse is matched by his strength of will; he never works more by instinct than by resolution; he knows what he would have and what he will do, and gains his end and does his work with full conscience of purpose and insistence of design. By the might of a great will seconded by the force of a great hand he won the place he holds against all odds of rivalry in a race of rival giants.

On the other hand, Mr. Swinburne is constantly liable on this same line to lapse into flagrant levity and perversity of taste; as in saying that he cannot consider Wordsworth "as mere poet" equal to Coleridge as mere poet; in speaking of Alfred de Musset as "the female page or attendant dwarf" of Byron and his poems as "decoctions of watered Byronism"; or in alluding jauntily and *en passant* to Gautier's *Mademoiselle de Maupin* as "the most perfect and exquisite book of modern times". To note, however, the points at which Mr. Swinburne's judgment hits the mark, or the points at which it misses it, is comparatively superfluous, inasmuch as both these cases seem to us essentially accidental. His book is not at all a book of judgment; it is a book of pure imagination. His genius is for style simply, and not in the least for thought nor for real analysis; he goes through the motions of criticism, and makes a considerable show of logic and philosophy, but with deep appreciation his writing seems to us to have very little to do. He is an imaginative commentator, often of a very splendid kind, but he is never a real interpreter and rarely a trustworthy guide. He is a writer, and a writer in constant quest of a theme. He has an inordinate sense of the picturesque, and he finds his theme in those subjects and those writers which gratify it. When they gratify it highly, he conceives a boundless relish for them; they give him his chance, and he turns on the deluge of his exorbitant homage. His imagination kindles, he abounds in their own sense, when they give him an inch he takes an ell, and quite loses sight of the subject in the entertainment he finds in his own word-spinning. In this respect he is extraordinarily accomplished: he very narrowly misses having a magnificent style. On the imaginative side, his style is almost complete, and seems capable of doing everything that picturesqueness demands. There are few writers of our day who could have produced this description of a thunderstorm at sea. Mr. Swinburne gives it to us as the likeness of Victor Hugo's genius:

> About midnight, the thunder-cloud was full overhead, full of incessant sound and fire, lightening and darkening so rapidly that it seemed to have life, and a delight in its life. At the same hour, the sky was clear to the west,

and all along the sea-line there sprang and sank as to music a restless dance or chase of summer lightning across the lower sky: a race and riot of lights, beautiful and rapid as a course of shining Oceanides along the tremulous floor of the sea. Eastward, at the same moment, the space of clear sky was higher and wider, a splendid semicircle of too intense purity to be called blue; it was of no colour nameable by man; and midway in it, between the stars and the sea, hung the motionless full moon; Artemis watching with serene splendour of scorn the battle of Titans and the revel of nymphs from her stainless and Olympian summit of divine indifferent light. Underneath and about us, the sea was paved with flame; the whole water trembled and hissed with phosphoric fire; even through the wind and thunder I could hear the crackling and sputtering of the water-sparks. In the same heaven and in the same hour there shone at once the three contrasted glories, golden and fiery and white, of moonlight, and of the double lightning, forked and sheet; and under all this miraculous heaven lay a flaming floor of water.

But with this extravagant development of the imagination there is no commensurate development either of the reason or of the moral sense. One of these defects is, to our mind, fatal to Mr. Swinburne's style; the other is fatal to his tone, to his temper, to his critical pretensions. His style is without measure, without discretion, without sense of what to take and what to leave; after a few pages, it becomes intolerably fatiguing. It is always listening to itself—always turning its head over its shoulders to see its train flowing behind it. The train shimmers and tumbles in a very gorgeous fashion, but the rustle of its embroidery is fatally importunate. Mr. Swinburne is a dozen times too verbose; at least one-half of his phrases are what the French call phrases in the air. One-half of his sentence is always a repetition, for mere fancy's sake and nothing more, of the meaning of the other half— a play upon its words, an echo, a reflection, a duplication. This trick, of course, makes a writer formidably prolix. What we have called the absence of the moral sense of the writer of these essays is, however, their most disagreeable feature, By this we do not mean that Mr. Swinburne is not didactic, nor edifying, nor devoted to pleading the cause of virtue. We mean simply that his moral plummet does not sink at all, and that when he pretends to drop it he is simply dabbling in the relatively very shallow pool of the picturesque. A sense of the picturesque so refined as Mr. Swinburne's will take one a great way, but it will by no means, in dealing with things whose great value is in what they tell us of human character, take one all the way. One breaks down with it (if one treats it as one's sole support) sooner or later in aesthetics; one breaks down with it very soon indeed in psychology.

We do not remember in this whole volume a single instance of delicate moral discrimination—a single case in which the moral note has been struck, in which the idea betrays the smallest acquaintance with the conscience. The moral realm for Mr. Swinburne is simply a brilliant chiaroscuro of costume and posture. This makes all Mr. Swinburne's magnificent talk about Victor Hugo's great criminals and monstrosities, about Shelley's Count Cenci, and Browning's Guido Franchesini, and about dramatic figures generally, quite worthless as anything but amusing fantasy. As psychology it is, to our sense, extremely puerile; for we do not mean simply to say that the author does not understand morality—a charge to which he would be probably quite indifferent; but that he does not at all understand immorality. Such a passage as his rhapsody upon Victor Hugo's Josiane ("such a pantheress may be such a poetess", etc.) means absolutely nothing. It is entertaining as pictorial writing—though even in this respect, as we have said, thanks to excess and redundancy, it is the picturesque spoiled rather than achieved; but as an attempt at serious analysis it seems to us, like many of its companions, simply ghastly—ghastly in its poverty of insight and its pretension to make mere lurid imagery do duty as thought.

6

CHARLES BAUDELAIRE

1876

As a brief discussion was lately carried on[1] touching the merits of the writer whose name we have prefixed to these lines, it may not be amiss to introduce him to some of those readers who must have observed the contest with little more than a vague sense of the strangeness of its subject. Charles Baudelaire is not a novelty in literature; his principal work[2] dates from 1857, and his career terminated a few years later. But his admirers have made a classic of him and elevated him to the rank of one of those subjects which are always in order. Even if we differ with them on this point, such attention as Baudelaire demands will not lead us very much astray. He is not, in quantity (whatever he may have been in quality), a formidable writer; having died young, he was not prolific, and the most noticeable of his original productions are contained in two small volumes.

His celebrity began with the publication of *Les Fleurs du Mal*, a collection of verses of which some had already appeared in periodicals. The *Revue des Deux Mondes* had taken the responsibility of introducing a few of them to the world—or rather, though it held them at the baptismal font of public opinion, it had declined to stand godfather. An accompanying note in the *Revue* disclaimed all editorial approval of their morality. This of course procured them a good many readers; and when, on its appearance, the volume we have mentioned was overhauled by the police a still greater number of persons desired to possess it. Yet in spite of the service rendered him by the censorship, Baudelaire has never become in any degree popular; the lapse of twenty years has seen but five editions of *Les Fleurs du Mal*. The foremost feeling of the reader of the present day will be one of surprise, and even amusement, at Baudelaire's audacities having provoked this degree of scandal. The world has travelled fast since then, and the French censorship must have been, in the year 1857, in a very prudish mood. There is little in *Les Fleurs du Mal* to make the reader of either French or

---

[1] There had been an exchange of letters on the subject in an American ournal.

[2] *Les Fleurs du Mal*, par Charles Baudelaire. Précédé d'une Notice par Théophile Gautier. Paris: Michel Lévy.

English prose and verse of the present day even open his eyes. We have passed through the fiery furnace and profited by experience. We are happier than Racine's heroine, who had not

> Su se faire un front qui ne rougit jamais.

Baudelaire's verses do not strike us as being dictated by a spirit of bravado—though we have heard that, in talk, it was his habit, to an even tiresome degree, to cultivate the quietly outrageous—to pile up monstrosities and blasphemies without winking and with the air of uttering proper commonplaces.

Les Fleurs du Mal is evidently a sincere book—so far as anything for a man of Baudelaire's temper and culture could be sincere. Sincerity seems to us to belong to a range of qualities with which Baudelaire and his friends were but scantily concerned. His great quality was an inordinate cultivation of the sense of the picturesque, and his care was for how things looked, and whether some kind of imaginative amuse- ment was not to be got out of them, much more than for what they meant and whither they led and what was their use in human life at large. The later editions of Les Fleurs du Mal (with some of the inter- dicted pieces still omitted and others, we believe, restored) contain a long preface by Théophile Gautier, which throws a curious side-light upon what the Spiritualist newspapers would call Baudelaire's "ment- ality". Of course Baudelaire is not to be held accountable for what Gautier says of him, but we cannot help judging a man in some degree by the company he keeps. To admire Gautier is certainly excellent taste, but to be admired by Gautier we cannot but regard as rather com- promising. He gives a magnificently picturesque account of the author of Les Fleurs du Mal, in which, indeed, the question of pure exactitude is evidently so very subordinate that it seems grossly ill-natured for us to appeal to such a standard. While we are reading him, however, we find ourselves wishing that Baudelaire's analogy with the author him- self were either greater or less. Gautier was perfectly sincere, because he dealt only with the picturesque and pretended to care only for appearances. But Baudelaire (who, to our mind, was an altogether inferior genius to Gautier) applied the same process of interpretation to things as regards which it was altogether inadequate; so that one is constantly tempted to suppose he cares more for his process—for making grotesquely-pictorial verse—than for the things themselves. On the whole, as we have said, this inference would be unfair. Baudelaire had a certain groping sense of the moral complexities of life, and if the best

that he succeeds in doing is to drag them down into the very turbid
element in which he himself plashes and flounders, and there present
them to us much besmirched and bespattered, this was not a want
of goodwill in him, but rather a dullness and permanent immaturity
of vision. For American readers, furthermore, Baudelaire is compromised by his having made himself the apostle of our own Edgar
Poe. He translated, very carefully and exactly, all of Poe's prose
writings, and, we believe, some of his very superficial verses. With all
due respect to the very original genius of the author of the *Tales of
Mystery*, it seems to us that to take him with more than a certain degree
of seriousness is to lack seriousness one's self. An enthusiasm for Poe
is the mark of a decidedly primitive stage of reflection. Baudelaire
thought him a profound philosopher, the neglect of whose golden
utterances stamped his native land with infamy. Nevertheless, Poe
was much the greater charlatan of the two, as well as the greater
genius.

Les Fleurs du Mal was a very happy title for Baudelaire's verses, but
it is not altogether a just one. Scattered flowers incontestably do bloom
in the quaking swamps of evil, and the poet who does not mind
encountering bad odours in his pursuit of sweet ones is quite at liberty
to go in search of them. But Baudelaire has, as a general thing, not
plucked the flowers—he has plucked the evil-smelling weeds (we take it
that he did not use the word flowers in a purely ironical sense) and he
has often taken up mere cupfuls of mud and bog-water. He had said
to himself that it was a great shame that the realm of evil and unclean
things should be fenced off from the domain of poetry; that it was full
of subjects, of chances and effects; that it had its light and shade, its
logic and its mystery; and that there was the making of some capital
verses in it. So he leaped the barrier and was soon immersed in it up
to his neck. Baudelaire's imagination was of a melancholy and sinister
kind, and, to a considerable extent, this plunging into darkness and
dirt was doubtless very spontaneous and disinterested. But he strikes
us on the whole as passionless, and this, in view of the unquestionable
pluck and acuteness of his fancy, is a great pity. He knew evil not by
experience, not as something within himself, but by contemplation
and curiosity, as something outside of himself, by which his own intellectual agility was not in the least discomposed, rather indeed (as
we say his fancy was of a dusky cast) agreeably flattered and stimulated.
In the former case, Baudelaire, with his other gifts, might have been a
great poet. But, as it is, evil for him begins outside and not inside, and

consists primarily of a great deal of lurid landscape and unclean furniture. This is an almost ludicrously puerile view of the matter. Evil is represented as an affair of blood and carrion and physical sickness—there must be stinking corpses and starving prostitutes and empty laudanum bottles in order that the poet shall be effectively inspired.

A good way to embrace Baudelaire at a glance is to say that he was, in his treatment of evil, exactly what Hawthorne was not—Hawthorne, who felt the thing at its source, deep in the human consciousness. Baudelaire's infinitely slighter volume of genius apart, he was a sort of Hawthorne reversed. It is the absence of this metaphysical quality in his treatment of his favourite subjects (Poe was his metaphysician, and his devotion sustained him through a translation of "Eureka!") that exposes him to that class of accusations of which M. Edmond Schérer's accusation of feeding upon *pourriture* is an example; and, in fact, in his pages we never know with what we are dealing. We encounter an inextricable confusion of sad emotions and vile things, and we are at a loss to know whether the subject pretends to appeal to our conscience or—we were going to say—to our olfactories. "Le Mal?" we exclaim; "you do yourself too much honour. This is not Evil; it is not the wrong; it is simply the nasty!" Our impatience is of the same order as that which we should feel if a poet, pretending to pluck "the flowers of good", should come and present us, as specimens, a rhapsody on plumcake and *eau de Cologne*. Independently of the question of his subjects, the charm of Baudelaire's verse is often of a very high order. He belongs to the class of geniuses in whom we ourselves find but a limited pleasure—the laborious, deliberate, economical writers, those who fumble a long time in their pockets before they bring out their hand with a coin in the palm. But the coin, when Baudelaire at last produced it, was often of a high value. He had an extraordinarily verbal instinct and an exquisite felicity of epithet. We cannot help wondering, however, at Gautier's extreme admiration for his endowment in this direction; it is the admiration of the writer who gushes for the writer who trickles. In one point Baudelaire is extremely remarkable—in his talent for suggesting associations. His epithets seem to have come out of old cupboards and pockets; they have a kind of magical mustiness. Moreover, his natural sense of the superficial picturesqueness of the miserable and the unclean was extremely acute; there may be a difference of opinion as to the advantage of possessing such a sense; but whatever it is worth Baudelaire had it in a high degree. One of his poems—

"To a Red-haired Beggar Girl"—is a masterpiece in the way of graceful expression of this high relish of what is shameful.

> Pour moi, poète chétif,
> Ton jeune corps maladif,
> Plein de taches de rousseur,
> A sa douceur.

Baudelaire repudiated with indignation the charge that he was what is called a realist, and he was doubtless right in doing so. He had too much fancy to adhere strictly to the real; he always embroiders and elaborates—endeavours to impart that touch of strangeness and mystery which is the very *raison d'être* of poetry. Baudelaire was a poet, and for a poet to be a realist is of course nonsense. The idea that Baudelaire imported into his theme was, as a general thing, an intensification of its repulsiveness, but it was at any rate ingenious. When he makes an invocation to "la Débauche aux bras immondes" one may be sure he means more by it than is evident to the vulgar—he means, that is, an intenser perversity. Occasionally he treats agreeable subjects, and his least sympathetic critics must make a point of admitting that his most successful poem is also his least morbid, and most touching; we allude to "Les Petites Vieilles"—a really masterly production. But if it represents the author's maximum, it is a note that he very rarely struck.

Baudelaire, of course, is a capital text for a discussion of the question as to the importance of the morality—or of the subject-matter in general—of a work of art; for he offers a rare combination of technical zeal and patience and of vicious sentiment. But even if we had space to enter upon such a discussion, we should spare our words; for argument on this point wears to our sense a really ridiculous aspect. To deny the relevancy of subject-matter and the importance of the moral quality of a work of art strikes us as, in two words, very childish. We do not know what the great moralists would say about the matter—they would probably treat it very good-humouredly; but that is not the question. There is very little doubt what the great artists would say. People of that temper feel that the whole thinking man is one, and that to count out the moral element in one's appreciation of an artistic total is exactly as sane as it would be (if the total were a poem) to eliminate all the words in three syllables, or to consider only such portions of it as had been written by candle-light. The crudity of sentiment of the advocates of "art for art" is often a striking example of the fact that a great deal of what is called culture may fail to dissipate a well-seated provincialism of spirit. They talk of morality as Miss Edgeworth's infantine heroes and heroines talk of "physic"—they allude to its being put into and kept out of work of art, put into and kept out of one's appreciation of the same, as if it were a coloured fluid kept in a big-labelled bottle in some mysterious intellectual closet. It is in reality simply a part of the essential richness of inspiration—it has nothing to do with the artistic process and it has everything to do with the artistic effect. The more a work of art feels it at its source, the richer it is; the less it feels it, the poorer it is. People of a large taste prefer rich works to poor ones and they are not inclined to assent to the assumption that the process is the whole work. We are safe in believing that all this is comfortably clear to most of those who have, in any degree, been initiated into art by production. For them the subject is as much a part of their work as their hunger is a part of their dinner. Baudelaire was not so far from being of this way of thinking as some of his admirers would persuade us; yet we may say on the whole that he was the victim of a grotesque illusion. He tried to make fine verses on ignoble subjects, and in our opinion he signally failed. He gives, as a poet, a perpetual impression of discomfort and pain. He went in search of corruption, and the ill-conditioned jade proved a thankless muse. The thinking reader, feeling himself, as a critic, all one, as we have said, finds the beauty perverted by the ugliness. What the poet wished, doubtless was to seem to be always in the poetic attitude; what the reader sees is a gentleman in a painful-looking posture, staring very hard at a mass of things from which, more intelligently, we avert our heads.

[7]

DANIEL DERONDA: A Conversation

1876

THEODORA, one day early in the autumn, sat on her verandah with a piece of embroidery, the design of which she made up as she proceeded, being careful, however, to have a Japanese screen before her, to keep her inspiration at the proper altitude. Pulcheria, who was paying her a visit, sat near her with a closed book, in a paper cover, in her lap. Pulcheria was playing with the pug-dog, rather idly, but Theodora was stitching, steadily and meditatively. "Well," said Theodora, at last, "I wonder what he accomplished in the East." Pulcheria took the little dog into her lap and made him sit on the book. "Oh," she replied, "they had tea-parties at Jerusalem—exclusively of ladies—and he sat in the midst and stirred his tea and made high-toned remarks. And then Mirah sang a little, just a little, on account of her voice being so weak. Sit still, Fido," she continued, addressing the little dog, "and keep your nose out of my face. But it's a nice little nose, all the same," she pursued, "a nice little short snub nose and not a horrid big Jewish nose. Oh, my dear, when I think what a collection of noses there must have been at that wedding!" At this moment Constantius steps upon the verandah from within, hat and stick in hand and his shoes a trifle dusty. He has some distance to come before he reaches the place where the ladies are sitting and this gives Pulcheria time to murmur, "Talk, of snub noses!" Constantius is presented by Theodora to Pulcheria, and he sits down and exclaims upon the admirable blueness of the sea; which lies in a straight band across the green of the little lawn, comments too upon the pleasure of having one side of one's verandah in the shade. Soon Fido, the little dog, still restless, jumps off Pulcheria's lap and reveals the book, which lies title upward. "Oh," says Constantius, "you have been finishing *Daniel Deronda*?" Then follows a conversation which it will be more convenient to present in another form.

THEODORA. Yes, Pulcheria has been reading aloud the last chapters to me. They are wonderfully beautiful.

CONSTANTIUS (after a moment's hesitation). Yes, they are very beautiful. I am sure you read well, Pulcheria, to give the fine passages their full value.

32

THEODORA. She reads well when she chooses, but I am sorry to say that in some of the fine passages of this last book she took quite a false tone. I couldn't have read them aloud myself; I should have broken down. But Pulcheria—would you really believe it?—when she couldn't go on it was not for tears, but for—the contrary.

CONSTANTIUS. For smiles? Did you really find it comical? One of my objections to *Daniel Deronda* is the absence of those delightfully humorous passages which enlivened the author's former works.

PULCHERIA. Oh, I think there are some places as amusing as anything in *Adam Bede* or *The Mill on the Floss*: for instance where, at the last, Deronda wipes Gwendolen's tears and Gwendolen wipes his.

CONSTANTIUS. Yes, I know what you mean. I can understand that situation presenting a slightly ridiculous image; that is, if the current of the story don't swiftly carry you past.

PULCHERIA. What do you mean by the current of the story? I never read a story with less current. It is not a river; it is a series of lakes. I once read of a group of little uneven ponds resembling, from a bird's-eye view, a looking-glass which had fallen upon the floor and broken, and was lying in fragments. That is what *Daniel Deronda* would look like, on a bird's-eye view.

THEODORA. Pulcheria found that comparison in a French novel. She is always reading French novels.

CONSTANTIUS. Ah, there are some very good ones.

PULCHERIA (perversely). I don't know; I think there are some very poor ones.

CONSTANTIUS. The comparison is not bad, at any rate. I know what you mean by *Daniel Deronda* lacking current. It has almost as little as *Romola*.

PULCHERIA. Oh, *Romola* is unpardonably slow; it is a kind of literary tortoise.

CONSTANTIUS. Yes, I know what you mean by that. But I am afraid you are not friendly to our great novelist.

THEODORA. She likes Balzac and George Sand and other impure writers.

CONSTANTIUS. Well, I must say I understand that.

PULCHERIA. My favourite novelist is Thackeray, and I am extremely fond of Miss Austen.

CONSTANTIUS. I understand that too. You read over *The Newcomes* and *Pride and Prejudice*.

PULCHERIA. No, I don't read them over now; I think them over. I have been making visits for a long time past to a series of friends, and I have spent the last six months in reading *Daniel Deronda* aloud. Fortune would have it that I should always arrive by the same train as the new number. I am accounted a frivolous, idle creature; I am not a disciple in the new school of embroidery, like Theodora; so I was immediately pushed into a chair and the book thrust into my hand, that I might lift up my voice and make peace between all the impatiences that were snatching at it. So I may claim at least that I have read every word of the work. I never skipped.

THEODORA. I should hope not, indeed!

CONSTANTIUS. And do you mean that you really didn't enjoy it?

PULCHERIA. I found it protracted, pretentious, pedantic.

CONSTANTIUS. I see; I can understand that.

THEODORA. Oh, you understand too much! This is the twentieth time you have used that formula.

CONSTANTIUS. What will you have? You know I must try to understand; it's my trade.

THEODORA. He means he writes reviews. Trying *not* to understand is what I call that trade!

CONSTANTIUS. Say then I take it the wrong way; that is why it has never made my fortune. But I do try to understand; it is my—my—— (He pauses.)

THEODORA. I know what you want to say. Your strong side.

PULCHERIA. And what is his weak side?

THEODORA. He writes novels.

CONSTANTIUS. I have written *one*. You can't call that a side. It's a little facet, at the most.

PULCHERIA. You talk as if you were a diamond. I should like to read it—not aloud!

CONSTANTIUS. You can't read it softly enough. But you, Theodora, you didn't find our book too "protracted"?

THEODORA. I should have liked it to continue indefinitely, to keep coming out always, to be one of the regular things of life.

PULCHERIA. Oh, come here, little dog! To think that *Daniel Deronda* might be perpetual when you, little short-nosed darling, can't last at the most more than nine or ten years!

THEODORA. A book like *Daniel Deronda* becomes part of one's life; one lives in it, or alongside of it. I don't hesitate to say that I have been living in this one for the last eight months. It is such a complete world George Eliot builds up; it is so vast, so much-embracing! It has such a firm earth and such an ethereal sky. You can turn into it and lose yourself in it.

PULCHERIA. Oh, easily, and die of cold and starvation!

THEODORA. I have been very near to poor Gwendolen and very near to that sweet Mirah. And the dear little Meyricks also; I know them intimately well.

PULCHERIA. The Meyricks, I grant you, are the best thing in the book.

THEODORA. They are a delicious family; I wish they lived in Boston. I consider Herr Klesmer almost Shakespearean, and his wife is almost as good. I have been near to poor grand Mordecai——

PULCHERIA. Oh, reflect, my dear; not too near!

THEODORA. And as for Deronda himself I freely confess that I am consumed with a hopeless passion for him. He is the most irresistible man in the literature of fiction.

PULCHERIA. He is not a man at all.

THEODORA. I remember nothing more beautiful than the description of his childhood, and that picture of his lying on the grass in the abbey cloister, a beautiful seraph-faced boy, with a lovely voice, reading history and asking his Scotch tutor why the Popes had so many nephews. He must have been delightfully handsome.

PULCHERIA. Never, my dear, with that nose! I am sure he had a nose and I hold that the author has shown great pusillanimity in her treatment of it. She has quite shirked it. The picture you speak of is very pretty, but a picture is not a person. And why is he always grasping his coat-collar, as if he wished to hang himself up? The author had an uncomfortable feeling that she must make him do something real, something visible and sensible, and she hit upon that clumsy figure. I don't see what you mean by saying you have been *near* those people; that is just what one is not. They produce no illusion. They are described and analysed to death, but we don't see them nor hear them nor touch them. Deronda clutches his coat-collar, Mirah crosses her feet, Mordecai talks like the Bible; but that doesn't make real figures of them. They have no existence outside of the author's study.

THEODORA. If you mean that they are nobly imaginative I quite agree with you; and if they say nothing to your own imagination the fault is yours, not theirs.

PULCHERIA. Pray don't say they are Shakespearean again. Shakespeare went to work another way.

CONSTANTIUS. I think you are both in a measure right; there is a distinction to be drawn. There are in *Daniel Deronda* the figures based upon observation and the figures based upon invention. This distinction, I know, is rather a rough one. There are no figures in any novel that are pure observation, and none that are pure invention. But either element may preponderate, and in those cases in which invention has preponderated George Eliot seems to me to have achieved at the best but so many brilliant failures.

THEODORA. And are *you* turning severe? I thought you admired her so much.

CONSTANTIUS. I defy any one to admire her more but one must discriminate. Speaking brutally, I consider *Daniel Deronda* the weakest of her books. It strikes me as very sensibly inferior to *Middlemarch* I have an immense opinion of *Middlemarch*.

PULCHERIA. Not having been obliged by circumstances to read *Middlemarch* to other people, I didn't read it at all. I couldn't read it to myself. I tried, but I broke down. I appreciated Rosamond, but I couldn't believe in Dorothea.

THEODORA (very gravely). So much the worse for you, Pulcheria. I have enjoyed *Daniel Deronda because* I had enjoyed *Middlemarch*. Why should you throw *Middlemarch* up against her? It seems to me that if a book is fine it is fine. I have enjoyed *Deronda* deeply, from beginning to end.

CONSTANTIUS. I assure you, so have I. I can read nothing of George Eliot's without enjoyment. I even enjoy her poetry, though I don't approve of it. In whatever she writes I enjoy her intelligence; it has space and air, like a fine landscape. The intellectual brilliancy of *Daniel Deronda* strikes me as very great, in excess of anything the author has done. In the first couple of numbers of the book this ravished me. I delighted in its deep, rich English tone, in which so many notes seemed melted together.

PULCHERIA. The tone is not English, it is German.

CONSTANTIUS. I understand that—if Theodora will allow me to say so. Little by little I began to feel that I cared less for certain notes than for others. I say it under my breath—I began to feel an occasional temptation to skip. Roughly speaking, all the Jewish burden of the story tended to weary me; it is this part that produces the poor illusion which I agree with Pulcheria in finding. Gwendolen and Grandcourt are admirable—Gwendolen is a masterpiece. She is known, felt and presented, psychologically, altogether in the grand manner. Beside her and beside her husband—a consummate picture of English brutality refined and distilled (for Grandcourt is before all things brutal), Deronda, Mordecai and Mirah are hardly more than shadows. They and their fortunes are all improvisation. I don't say anything against improvisation. When it succeeds it has a surpassing charm. But it must succeed. With George Eliot it seems to me to succeed, but a little less than one would expect of her talent. The story of Deronda's life, his mother's story, Mirah's story, are quite the sort of thing one finds in George Sand. But they are really not so good as they would be in George Sand. George Sand would have carried it off with a lighter hand.

THEODORA. Oh, Constantius, how can you compare George Eliot's novels to that woman's? It is sunlight and moonshine.

PULCHERIA. I really think the two writers are very much alike. They are both very voluble, both addicted to moralizing and philosophizing à tout bout de champ, both inartistic.

CONSTANTIUS. I see what you mean. But George Eliot is solid, and George Sand is liquid. When occasionally George Eliot liquefies—as in the history of Deronda's birth, and in that of Mirah—it is not to so crystalline a clearness as the author of Consuelo and André. Take Mirah's long narrative of her adventures, when she unfolds them to Mrs. Meyrick. It is arranged, it is artificial, ancien jeu, quite in the George Sand manner. But George Sand would have done it better. The false tone would have remained, but it would have been more persuasive. It would have been a fib, but the fib would have been neater.

THEODORA. I don't think fibbing neatly a merit, and I don't see what is to be gained by such comparisons. George Eliot is pure and George Sand is impure; how can you compare them? As for the Jewish element in Deronda, I think it a very fine idea; it's a noble subject. Wilkie Collins and Miss Braddon would not have thought of it, but that does not condemn it. It shows a large conception of what one may do in a novel. I heard you say, the other day, that most novels were so trivial—that they had no general ideas. Here is a general idea, the idea interpreted by Deronda. I have never disliked the Jews as some people do; I am not like Pulcheria, who sees a Jew in every bush. I wish there were one; I would cultivate shrubbery. I have known too many clever and charming Jews; I have known none that were not clever.

PULCHERIA. Clever, but not charming.

CONSTANTIUS. I quite agree with you as to Deronda's going in for the Jews and turning out a Jew himself being a fine subject, and this

quite apart from the fact of whether such a thing as a Jewish revival be
at all a possibility. If it be a possibility, so much the better—so much
the better for the subject, I mean.

PULCHERIA. *A la bonne heure!*

CONSTANTIUS. I rather suspect it is not a possibility; that the Jews
in general take themselves much less seriously than that. They have
other fish to fry. George Eliot takes them as a person outside of
Judaism—aesthetically. I don't believe that is the way they take
themselves.

PULCHERIA. They have the less excuse then for keeping themselves
so dirty.

THEODORA. George Eliot must have known some delightful
Jews.

CONSTANTIUS. Very likely; but I shouldn't wonder if the most
delightful of them had smiled a trifle, here and there, over her book.
But that makes nothing, as Herr Klesmer would say. The subject
is a noble one. The idea of depicting a nature able to feel and worthy
to feel the sort of inspiration that takes possession of Deronda, of
depicting it sympathetically, minutely and intimately—such an idea
has great elevation. There is something very fascinating in the mission
that Deronda takes upon himself. I don't quite know what it means,
I don't understand more than half of Mordecai's rhapsodies, and I
don't perceive exactly what practical steps could be taken. Deronda
could go about and talk with clever Jews—not an unpleasant life.

PULCHERIA. All that seems to me so unreal that when at the end the
author finds herself confronted with the necessity of making him start
for the East by the train, and announces that Sir Hugo and Lady
Mallinger have given his wife "a complete Eastern outfit", I descend
to the ground with a ludicrous jump.

CONSTANTIUS. Unreal, if you please; that is no objection to it; it
greatly tickles my imagination. I like extremely the idea of Mordecai
believing, without ground of belief, that if he only wait, a young man
on whom nature and society have centred all their gifts will come to
him and receive from his hands the precious vessel of his hopes. It is
romantic, but it is not vulgar romance; it is finely romantic. And there
is something very fine in the author's own feeling about Deronda.
He is a very liberal creation. He is, I think, a failure—a brilliant failure;
if he had been a success I should call him a splendid creation. The author
meant to do things very handsomely for him; she meant apparently
to make a faultless human being.

PULCHERIA. She made a dreadful prig.

CONSTANTIUS. He *is* rather priggish, and one wonders that so clever a woman as George Eliot shouldn't see it.

PULCHERIA. He has no blood in his body. His attitude at moments is like that of a high-priest in a *tableau vivant*.

THEODORA. Pulcheria likes the little gentlemen in the French novels who take good care of their attitudes, which are always the same attitude, the attitude of "conquest"—of a conquest that tickles their vanity. Deronda has a contour that cuts straight through the middle of all that. He is made of a stuff that isn't dreamt of in their philosophy.

PULCHERIA. Pulcheria likes very much a novel which she read three or four years ago, but which she has not forgotten. It was by Ivan Turgénieff, and it was called *On the Eve*. Theodora has read it, I know, because she admires Turgénieff, and Constantius has read it, I suppose, because he has read everything.

CONSTANTIUS. If I had no reason but that for my reading, it would be small. But Turgénieff is my man.

PULCHERIA. You were just now praising George Eliot's general ideas. The tale of which I speak contains in the portrait of the hero very much such a general idea as you find in the portrait of Deronda. Don't you remember the young Bulgarian student, Inssaroff, who gives himself the mission of rescuing his country from its subjection to the Turks? Poor man, if he had foreseen the horrible summer of 1876! His character is the picture of a race-passion, of patriotic hopes and dreams. But what a difference in the vividness of the two figures. Inssaroff is a man; he stands up on his feet; we see him, hear him, touch him. And it has taken the author but a couple of hundred pages— not eight volumes—to do it.

THEODORA. I don't remember Inssaroff at all, but I perfectly remember the heroine, Helena. She is certainly most remarkable, but, remarkable as she is, I should never dream of calling her as wonderful as Gwendolen.

CONSTANTIUS. Turgénieff is a magician, which I don't think I should call George Eliot. One is a poet, the other is a philosopher. One cares for the aspect of things and the other cares for the reason of things. George Eliot, in embarking with Deronda, took aboard, as it were, a far heavier cargo than Turgénieff with his Inssaroff. She proposed, consciously, to strike more notes.

PULCHERIA. Oh, consciously, yes!

CONSTANTIUS. George Eliot wished to show the possible picturesqueness—the romance, as it were—of a high moral tone. Deronda is a
moralist, a moralist with a rich complexion.

THEODORA. It is a most beautiful nature. I don't know anywhere a
more complete, a more deeply analysed portrait of a great nature. We
praise novelists for wandering and creeping so into the small corners of
the mind. That is what we praise Balzac for when he gets down upon
all fours to crawl through *Le Père Goriot* or *Les Parents Pauvres*. But
I must say I think it a finer thing to unlock with as firm a hand as
George Eliot some of the greater chambers of human character.
Deronda is in a manner an ideal character, if you will, but he seems to
me triumphantly married to reality. There are some admirable things
said about him; nothing can be finer than those pages of description of
his moral temperament in the fourth book—his elevated way of looking
at things, his impartiality, his universal sympathy, and at the same time
his fear of their turning into mere irresponsible indifference. I remember some of it verbally: "He was ceasing to care for knowledge
—he had no ambition for practice—unless they could be gathered up
into one current with his emotions."

PULCHERIA. Oh, there is plenty about his emotions. Everything
about him is "emotive". That bad word occurs on every fifth page.

THEODORA. I don't see that it is a bad word.

PULCHERIA. It may be good German, but it is poor English.

THEODORA. It is not German at all; it is Latin. So, my dear!

PULCHERIA. As I say, then, it is not English.

THEODORA. This is the first time I ever heard that George Eliot's
style was bad!

CONSTANTIUS. It is admirable; it has the most delightful and the most
intellectually comfortable suggestions. But it is occasionally a little
too long-sleeved, as I may say. It is sometimes too loose a fit for the
thought, a little baggy.

THEODORA. And the advice he gives Gwendolen, the things he says
to her, they are the very essence of wisdom, of warm human wisdom,
knowing life and feeling it. "Keep your fear as a safeguard, it may
make consequences passionately present to you." What can be better
than that?

PULCHERIA. Nothing perhaps. But what can be drearier than a
novel in which the function of the hero—young, handsome and
brilliant—is to give didactic advice, in a proverbial form, to the young,
beautiful and brilliant heroine?

CONSTANTIUS. That is not putting it quite fairly. The function of Deronda is to make Gwendolen fall in love with him, to say nothing of falling in love himself with Mirah.

PULCHERIA. Yes, the less said about that the better. All we know about Mirah is that she has delicate rings of hair, sits with her feet crossed, and talks like an article in a new magazine.

CONSTANTIUS. Deronda's function of adviser to Gwendolen does not strike me as so ridiculous. He is not nearly so ridiculous as if he were lovesick. It is a very interesting situation—that of a man with whom a beautiful woman in trouble falls in love and yet whose affections are so preoccupied that the most he can do for her in return is to enter kindly and sympathetically into her position, pity her and talk to her. George Eliot always gives us something that is strikingly and ironically characteristic of human life; and what savours more of the essential crookedness of our fate than the sad cross-purposes of these two young people? Poor Gwendolen's falling in love with Deronda is part of her own luckless history, not of his.

THEODORA. I do think he takes it to himself rather too little. No man had ever so little vanity.

PULCHERIA. It is very inconsistent, therefore, as well as being extremely impertinent and ill-mannered, his buying back and sending to her her necklace at Leubronn.

CONSTANTIUS. Oh, you must concede that; without it there would have been no story. A man writing of him, however, would certainly have made him more peccable. As George Eliot lets herself go, in that quarter, she becomes delightfully, almost touchingly, feminine. It is like her making Romola go to housekeeping with Tessa, after Tito Melema's death; like her making Dorothea marry Will Ladislaw. If Dorothea had married any one after her misadventure with Casaubon she would have married a trooper.

THEODORA. Perhaps some day Gwendolen will marry Rex.

PULCHERIA. Pray, who is Rex?

THEODORA. Why, Pulcheria, how can you forget?

PULCHERIA. Nay, how can I remember? But I recall such a name in the dim antiquity of the first or second book. Yes, and then he is pushed to the front again at the last, just in time not to miss the falling of the curtain. Gwendolen will certainly not have the audacity to marry any one we know so little about.

CONSTANTIUS. I have been wanting to say that there seems to me to be two very distinct elements in George Eliot—a spontaneous one and an artificial one. There is what she is by inspiration and what she is because it is expected of her. These two heads have been very perceptible in her recent writings; they are much less noticeable in her early ones.

THEODORA. You mean that she is too scientific? So long as she remains the great literary genius that she is, how can she be too scientific? She is simply permeated with the highest culture of the age.

PULCHERIA. She talks too much about the "dynamic quality" of people's eyes. When she uses such a phrase as that in the first sentence in her book she is not a great literary genius, because she shows a want of tact. There can't be a worse limitation.

CONSTANTIUS. The "dynamic quality" of Gwendolen's glance has made the tour of the world.

THEODORA. It shows a very low level of culture on the world's part to be agitated by a term perfectly familiar to all decently-educated people.

PULCHERIA. I don't pretend to be decently educated; pray tell me what it means.

CONSTANTIUS (promptly). I think Pulcheria has hit it in speaking of a want of tact. In the manner of the book, throughout, there is something that one may call a want of tact. The epigraphs in verse are a want of tact; they are sometimes, I think, a trifle more pretentious than really pregnant; the importunity of the moral reflections is a want of tact; the very diffuseness is a want of tact. But it comes back to what I said just now about one's sense of the author writing under a sort of external pressure. I began to notice it in *Felix Holt*; I don't think I had before. She strikes me as a person who certainly has naturally a taste for general considerations, but who has fallen upon an age and a circle which have compelled her to give them an exaggerated attention. She does not strike me as naturally a critic, less still as naturally a sceptic; her spontaneous part is to observe life and to feel it, to feel it with admirable depth. Contemplation, sympathy and faith—something like that, I should say, would have been her natural scale. If she had fallen upon an age of enthusiastic assent to old articles of faith, it seems to me possible that she would have had a more perfect, a more consistent and graceful development than she has actually had. If she had cast herself into such a current—her genius being equal—it might have carried her to splendid distances. But she has chosen to go into criticism, and to the critics she addresses her work; I mean the critics of the universe. Instead of feeling life itself, it is "views" upon life that she tries to feel.

PULCHERIA. She is the victim of a first-class education. I am so glad!

CONSTANTIUS. Thanks to her admirable intellect she philosophizes very sufficiently; but meanwhile she has given a chill to her genius. She has come near spoiling an artist.

PULCHERIA. She has quite spoiled one. Or rather I shouldn't say that, because there was no artist to spoil. I maintain that she is not an artist. An artist could never have put a story together so monstrously ill. She has no sense of form.

THEODORA. Pray, what could be more artistic than the way that Deronda's paternity is concealed till almost the end, and the way we are made to suppose Sir Hugo is his father?

PULCHERIA. And Mirah his sister. How does that fit together? I was as little made to suppose he was not a Jew as I cared when I found out he was. And his mother popping up through a trap-door and popping down again, at the last, in that scrambling fashion! His mother is very bad.

CONSTANTIUS. I think Deronda's mother is one of the unvivified characters; she belongs to the cold half of the book. All the Jewish part is at bottom cold; that is my only objection. I have enjoyed it because my fancy often warms cold things; but beside Gwendolen's history it is like the empty half of the lunar disk beside the full one. It is admirably studied, it is imagined, it is understood, but it is not embodied. One feels this strongly in just those scenes between Deronda and his mother; one feels that one has been appealed to on rather an artificial ground of interest. To make Deronda's reversion to his native faith more dramatic and profound, the author has given him a mother who on very arbitrary grounds, apparently, has separated herself from this same faith and who has been kept waiting in the wings, as it were, for many acts, to come on and make her speech and say so. This moral situation of hers we are invited retrospectively to appreciate. But we hardly care to do so.

PULCHERIA. I don't *see* the princess, in spite of her flame-coloured robe. Why should an actress and prima-donna care so much about religious matters?

THEODORA. It was not only that; it was the Jewish race she hated, Jewish manners and looks. You, my dear, ought to understand that.

PULCHERIA. I do, but I am not a Jewish actress of genius; I am not what Rachel was. If I were I should have other things to think about.

CONSTANTIUS. Think now a little about poor Gwendolen.

PULCHERIA. I don't care to think about her. She was a second-rate English girl who got into a flutter about a lord.

THEODORA. I don't see that she is worse than if she were a first-rate American girl who should get into exactly the same flutter.

PULCHERIA. It wouldn't be the same flutter at all; it wouldn't be any flutter. She wouldn't be afraid of the lord, though she might be amused at him.

THEODORA. I am sure I don't perceive whom Gwendolen was afraid of. She was afraid of her misdeed—her broken promise—after she had committed it, and through that fear she was afraid of her husband. Well she might be! I can imagine nothing more vivid than the sense we get of his absolutely clammy selfishness.

PULCHERIA. She was not afraid of Deronda when, immediately after her marriage and without any but the most casual acquaintance with him, she begins to hover about him at the Mallingers' and to drop little confidences about her conjugal woes. That seems to me very indelicate; ask any woman.

CONSTANTIUS. The very purpose of the author is to give us an idea of the sort of confidence that Deronda inspired—its irresistible potency.

PULCHERIA. A lay father-confessor—horrid!

CONSTANTIUS. And to give us an idea also of the acuteness of Gwendolen's depression, of her haunting sense of impending trouble.

THEODORA. It must be remembered that Gwendolen was in love with Deronda from the first, long before she knew it. She didn't know it, poor girl, but that was it.

PULCHERIA. That makes the matter worse. It is very disagreeable to see her hovering and rustling about a man who is indifferent to her.

THEODORA. He was not indifferent to her, since he sent her back her necklace.

PULCHERIA. Of all the delicate attentions to a charming girl that I ever heard of, that little pecuniary transaction is the most felicitous.

CONSTANTIUS. You must remember that he had been *en rapport* with her at the gaming-table. She had been playing in defiance of his observation, and he, continuing to observe her, had been in a measure responsible for her loss. There was a tacit consciousness of this between them. You may contest the possibility of tacit consciousness going so far, but that is not a serious objection. You may point out two or three weak spots in detail; the fact remains that Gwendolen's whole history is vividly told. And see how the girl is known, inside out, how thoroughly she is felt and understood. It is the most *intelligent* thing in all George Eliot's writing, and that is saying much. It is so deep, so true, so complete, it holds such a wealth of psychological detail, it is more than masterly.

THEODORA. I don't know where the perception of character has sailed closer to the wind.

PULCHERIA. The portrait may be admirable, but it has one little fault. You don't care a straw for the original. Gwendolen is not an interesting girl, and when the author tries to invest her with a deep tragic interest she does so at the expense of consistency. She has made her at the outset too light, too flimsy; tragedy has no hold on such a girl.

THEODORA. You are hard to satisfy. You said this morning that Dorothea was too heavy, and now you find Gwendolen too light. George Eliot wished to give us the perfect counterpart of Dorothea. Having made one portrait she was worthy to make the other.

PULCHERIA. She has committed the fatal error of making Gwendolen vulgarly, pettily, drily selfish. She was *personally* selfish.

THEODORA. I know nothing more personal than selfishness.

PULCHERIA. I am selfish, but I don't go about with my chin out like that; at least I hope I don't. She was an odious young woman, and one can't care what becomes of her. When her marriage turned out ill she would have become still more hard and positive; to make her soft and appealing is very bad logic. The second Gwendolen doesn't belong to the first.

CONSTANTIUS. She is perhaps at the first a little childish for the weight of interest she has to carry, a little too much after the pattern of the unconscientious young ladies of Miss Yonge and Miss Sewell.

THEODORA. Since when is it forbidden to make one's heroine young? Gwendolen is a perfect picture of youthfulness—its eagerness, its presumption, its preoccupation with itself, its vanity and silliness, its sense of its own absoluteness. But she is extremely intelligent and clever, and therefore tragedy *can* have a hold upon her. Her conscience doesn't make the tragedy; that is an old story and, I think, a secondary form of suffering. It is the tragedy that makes her conscience, which then reacts upon it; and I can think of nothing more powerful than the way in which the growth of her conscience is traced, nothing more touching than the picture of its helpless maturity.

CONSTANTIUS. That is perfectly true. Gwendolen's history is

admirably typical—as most things are with George Eliot: it is the very stuff that human life is made of. What is it made of but the discovery by each of us that we are at the best but a rather ridiculous fifth wheel to the coach, after we have sat cracking our whip and believing that we are at least the coachman in person? We think we are the main hoop to the barrel, and we turn out to be but a very incidental splinter in one of the staves. The universe forcing itself with a slow, inexorable pressure into a narrow, complacent, and yet after all extremely sensitive mind, and making it ache with the pain of the process—that is Gwendolen's story. And it becomes completely characteristic in that her supreme perception of the fact that the world is whirling past her is in the disappointment not of a base but of an exalted passion. The very chance to embrace what the author is so fond of calling a "larger life" seems refused to her. She is punished for being narrow, and she is not allowed a chance to expand. Her finding Deronda pre-engaged to go to the East and stir up the race-feeling of the Jews strikes me as a wonderfully happy invention. The irony of the situation, for poor Gwendolen, is almost grotesque, and it makes one wonder whether the whole heavy structure of the Jewish question in the story was not built up by the author for the express purpose of giving it proper force to this particular stroke.

THEODORA. George Eliot's intentions are extremely complex, The mass is for each detail and each detail is for the mass.

PULCHERIA. She is very fond of deaths by drowning. Maggie Tulliver and her brother are drowned, Tito Melema is drowned, Mr. Grandcourt is drowned. It is extremely unlikely that Grandcourt should not have known how to swim.

CONSTANTIUS. He did, of course, but he had a cramp. It served him right. I can't imagine a more consummate representation of the most detestable kind of Englishman—the Englishman who thinks it low to articulate. And in Grandcourt the type and the individual are so happily met: the type with its sense of the proprieties and the individual with his absence of all sense. He is the apotheosis of dryness, a human expression of the simple idea of the perpendicular.

THEODORA. Mr. Casaubon, in *Middlemarch*, was very dry too; and yet what a genius it is that can give us two disagreeable husbands who are so utterly different!

PULCHERIA. You must count the two disagreeable wives too— Rosamond Vincy and Gwendolen. They are very much alike. I know the author didn't mean it; it proves how common a type the worldly, *pincée*, selfish young woman seemed to her. They are both disagreeable; you can't get over that.

CONSTANTIUS. There is something in that, perhaps. I think, at any rate, that the secondary people here are less delightful than in *Middlemarch*; there is nothing so good as Mary Garth and her father, or the little old lady who steals sugar, or the parson who is in love with Mary, or the country relatives of old Mr. Featherstone. Rex Gascoigne is not so good as Fred Vincy.

THEODORA. Mr. Gascoigne is admirable, and Mrs. Davilow is charming.

PULCHERIA. And you must not forget that you think Herr Klesmer "Shakespearean". Wouldn't "Wagnerian" be high enough praise?

CONSTANTIUS. Yes, one must make an exception with regard to the Klesmers and the Meyricks. They are delightful, and as for Klesmer himself, and Hans Meyrick, Theodora may maintain her epithet. Shakespearean characters are characters that are born of the *overflow* of observation—characters that make the drama seem multitudinous, like life. Klesmer comes in with a sort of Shakespearean "value", as a painter would say, and so, in a different tone, does Hans Meyrick. They spring from a much peopled mind.

THEODORA. I think Gwendolen's confrontation with Klesmer one of the finest things in the book.

CONSTANTIUS. It is like everything in George Eliot; it will bear thinking of.

PULCHERIA. All that is very fine, but you cannot persuade me that *Deronda* is not a very ponderous and ill-made story. It has nothing that one can call a subject. A silly young girl and a solemn, sapient young man who doesn't fall in love with her! That is the *donnée* of eight monthly volumes. I call it very flat. Is that what the exquisite art of Thackeray and Miss Austen and Hawthorne has come to? I would as soon read a German novel outright.

THEODORA. There is something higher than form—there is spirit.

CONSTANTIUS. I am afraid Pulcheria is sadly aesthetic. She had better confine herself to Mérimée.

PULCHERIA. I shall certainly to-day read over *La Double Méprise*.

THEODORA. Oh, my dear, *y pensez-vous?*

CONSTANTIUS. Yes, I think there is little art in *Deronda*, but I think there is a vast amount of life. In life without art you can find your account; but art without life is a poor affair. The book is full of the world.

THEODORA. It is full of beauty and knowledge, and that is quite art enough for me.

PULCHERIA (to the little dog). We are silenced, darling, but we are not convinced, are we? (The pug begins to bark.) No, we are not even silenced. It's a young woman with two bandboxes.

THEODORA. Oh, it must be our muslins.

CONSTANTIUS (rising to go). I see what you mean.

8

THE ART OF FICTION

1884

I SHOULD not have affixed so comprehensive a title to these few remarks, necessarily wanting in any completeness upon a subject the full consideration of which would carry us far, did I not seem to discover a pretext for my temerity in the interesting pamphlet lately published under this name by Mr. Walter Besant. Mr. Besant's lecture at the Royal Institution—the original form of his pamphlet—appears to indicate that many persons are interested in the art of fiction, and are not indifferent to such remarks, as those who practise it may attempt to make about it. I am therefore anxious not to lose the benefit of this favourable association, and to edge in a few words under cover of the attention which Mr. Besant is sure to have excited. There is something very encouraging in his having put into form certain of his ideas on the mystery of story-telling.

It is a proof of life and curiosity—curiosity on the part of the brotherhood of novelists as well as on the part of their readers. Only a short time ago it might have been supposed that the English novel was not what the French call *discutable*. It had no air of having a theory, a conviction, a consciousness of itself behind it—of being the expression of an artistic faith, the result of choice and comparison. I do not say it was necessarily the worse for that: it would take much more courage than I possess to intimate that the form of the novel as Dickens and Thackeray (for instance) saw it had any taint of incompleteness. It was, however, *naïf* (if I may help myself out with another French word); and evidently if it be destined to suffer in any way for having lost its *naïveté* it has now an idea of making sure of the corresponding advantages. During the period I have alluded to there was a comfortable, good-humoured feeling abroad that a novel is a novel, as a pudding is a pudding, and that our only business with it could be to swallow it. But within a year or two, for some reason or other, there have been signs of returning animation—the era of discussion would appear to have been to a certain extent opened. Art lives upon discussion, upon experiment, upon curiosity, upon variety of attempt, upon the exchange of views and the comparison of stand-points; and there is a presumption that those times when no one has anything particular to

49

say about it, and has no reason to give for practice or preference, though they may be times of honour, are not times of development—are times, possibly even, a little of dullness. The successful application of any art is a delightful spectacle, but the theory too is interesting; and though there is a great deal of the latter without the former I suspect there has never been a genuine success that has not had a latent core of conviction. Discussion, suggestion, formulation, these things are fertilizing when they are frank and sincere. Mr. Besant has set an excellent example in saying what he thinks, for his part, about the way in which fiction should be written, as well as about the way in which it should be published; for his view of the "art", carried on into an appendix, covers that too. Other labourers in the same field will doubtless take up the argument, they will give it the light of their experience, and the effect will surely be to make our interest in the novel a little more what it had for some time threatened to fail to be—a serious, active, inquiring interest, under protection of which this delightful study may, in moments of confidence, venture to say a little more what it thinks of itself.

It must take itself seriously for the public to take it so. The old superstition about fiction being "wicked" has doubtless died out in England; but the spirit of it lingers in a certain oblique regard directed toward any story which does not more or less admit that it is only a joke. Even the most jocular novel feels in some degree the weight of the prescription that was formerly directed against literary levity: the jocularity does not always succeed in passing for orthodoxy. It is still expected, though perhaps people are ashamed to say it, that a production which is after all only a "make-believe" (for what else is a "story"?) shall be in some degree apologetic—shall renounce the pretension of attempting really to represent life. This, of course, any sensible, wide-awake story declines to do, for it quickly perceives that the tolerance granted to it on such a condition is only an attempt to stifle it disguised in the form of generosity. The old evangelical hostility to the novel, which was as explicit as it was narrow and which regarded it as little less favourable to our immortal part than a stage-play, was in reality far less insulting. The only reason for the existence of a novel is that it does attempt to represent life. When it relinquishes this attempt, the same attempt that we see on the canvas of the painter, it will have arrived at a very strange pass. It is not expected of the picture that it will make itself humble in order to be forgiven; and the analogy between the art of the painter and the art of the novelist is, so far as I am able to see, complete. Their inspiration is the same, their process (allowing for the different quality of the vehicle) is the same, their success is the same. They may learn from each other, they may explain and sustain each other. Their cause is the same, and the honour of one is the honour of another. The Mahometans think a picture an unholy thing, but it is a long time since any Christian did, and it is therefore the more odd that in the Christian mind the traces (dissimulated though they may be) of a suspicion of the sister art should linger to this day. The only effectual way to lay it to rest is to emphasize the analogy to which I just alluded—to insist on the fact that as the picture is reality, so the novel is history. That is the only general description (which does it justice) that we may give of the novel. But history also is allowed to represent life; it is not, any more than painting, expected to apologize. The subject-matter of fiction is stored up likewise in documents and records, and if it will not give itself away, as they say in California, it must speak with assurance, with the tone of the historian. Certain accomplished novelists have a habit of giving themselves away which must often bring tears to the eyes of people who take their fiction seriously. I was lately struck, in reading over many pages of Anthony Trollope, with his want of discretion in this particular. In a digression, a parenthesis or an aside, he concedes to the reader that he and this trusting friend are only "making believe". He admits that the events he narrates have not really happened, and that he can give his narrative any turn the reader may like best. Such a betrayal of a sacred office seems to me, I confess, a terrible crime; it is what I mean by the attitude of apology, and it shocks me every whit as much in Trollope as it would have shocked me in Gibbon or Macaulay. It implies that the novelist is less occupied in looking for the truth (the truth, of course I mean, that he assumes, the premises that we must grant him, whatever they may be) than the historian, and in doing so it deprives him at a stroke of all his standing-room. To represent and illustrate the past, the actions of men, is the task of either writer, and the only difference that I can see is, in proportion as he succeeds, to the honour of the novelist, consisting as it does in his having more difficulty in collecting his evidence, which is so far from being purely literary. It seems to me to give him a great character, the fact that he has at once so much in common with the philosopher and the painter; this double analogy is a magnificent heritage.

It is of all this evidently that Mr. Besant is full when he insists upon the fact that fiction is one of the *fine* arts, deserving in its turn of all

the honours and emoluments that have hitherto been reserved for the
successful profession of music, poetry, painting, architecture. It is
impossible to insist too much on so important a truth, and the place
that Mr. Besant demands for the work of the novelist may be represented, a trifle abstractly, by saying that he demands not only that
it shall be reputed artistic, but that it shall be reputed very artistic
indeed. It is excellent that he should have struck this note, for his doing
so indicates that there was need of it, that his proposition may be to
many people a novelty. One rubs one's eyes at the thought; but the
rest of Mr. Besant's essay confirms the revelation. I suspect in truth
that it would be possible to confirm it still further, and that one would
not be far wrong in saying that in addition to the people to whom it
has never occurred that a novel ought to be artistic, there are a great
many others who, if this principle were urged upon them, would be
filled with indefinable mistrust. They would find it difficult to explain
their repugnance, but it would operate strongly to put them on their
guard. "Art", in our Protestant communities, where so many things
have got so strangely twisted about, is supposed in certain circles to
have some vaguely injurious effect upon those who make it an important consideration, who let it weigh in the balance. It is assumed to
be opposed in some mysterious manner to morality, to amusement,
to instruction. When it is embodied in the work of the painter (the
sculptor is another affair!) you know what it is: it stands there before
you, in the honesty of pink and green and a gilt frame; you can see
the worst of it at a glance, and you can be on your guard. But when it
is introduced into literature it becomes more insidious—there is danger
of its hurting you before you know it. Literature should be either
instructive or amusing, and there is in many minds an impression that
these artistic preoccupations, the search for form, contribute to neither
end, interfere indeed with both. They are too frivolous to be edifying,
and too serious to be diverting; and they are moreover priggish and
paradoxical and superfluous. That, I think, represents the manner in
which the latent thought of many people who read novels as an exercise in skipping would explain itself if it were to become articulate.
They would argue, of course, that a novel ought to be "good", but
they would interpret this term in a fashion of their own, which indeed
would vary considerably from one critic to another. One would say
that being good means representing virtuous and aspiring characters,
placed in prominent positions; another would say that it depends on a
"happy ending", on a distribution at the last of prizes, pensions, hus-

bands, wives, babies, millions, appended paragraphs, and cheerful remarks. Another still would say that it means being full of incident and
movement, so that we shall wish to jump ahead, to see who was the
mysterious stranger, and if the stolen will was ever found, and shall
not be distracted from this pleasure by any tiresome analysis or "description". But they would all agree that the "artistic" idea would spoil
some of their fun. One would hold it accountable for all the description,
another would see it revealed in the absence of sympathy. Its hostility
to a happy ending would be evident, and it might even in some cases
render any ending at all impossible. The "ending" of a novel is, for
many persons, like that of a good dinner, a course of dessert and ices,
and the artist in fiction is regarded as a sort of meddlesome doctor who
forbids agreeable aftertastes. It is therefore true that this conception
of Mr. Besant's of the novel as a superior form encounters not only a
negative but a positive indifference. It matters little that as a work of
art it should really be as little or as much of its essence to supply happy
endings, sympathetic characters, and an objective tone, as if it were a
work of mechanics: the association of ideas, however incongruous,
might easily be too much for it if an eloquent voice were not sometimes
raised to call attention to the fact that it is at once as free and as serious
a branch of literature as any other.

Certainly this might sometimes be doubted in presence of the
enormous number of works of fiction that appeal to the credulity of
our generation, for it might easily seem that there could be no great
character in a commodity so quickly and easily produced. It must be
admitted that good novels are much compromised by bad ones, and
that the field at large suffers discredit from overcrowding. I think,
however, that this injury is only superficial, and that the super-
abundance of written fiction proves nothing against the principle itself.
It has been vulgarized, like all other kinds of literature, like everything
else to-day, and it has proved more than some kinds accessible to vulgarization. But there is as much difference as there ever was between
a good novel and a bad one: the bad is swept with all the daubed
canvases and spoiled marble into some unvisited limbo, or infinite
rubbish-yard beneath the back-windows of the world, and the good
subsists and emits its light and stimulates our desire for perfection. As
I shall take the liberty of making but a single criticism of Mr. Besant,
whose tone is so full of the love of his art, I may as well have done with
it at once. He seems to me to mistake in attempting to say so definitely
beforehand what sort of an affair the good novel will be. To indicate

the danger of such an error as that has been the purpose of these few
pages; to suggest that certain traditions on the subject, applied *a priori*,
have already had much to answer for, and that the good health of an
art which undertakes so immediately to reproduce life must demand
that it be perfectly free. It lives upon exercise, and the very meaning
of exercise is freedom. The only obligation to which in advance we
may hold a novel, without incurring the accusation of being arbitrary,
is that it be interesting. That general responsibility rests upon it, but
it is the only one I can think of. The ways in which it is at liberty to
accomplish this result (of interesting us) strike me as innumerable, and
such as can only suffer from being marked out or fenced in by prescription. They are as various as the temperament of man, and they are
successful in proportion as they reveal a particular mind, different
from others. A novel is in its broadest definition a personal, a direct
impression of life: that, to begin with, constitutes its value, which is
greater or less according to the intensity of the impression. But there
will be no intensity at all, and therefore no value, unless there is freedom
to feel and say. The tracing of a line to be followed, of a tone to be
taken, of a form to be filled out is a limitation of that freedom and a
suppression of the very thing that we are most curious about. The
form, it seems to me, is to be appreciated after the fact: then the
author's choice has been made, his standard has been indicated; then
we can follow lines and directions and compare tones and resemblances.
Then in a word we can enjoy one of the most charming of pleasures,
we can estimate quality, we can apply the test of execution. The execution belongs to the author alone; it is what is most personal to him,
and we measure him by that. The advantage, the luxury, as well as the
torment and responsibility of the novelist, is that there is no limit to
what he may attempt as an executant—no limit to his possible experiments, efforts, discoveries, successes. Here it is especially that he
works, step by step, like his brother of the brush, of whom we may
always say that he has painted his picture in a manner best known to
himself. His manner is his secret, not necessarily a jealous one. He
cannot disclose it as a general thing if he would; he would be at a loss
to teach it to others. I say this with a due recollection of having insisted on the community of method of the artist who paints a picture
and the artist who writes a novel. The painter *is* able to teach the rudiments of his practice, and it is possible, from the study of good work
(granted the aptitude), both to learn how to paint and to learn how to
write. Yet it remains true, without injury to the *rapprochement*, that

the literary artist would be obliged to say to his pupil much more than the other, "Ah, well, you must do it as you can!" It is a question of degree, a matter of delicacy. If there are exact sciences, there are also exact arts, and the grammar of painting is so much more definite that it makes the difference.

I ought to add, however, that if Mr. Besant says at the beginning of his essay that the "laws of fiction may be laid down and taught with as much precision and exactness as the laws of harmony, perspective, and proportion", he mitigates what might appear to be an extravagance by applying his remark to "general" laws, and by expressing most of these rules in a manner with which it would certainly be unaccommodating to disagree. That the novelist must write from his experience, that his "characters must be real and such as might be met with in actual life": that "a young lady brought up in a quiet country village should avoid descriptions of garrison life", and "a writer whose friends and personal experiences belong to the lower middle-class should carefully avoid introducing his characters into society"; that one should enter one's notes in a common-place book; that one's figures should be clear in outline; that making them clear by some trick of speech or of carriage is a bad method, and "describing them at length" is a worse one; that English Fiction should have a "conscious moral purpose"; that "it is almost impossible to estimate too highly the value of careful workmanship—that is, of style"; that "the most important point of all is the story", that "the story is everything": these are principles with most of which it is surely impossible not to sympathize. That remark about the lower middle-class writer and his knowing his place is perhaps rather chilling; but for the rest I should find it difficult to dissent from any one of these recommendations. At the same time, I should find it difficult positively to assent to them, with the exception, perhaps, of the injunction as to entering one's notes in a common-place book. They scarcely seem to me to have the quality that Mr. Besant attributes to the rules of the novelist—the "precision and exactness" of "the laws of harmony, perspective, and proportion". They are suggestive, they are even inspiring, but they are not exact, though they are doubtless as much so as the case admits of: which is a proof of that liberty of interpretation for which I just contended. For the value of these different injunctions—so beautiful and so vague—is wholly in the meaning one attaches to them. The characters, the situation, which strike one as real will be those that touch and interest one most, but the measure of reality is very difficult to fix.

The reality of Don Quixote or of Mr. Micawber is a very delicate
shade; it is a reality so coloured by the author's vision that, vivid as it
may be, one would hesitate to propose it as a model: one would
expose one's self to some very embarrassing questions on the part of a
pupil. It goes without saying that you will not write a good novel
unless you possess the sense of reality; but it will be difficult to give
you a recipe for calling that sense into being. Humanity is immense,
and reality has a myriad forms; the most one can affirm is that some of
the flowers of fiction have the odour of it, and others have not; as for
telling you in advance how your nosegay should be composed, that is
another affair. It is equally excellent and inconclusive to say that one
must write from experience; to our supposititious aspirant such a
declaration might savour of mockery. What kind of experience is
intended, and where does it begin and end? Experience is never
limited, and it is never complete; it is an immense sensibility, a kind
of huge spider-web of the finest silken threads suspended in the chamber
of consciousness, and catching every air-borne particle in its tissue. It
is the very atmosphere of the mind; and when the mind is imaginative
—much more when it happens to be that of a man of genius—it takes
to itself the faintest hints of life, it converts the very pulses of the air
into revelations. The young lady living in a village has only to be a
damsel upon whom nothing is lost to make it quite unfair (as it seems
to me) to declare to her that she shall have nothing to say about the
military. Greater miracles have been seen than that, imagination
assisting, she should speak the truth about some of these gentlemen.
I remember an English novelist, a woman of genius, telling me that she
was much commended for the impression she had managed to give in
one of her tales of the nature and way of life of the French Protestant
youth. She had been asked where she learned so much about this
recondite being, she had been congratulated on her peculiar opportunities. These opportunities consisted in her having once, in Paris, as
she ascended a staircase, passed an open door where, in the household
of a *pasteur*, some of the young Protestants were seated at table round
a finished meal. The glimpse made a picture; it lasted only a moment,
but that moment was experience. She had got her direct personal
impression, and she turned out her type. She knew what youth was,
and what Protestantism; she also had the advantage of having seen
what it was to be French, so that she converted these ideas into a
concrete image and produced a reality. Above all, however, she was
blessed with the faculty which when you give it an inch takes an ell,

and which for the artist is a much greater source of strength than any accident of residence or of place in the social scale. The power to guess the unseen from the seen, to trace the implication of things, to judge the whole piece by the pattern, the condition of feeling life in general so completely that you are well on your way to knowing any particular corner of it—this cluster of gifts may almost be said to constitute experience, and they occur in country and in town and in the most differing stages of education. If experience consists of impressions, it may be said that impressions *are* experience, just as (have we not seen it?) they are the very air we breathe. Therefore, if I should certainly say to a novice, "Write from experience and experience only", I should feel that this was rather a tantalizing monition if I were not careful immediately to add, "Try to be one of the people on whom nothing is lost!"

I am far from intending by this to minimize the importance of exactness—of truth of detail. One can speak best from one's own taste, and I may therefore venture to say that the air of reality (solidity of specification) seems to me to be the supreme virtue of a novel—the merit on which all its other merits (including that conscious moral purpose of which Mr. Besant speaks) helplessly and submissively depend. If it be not there they are all as nothing, and if these be there, they owe their effect to the success with which the author has produced the illusion of life. The cultivation of this success, the study of this exquisite process form, to my taste, the beginning and the end of the art of the novelist. They are his inspiration, his despair, his reward, his torment, his delight. It is here in very truth that he competes with life; it is here that he competes with his brother the painter in *his* attempt to render the look of things, the look that conveys their meaning, to catch the colour, the relief, the expression, the surface, the substance of the human spectacle. It is in regard to this that Mr. Besant is well inspired when he bids him take notes. He cannot possibly take too many, he cannot possibly take enough. All life solicits him, and to "render" the simplest surface, to produce the most momentary illusion, is a very complicated business. His case would be easier, and the rule would be more exact, if Mr. Besant had been able to tell him what notes to take. But this, I fear, he can never learn in any manual; it is the business of his life. He has to take a great many in order to select a few, he has to work them up as he can, and even the guides and philosophers who might have most to say to him must leave him alone when it comes to the application of precepts, as we leave the painter in communion with his palette. That his characters "must be clear in outline", as Mr. Besant says—he feels that down to his boots; but how he shall make them so is a secret between his good angel and himself. It would be absurdly simple if he could be taught that a great deal of "description" would make them so, or that on the contrary the absence of description and the cultivation of dialogue, or the absence of dialogue and the multiplication of "incident", would rescue him from his difficulties. Nothing, for instance, is more possible than that he be of a turn of mind for which this odd, literal opposition of description and dialogue, incident and description, has little meaning and light. People often talk of these things as if they had a kind of internecine distinctness, instead of melting into each other at every breath, and being intimately associated parts of one general effort of expression. I cannot imagine composition existing in a series of blocks, nor conceive, in any novel worth discussing at all, of a passage of description that is not in its intention narrative, a passage of dialogue that is not in its intention descriptive, a touch of truth of any sort that does not partake of the nature of incident, or an incident that derives its interest from any other source than the general and only source of the success of a work of art—that of being illustrative. A novel is a living thing, all one and continuous, like any other organism, and in proportion as it lives will it be found, I think, that in each of the parts there is something of each of the other parts. The critic who over the close texture of a finished work shall pretend to trace a geography of items will mark some frontiers as artificial, I fear, as any that have been known to history. There is an old-fashioned distinction between the novel of character and the novel of incident which must have cost many a smile to the intending fabulist who was keen about his work. It appears to me as little to the point as the equally celebrated distinction between the novel and the romance—to answer as little to any reality. There are bad novels and good novels, as there are bad pictures and good pictures; but that is the only distinction in which I see any meaning, and I can as little imagine speaking of a novel of character as I can imagine speaking of a picture of character. When one says picture one says of character, when one says novel one says of incident, and the terms may be transposed at will. What is character but the determination of incident? What is incident but the illustration of character? What is either a picture or a novel that is *not* of character? What else do we seek in it and find in it? It is an incident for a woman to stand up with her hand resting on a table and look out at you in a certain way; or if it be not an incident I think it will be hard to say what it is. At the same time it is an expression of character. If you say you don't see it (character in *that—allons donc!*), this is exactly what the artist who has reasons of his own for thinking he *does* see it undertakes to show you. When a young man makes up his mind that he has not faith enough after all to enter the church as he intended, that is an incident, though you may not hurry to the end of the chapter to see whether perhaps he doesn't change once more. I do not say that these are extraordinary or startling incidents. I do not pretend to estimate the degree of interest proceeding from them, for this will depend upon the skill of the painter. It sounds almost puerile to say that some incidents are intrinsically much more important than others, and I need not take this precaution after having professed my sympathy for the major ones in remarking that the only classification of the novel that I can understand is into that which has life and that which has it not.

The novel and the romance, the novel of incident and that of character—these clumsy separations appear to me to have been made by critics and readers for their own convenience, and to help them out of some of their occasional queer predicaments, but to have little reality or interest for the producer, from whose point of view it is of course that we are attempting to consider the art of fiction. The case is the same with another shadowy category which Mr. Besant apparently is disposed to set up—that of the "modern English novel"; unless indeed it be that in this matter he has fallen into an accidental confusion of stand-points. It is not quite clear whether he intends the remarks in which he alludes to it to be didactic or historical. It is as difficult to suppose a person intending to write a modern English as to suppose him writing an ancient English novel: that is a label which begs the question. One writes the novel, one paints the picture, of one's language and of one's time, and calling it modern English will not, alas! make the difficult task any easier. No more, unfortunately, will calling this or that work of one's fellow-artist a romance—unless it be, of course, simply for the pleasantness of the thing, as for instance when Hawthorne gave this heading to his story of *Blithedale*. The French, who have brought the theory of fiction to remarkable completeness, have but one name for the novel, and have not attempted smaller things in it, that I can see, for that. I can think of no obligation to which the "romancer" would not be held equally with the novelist; the standard of execution is equally high for each. Of course it is of execution that we are talking—that being the only point of a novel that is open to contention. This is perhaps too often lost sight of, only to produce interminable confusions and cross-purposes. We must grant the artist his subject, his idea, his *donnée*: our criticism is applied only to what he makes of it. Naturally I do not mean that we are bound to like it or find it interesting: in case we do not our course is perfectly simple—to let it alone. We may believe that of a certain idea even the most sincere novelist can make nothing at all, and the event may perfectly justify our belief; but the failure will have been a failure to execute, and it is in the execution that the fatal weakness is recorded. If we pretend to respect the artist at all, we must allow him his freedom of choice, in the face, in particular cases, of innumerable presumptions that the choice will not fructify. Art derives a considerable part of its beneficial exercise from flying in the face of presumptions, and some of the most interesting experiments of which it is capable are hidden in the bosom of common things. Gustave Flaubert has written a story about the devotion of a servant-girl to a parrot, and the production, highly finished as it is, cannot on the whole be called a success. We are perfectly free to find it flat, but I think it might have been interesting; and I, for my part, am extremely glad he should have written it; it is a contribution to our knowledge of what can be done—or what cannot. Ivan Turgénieff has written a tale about a deaf and dumb serf and a lap-dog, and the thing is touching, loving, a little masterpiece. He struck the note of life where Gustave Flaubert missed it—he flew in the face of a presumption and achieved a victory.

Nothing, of course, will ever take the place of the good old fashion of "liking" a work of art or not liking it: the most improved criticism will not abolish that primitive, that ultimate test. I mention this to guard myself from the accusation of intimating that the idea, the subject, of a novel or a picture, does not matter. It matters, to my sense, in the highest degree, and if I might put up a prayer it would be that artists should select none but the richest. Some, as I have already hastened to admit, are much more remunerative than others, and it would be a world happily arranged in which persons intending to treat them should be exempt from confusions and mistakes. This fortunate condition will arrive only, I fear, on the same day that critics become purged from error. Meanwhile, I repeat, we do not judge the artist with fairness unless we say to him.

Oh, I grant you your starting-point, because if I did not I should seem to prescribe to you, and heaven forbid I should take that responsibility. If I pretend to tell you what you must not take, you will call upon me to tell you then what you must take; in which case I shall be prettily caught. Moreover, it isn't till I have accepted your data that I can begin to measure you. I have the standard, the pitch; I have no right to tamper with your flute and then criticize your music. Of course I may not care for your idea at all; I may think it silly, or stale, or unclean; in which case I wash my hands of you altogether. I may content myself with believing that you will not have succeeded in being interesting, but I shall, of course, not attempt to demonstrate it, and you will be as indifferent to me as I am to you. I needn't remind you that there are all sorts of tastes: who can know it better? Some people, for excellent reasons, don't like to read about carpenters; others for reason even better, don't like to read about courtesans. Many object to Americans. Others (I believe they are mainly editors and publishers) won't look at Italians. Some readers don't like quiet subjects; others don't like bustling ones. Some enjoy a complete illusion, others the consciousness of large concessions. They choose their novels accordingly, and if they don't care about your idea they won't, *a fortiori*, care about your treatment.

So that it comes back very quickly, as I have said, to the liking: in spite of M. Zola, who reasons less powerfully than he represents, and who will not reconcile himself to this absoluteness of taste, thinking that there are certain things that people ought to like, and that they can be made to like. I am quite at a loss to imagine anything (at any rate in this matter of fiction) that people *ought* to like or to dislike. Selection will be sure to take care of itself, for it has a constant motive behind it. That motive is simply experience. As people feel life, so they will feel the art that is most closely related to it. This closeness of relation is what we should never forget in talking of the effort of the novel. Many people speak of it as a factitious, artificial form, a product of ingenuity, the business of which is to alter and arrange the things that surround us, to translate them into conventional, traditional moulds. This, however, is a view of the matter which carries us but a very short way, condemns the art to an eternal repetition of a few familiar *clichés*, cuts short its development and leads us straight up to a dead wall. Catching the very note and trick, the strange irregular rhythm of life, that is the attempt whose strenuous force keeps Fiction upon her feet. In proportion as in what she offers us we see life *without* rearrangement do we feel that we are touching the truth; in proportion as we see it *with* arrangement do we feel that we are being put off with a substitute, a compromise and convention. It is not uncommon to hear an extraordinary assurance of remark in regard to this matter of rearranging, which is often spoken of as if it were the last word of art. Mr. Besant seems to me in danger of falling into the great error with his rather unguarded talk about "selection". Art is essentially selection, but it is a selection whose main care is to be typical, to be inclusive. For many people art means rose-coloured window-panes, and selection means picking a bouquet for Mrs. Grundy. They will tell you glibly that artistic considerations have nothing to do with the disagreeable, with the ugly; they will rattle off shallow common-places about the province of art and the limits of art till you are moved to some wonder in return as to the province and the limits of ignorance. It appears to me that no one can ever have made a seriously artistic attempt without becoming conscious of an immense increase—a kind of revelation—of freedom. One perceives in that case—by the light of a heavenly ray—that the province of art is all life, all feeling, all observation, all vision. As Mr. Besant so justly intimates, it is all experience. That is a sufficient answer to those who maintain that it must not touch the sad things of life, who stick into its divine unconscious bosom little prohibitory inscriptions on the end of sticks, such as we see in public gardens—"It is forbidden to walk on the grass; it is forbidden to touch the flowers; it is not allowed to introduce dogs or to remain after dark; it is requested to keep to the right." The young aspirant in the line of fiction whom we continue to imagine will do nothing without taste, for in that case his freedom would be of little use to him; but the first advantage of his taste will be to reveal to him the absurdity of the little sticks and tickets. If he have taste, I must add, of course he will have ingenuity, and my disrespectful reference to that quality just now was not meant to imply that it is useless in fiction. But it is only a secondary aid; the first is a capacity for receiving straight impressions.

Mr. Besant has some remarks on the question of "the story" which I shall not attempt to criticize, though they seem to me to contain a singular ambiguity, because I do not think I understand them. I cannot see what is meant by talking as if there were a part of a novel which is the story and part of it which for mystical reasons is not—unless indeed the distinction be made in a sense in which it is difficult to suppose that any one should attempt to convey anything. "The story", if it represents anything, represents the subject, the idea, the *donnée* of the novel; and there is surely no "school"—Mr. Besant speaks of a school—which urges that a novel should be all treatment and no subject. There must assuredly be something to treat; every school is intimately conscious of that. This sense of the story being the idea, the starting-point, of the novel, is the only one that I see in which it can be spoken of as something different from its organic

whole; and since in proportion as the work is successful the idea per-
meates and penetrates it, informs and animates it, so that every word
and every punctuation-point contribute directly to the expression, in
that proportion do we lose our sense of the story being a blade which
may be drawn more or less out of its sheath. The story and the novel,
the idea and the form, are the needle and thread, and I never heard of a
guild of tailors who recommended the use of the thread without the
needle, or the needle without the thread. Mr. Besant is not the only
critic who may be observed to have spoken as if there were certain
things in life which constitute stories, and certain others which do not.
I find the same odd implication in an entertaining article in the *Pall
Mall Gazette*, devoted, as it happens, to Mr. Besant's lecture. "The
story is the thing!" says this graceful writer, as if with a tone of opposition to some other idea. I should think it was, as every painter who,
as the time for "sending in" his picture looms in the distance, finds
himself still in quest of a subject—as every belated artist not fixed
about his theme will heartily agree. There are some subjects which
speak to us and others which do not, but he would be a clever man
who should undertake to give a rule—an *index expurgatorius*—by which
the story and the no-story should be known apart. It is impossible (to
me at least) to imagine any such rule which shall not be altogether
arbitrary. The writer in the *Pall Mall* opposes the delightful (as I
suppose) novel of *Margot la Balafrée* to certain tales in which "Bostonian
'nymphs' appear to have 'rejected English dukes for psychological
reasons'". I am not acquainted with the romance just designated,
and can scarcely forgive the *Pall Mall* critic for not mentioning the
name of the author, but the title appears to refer to a lady who may
have received a scar in some heroic adventure. I am inconsolable at
not being acquainted with this episode, but am utterly at a loss to see
why it is a story when the rejection (or acceptance) of a duke is not,
and why a reason, psychological or other, is not a subject when a
cicatrix is. They are all particles of the multitudinous life with which
the novel deals, and surely no dogma which pretends to make it lawful
to touch the one and unlawful to touch the other will stand for a
moment on its feet. It is the special picture that must stand or fall,
according as it seem to possess truth or to lack it. Mr. Besant does not,
to my sense, light up the subject by intimating that a story must, under
penalty of not being a story, consist of "adventures". Why of adventures more than of green spectacles? He mentions a category of impossible things, and among them he places "fiction without adventure".

Why without adventure, more than without matrimony, or celibacy, or parturition, or cholera, or hydropathy, or Jansenism? This seems to me to bring the novel back to the hapless little *rôle* of being an artificial, ingenious thing—bring it down from its large, free character of an immense and exquisite correspondence with life. And what *is* adventure, when it comes to that, and by what sign is the listening pupil to recognize it? It is an adventure—an immense one—for me to write this little article; and for a Bostonian nymph to reject an English duke is an adventure only less stirring, I should say, than for an English duke to be rejected by a Bostonian nymph. I see dramas within dramas in that, and innumerable points of view. A psychological reason is, to my imagination, an object adorably pictorial; to catch the tint of its complexion—I feel as if that idea might inspire one to Titianesque efforts. There are few things more exciting to me, in short, than a psychological reason, and yet, I protest, the novel seems to me the most magnificent form of art. I have just been reading at the same time, the delightful story of *Treasure Island*, by Mr. Robert Louis Stevenson and, in a manner less consecutive, the last tale from M. Edmond de Goncourt, which is entitled *Chérie*. One of these works treats of murders, mysteries, islands of dreadful renown, hair-breadth escapes, miraculous coincidences and buried doubloons. The other treats of a little French girl who lived in a fine house in Paris, and died of wounded sensibility because no one would marry her. I call *Treasure Island* delightful, because it appears to me to have succeeded wonderfully in what it attempts; and I venture to bestow no epithet upon *Chérie*, which strikes me as having failed deplorably in what it attempts—that is in tracing the development of the moral consciousness of a child. But one of these productions strikes me as exactly as much of a novel as the other, and as having a "story" quite as much. The moral consciousness of a child is as much a part of life as the islands of the Spanish Main, and the one sort of geography seems to me to have those "surprises" of which Mr. Besant speaks quite as much as the other. For myself (since it comes back in the last resort, as I say, to the preference of the individual), the picture of the child's experience has the advantage that I can at successive steps (an immense luxury, near to the "sensual pleasure" of which Mr. Besant's critic in the *Pall Mall* speaks) say Yes or No, as it may be, to what the artist puts before me. I have been a child in fact, but I have been on a quest for a buried treasure only in supposition, and it is a simple accident that with M. de Goncourt I should have for the most part to say No. With George

Eliot, when she painted that country with a far other intelligence, I always said Yes.

The most interesting part of Mr. Besant's lecture is unfortunately the briefest passage—his very cursory allusion to the "conscious moral purpose" of the novel. Here again it is not very clear whether he be recording a fact or laying down a principle; it is a great pity that in the latter case he should not have developed his idea. This branch of the subject is of immense importance, and Mr. Besant's few words point to considerations of the widest reach, not to be lightly disposed of. He will have treated the art of fiction but superficially who is not prepared to go every inch of the way that these considerations will carry him. It is for this reason that at the beginning of these remarks I was careful to notify the reader that my reflections on so large a theme have no pretension to be exhaustive. Like Mr. Besant, I have left the question of the morality of the novel till the last, and at the last I find I have used up my space. It is a question surrounded with difficulties, as witness the very first that meets us, in the form of a definite question, on the threshold. Vagueness, in such a discussion, is fatal, and what is the meaning of your morality and your conscious moral purpose? Will you not define your terms and explain how (a novel being a picture) a picture can be either moral or immoral? You wish to paint a moral picture or carve a moral statue: will you not tell us how you would set about it? We are discussing the Art of Fiction; questions of art are questions (in the widest sense) of execution; questions of morality are quite another affair, and will you not let us see how it is that you find it so easy to mix them up? These things are so clear to Mr. Besant that he has deduced from them a law which he sees embodied in English Fiction, and which is "a truly admirable thing and a great cause for congratulation". It is a great cause for congratulation indeed when such thorny problems become as smooth as silk. I may add that in so far as Mr. Besant perceives that in point of fact English Fiction has addressed itself preponderantly to these delicate questions he will appear to many people to have made a vain discovery. They will have been positively struck, on the contrary, with the moral timidity of the usual English novelist; with his (or with her) aversion to face the difficulties with which on every side the treatment of reality bristles. He is apt to be extremely shy (whereas the picture that Mr. Besant draws is a picture of boldness), and the sign of his work, for the most part, is a cautious silence on certain subjects. In the English novel (by which of course I mean the American as well), more than in any other, there is a traditional difference between that which people know and that which they agree to admit that they know, that which they see and that which they speak of, that which they feel to be a part of life and that which they allow to enter into literature. There is the great difference, in short, between what they talk of in conversation and what they talk of in print. The essence of moral energy is to survey the whole field, and I should directly reverse Mr. Besant's remark and say not that the English novel has a purpose, but that it has a diffidence. To what degree a purpose in a work of art is a source of corruption I shall not attempt to inquire; the one that seems to me least dangerous is the purpose of making a perfect work. As for our novel, I may say lastly on this score that as we find it in England to-day it strikes me as addressed in a large degree to "young people", and that this in itself constitutes a presumption that it will be rather shy. There are certain things which it is generally agreed not to discuss, not even to mention, before young people. That is very well, but the absence of discussion is not a symptom of the moral passion. The purpose of the English novel—"a truly admirable thing, and a great cause for congratulation" —strikes me therefore as rather negative.

There is one point at which the moral sense and the artistic sense lie very near together; that is in the light of the very obvious truth that the deepest quality of a work of art will always be the quality of the mind of the producer. In proportion as that intelligence is fine will the novel, the picture, the statue partake of the substance of beauty and truth. To be constituted of such elements is, to my vision, to have purpose enough. No good novel will ever proceed from a superficial mind; that seems to me an axiom which, for the artist in fiction, will cover all needful moral ground: if the youthful aspirant take it to heart it will illuminate for him many of the mysteries of "purpose". There are many other useful things that might be said to him, but I have come to the end of my article, and can only touch them as I pass. The critic in the *Pall Mall Gazette*, whom I have already quoted, draws attention to the danger, in speaking of the art of fiction, of generalizing. The danger that he has in mind is rather, I imagine, that of particularizing, for there are some comprehensive remarks which, in addition to those embodied in Mr. Besant's suggestive lecture, might without fear of misleading him be addressed to the ingenuous student. I should remind him first of the magnificence of the form that is open to him, which offers to sight so few restrictions and such innumerable opportunities. The other arts, in comparison, appear confined and hampered;

the various conditions under which they are exercised are so rigid and definite. But the only condition that I can think of attaching to the composition of the novel is, as I have already said, that it be sincere. This freedom is a splendid privilege, and the first lesson of the young novelist is to learn to be worthy of it.

Enjoy it as it deserves [I should say to him]; take possession of it, explore it to its utmost extent, publish it, rejoice in it. All life belongs to you, and do not listen either to those who would shut you up into corners of it and tell you that it is only here and there that art inhabits, or to those who would persuade you that this heavenly messenger wings her way outside of life altogether, breathing a superfine air, and turning away her head from the truth of things. There is no impression of life, no manner of seeing it and feeling it, to which the plan of the novelist may not offer a place; you have only to remember that talents so dissimilar as those of Alexandre Dumas and Jane Austen, Charles Dickens and Gustave Flaubert have worked in this field with equal glory. Do not think too much about optimism and pessimism; try and catch the colour of life itself. In France to-day we see a prodigious effort (that of Emile Zola, to whose solid and serious work no explorer of the capacity of the novel can allude without respect), we see an extraordinary effort vitiated by a spirit of pessimism on a narrow basis. M. Zola is magnificent, but he strikes an English reader as ignorant; he has an air of working in the dark; if he had as much light as energy, his results would be of the highest value. As for the aberrations of a shallow optimism, the ground (of English fiction especially) is strewn with their brittle particles as with broken glass. If you must indulge in conclusions, let them have the taste of a wide knowledge. Remember that your first duty is to be as complete as possible—to make as perfect a work. Be generous and delicate and pursue the prize.

9

EMERSON

1887

MR. ELLIOT CABOT has made a very interesting contribution to a class of books of which our literature, more than any other, offers admirable examples: he has given us a biography[1] intelligently and carefully composed. These two volumes are a model of responsible editing— I use that term because they consist largely of letters and extracts from letters: nothing could resemble less the manner in which the mere bookmaker strings together his frequently questionable pearls and shovels the heap into the presence of the public. Mr. Cabot has selected, compared, discriminated, steered an even course between meagreness and redundancy, and managed to be constantly and happily illustrative. And his work, moreover, strikes us as the better done from the fact that it stands for one of the two things that make an absorbing memoir a good deal more than for the other. If these two things be the conscience of the writer and the career of his hero, it is not difficult to see on which side the biographer of Emerson has found himself strongest. Ralph Waldo Emerson was a man of genius, but he led for nearly eighty years a life in which the sequence of events had little of the rapidity, or the complexity, that a spectator loves. There is something we miss very much as we turn these pages—something that has a kind of accidental, inevitable presence in almost any personal record— something that may be most definitely indicated under the name of colour. We lay down the book with a singular impression of paleness —an impression that comes partly from the tone of the biographer and partly from the moral complexion of his subject, but mainly from the vacancy of the page itself. That of Emerson's personal history is condensed into the single word Concord, and all the condensation in the world will not make it look rich. It presents a most continuous surface. Mr. Matthew Arnold, in his *Discourses in America*, contests Emerson's complete right to the title of a man of letters; yet letters surely were the very texture of his history. Passions, alternations, affairs, adventures had absolutely no part in it. It stretched itself out in enviable quiet—a quiet in which we hear the jotting of the pencil

---

[1] *A Memoir of Ralph Waldo Emerson*, by James Elliot Cabot. Two volumes: London, 1887.

in the notebook. It is the very life for literature (I mean for one's own, not that of another): fifty years of residence in the home of one's fore-fathers, pervaded by reading, by walking in the woods and the daily addition of sentence to sentence.

If the interest of Mr. Cabot's pencilled portrait is incontestable and yet does not spring from variety, it owes nothing either to a source from which it might have borrowed much and which it is impossible not to regret a little that he has so completely neglected: I mean a greater reference to the social conditions in which Emerson moved, the company he lived in, the moral air he breathed. If his biographer had allowed himself a little more of the ironic touch, had put himself once in a way under the protection of Sainte-Beuve and had attempted something of a general picture, we should have felt that he only went with the occasion. I may over-estimate the latent treasures of the field, but it seems to me there was distinctly an opportunity—an opportunity to make up moreover in some degree for the white tint of Emerson's career considered simply in itself. We know a man imperfectly until we know his society, and we but half know a society until we know its manners. This is especially true of a man of letters, for manners lie very close to literature. From those of the New England world in which Emerson's character formed itself Mr. Cabot almost averts his lantern, though we feel sure that there would have been delightful glimpses to be had and that he would have been in a position—that is that he has all the knowledge that would enable him—to help us to them. It is as if he could not trust himself, knowing the subject only too well. This adds to the effect of extreme discretion that we find in his volumes, but it is the cause of our not finding certain things, certain figures and scenes, evoked. What is evoked is Emerson's pure spirit, by a copious, sifted series of citations and comments. But we must read as much as possible between the lines, and the picture of the transcendental time (to mention simply one corner) has yet to be painted—the lines have yet to be bitten in. Meanwhile we are held and charmed by the image of Emerson's mind and the extreme appeal which his physiognomy makes to our art of discrimination. It is so fair, so uniform and impersonal, that its features are simply fine shades, the gradations of tone of a surface whose proper quality was of the smoothest and on which nothing was reflected with violence. It is a pleasure of the critical sense to find, with Mr. Cabot's extremely intelligent help, a notation for such delicacies.

We seem to see the circumstances of our author's origin, immediate and remote, in a kind of high, vertical moral light, the brightness of a society at once very simple and very responsible. The rare singleness that was in his nature (so that he was *all* the warning moral voice, without distraction or counter-solicitation), was also in the stock he sprang from, clerical for generations, on both sides, and clerical in the Puritan sense. His ancestors had lived long (for nearly two centuries) in the same corner of New England, and during that period had preached and studied and prayed and practised. It is impossible to imagine a spirit better prepared in advance to be exactly what it was —better educated for its office in its far-away unconscious beginnings. There is an inner satisfaction in seeing so straight, although so patient, a connection between the stem and the flower, and such a proof that when life wishes to produce something exquisite in quality she takes her measures many years in advance. A conscience like Emerson's could not have been turned off, as it were, from one generation to another: a succession of attempts, a long process of refining, was required. His perfection, in his own line, comes largely from the non-interruption of the process.

As most of us are made up of ill-assorted pieces, his reader, and Mr. Cabot's, envies him this transmitted unity, in which there was no mutual hustling or crowding of elements. It must have been a kind of luxury to be—that is to feel—so homogeneous, and it helps to account for his serenity, his power of acceptance, and that absence of personal passion which makes his private correspondence read like a series of beautiful circulars or expanded cards *pour prendre congé*. He had the equanimity of a result; nature had taken care of him and he had only to speak. He accepted himself as he accepted others, accepted everything; and his absence of eagerness, or in other words his modesty, was that of a man with whom it is not a question of success, who has nothing invested or at stake. The investment, the stake, was that of the race, of all the past Emersons and Bulkeleys and Waldos. There is much that makes us smile, to-day, in the commotion produced by his secession from the mild Unitarian pulpit: we wonder at a condition of opinion in which any utterance of his should appear to be wanting in superior piety—in the essence of good instruction. All that is changed: the great difference has become the infinitely small, and we admire a state of society in which scandal and schism took on no darker hue; but there is even yet a sort of drollery in the spectacle of a body of people among whom the author of *The American Scholar* and of the Address of 1838 at the Harvard Divinity College passed for profane, and who failed to see that he only gave his plea for the spiritual life the advantage of a brilliant expression. They were so provincial as to think that brilliancy came ill-recommended, and they were shocked at his ceasing to care for the prayer and the sermon. They might have perceived that he *was* the prayer and the sermon: not in the least a secularizer, but in his own subtle insinuating way a sanctifier.

Of the three periods into which his life divides itself, the first was (as in the case of most men) that of movement, experiment, and selection—that of effort too and painful probation. Emerson had his message, but he was a good while looking for his form—the form which, as he himself would have said, he never completely found and of which it was rather characteristic of him that his later years (with their growing refusal to give him the *word*), wishing to attack him in his most vulnerable point, where his tenure was least complete, had in some degree the effect of despoiling him. It all sounds rather bare and stern, Mr. Cabot's account of his youth and early manhood, and we get an impression of a terrible paucity of alternatives. If he would be neither a farmer nor a trader he could "teach school"; that was the main resource and a part of the general educative process of the young New Englander who proposed to devote himself to the things of the mind. There was an advantage in the nudity, however, which was that, in Emerson's case at least, the things of the mind did get themselves admirably well considered. If it be his great distinction and his special sign that he had a more vivid conception of the moral life than anyone else, it is probably not fanciful to say that he owed it in part to the limited way in which he saw our capacity for living illustrated. The plain, God-fearing, practical society which surrounded him was not fertile in variations: it had great intelligence and energy, but it moved altogether in the straightforward direction. On three occasions later—three journeys to Europe—he was introduced to a more complicated world; but his spirit, his moral taste, as it were, abode always within the undecorated walls of his youth. There he could dwell with that ripe unconsciousness of evil which is one of the most beautiful signs by which we know him. His early writings are full of quaint animadversion upon the vices of the place and time, but there is something charmingly vague, light and general in the arraignment. Almost the worst he can say is that these vices are negative and that his fellow-townsmen are not heroic. We feel that his first impressions were gathered in a community from which misery and extravagance, and either extreme, of any sort, were equally absent. What the life of New

England fifty years ago offered to the observer was the common lot, in a kind of achromatic picture, without particular intensifications. It was from this table of the usual, the merely typical joys and sorrows that he proceeded to generalize—a fact that accounts in some degree for a certain inadequacy and thinness in his enumerations. But it helps to account also for his direct, intimate vision of the soul itself—not in its emotions, its contortions and perversions, but in its passive, exposed, yet healthy form. He knows the nature of man and the long tradition of its dangers; but we feel that whereas he can put his finger on the remedies, lying for the most part, as they do, in the deep recesses of virtue, of the spirit, he has only a kind of hearsay, uninformed acquaintance with the disorders. It would require some ingenuity, the reader may say too much, to trace closely this correspondence between his genius and the frugal, dutiful, happy but decidedly lean Boston of the past, where there was a great deal of will but very little fulcrum—like a ministry without an opposition.

The genius itself it seems to me impossible to contest—I mean the genius for seeing character as a real and supreme thing. Other writers have arrived at a more complete expression: Wordsworth and Goethe, for instance, give one a sense of having found their form, whereas with Emerson we never lose the sense that he is still seeking it. But no one has had so steady and constant, and above all so natural, a vision of what we require and what we are capable of in the way of aspiration and independence. With Emerson it is ever the special capacity for moral experience—always that and only that. We have the impression, somehow, that life had never bribed him to look at anything but the soul; and indeed in the world in which he grew up and lived the bribes and lures, the beguilements and prizes, were few. He was in an admirable position for showing, what he constantly endeavoured to show, that the prize was within. Any one who in New England at that time could do that was sure of success, of listeners and sympathy: most of all, of course, when it was a question of doing it with such a divine persuasiveness. Moreover, the way in which Emerson did it added to the charm—by word of mouth, face to face, with a rare, irresistible voice and a beautiful mild, modest authority. If Mr. Arnold is struck with the limited degree in which he was a man of letters I suppose it is because he is more struck with his having been, as it were, a man of lectures. But the lecture surely was never more purged of its grossness—the quality in it that suggests a strong light and a big brush—than as it issued from Emerson's lips; so far from being a vulgarization, it was simply the esoteric made audible, and instead of treating the few as the many, after the usual fashion of gentlemen on platforms, he treated the many as the few. There was probably no other society at that time in which he would have got so many persons to understand that; for we think the better of his audience as we read him, and wonder where else people would have had so much moral attention to give. It is to be remembered however that during the winter of 1847–48, on the occasion of his second visit to England, he found many listeners in London and in provincial cities. Mr. Cabot's volumes are full of evidence of the satisfactions he offered, the delights and revelations he may be said to have promised, to a race which had to seek its entertainment, its rewards and consolations, almost exclusively in the moral world. But his own writings are fuller still; we find an instance almost wherever we open them.

> All these great and transcendent properties are ours . . . Let us find room for this great guest in our small houses . . . Where the heart is, there the muses, there the gods sojourn, and not in any geography of fame. Massachusetts, Connecticut River, and Boston Bay, you think paltry places, and the ear loves names of foreign and classic topography. But here we are, and if we will tarry a little we may come to learn that here is best . . . The Jerseys were handsome enough ground for Washington to tread, and London streets for the feet of Milton . . . That country is fairest which is inhabited by the noblest minds.

We feel, or suspect, that Milton is thrown in as a hint that the London streets are no such great place, and it all sounds like a sort of pleading consolation against bleakness.

The beauty of a hundred passages of this kind in Emerson's pages is that they are effective, that they do come home, that they rest upon insight and not upon ingenuity, and that if they are sometimes obscure it is never with the obscurity of paradox. We seem to see the people turning out into the snow after hearing them, glowing with a finer glow than even the climate could give and fortified for a struggle with overshoes and the east wind.

> Look to it first and only, that fashion, custom, authority, pleasure, and money, are nothing to you, are not as bandages over your eyes, that you cannot see; but live with the privilege of the immeasurable mind. Not too anxious to visit periodically all families and each family in your parish connection, when you meet one of these men or women be to them a divine man; be to them thought and virtue; let their timid aspirations find in you a friend; let their trampled instincts be genially tempted out in your atmosphere;

let their doubts know that you have doubted, and their wonder feel that you
have wondered.

When we set against an exquisite passage like that, or like the familiar
sentences that open the essay on History ("He that is admitted to the
right of reason is made freeman of the whole estate. What Plato has
thought, he may think; what a saint has felt, he may feel; what at any
time has befallen any man, he can understand"); when we compare
the letters, cited by Mr. Cabot, to his wife from Springfield, Illinois
(January 1853), we feel that his spiritual tact needed to be very just,
but that if it was so it must have brought a blessing.

> Here I am in the deep mud of the prairies, misled I fear into this bog, not
> by a will-of-the-wisp, such as shine in bogs, but by a young New Hampshire
> editor, who over-estimated the strength of both of us, and fancied I should
> glitter in the prairie and draw the prairie birds and waders. It rains and
> thaws incessantly, and if we step off the short street we go up to the shoulders,
> perhaps in mud. My chamber is a cabin; my fellow-boarders are legislators . . .
> Two or three governors or ex-governors live in the house . . . I cannot
> command daylight and solitude for study or for more than a scrawl. . . .

And another extract:

> A cold, raw country this, and plenty of night-travelling and arriving at
> four in the morning to take the last and worst bed in the tavern. Advancing
> day brings mercy and favour to me, but not the sleep . . . Mercury 15° below
> zero . . . I find well-disposed, kindly people among these sinewy farmers of
> the North, but in all that is called cultivation they are only ten years old.

He says in another letter (in 1860), "I saw Michigan and its forests
and the Wolverines pretty thoroughly"; and on another page Mr.
Cabot shows him as speaking of his engagements to lecture in the
West as the obligation to "wade, and freeze, and ride, and run, and
suffer all manner of indignities". This was not New England, but as
regards the country districts throughout, at that time, it was a question
of degree. Certainly never was the fine wine of philosophy carried to
remoter or queerer corners: never was a more delicate diet offered to
"two or three governors, or ex-governors", living in a cabin. It was
Mercury, shivering in a mackintosh, bearing nectar and ambrosia to
the gods whom he wished those who lived in cabins to endeavour to
feel that they might be.

I have hinted that the will, in the old New England society was a
clue without a labyrinth; but it had its use, nevertheless, in helping the

young talent to find its mould. There were few or none ready-made: tradition was certainly not so oppressive as might have been inferred from the fact that the air swarmed with reformers and improvers. Of the patient, philosophic manner in which Emerson groped and waited, through teaching the young and preaching to the adult, for his particular vocation, Mr. Cabot's first volume gives a full and orderly account. His passage from the Unitarian pulpit to the lecture-desk was a step which at this distance of time can hardly help appearing to us short, though he was long in making it, for even after ceasing to have a parish of his own he freely confounded the two, or willingly, at least, treated the pulpit as a platform. "The young people and the mature hint at odium and the aversion of faces, to be presently encountered in society," he writes in his journal in 1838; but in point of fact the quiet drama of his abdication was not to include the note of suffering. The Boston world might feel disapproval, but it was far too kindly to make this sentiment felt as a weight: every element of martyrdom was there but the important ones of the cause and the persecutors. Mr. Cabot marks the lightness of the penalties of dissent; if they were light in somewhat later years for the transcendentalists and fruit-eaters they could press but little on a man of Emerson's distinction, to whom, all his life, people went not to carry but to ask the right word. There was no consideration to give up, he could not have been one of the dingy if he had tried; but what he did renounce in 1838 was a material profession. He was "settled", and his indisposition to administer the communion unsettled him. He calls the whole business, in writing to Carlyle, "a tempest in our washbowl"; but it had the effect of forcing him to seek a new source of income. His wants were few and his view of life severe, and this came to him, little by little, as he was able to extend the field in which he read his discourses. In 1835, upon his second marriage, he took up his habitation at Concord, and his life fell into the shape it was, in a general way, to keep for the next half-century. It is here that we cannot help regretting that Mr. Cabot had not found it possible to treat his career a little more pictorially. Those fifty years of Concord—at least the earlier part of them—would have been a subject bringing into play many odd figures, many human incongruities: they would have abounded in illustrations of the primitive New England character, especially during the time of its queer search for something to expend itself upon. Objects and occupations have multiplied since then, and now there is no lack; but fifty years ago the expanse was wide and free, and we get the impression of a conscience gasping in the void, panting for sensations, with something of the movement of the gills of a landed fish. It would take a very fine point to sketch Emerson's benignant, patient, inscrutable countenance during the various phases of this democratic communion; but the picture, when complete, would be one of the portraits, half a revelation and half an enigma, that suggest and fascinate. Such a striking personage as old Miss Mary Emerson, our author's aunt, whose high intelligence and temper were much of an influence in his earlier years, has a kind of tormenting representative value: we want to see her from head to foot, with her frame and her background; having (for we happen to have it) an impression that she was a very remarkable specimen of the transatlantic Puritan stock, a spirit that would have dared the devil. We miss a more liberal handling, are tempted to add touches of our own, and end by convincing ourselves that Miss Mary Moody Emerson, grim intellectual virgin and daughter of a hundred ministers, with her local traditions and her combined love of empire and of speculation, would have been an inspiration for a novelist. Hardly less so the charming Mrs. Ripley, Emerson's life-long friend and neighbour, most delicate and accomplished of women, devoted to Greek and to her house, studious, simple and dainty—an admirable example of the old-fashioned New England lady. It was a freak of Miss Emerson's somewhat sardonic humour to give her once a broomstick to carry across Boston Common (under the pretext of a "moving"), a task accepted with docility but making of the victim the most benignant witch ever equipped with that utensil.

These ladies, however, were very private persons and not in the least of the reforming tribe: there are others who would have peopled Mr. Cabot's page to whom he gives no more than a mention. We must add that it is open to him to say that their features have become faint and indistinguishable to-day without more research than the question is apt to be worth: they are embalmed—in a collective way—the apprehensible part of them, in Mr. Frothingham's clever *History of Transcendentalism in New England*. This must be admitted to be true of even so lively a "factor", as we say nowadays, as the imaginative, talkative, intelligent and finally Italianized and shipwrecked Margaret Fuller: she is now one of the dim, one of Carlyle's "then-celebrated" at most. It seemed indeed as if Mr. Cabot rather grudged her a due place in the record of the company that Emerson kept, until we came across the delightful letter he quotes toward the end of his first volume —a letter interesting both as a specimen of inimitable, imperceptible edging away, and as an illustration of the curiously generalized way, as if with an implicit protest against personalities, in which his intercourse, epistolary and other, with his friends was conducted. There is an extract from a letter to his aunt on the occasion of the death of a deeply-loved brother (his own) which reads like a passage from some fine old chastened essay on the vanity of earthly hopes: strangely unfamiliar, considering the circumstances. Courteous and humane to the furthest possible point, to the point of an almost profligate surrender of his attention, there was no familiarity in him, no personal avidity. Even his letters to his wife are courtesies, they are not familiarities. He had only one style, one manner, and he had it for everything—even for himself, in his notes, in his journals. But he had it in perfection for Miss Fuller; he retreats, smiling and flattering, on tiptoe, as if he were advancing. "She ever seems to crave," he says in his journal, "something which I have not, or have not for her." What he had was doubtless not what she craved, but the letter in question should be read to see how the modicum was administered. It is only between the lines of such a production that we read that a part of her effect upon him was to bore him; for his system was to practise a kind of universal passive hospitality—he aimed at nothing less. It was only because he was so deferential that he could be so detached; he had polished his aloofness till it reflected the image of his solicitor. And this was not because he was an "uncommunicating egotist", though he amuses himself with saying so to Miss Fuller: egotism is the strongest of passions, and he was altogether passionless. It was because he had no personal, just as he had almost no physical wants. "Yet I plead not guilty to the malice prepense. 'Tis imbecility, not contumacy, though perhaps somewhat more odious. It seems very just, the irony with which you ask whether you may be trusted and promise such docility. Alas, we will all promise, but the prophet loiters." He would not say even to himself that she bored him; he had denied himself the luxury of such easy and obvious short cuts. There is a passage in the lecture (1844) called "Man the Reformer", in which he hovers round and round the idea that the practice of trade, in certain conditions likely to beget an underhand competition, does not draw forth the nobler parts of character, till the reader is tempted to interrupt him with, "Say at once that it is impossible for a gentleman!"

So he remained always, reading his lectures in the winter, writing them in the summer, and at all seasons taking wood-walks and looking for hints in old books.

Delicious summer stroll through the pastures . . . On the steep park of Conantum I have the old regret—is all this beauty to perish? Shall none re-make this sun and wind; the sky-blue river; the river-blue sky; the yellow meadow, spotted with sacks and sheets of cranberry-gatherers; the red bushes; the iron-gray house, just the colour of the granite rocks; the wild orchard?

His observation of Nature was exquisite—always the direct, irre-sistible impression.

The hawking of the wild geese flying by night; the thin note of the companionable titmouse in the winter day; the fall of swarms of flies in autumn, from combats high in the air, pattering down on the leaves like rain; the angry hiss of the wood-birds; the pine throwing out its pollen for the benefit of the next century. . . . (*Literary Ethics.*)

I have said there was no familiarity in him, but he was familiar with woodland creatures and sounds. Certainly, too, he was on terms of free association with his books, which were numerous and dear to him; though Mr. Cabot says, doubtless with justice, that his depend-ence on them was slight and that he was not "intimate" with his authors. They did not feed him but they stimulated; they were not his meat but his wine—he took them in sips. But he needed them and liked them; he had volumes of notes from his reading, and he could not have produced his lectures without them. He liked literature as a thing to refer to, liked the very names of which it is full, and used them, especially in his later writings, for purposes of ornament, to dress the dish, sometimes with an unmeasured profusion. I open *The Conduct of Life* and find a dozen on the page. He can easily say of course, that he follows a better one—that of his well-loved and irrepressibly allusive Montaigne. In his own bookishness there is a certain contradiction, just as there is a latent incompleteness in his whole literary side. In-dependence, the return to nature, the finding out and doing for one's self, was ever what he most highly recommended; and yet he is con-stantly reminding his readers of the conventional signs and consecrations —of what other men have done. This was partly because the inde-pendence that he had in his eye was an independence without ill-nature, without rudeness (though he likes that word), and full of gentle amiabilities, curiosities and tolerances; and partly it is a simple matter of form, a literary expedient, confessing its character—on the part of one who had never really mastered the art of composition—of continuous expression. Charming to many a reader, charming yet ever slightly droll, will remain Emerson's frequent invocation of the "scholar"; there is such a friendly vagueness and convenience in it. It is of the scholar that he expects all the heroic and uncomfortable things, the concentrations and relinquishments, that make up the noble life. We fancy this personage looking up from his book and arm-chair a little ruefully and saying, "Ah, but why *me* always and only? Why so much of me, and is there no one else to share the responsibility?" "Neither years nor books have yet availed to extirpate a prejudice then rooted in me [when as a boy he first saw the graduates of his college assembled at their anniversary], that a scholar is the favourite of heaven and earth, the excellency of his country, the happiest of men."

In truth, by this term he means simply the cultivated man, the man who has had a liberal education, and there is a voluntary plainness in his use of it—speaking of such people as the rustic, or the vulgar, speak of those who have a tincture of books. This is characteristic of his humility—that humility which was nine-tenths a plain fact (for it is easy for persons who have at bottom a great fund of indifference to be humble), and the remaining tenth a literary habit. Moreover an American reader may be excused for finding in it a pleasant sign of that prestige, often so quaintly and indeed so extravagantly acknowledged, which a connection with literature carries with it among the people of the United States. There is no country in which it is more freely admitted to be a distinction—*the* distinction; or in which so many persons have become eminent for showing it even in a slight degree. Gentlemen and ladies are celebrated there on this ground who would not on the same ground, though they might on another, be celebrated anywhere else. Emerson's own tone is an echo of that, when he speaks of the scholar—not of the banker, the great merchant, the legislator, the artist—as the most distinguished figure in the society about him. It is because he has most to give up that he is appealed to for efforts and sacrifices. "Meantime I know that a very different estimate of the scholar's profession prevails in this country," he goes on to say in the address from which I last quoted (the *Literary Ethics*), "and the importunity with which society presses its claim upon young men tends to pervert the views of the youth in respect to the culture of the intellect." The manner in which that is said represents, surely, a serious mistake: with the estimate of the scholar's profession which then prevailed in New England Emerson could have had no quarrel; the ground of his lamentation was another side of the matter. It was not a question

of estimate, but of accidental practice. In 1838 there were still so many
things of prime material necessity to be done that reading was driven
to the wall; but the reader was still thought the cleverest, for he found
time as well as intelligence. Emerson's own situation sufficiently indicates it. In what other country, on sleety winter nights, would provincial and bucolic populations have gone forth in hundreds for the
cold comfort of a literary discourse? The distillation anywhere else
would certainly have appeared too thin, the appeal too special. But for
many years the American people of the middle regions, outside of a
few cities, had in the most rigorous seasons no other recreation. A
gentleman, grave or gay, in a bare room, with a manuscript, before a
desk, offered the reward of toil, the refreshment of pleasure, to the
young, the middle-aged and the old of both sexes. The hour was
brightest, doubtless, when the gentleman was gay, like Doctor Oliver
Wendell Holmes. But Emerson's gravity never sapped his career, any
more than it chilled the regard in which he was held among those
who were particularly his own people. It was impossible to be more
honoured and cherished, far and near, than he was during his long
residence in Concord, or more looked upon as the principal gentleman
in the place. This was conspicuous to the writer of these remarks on
the occasion of the curious, sociable, cheerful public funeral made for
him in 1882 by all the countryside, arriving, as for the last honours to
the first citizen, in trains, in waggons, on foot, in multitudes. It was a
popular manifestation, the most striking I have ever seen provoked
by the death of a man of letters.

If a picture of that singular and very illustrative institution the old
American lecture-system would have constituted a part of the filling-
in of the ideal memoir of Emerson, I may further say, returning to the
matter for a moment, that such a memoir would also have had a
chapter for some of those Concord-haunting figures which are not
so much interesting in themselves as interesting because for a season
Emerson thought them so. And the pleasure of that would be partly
that it would push us to inquire how interesting he did really think
them. That is, it would bring up the question of his inner reserves
and scepticisms, his secret ennuis and ironies, the way he sympathized
for courtesy and then, with his delicacy and generosity, in a world
after all given much to the literal, let his courtesy pass for adhesion—
a question particularly attractive to those for whom he has, in general,
a fascination. Many entertaining problems of that sort present themselves for such readers: there is something indefinable for them in the

mixture of which he was made—his fidelity as an interpreter of the so-called transcendental spirit and his freedom from all wish for any personal share in the effect of his ideas. He drops them, sheds them, diffuses them, and we feel as if there would be a grossness in holding him to anything so temporal as a responsibility. He had the advantage, for many years, of having the question of application assumed for him by Thoreau, who took upon himself to be, in the concrete, the sort of person that Emerson's "scholar" was in the abstract, and who paid for it by having a shorter life than that fine adumbration. The application, with Thoreau, was violent and limited (it became a matter of prosaic detail, the non-payment of taxes, the non-wearing of a neck-tie, the preparation of one's food one's self, the practice of a rude sincerity—all things not of the essence), so that, though he wrote some beautiful pages, which read like a translation of Emerson into the sounds of the field and forest and which no one who has ever loved nature in New England, or indeed anywhere, can fail to love, he suffers something of the *amoindrissement* of eccentricity. His master escapes that reduction altogether. I call it an advantage to have had such a pupil as Thoreau; because for a mind so much made up of reflection as Emerson's everything comes under that head which prolongs and reanimates the process—produces the return, again and yet again, on one's impressions. Thoreau must have had this moderating and even chastening effect. It did not rest, moreover, with him alone; the advantage of which I speak was not confined to Thoreau's case. In 1837 Emerson (in his journal) pronounced Mr. Bronson Alcott the most extraordinary man and the highest genius of his time: the sequence of which was that for more than forty years after that he had the gentleman living but half a mile away. The opportunity for the return, as I have called it, was not wanting.

His detachment is shown in his whole attitude toward the transcendental movement—that remarkable outburst of Romanticism on Puritan ground, as Mr. Cabot very well names it. Nothing can be more ingenious, more sympathetic and charming, than Emerson's account and definition of the matter in his lecture (of 1842) called "The Transcendentalist"; and yet nothing is more apparent from his letters and journals than that he regarded any such label or banner as a mere tiresome flutter. He liked to taste but not to drink—least of all to become intoxicated. He liked to explain the transcendentalists but did not care at all to be explained by them: a doctrine "whereof you know I am wholly guiltless", he says to his wife in 1842, "and which is

spoken of as a known and fixed element, like salt or meal. So that I
have to begin with endless disclaimers and explanations: 'I am not
the man you take me for.' " He was never the man any one took him
for, for the simple reason that no one could possibly take him for the
elusive, irreducible, merely gustatory spirit for which he took himself.

> It is a sort of maxim with me never to harp on the omnipotence of limi-
> tations. Least of all do we need any suggestion of checks and measures; as
> if New England were anything else . . . Of so many fine people it is true that
> being so much they ought to be a little more, and missing that are naught.
> It is a sort of King Rene period; there is no doing, but rare thrilling prophecy
> from bands of competing minstrels.

That is his private expression about a large part of a ferment in
regard to which his public judgment was that—

> That indeed constitutes a new feature in their portrait, that they are the
> most exacting and extortionate critics . . . These exacting children advertise
> us of our wants. There is no compliment, no smooth speech with them;
> they pay you only this one compliment of insatiable expectation; they aspire,
> they severely exact, and if they only stand fast in this watch-tower, and stand
> fast unto the end, and without end, then they are terrible friends, whereof
> poet and priest cannot but stand in awe; and what if they eat clouds and drink
> wind, they have not been without service to the race of man.

That was saying the best for them, as he always said it for everything;
but it was the sense of their being "bands of competing minstrels" and
their camp being only a "measure and check", in a society too sparse
for a synthesis, that kept him from wishing to don their uniform. This
was after all but a misfitting imitation of his natural wear, and what
he would have liked was to put that off—he did not wish to button
it tighter. He said the best for his friends of the Dial, of Fruitlands
and Brook Farm, in saying that they were fastidious and critical; but
he was conscious in the next breath that what there was around them
to be criticized was mainly a negative. Nothing is more perceptible
to-day than that their criticism produced no fruit—that it was little
else than a very decent and innocent recreation—a kind of Puritan
carnival. The New England world was for much the most part very
busy, but the Dial and Fruitlands and Brook Farm were the amusement
of the leisure-class. Extremes meet, and as in older societies that class
is known principally by its connection with castles and carriages, so
at Concord it came, with Thoreau and Mr. W. H. Channing, out of
the cabin and the wood-lot.

Emerson was not moved to believe in their fastidiousness as a productive principle even when they directed it upon abuses which he abundantly recognized. Mr. Cabot shows that he was by no means one of the professional abolitionists or philanthropists—never an enrolled "humanitarian".

> We talk frigidly of Reform until the walls mock us. It is that of which a man should never speak, but if he have cherished it in his bosom he should steal to it in darkness, as an Indian to his bride . . . Does he not do more to abolish slavery who works all day steadily in his own garden, than he who goes to the abolition meeting and makes a speech? He who does his own work frees a slave.

I must add that even while I transcribe these words there comes to me the recollection of the great meeting in the Boston Music Hall, on the first day of 1863, to celebrate the signing by Mr. Lincoln of the proclamation freeing the Southern slaves—of the momentousness of the occasion, the vast excited multitude, the crowded platform and the tall, spare figure of Emerson, in the midst, reading out the stanzas that were published under the name of the Boston Hymn. They are not the happiest he produced for an occasion—they do not compare with the verses on the "embattled farmers", read at Concord in 1857, and there is a certain awkwardness in some of them. But I well remember the immense effect with which his beautiful voice pronounced the lines—

> Pay ransom to the owner
> And fill the bag to the brim.
> Who is the owner? The slave is owner,
> And ever was. Pay *him*!

And Mr. Cabot chronicles the fact that the *gran' rifiuto*—the great backsliding of Mr. Webster when he cast his vote in Congress for the Fugitive Slave Law of 1850—was the one thing that ever moved him to heated denunciation. He felt Webster's apostasy as strongly as he had admired his genius. "Who has not helped to praise him? Simply he was the one American of our time whom we could produce as a finished work of nature." There is a passage in his journal (not a rough jotting, but, like most of the entries in it, a finished piece of writing), which is admirably descriptive of the wonderful orator and is moreover one of the very few portraits, or even personal sketches, yielded by Mr. Cabot's selections. It shows that he could observe the human figure and "render" it to good purpose.

His splendid wrath, when his eyes become fire, is good to see, so intellectual it is—the wrath of the fact and the case he espouses, and not at all personal to himself . . . These village parties must be dish-water to him, yet he shows himself just good-natured, just nonchalant enough; and he has his own way, without offending any one or losing any ground . . . His expensiveness seems necessary to him; were he too prudent a Yankee it would be a sad deduction from his magnificence. I only wish he would not truckle [to the slave-holders]. I do not care how much he spends.

I doubtless appear to have said more than enough, yet I have passed by many of the passages I had marked for transcription from Mr. Cabot's volumes. There is one, in the first, that makes us stare as we come upon it, to the effect that Emerson "could see nothing in Shelley, Aristophanes, Don Quixote, Miss Austen, Dickens". Mr. Cabot adds that he rarely read a novel, even the famous ones (he has a point of contact here as well as, strangely enough, on two or three other sides with that distinguished moralist M. Ernest Renan, who, like Emerson, was originally a dissident priest and cannot imagine why people should write works of fiction); and thought Dante "a man to put into a museum, but not into your house; another Zerah Colburn; a prodigy of imaginative function, executive rather than contemplative or wise". The confession of an insensibility ranging from Shelley to Dickens and from Dante to Miss Austen and taking Don Quixote and Aristophanes on the way, is a large allowance to have to make for a man of letters, and may appear to confirm but slightly any claim of intellectual hospitality and general curiosity put forth for him. The truth, was that, sparely constructed as he was and formed not wastefully, not with material left over, as it were, for a special function, there were certain chords in Emerson that did not vibrate at all. I well remember my impression of this on walking with him in the autumn of 1872 through the galleries of the Louvre and, later that winter, through those of the Vatican: his perception of the objects contained in these collections was of the most general order. I was struck with the anomaly of a man so refined and intelligent being so little spoken to by works of art. It would be more exact to say that certain chords were wholly absent; the tune was played, the tune of life and literature, altogether on those that remained. They had every wish to be equal to their office, but one feels that the number was short—that some notes could not be given. Mr. Cabot makes use of a singular phrase when he says, in speaking of Hawthorne, for several years our author's neighbour at Concord and a little—a very little we gather—his companion, that Emerson was unable to read his novels—he thought them "not worthy of him". This is a judgment odd almost to fascination—we circle round it and turn it over and over; it contains so elusive an ambiguity. How highly he must have esteemed the man of whose genius *The House of the Seven Gables* and *The Scarlet Letter* gave imperfectly the measure, and how strange that he should not have been eager to read almost anything that such a gifted being might have let fall! It was a rare accident that made them live almost side by side so long in the same small New England town, each a fruit of a long Puritan stem, yet with such a difference of taste. Hawthorne's vision was all for the evil and sin of the world; a side of life as to which Emerson's eyes were thickly bandaged. There were points as to which the latter's conception of right could be violated, but he had no great sense of wrong—a strangely limited one, indeed, for a moralist—no sense of the dark, the foul, the base. There was certain complications in life which he never suspected. One asks one's self whether that is why he did not care for Dante and Shelley and Aristophanes and Dickens, their works containing a considerable reflection of human perversity. But that still leaves the indifference to Cervantes and Miss Austen unaccounted for.

It has not, however, been the ambition of these remarks to account for everything, and I have arrived at the end without even pointing to the grounds on which Emerson justifies the honours of biography, discussion and illustration. I have assumed his importance and continuance, and shall probably not be gainsaid by those who read him. Those who do not will hardly rub him out. Such a book as Mr. Cabot's subjects a reputation to a test—leads people to look it over and hold it up to the light, to see whether it is worth keeping in use or even putting away in a cabinet. Such a revision of Emerson has no relegating consequences. The result of it is once more the impression that he serves and will not wear out, and that indeed we cannot afford to drop him. His instrument makes him precious. He did something better than any one else; he had a particular faculty, which has not been surpassed, for speaking to the soul in a voice of direction and authority. There have been many spiritual voices appealing, consoling, reassuring, exhorting, or even denouncing and terrifying, but none has had just that firmness and just that purity. It penetrates further, it seems to go back to the roots of our feelings, to where conduct and manhood begin; and moreover, to us to-day, there is something in it that says that it is connected somehow with the virtue of the world, has wrought and achieved, lived in thousands of minds, produced a mass of character and life. And there is this further sign of Emerson's singular power, that he is a striking exception to the general rule that writings live in the last resort by their form; that they owe a large part of their fortune to the art with which they have been composed. It is hardly too much, or too little, to say of Emerson's writings in general that they were not composed at all. Many and many things are beautifully said; he had felicities, inspirations, unforgettable phrases; he had frequently an exquisite eloquence.

> O my friends, there are resources in us on which we have not yet drawn. There are men who rise refreshed on hearing a threat; men to whom a crisis which intimidates and paralyses the majority—demanding not the faculties of prudence and thrift, but comprehension, immovableness, the readiness of sacrifice, comes graceful and beloved as a bride . . . But these are heights that we can scarce look up to and remember without contrition and shame. Let us thank God that such things exist.

None the less we have the impression that that search for a fashion and a manner on which he was always engaged never really came to a conclusion; it draws itself out through his later writings—it drew itself out through his later lectures, like a sort of renunciation of success. It is not on these, however, but on their predecessors, that his reputation will rest. Of course the way he spoke was the way that was on the whole most convenient to him; but he differs from most men of letters of the same degree of credit in failing to strike us as having achieved a style. This achievement is, as I say, usually the bribe or toll-money on the journey to posterity; and if Emerson goes his way, as he clearly appears to be doing, on the strength of his message alone, the case will be rare, the exception striking, and the honour great.

10

GUY DE MAUPASSANT

1888

I

THE first artists, in any line, are doubtless not those whose general ideas about their art are most often on their lips—those who most abound in precept, apology, and formula and can best tell us the reasons and the philosophy of things. We know the first usually by their energetic practice, the constancy with which they apply their principles, and the serenity with which they leave us to hunt for their secret in the illustration, the concrete example. None the less it often happens that a valid artist utters his mystery, flashes upon us for a moment the light by which he works, shows us the rule by which he holds it just that he should be measured. This accident is happiest, I think, when it is soonest over; the shortest explanations of the products of genius are the best, and there is many a creator of living figures whose friends, however full of faith in his inspiration, will do well to pray for him when he sallies forth into the dim wilderness of theory. The doctrine is apt to be so much less inspired than the work, the work is often so much more intelligent than the doctrine. M. Guy de Maupassant has lately traversed with a firm and rapid step a literary crisis of this kind; he has clambered safely up the bank at the further end of the morass. If he has relieved himself in the preface to *Pierre et Jean*, the last-published of his tales, he has also rendered a service to his friends; he has not only come home in a recognizable plight, escaping gross disaster with a success which even his extreme good sense was far from making in advance a matter of course, but he has expressed in intelligible terms (that by itself is a ground of felicitation) his most general idea, his own sense of his direction. He has arranged, as it were, the light in which he wishes to sit. If it is a question of attempting, under however many disadvantages, a sketch of him, the critic's business therefore is simplified: there will be no difficulty in placing him, for he himself has chosen the spot, he has made the chalk-mark on the floor.

I may as well say at once that in dissertation M. de Maupassant does not write with his best pen; the philosopher in his composition is perceptibly inferior to the story-teller. I would rather have written

half a page of *Boule de Suif* than the whole of the introduction to
Flaubert's *Letters to Madame Sand*; and his little disquisition on the
novel in general, attached to that particular example of it which
he has just put forth,[1] is considerably less to the point than the masterpiece which it ushers in. In short, as a commentator M. de Maupassant
is slightly common, while as an artist he is wonderfully rare. Of course
we must, in judging a writer, take one thing with another, and if I
could make up my mind that M. de Maupassant is weak in theory, it
would almost make me like him better, render him more approachable,
give him the touch of softness that he lacks, and show us a human flaw.
The most general quality of the author of *La Maison Tellier* and *Bel-
Ami*, the impression that remains last after the others have been
accounted for, is an essential hardness—hardness of form, hardness of
nature; and it would put us more at ease to find that if the fact with
him (the fact of execution) is so extraordinarily definite and adequate,
his explanations, after it, were a little vague and sentimental. But I
am not so sure that he must even be held foolish to have noticed the
race of critics: he is at any rate so much less foolish than several of that
fraternity. He has said his say concisely and as if he were saying it
once for all. In fine, his readers must be grateful to him for such a
passage as that in which he remarks that whereas the public at large
very legitimately says to a writer, "Console me, amuse me, terrify
me, make me cry, make me dream, or make me think," what the
sincere critic says is, "Make me something fine in the form that shall
suit you best, according to your temperament." This seems to me to
put into a nutshell the whole question of the different classes of fiction,
concerning which there has recently been so much discourse. There
are simply as many different kinds as there are persons practising the
art, for if a picture, a tale, or a novel be a direct impression of life
(and that surely constitutes its interest and value), the impression will
vary according to the plate that takes it, the particular structure and
mixture of the recipient.

I am not sure that I know what M. de Maupassant means when he
says, "The critic shall appreciate the result only according to the nature
of the effort; he has no right to concern himself with tendencies."
The second clause of that observation strikes me as rather in the air,
thanks to the vagueness of the last word. But our author adds to the
definiteness of his contention when he goes on to say that any form of
the novel is simply a vision of the world from the stand-point of a

[1] *Pierre et Jean.* Paris: Ollendorff, 1888.

person constituted after a certain fashion, and that it is therefore absurd to say that there is, for the novelist's use, only one reality of things. This seems to me commendable, not as a flight of metaphysics, hovering over bottomless gulfs of controversy, but, on the contrary, as a just indication of the vanity of certain dogmatisms. The particular way we see the world is our particular illusion about it, says M. de Maupassant, and this illusion fits itself to our organs and senses; our receptive vessel becomes the furniture of *our* little plot of the universal consciousness.

How childish, moreover, to believe in reality, since we each carry our own in our thought and in our organs. Our eyes, our ears, our sense of smell, of taste, differing from one person to another, create as many truths as there are men upon earth. And our minds, taking instruction from these organs, so diversely impressed, understand, analyse, judge, as if each of us belonged to a different race. Each one of us, therefore, forms for himself an illusion of the world, which is the illusion poetic, or sentimental, or joyous, or melancholy, or unclean, or dismal, according to his nature. And the writer has no other mission than to reproduce faithfully this illusion, with all the contrivances of art that he has learned and has at his command. The illusion of beauty, which is a human convention! The illusion of ugliness, which is a changing opinion! The illusion of truth, which is never immutable! The illusion of the ignoble, which attracts so many! The great artists are those who make humanity accept their particular illusion. Let us, therefore, not get angry with any one theory, since every theory is the generalized expression of a temperament asking itself questions.

What is interesting in this is not that M. de Maupassant happens to hold that we have no universal measure of the truth, but that it is the last word on a question of art from a writer who is rich in experience and has had success in a very rare degree. It is of secondary importance that our impression should be called, or not called, an illusion; what is excellent is that our author has stated more neatly than we have lately seen it done that the value of the artist resides in the clearness with which he gives forth that impression. His particular organism constitutes a *case*, and the critic is intelligent in proportion as he apprehends and enters into that case. To quarrel with it because it is not another, which it could not possibly have been without a wholly different outfit, appears to M. de Maupassant a deplorable waste of time. If this appeal to our disinterestedness may strike some readers as chilling (through their inability to conceive of any other form than the one they like—a limitation excellent for a reader but poor for a judge), the occasion happens to be none of the best for saying so, for M. de Maupassant himself precisely presents all the symptoms of a "case" in the most striking way, and shows us how far the consideration of them may take us. Embracing such an opportunity as this, and giving ourselves to it freely, seems to me indeed to be a course more fruitful in valid conclusions, as well as in entertainment by the way, than the more common method of establishing one's own premises. To make clear to ourselves those of the author of *Pierre et Jean*—those to which he is committed by the very nature of his mind—is an attempt that will both stimulate and repay curiosity. There is no way of looking at his work less dry, less academic, for as we proceed from one of his peculiarities to another, the whole horizon widens, yet without our leaving firm ground, and we see ourselves landed, step by step, in the most general questions—those explanations of things which reside in the race, in the society. Of course there are cases and cases, and it is the salient ones that the disinterested critic is delighted to meet.

What makes M. de Maupassant salient is two facts: the first of which is that his gifts are remarkably strong and definite, and the second that he writes directly *from* them, as it were: holds the fullest, the most uninterrupted—I scarcely know what to call it—the boldest communication with them. A case is poor when the cluster of the artist's sensibilities is small, or they themselves are wanting in keenness, or else when the personage fails to admit them—either through ignorance, or diffidence, or stupidity, or the error of a false ideal—to what may be called, a legitimate share in his attempt. It is, I think, among English and American writers that this latter accident is most liable to be misled by some convention or other as to the sort of feeler we *ought* to put forth, forgetting that the best one will be the one that nature happens to have given us. We have doubtless often enough the courage of our opinions (when it befalls that we have opinions), but we have not so constantly that of our perceptions. There is a whole side of our perceptive apparatus that we in fact neglect, and there are probably many among us who would erect this tendency into a duty. M. de Maupassant neglects nothing that he possesses; he cultivates his garden with admirable energy; and if there is a flower you miss from the rich parterre, you may be sure that it could not possibly have been raised, his mind not containing the soil for it. He is plainly of the opinion that the first duty of the artist, and the thing that makes him most useful to his fellow-men, is to master his instrument, whatever it may happen to be.

His own is that of the senses, and it is through them alone, or almost alone, that life appeals to him; it is almost alone by their help that he describes it, that he produces brilliant works. They render him this great assistance because they are evidently, in his constitution, extraordinarily alive; there is scarcely a page in all his twenty volumes that does not testify to their vivacity. Nothing could be further from his thought than to disavow them and to minimize their importance. He accepts them frankly, gratefully, works them, rejoices in them. If he were told that there are many English writers who would be sorry to go with him in this, he would, I imagine, staring, say that that is about what was to have been expected of the Anglo-Saxon race, or even that many of them probably could not go with him if they would. Then he would ask how our authors can be so foolish as to sacrifice such a *moyen*, how they can afford to, and exclaim, "They must be pretty works, those they produce, and give a fine, true, complete account of life, with such omissions, such lacunæ!" M. de Maupassant's productions teach us, for instance, that his sense of smell is exceptionally acute—as acute as that of those animals of the field and forest whose subsistence and security depend upon it. It might be thought that he would, as a student of the human race, have found an abnormal development of this faculty embarrassing, scarcely knowing what to do with it, where to place it. But such an apprehension betrays an imperfect conception of his directness and resolution, as well as of his constant economy of means. Nothing whatever prevents him from representing the relations of men and women as largely governed by the scent of the parties. Human life in his pages (would this not be the most general description he would give of it?) appears for the most part as a sort of concert of odours, and his people are perpetually engaged, or he is engaged on their behalf, in sniffing up and distinguishing them, in some pleasant or painful exercise of the nostril. "If everything in life speaks to the nostril, why on earth shouldn't we say so?" I suppose him to inquire; "and what a proof of the empire of poor conventions and hypocrisies, *chez vous autres*, that you should pretend to describe and characterize, and yet take no note (or so little that it comes to the same thing) of that essential sign!"

Not less powerful is his visual sense, the quick, direct discrimination of his eye, which explains the singularly vivid concision of his descriptions. These are never prolonged nor analytic, have nothing of enumeration, of the quality of the observer, who counts the items to be sure he has made up the sum. His eye *selects* unerringly, unscrupulously, almost impudently—catches the particular thing in which the character of the object or the scene resides, and, by expressing it with the artful brevity of a master, leaves a convincing, original picture. If he is inveterately synthetic, he is never more so than in the way he brings this hard, short, intelligent gaze to bear. His vision of the world is for the most part a vision of ugliness, and even when it is not, there is in his easy power to generalize a certain absence of love, a sort of bird's-eye-view contempt. He has none of the superstitions of observation, none of our English indulgences, our tender and often imaginative superficialities. If he glances into a railway carriage bearing its freight into the Parisian suburbs of a summer Sunday, a dozen dreary lives map themselves out in a flash.

> There were stout ladies in farcical clothes, those middle-class goodwives of the *banlieue* who replace the distinction they don't possess by an irrelevant dignity; gentlemen weary of the office, with sallow faces and twisted bodies, and one of their shoulders a little forced up by perpetual bending at work over a table. Their anxious, joyless faces spoke moreover of domestic worries, incessant needs for money, old hopes finally shattered; for they all belonged to the army of poor threadbare devils who vegetate frugally in a mean little plaster house, with a flower-bed for a garden.

Even in a brighter picture, such as the admirable vignette of the drive of Madame Tellier and her companions, the whole thing is an impression, as painters say nowadays, in which the figures are cheap. The six women at the station clamber into a country cart and go jolting through the Norman landscape to the village.

> But presently the jerky trot of the nag shook the vehicle so terribly that the chairs began to dance, tossing up the travellers to right, to left, with movements like puppets, scared grimaces, cries of dismay suddenly interrupted by a more violent bump. They clutched the sides of the trap, their bonnets turned over on to their backs, or upon the nose or the shoulder; and the white horse continued to go, thrusting out his head and straightening the little tail, hairless like that of a rat, with which from time to time he whisked his buttocks. Joseph Rivet, with one foot stretched upon the shaft, the other leg bent under him, and his elbows very high, held the reins and emitted from his throat every moment a kind of cluck which caused the animal to prick up his ears and quicken his pace. On either side of the road the green country stretched away. The colza, in flower, produced in spots a great carpet of undulating yellow, from which there rose a strong, wholesome smell, a smell penetrating and pleasant, carried very far by the breeze. In the tall rye the cornflowers held up their little azure heads, which the women wished to pluck; but M. Rivet refused to stop. Then, in some place,

a whole field looked as if it were sprinkled with blood, it was so crowded with poppies. And in the midst of the great level, taking colour in this fashion from the flowers of the soil, the trap passed on with the jog of the white horse, seeming itself to carry a nosegay of richer hues; it disappeared behind the big trees of a farm, to come out again where the foliage stopped and parade afresh through the green and yellow crops, pricked with red or blue, its blazing cartload of women, which receded in the sunshine.

As regards the other sense, the sense *par excellence*, the sense which we scarcely mention in English fiction, and which I am not very sure I shall be allowed to mention in an English periodical, M. de Maupassant speaks for that, and of it, with extraordinary distinctness and authority. To say that it occupies the first place in his picture is to say too little; it covers in truth the whole canvas, and his work is little else but a report of its innumerable manifestations. These manifestations are not, for him, so many incidents of life; they are life itself, they represent the standing answer to any question that we may ask about it. He describes them in detail, with a familiarity and a frankness which leave nothing to be added; I should say with singular truth, if I did not consider that in regard to this article he may be taxed with a certain exaggeration. M. de Maupassant would doubtless affirm that where the empire of the sexual sense is concerned, no exaggeration is possible: nevertheless it may be said that whatever depths may be discovered by those who dig for them, the impression of the human spectacle for him who takes it as it comes has less analogy with that of the monkey's cage than this admirable writer's account of it. I speak of the human spectacle as we Anglo-Saxons see it—as we Anglo-Saxons pretend we see it, M. de Maupassant would possibly say.

At any rate, I have perhaps touched upon this peculiarity sufficiently to explain my remark that his point of view is almost solely that of the senses. If he is a very interesting case, this makes him also an embarrassing one, embarrassing and mystifying for the moralist. I may as well admit that no writer of the day strikes me as equally so. To find M. de Maupassant a lion in the path—that may seem to some people a singular proof of want of courage; but I think the obstacle will not be made light of by those who have really taken the measure of the animal. We are accustomed to think, we of the English faith, that a cynic is a living advertisement of his errors, especially in proportion as he is a thorough-going one; and M. de Maupassant's cynicism, unrelieved as it is, will not be disposed of off-hand by a critic of a competent literary sense. Such a critic is not slow to perceive, to his no small confusion, that though judging from usual premises, the author of *Bel-Ami* ought to be a warning, he somehow is not. His baseness, as it pervades him, ought to be written all over him; yet somehow there are there certain aspects—and those commanding, as the house-agents say—in which it is not in the least to be perceived. It is easy to exclaim that if he judges life only from the point of view of the senses, many are the noble and exquisite things that he must leave out. What he leaves out has no claim to get itself considered till after we have done justice to what he takes in. It is this positive side of M. de Maupassant that is most remarkable—the fact that his literary character is so complete and edifying. "Auteur à peu près irréprochable dans un genre qui ne l'est pas," as that excellent critic M. Jules Lemaître says of him, he disturbs us by associating a conscience and a high standard with a temper long synonymous, in our eyes, with an absence of scruples. The situation would be simpler certainly if he were a bad writer; but none the less it is possible, I think, on the whole, to circumvent him, even without attempting to prove that after all he is one.

The latter part of his introduction to *Pierre et Jean* is less felicitous than the beginning but we learn from it—and this is interesting—that he regards the analytic fashion of telling a story, which has lately begotten in his own country some such remarkable experiments (few votaries as it has attracted among ourselves), as very much less profitable than the simple epic manner which "avoids with care all complicated explanations, all dissertations upon motives, and confines itself to making persons and events pass before our eyes". M. de Maupassant adds that in his view "psychology should be hidden in a book, as it is hidden in reality under the facts of existence. The novel conceived in this manner gains interest, movement, colour, the bustle of life." When it is a question of an artistic process, we must always mistrust very sharp distinctions, for there is surely in every method a little of every other method. It is as difficult to describe an action without glancing at its motive, its moral history, as it is to describe a motive without glancing at its practical consequence. Our history and our fiction are what we do; but it surely is not more easy to determine where what we do begins than to determine where it ends—notoriously a hopeless task. Therefore it would take a very subtle sense to draw a hard and fast line on the borderland of explanation and illustration. If psychology be hidden in life, as, according to M. de Maupassant, it should be in a book, the question immediately comes up, "From whom is it hidden?" From some people, no doubt, but very much less from others; and all depends upon the observer, the nature of one's observation, and one's curiosity. For some people motives, reasons, relations, explanations, are a part of the very surface of the drama, with the footlights beating full upon them. For me an act, an incident, an attitude, may be a sharp, detached, isolated thing, of which I give a full account in saying that in such and such a way it came off. For you it may be hung about with implications, with relations, and conditions as necessary to help you to recognize it as the clothes of your friends are to help you know them in the street. You feel that they would seem strange to you without petticoats and trousers.

M. de Maupassant would probably urge that the right thing is to know, or to guess, how events come to pass, but to say as little about it as possible. There are matters in regard to which he feels the importance of being explicit, but that is not one of them. The contention to which I allude strikes me as rather arbitrary, so difficult is it to put one's finger upon the reason why, for instance, there should be so little mystery about what happened to Christiane Andermatt, in *Mont-Oriol*, when she went to walk on the hills with Paul Brétigny, and so much, say, about the forces that formed her for that gentleman's convenience, or those lying behind any other odd collapse that our author may have related. The rule misleads, and the best rule certainly is the tact of the individual writer, which will adapt itself to the material as the material comes to him. The cause we plead is ever pretty sure to be the cause of our idiosyncrasies, and if M. de Maupassant thinks meanly of "explanations", it is, I suspect, that they come to him in no great affluence. His view of the conduct of man is so simple as scarcely to require them; and indeed so far as they are needed he *is*, virtually, explanatory. He deprecates reference to motives, but there is one, covering an immense ground in his horizon, as I have already hinted, to which he perpetually refers. If the sexual impulse be not a moral antecedent, it is none the less the wire that moves almost all M. de Maupassant's puppets, and as he has not hidden it, I cannot see that he has eliminated analysis or made a sacrifice to discretion. His pages are studded with that particular analysis; he is constantly peeping behind the curtain, telling us what he discovers there. The truth is that the admirable system of simplification which makes his tales so rapid and so concise (especially his shorter ones, for his novels in some degree, I think, suffer from it) strikes us as not in the least a conscious intellectual effort, a selective, comparative process. He tells us all he knows, all he suspects, and if these things take no

account of the moral nature of man, it is because he has no windows
looking in that direction, and not because artistic scruples have compelled him to close it up. The very compact mansion in which he
dwells presents on that side a perfectly dead wall.

This is why, if his axiom that you produce the effect of truth better
by painting people from the outside than from the inside has a large
utility, his example is convincing in a much higher degree. A writer
is fortunate when his theory and his limitations so exactly correspond,
when his curiosities may be appeased with such precision and promptitude. M. de Maupassant contends that the most that the analytic
novelist can do is to put himself—his own peculiarities—into the
costume of the figure analysed. This may be true, but if it applies to
one manner of representing people who are not ourselves, it applies also
to any other manner. It is the limitation, the difficulty of the novelist,
to whatever clan or camp he may belong. M. de Maupassant is remarkably objective and impersonal, but he would go too far if he were
to entertain the belief that he has kept himself out of his books. They
speak of him eloquently, even if it only be to tell us how easy—how
easy, given his talent of course—he has found this impersonality. Let
us hasten to add that in the case of describing a character it is doubtless
more difficult to convey the impression of something that is not one's
self (the constant effort, however delusive at bottom, of the novelist)
than in the case of describing some object more immediately visible.
The operation is more delicate, but that circumstance only increases
the beauty of the problem.

On the question of style our author has some excellent remarks;
we may be grateful indeed for every one of them, save an odd reflection about the way to "become original" if we happen not to be
so. The recipe for this transformation, it would appear, is to sit down
in front of a blazing fire, or a tree in a plain, or any object we encounter
in the regular way of business, and remain there until the tree, or the
fire, or the object, whatever it be, become different for us from all
other specimens of the same class. I doubt whether this system would
always answer, for surely the resemblance is what we wish to discover,
quite as much as the difference, and the best way to preserve it is not
to look for something opposed to it. Is not this indication of the road
to take to become, as a writer, original touched with the same fallacy
as the recommendation about eschewing analysis? It is the only naïveté
I have encountered in M. de Maupassant's many volumes. The best
originality is the most unconscious, and the best way to describe a

tree is the way in which it has struck us. "Ah, but we don't always know how it has struck us," the answer to that may be, "and it takes some time and ingenuity—much fasting and prayer—to find out." If we do not know, it probably has not struck us very much: so little indeed that our inquiry had better be relegated to that closed chamber of an artist's meditations, that sacred back kitchen, which no *a priori* rule can light up. The best thing the artist's adviser can do in such a case is to trust him and turn away, to let him fight the matter out with his conscience. And be this said with a full appreciation of the degree in which M. de Maupassant's observations on the whole question of a writer's style, at the point we have come to to-day, bear the stamp of intelligence and experience. His own style is of so excellent a tradition that the presumption is altogether in favour of what he may have to say.

He feels oppressively, discouragingly, as many another of his country-men must have felt—for the French have worked their language as no other people have done—the penalty of coming at the end of three centuries of literature, the difficulty of dealing with an instrument of expression so worn by friction, of drawing new sounds from the old familiar pipe. "When we read, so saturated with French writing as we are that our whole body gives us the impression of being a paste made of words, do we ever find a line, a thought, which is not familiar to us, and of which we have not had at least a confused presentiment?" And he adds that the matter is simple enough for the writer who only seeks to amuse the public by means already known; he attempts little, and he produces "with confidence, in the candour of his mediocrity", works which answer no question and leave no trace. It is he who wants to do more than this that has less and less an easy time of it. Everything seems to him to have been done, every effect produced, every com-bination already made. If he be a man of genius, his trouble is lightened, for mysterious ways are revealed to him, and new combinations spring up for him even after novelty is dead. It is to the simple man of taste and talent, who has only a conscience and a will, that the situation may sometimes well appear desperate; he judges himself as he goes, and he can only go step by step over ground where every step is already a footprint.

If it be a miracle whenever there is a fresh tone, the miracle has been wrought for M. de Maupassant. Or is he simply a man of genius to whom short cuts have been disclosed in the watches of the night? At any rate he has had faith—religion has come to his aid; I mean the religion of his mother tongue, which he has loved well enough to be

patient for her sake. He has arrived at the peace which passeth understanding, at a kind of conservative piety. He has taken his stand on
simplicity, on a studied sobriety, being persuaded that the deepest
science lies in that direction rather than in the multiplication of new
terms, and on this subject he delivers himself with superlative wisdom.

> There is no need of the queer, complicated, numerous, and Chinese
> vocabulary which is imposed on us to-day under the name of artistic writing,
> to fix all the shades of thought; the right way is to distinguish with an extreme
> clearness all those modifications of the value of a word which come from the
> place it occupies. Let us have fewer nouns, verbs and adjectives of an almost
> imperceptible sense, and more different phrases variously constructed, in-
> geniously cast, full of the science of sound and rhythm. Let us have an
> excellent general form rather than be collectors of rare terms.

M. de Maupassant's practice does not fall below his exhortation (though
I must confess that in the foregoing passage he makes use of the detestable expression "stylist", which I have not reproduced). Nothing can
exceed the masculine firmness, the quiet force of his own style, in
which every phrase is a close sequence, every epithet a paying piece,
and the ground is completely cleared of the vague, the ready-made
and the second-best. Less than any one to-day does he beat the air;
more than any one does he hit out from the shoulder.

II

He has produced a hundred short tales and only four regular novels;
but if the tales deserve the first place in any candid appreciation of his
talent it is not simply because they are so much the more numerous:
they are also more characteristic; they represent him best in his originality, and their brevity, extreme in some cases, does not prevent them
from being a collection of masterpieces. (They are very unequal, and
I speak of the best.) The little story is but scantily relished in England,
where readers take their fiction rather by the volume than by the page,
and the novelist's idea is apt to resemble one of those old-fashioned
carriages which require a wide court to turn round. In America, where
it is associated pre-eminently with Hawthorne's name, with Edgar
Poe's, and with that of Mr. Bret Harte, the short tale has had a better
fortune. France, however, has been the land of its great prosperity,
and M. de Maupassant had from the first the advantage of addressing
a public accustomed to catch on, as the modern phrase is, quickly.

In some respects, it may be said, he encountered prejudices too friendly, for he found a tradition of indecency ready made to his hand. I say indecency with plainness, though my indication would perhaps please better with another word, for we suffer in English from a lack of roundabout names for the *conte leste*—that element for which the French, with their *grivois*, their *gaillard*, their *égrillard*, their *gaudriole*, have so many convenient synonyms. It is an honoured tradition in France that the little story, in verse or in prose, should be liable to be more or less obscene (I can think only of that alternative epithet), though I hasten to add that among literary forms it does not monopolize the privilege. Our uncleanness is less producible—at any rate it is less produced.

For the last ten years our author has brought forth with regularity these condensed compositions, of which, probably, to an English reader, at a first glance, the most universal sign will be their licentiousness. They really partake of this quality, however, in a very differing degree, and a second glance shows that they may be divided into numerous groups. It is not fair, I think, even to say that what they have most in common is their being extremely *lestes*. What they have most in common is their being extremely strong, and after that their being extremely brutal. A story may be obscene without being brutal, and *vice versa*, and M. de Maupassant's contempt for those interdictions which are supposed to be made in the interest of good morals is but an incident—a very large one indeed—of his general contempt. A pessimism so great that its alliance with the love of good work, or even with the calculation of the sort of work that pays best in a country of style, is, as I have intimated, the most puzzling of anomalies (for it would seem in the light of such sentiments that nothing is worth anything); this cynical strain is the sign of such gems of narration as *La Maison Tellier*, *L'Histoire d'une fille de ferme*, *L'Ane*, *Le Chien*, *Mademoiselle Fifi*, *Monsieur Parent*, *L'Héritage*, *En Famille*, *Le Baptême*, *Le Père Amable*. The author fixes a hard eye on some small spot of human life, usually some ugly, dreary, shabby, sordid one, takes up the particle, and squeezes it either till it grimaces or till it bleeds. Sometimes the grimace is very droll, sometimes the wound is very horrible; but in either case the whole thing is real, observed, noted, and represented, not an invention or a castle in the air. M. de Maupassant sees human life as a terribly ugly business relieved by the comical, but even the comedy is for the most part the comedy of misery, of avidity, of ignorance, helplessness, and grossness. When his laugh is not for these

things, it is for the little *saletés* (to use one of his own favourite words)
of luxurious life, which are intended to be prettier, but which can
scarcely be said to brighten the picture. I like *La Bête à Maître Bel-
homme*, *La Ficelle*, *Le Petit Fût*, *Le Cas de Madame Luneau*, *Tribuneaux
rustiques*, and many others of this category much better than his anecdotes of the mutual confidences of his little *marquises* and *baronnes*.

Not counting his novels for the moment, his tales may be divided
into the three groups of those which deal with the Norman peasantry,
those which deal with the *petit employé* and small shopkeeper, usually
in Paris, and the miscellaneous, in which the upper walks of life are
represented, and the fantastic, the whimsical, the weird, and even the
supernatural, figure as well as the unexpurgated. These last things
range from *Le Horla* (which is not a specimen of the author's best
vein—the only occasion on which he has the weakness of imitation
is when he strikes us as emulating Edgar Poe) to *Miss Harriet*, and from
Boule de Suif (a triumph) to that almost inconceivable little growl of
Anglophobia, *Découverte*—inconceivable I mean in its irresponsibility
and ill-nature on the part of a man of M. de Maupassant's distinction;
passing by such little perfections as *Petit Soldat*, *L'Abandonné*, *Le Collier*
(the list is too long for complete enumeration), and such gross imperfections (for it once in a while befalls our author to go woefully astray)
as *La Femme de Paul*, *Châli*, *Les Sœurs Rondoli*. To these might almost
be added as a special category the various forms in which M. de Maupassant relates adventures in railway carriages. Numerous, to his
imagination, are the pretexts for enlivening fiction afforded by first,
second, and third class compartments; the accidents (which have
nothing to do with the conduct of the train) that occur there constitute
no inconsiderable part of our earthly transit.

It is surely by his Norman peasant that his tales will live; he knows
this worthy as if he had made him, understands him down to the
ground, puts him on his feet with a few of the freest, most plastic
touches. M. de Maupassant does not admire him, and he is such a
master of the subject that it would ill become an outsider to suggest
a revision of judgment. He is a part of the contemptible furniture of
the world, but on the whole, it would appear, the most grotesque
part of it. His caution, his canniness, his natural astuteness, his stingi-
ness, his general grinding sordidness, are as unmistakable as that quaint
and brutish dialect in which he expresses himself, and on which our
author plays like a virtuoso. It would be impossible to demonstrate
with a finer sense of the humour of the thing the fatuities and densities

of his ignorance, the bewilderments of his opposed appetites, the over-reachings of his caution. His existence has a gay side, but it is apt to be the barbarous gaiety commemorated in *Farce Normande*, an anecdote which, like many of M. de Maupassant's anecdotes, it is easier to refer the reader to than to repeat. If it is most convenient to place *La Maison Tellier* among the tales of the peasantry, there is no doubt that it stands at the head of the list. It is absolutely unadapted to the perusal of ladies, and young persons, but it shares this peculiarity with most of its fellows so that to ignore it on that account would be to imply that we must forswear M. de Maupassant altogether, which is an incongruous and insupportable conclusion. Every good story is of course both a picture and an idea, and the more they are interfused the better the problem is solved. In *La Maison Tellier* they fit each other to perfection; the capacity for sudden innocent delights latent in natures which have lost their innocence is vividly illustrated by the singular scenes to which our acquaintance with Madame and her staff (little as it may be a thing to boast of) successively introduces us. The breadth, the freedom, and brightness of all this give the measure of the author's talent, and of that large, keen way of looking at life which sees the pathetic and the droll, the stuff of which the whole piece is made, in the queerest and humblest patterns. The tone of *La Maison Tellier* and the few compositions which closely resemble it, expresses M. de Maupassant's nearest approach to geniality. Even here, however, it is the geniality of the showman exhilarated by the success with which he feels that he makes his mannikins (and especially his womankins) caper and squeak, and who after the performance tosses them into their box with the irreverence of a practised hand. If the pages of the author of *Bel-Ami* may be searched almost in vain for a manifestation of the sentiment of respect, it is naturally not by Mme Tellier and her charges that we must look most to see it called forth; but they are among the things that please him most.

Sometimes there is a sorrow, a misery, or even a little heroism, that he handles with a certain tenderness (*Une Vie* is the capital example of this), without insisting on the poor, the ridiculous, or, as he is fond of saying, the bestial side of it. Such an attempt, admirable in its sobriety and delicacy, is the sketch, in *L'Abandonné*, of the old lady and gentleman, Mme de Cadour and M. d'Apreval, who, staying with the husband of the former at a little watering-place on the Normandy coast, take a long, hot walk on a summer's day, on a straight, white road, into the interior, to catch a clandestine glimpse of a young farmer, their illegitimate son. He has been pensioned, he is ignorant of his origin, and is a commonplace and unconciliatory rustic. They look at him, in his dirty farmyard, and no sign passes between them; then they turn away and crawl back, in melancholy silence, along the dull French road. The manner in which this dreary little occurrence is related makes it as large as a chapter of history. There is tenderness in *Miss Harriet*, which sets forth how an English old maid, fantastic, hideous, sentimental, and tract-distributing, with a smell of india-rubber, fell in love with an irresistible French painter, and drowned herself in the well because she saw him kissing the maid-servant; but the figure of the lady grazes the farcical. Is it because we know Miss Harriet (if we are not mistaken in the type the author has had in his eye) that we suspect the good spinster was not so weird and desperate, addicted though her class may be, as he says, to "haunting all the *tables d'hôte* in Europe, to spoiling Italy, poisoning Switzerland, making the charming towns of the Mediterranean uninhabitable, carrying every-where their queer little manias, their *mœurs de vestales pétrifiées*, their indescribable garments, and that odour of india-rubber which makes one think that at night they must be slipped into a case?" What would Miss Harriet have said to M. de Maupassant's friend, the hero of the *Découverte*, who, having married a little Anglaise because he thought she was charming when she spoke broken French, finds she is very flat as she becomes more fluent, and has nothing more urgent than to denounce her to a gentleman he meets on the steam-boat, and to relieve his wrath in ejaculations of "Sales Anglais"?

M. de Maupassant evidently knows a great deal about the army of clerks who work under government, but it is a terrible tale that he has to tell of them and of the *petit bourgeois* in general. It is true that he has treated the *petit bourgeois* in *Pierre et Jean* without holding him up to our derision, and the effort has been so fruitful, that we owe to it the work for which, on the whole, in the long list of his successes, we are most thankful. But of *Pierre et Jean*, a production neither comic nor cynical (in the degree, that is, of its predecessors), but serious and fresh I will speak anon. In *Monsieur Parent*, *L'Héritage*, *En Famille*, *Une Partie de campagne*, *Promenade*, and many other pitiless little pieces, the author opens the window wide to his perception of everything mean, narrow, and sordid. The subject is ever the struggle for existence in hard conditions, lighted up simply by more or less *polissonnerie*. Nothing is more striking to an Anglo-Saxon reader than the omission of all the other lights, those with which our imagination, and I think it ought to be said our observation, is. familiar, and which our own works of fiction at any rate do not permit us to forget: those of which the most general description is that they spring from a certain mixture of good humour and piety—piety, I mean, in the civil and domestic sense quite as much as in the religious. The love of sport, the sense of decorum, the necessity for action, the habit of respect, the absence of irony, the pervasiveness of childhood, the expansive tendency of the race, are a few of the qualities (the analysis might, I think, be pushed much further) which ease us off, mitigate our tension and irritation, rescue us from the nervous exasperation which is almost the commonest element of life as depicted by M. de Maupassant. No doubt there is in our literature an immense amount of conventional blinking, and it may be questioned whether pessimistic representation in M. de Maupassant's manner does not follow his particular original more closely than our perpetual quest of pleasantness (does not Mr. Rider Haggard make even his African carnage pleasant?) adheres to the lines of the world we ourselves know.

Fierce indeed is the struggle for existence among even our pious and good-humoured millions, and it is attended with incidents as to which after all little testimony is to be extracted from our literature of fiction. It must never be forgotten that the optimism of that literature is partly the optimism of woman and of spinsters; in other words the optimism of ignorance as well as of delicacy. It might be supposed that the French, with their mastery of the *arts d'agrément*, would have more consolations than we, but such is not the account of the matter given by the new generation of painters. To the French we seem superficial, and we are certainly open to the reproach; but none the less even to the infinite majority of readers of good faith there will be a wonderful want of correspondence between the general picture of *Bel-Ami*, of *Mont-Oriol*, of *Une Vie*, *Yvette* and *En Famille*, and our own vision of reality. It is an old impression of course that the satire of the French has a very different tone from ours; but few English readers will admit that the feeling of life is less in ours than in theirs. The feeling of life is evidently, *de part et d'autre*, a very different thing. If in ours, as the novel illustrates it, there are superficialities, there are also qualities which are far from being negatives and omissions: a large imagination and (is it fatuous to say?) a large experience of the positive kind. Even those of our novelists whose manner is most ironic pity life more and hate it less than M. de Maupassant and his great initiator Flaubert. It comes back I suppose to our good-humour (which may apparently also be an artistic force); at any rate, we have reserves about our shames and our sorrows, indulgences and tolerances about our Philistinism, forbearances about our blows, and a general friendliness of conception about our possibilities, which take the cruelty from our self-derision and operate in the last resort as a sort of tribute to our freedom. There is a horrible, admirable scene in *Monsieur Parent*, which is a capital example of triumphant ugliness. The harmless gentleman who gives his name to the tale has an abominable wife, one of whose offensive attributes is a lover (unsuspected by her husband), only less impudent than herself. M. Parent comes in from a walk with his little boy, at dinner-time to encounter suddenly in his abused, dishonoured, deserted home, convincing proof of her misbehaviour. He waits and waits dinner for her, giving her the benefit of every doubt; but when at last she enters, late in the evening, accompanied by the partner of her guilt, there is a tremendous domestic concussion. It is to the peculiar vividness of this scene that I allude, the way we hear it and see it, and its most repulsive details are evoked for us: the sordid confusion, the vulgar noise, the disordered table and ruined dinner, the shrill insolence of the wife, her brazen mendacity, the scared inferiority of the lover, the mere momentary heroics of the weak husband, the scuffle and somersault, the eminently unpoetic justice with which it all ends.

When Thackeray relates how Arthur Pendennis goes home to take pot-luck with the insolvent Newcomes at Boulogne, and how the dreadful Mrs. Mackenzie receives him, and how she makes a scene, when the frugal repast is served, over the diminished mutton-bone, we feel that the notation of that order of misery goes about as far as we can bear it. But this is child's play to the history of M. and Mme Caravan and their attempt, after the death (or supposed death) of the husband's mother, to transfer to their apartment before the arrival of the other heirs certain miserable little articles of furniture belonging to the deceased, together with the frustration of the manœuvre not only by the grim resurrection of the old woman (which is a sufficiently fantastic item), but by the shock of battle when a married daughter and her husband appear. No one gives us like M. de Maupassant the odious words exchanged on such an occasion as that: no one depicts with so just a hand the feelings of small people about small things. These feelings are very apt to be "fury"; that word is of strikingly frequent occurrence in his pages. *L'Héritage* is a drama of private life in the little world of the Ministère de la Marine—a world, according to M.

de Maupassant, of dreadful little jealousies and ineptitudes. Readers of a robust complexion should learn how the wretched M. Lesable was handled by his wife and her father on his failing to satisfy their just expectations, and how he comported himself in the singular situation thus prepared for him. The story is a model of narration, but it leaves our poor average humanity dangling like a beaten rag.

Where does M. de Maupassant find the great multitude of his detestable women? or where at least does he find the courage to represent them in such colours? Jeanne de Lamare, in *Une Vie*, receives the outrages of fate with a passive fortitude; and there is something touching in Mme Roland's *âme tendre de caissière*, as exhibited in *Pierre et Jean*. But for the most part M. de Maupassant's heroines are a mixture of extreme sensuality and extreme mendacity. They are a large element in that general disfigurement, that *illusion de l'ignoble, qui attire tant d'êtres*, which makes the perverse or the stupid side of things the one which strikes him first, which leads him, if he glances at a group of nurses and children sunning themselves in a Parisian square, to notice primarily the *yeux de brute* of the nurses; or if he speaks of the longing for a taste of the country which haunts the shopkeeper fenced in behind his counter, to identify it as the *amour bête de la nature;* or if he has occasion to put the boulevards before us on a summer's evening, to seek his effect in these terms: "The city, as hot as a stew, seemed to sweat in the suffocating night. The drains puffed their pestilential breath from their mouths of granite, and the underground kitchens poured into the streets, through their low windows, the infamous miasmas of their dishwater and old sauces." I do not contest the truth of such indications, I only note the particular selection and their seeming to the writer the most *apropos*.

Is it because of the inadequacy of these indications when applied to the long stretch that M. de Maupassant's novels strike us as less complete, in proportion to the talent expended upon them, than his *contes* and *nouvelles*? I make this invidious distinction in spite of the fact that *Une Vie* (the first of the novels in the order of time) is a remarkably interesting experiment, and that *Pierre et Jean* is, so far as my judgment goes, a faultless production. *Bel-Ami* is full of the bustle and the crudity of life (its energy and expressiveness almost bribe one to like it), but it has the great defect that the physiological explanation of things here too visibly contracts the problem in order to meet it. The world represented is too special, too little inevitable, too much to take or to leave as we like—a world in which every man is a cad and every woman a harlot. M. de Maupassant traces the career of a finished blackguard who succeeds in life through women, and he represents him primarily as succeeding in the profession of journalism. His colleagues and his mistresses are as depraved as himself, greatly to the injury of the ironic idea, for the real force of satire would have come from seeing him engaged and victorious with natures better than his own. It may be remarked that this was the case with the nature of Mme Walter; but the reply to that is—hardly! Moreover the author's whole treatment of the episode of Mme Walter is the thing on which his admirers have least to congratulate him. The taste of it is so atrocious, that it is difficult to do justice to the way it is made to stand out. Such an instance as this pleads with irresistible eloquence, as it seems to me, the cause of that salutary diffidence or practical generosity which I mentioned on a preceding page. I know not the English or American novelist who could have written this portion of the history of *Bel-Ami* if he would. But I also find it impossible to conceive of a member of that fraternity who would have written it if he could. The subject of *Mont-Oriol* is full of queerness to the English mind. Here again the picture has much more importance than the idea, which is simply that a gentleman, if he happen to be a low animal, is liable to love a lady very much less if she presents him with a pledge of their affection. It need scarcely be said that the lady and gentleman who in M. de Maupassant's pages exemplify this interesting truth are not united in wedlock—that is with each other.

M. de Maupassant tells us that he has imbibed many of his principles from Gustave Flaubert, from the study of his works as well as, formerly, the enjoyment of his words. It is in *Une Vie* that Flaubert's influence is most directly traceable, for the thing has a marked analogy with *L'Education sentimentale*. That is, it is the presentation of a simple piece of a life (in this case a long piece), a series of observations upon an episode *quelconque*, as the French say, with the minimum of arrangement of the given objects. It is an excellent example of the way the impression of truth may be conveyed by that form, but it would have been a still better one if in his search for the effect of dreariness (the effect of dreariness may be said to be the subject of *Une Vie*, so far as the subject is reducible) the author had not eliminated excessively. He has arranged, as I say, as little as possible; the necessity of a "plot" has in no degree imposed itself upon him, and his effort has been to give the uncomposed, unrounded look of life, with its accidents, its broken rhythm, its queer resemblance to the famous description of "Bradshaw"—a compound of trains that start but don't arrive, and trains that arrive but don't start. It is almost an arrangement of the history of poor Mme de Lamare to have left so many things out of it, for after all she is described in very few of the relations of life. The principal ones are there certainly; we see her as a daughter, a wife, and a mother, but there is a certain accumulation of secondary experience that marks any passage from youth to old age which is a wholly absent element in M. de Maupassant's narrative, and the supression of which gives the thing a tinge of the arbitrary. It is in the power of this secondary experience to make a great difference, but nothing makes any difference for Jeanne de Lamare as M. de Maupassant puts her before us. Had she no other points of contact than those he describes?—no friends, no phases, no episodes, no chances, none of the miscellaneous *remplissage* of life? No doubt M. de Maupassant would say that he has had to select, that the most comprehensive enumeration is only a condensation, and that, in accordance with the very just principles enunciated in that preface to which I have perhaps too repeatedly referred, he has sacrificed what is uncharacteristic to what is characteristic. It characterizes the career of this French country lady of fifty years ago that its long gray expanse should be seen as peopled with but five or six figures. The essence of the matter is that she was deceived in almost every affection, and that essence is given if the persons who deceived her are given.

The reply is doubtless adequate, and I have only intended my criticism to suggest the degree of my interest. What it really amounts to is that if the subject of this artistic experiment had been the existence of an English lady, even a very dull one, the air of verisimilitude would have demanded that she should have been placed in a denser medium. *Une Vie* may after all be only a testimony to the fact of the melancholy void of the coast of Normandy, even within a moderate drive of a great seaport, under the Restoration and Louis Philippe. It is especially to be recommended to those who are interested in the question of what constitutes a "story", offering as it does the most definite sequences at the same time that it has nothing that corresponds to the usual idea of a plot, and closing with an implication that finds us prepared. The picture again in this case is much more dominant than the idea, unless it be an idea that loneliness and grief are terrible. The picture, at any rate, is full of truthful touches, and the work has the merit and the charm that it is the most delicate of the author's productions and the least hard. In none other has he occupied himself so continuously with so innocent a figure as his soft, bruised heroine; in none other has he paid our poor blind human history the compliment (and this is remarkable, considering the flatness of so much of the particular subject) of finding it so little *bête*. He may think it, here, but comparatively he does not say it. He almost betrays a sense of moral things. Jeanne is absolutely passive, she has no moral spring, no active moral life, none of the edifying attributes of character (it costs her apparently as little as may be in the way of a shock, a complication of feeling, to discover, by letters, after her mother's death, that this lady has not been the virtuous woman she has supposed); but her chronicler has had to handle the immaterial forces of patience and renunciation, and this has given the book a certain purity, in spite of two or three "physiological" passages that come in with violence—a violence the greater as we feel it to be a result of selection. It is very much a mark of M. de Maupassant that on the most striking occasion, with a single exception, on which his picture is not a picture of libertinage it is a picture of unmitigated suffering. Would he suggest that these are the only alternatives?

The exception that I here allude to is for *Pierre et Jean*, which I have left myself small space to speak of. Is it because in this masterly little novel there is a show of those immaterial forces which I just mentioned, and because Pierre Roland is one of the few instances of operative character that can be recalled from so many volumes, that many readers will place M. de Maupassant's latest production altogether at the head of his longer ones? I am not sure, inasmuch as after all the character in question is not extraordinarily distinguished, and the moral problem not presented in much complexity. The case is only relative. Perhaps it is not of importance to fix the reasons of preference in respect to a piece of writing so essentially a work of art and of talent. *Pierre et Jean* is the best of M. de Maupassant's novels mainly because M. de Maupassant has never before been so clever. It is a pleasure to see a mature talent able to renew itself, strike another note, and appear still young. This story suggests the growth of a perception that everything has not been said about the actors on the world's stage when they are represented either as helpless victims or as mere bundles of appetites. There is an air of responsibility about Pierre Roland, the person on whose behalf the tale is mainly told, which almost constitutes a pledge. An inquisitive critic may ask why in this particular case M. de Maupassant should have stuck to the *petit bourgeois*, the circumstances not being such as to typify that class more than another. There are reasons indeed which on reflection are perceptible; it was necessary that his people should be poor, and necessary even that to attenuate Madame Roland's misbehaviour she should have had the excuse of the contracted life of a shopwoman in the Rue Montmartre. Were the inquisitive critic slightly malicious as well, he might suspect the author of a fear that he should seem to give way to the *illusion du beau* if in addition to representing the little group in *Pierre et Jean* as persons of about the normal conscience he had also represented them as of the cultivated class. If they belong to the humble life this belittles and— I am still quoting the supposedly malicious critic—M. de Maupassant *must*, in one way or the other, belittle. To the English reader it will appear, I think, that Pierre and Jean are rather more of the cultivated class than two young Englishmen in the same social position. It belongs to the drama that the struggle of the elder brother—educated, proud, and acute—should be partly with the pettiness of his opportunities. The author's choice of a *milieu*, moreover, will serve to English readers as an example of how much more democratic contemporary French fiction is than that of his own country. The greater part of it—almost all the work of Zola and of Daudet, the best of Flaubert's novels, and the best of those of the brothers De Goncourt—treat of that vast, dim section of society which, lying between those luxurious walks on whose behalf there are easy presuppositions and that darkness of misery which, in addition to being picturesque, brings philanthropy also to the writer's aid, constitutes really, in extent and expressiveness, the substance of any nation. In England, where the fashion of fiction still sets mainly to the country house and the hunting-field, and yet more novels are published than anywhere else in the world, that thick twilight of mediocrity of condition has been little explored. May it yield triumphs in the years to come!

It may seem that I have claimed little for M. de Maupassant, so far as English readers are concerned with him, in saying that after publishing twenty improper volumes he has at last published a twenty-first, which is neither indecent nor cynical. It is not this circumstance that has led me to dedicate so many pages to him, but the circumstance that in producing all the others he yet remained, for those who are interested in these matters, a writer with whom it was impossible not to reckon. This is why I called him, to begin with, so many ineffectual names: a rarity, a"case", an embarrassment, a lion in the path. He is still in the path as I conclude these observations, but I think that in making them we have discovered a legitimate way round. If he is a master of his art and it is discouraging to find what low views are compatible with mastery, there is satisfaction, on the other hand, in learn- ing on what particular condition he holds his strange success. This con- dition, it seems to me, is that of having totally omitted one of the items of the problem, an omission which has made the problem so much easier that it may almost be described as a short cut to a solution. The question is whether it be a fair cut. M. de Maupassant has simply skipped the whole reflective part of his men and women—that reflective part which governs conduct and produces character. He may say that he does not see it, does not know it; to which the answer is, "So much the better for you, if you wish to describe life without it. The strings you pull are by so much the less numerous, and you can therefore pull those that remain with greater promptitude, consequently with greater firmness, with a greater air of knowledge." Pierre Roland, I repeat, shows a capacity for reflection, but I cannot think who else does, among the thousand figures who com- pete with him—I mean for reflection addressed to anything higher than the gratification of an instinct. We have an impression that M. d'Apreval and Mme de Cador reflect, as they trudge back from their mournful excursion, but that indication is not pushed very far. An aptitude for this exercise is a part of disciplined manhood, and discip- lined manhood M. de Maupassant has simply not attempted to re- present. I can remember no instance in which he sketches any con- siderable capacity for conduct, and his women betray that capacity as little as his men. I am much mistaken if he has once painted a gentle- man, in the English sense of the term. His gentlemen, like Paul Brétigny and Gontran de Ravenel, are guilty of the most extraor- dinary deflections. For those who are conscious of this element in life, look for it and like it, the gap will appear to be immense. It will lead them to say, "No wonder you have a contempt if that is the way you limit the field. No wonder you judge people roughly if that is the way you see them. Your work, on your premises, remains the admirable thing it is, but is your 'case' not adequately explained?"

The erotic element in M. de Maupassant, about which much more might have been said, seems to me to be explained by the same limit- ation, and explicable in a similar way wherever else its literature occurs in excess. The carnal side of man appears the most characteristic if you look at it a great deal; and you look at it a great deal if you do not look at the other, at the side by which he reacts against his weaknesses, his defeats. The more you look at the other, the less the whole busi- ness to which French novelists have ever appeared to English readers to give a disproportionate place—the business, as I may say, of the senses—will strike you as the only typical one. Is not this the most useful reflection to make in regard to the famous question of the morality, the decency, of the novel? It is the only one, it seems to me, that will meet the case as we find the case to-day. Hard and fast rules, *a priori* restrictions, mere interdictions (you shall not speak of this, you shall not look at that) have surely served their time, and will in the nature of the case never strike an energetic talent as anything but arbitrary. A healthy, living and growing art, full of curiosity and fond of exercise, has an indefeasible mistrust of rigid prohibitions. Let us then leave this magnificent art of the novelist to itself and to its perfect freedom, in the faith that one example is as good as another, and that our fiction will always be decent enough if it be sufficiently general. Let us not be alarmed at this prodigy (though prodigies are alarming) of M. de Maupassant, who is at once so licentious and so impeccable, but gird ourselves up with the conviction that another point of view will yield another perfection.

11

THE JOURNAL OF THE BROTHERS DE GONCOURT

1888

I CAN scarcely forbear beginning these limited remarks on an interesting subject with a regret—the regret that I had not found the right occasion to make them two or three years ago. This is not because since that time the subject has become less attaching, but precisely because it has become more so, has become so absorbing that I am oppressively conscious of the difficulty of treating it. It was never, I think, an easy one; inasmuch as for persons interested in questions of literature, of art, of form, in the general question of the observation of life for an artistic purpose, the appeal and the solicitation of Edmond and Jules de Goncourt were essentially not simple and soothing. The manner of this extraordinary pair, their temper, their strenuous effort and conscious system, suggested anything but a quick solution of the problems that seemed to hum in our ears as we read; suggested it almost as little indeed as their curious, uncomfortable style, with its multiplied touches and pictorial verbosity, was apt to evoke an immediate vision of the objects to which it made such sacrifices of the synthetic and rhythmic. None the less, if one liked them well enough to persist, one ended by making terms with them; I allude to the liking as conditional because it appears to be a rule of human relations that it is by no means always a sufficient bond of sympathy for people to care for the same things: there may be so increasing a divergence when they care for them in different ways The great characteristic of the way of the brothers De Goncourt was that it was extraordinarily "modern"; so illustrative of feelings that had not yet found intense expression in literature that it made at last the definite standpoint, the common ground and the clear light for taking one's view of them. They bristled (the word is their own) with responsible professions, and took us further into the confidence of their varied sensibility than we always felt it important to penetrate; but the formula that expressed them remained well in sight. They were historians and observers who were painters; they composed biographies, they told stories, with the palette always on their thumb.

Now, however, all that is changed and the case is infinitely more complicated. M. Edmond de Goncourt has published, at intervals of a few months, the *Journal* kept for twenty years by his brother and himself, and the *Journal* makes all the difference. The situation was comparatively manageable before, but now it strikes us as extremely embarrassing. M. Edmond de Goncourt has mixed the cards in the most extraordinary way; he has shifted his position with a carelessness of consequences of which I know no other example. Who can recall an instance of an artist's having it in his power to deprive himself of the advantage of the critical perspective in which he stands, and being eager to use that power?

That MM. de Goncourt should have so faithfully carried on their *Journal* is a very interesting and remarkable fact, as to which there will be much to say; but it has almost a vulgarly usual air in comparison with the circumstance that one of them has judged best to give the document to the light. If it be true that the elder and surviving brother has held a part of it back, that only adds to the judicious, responsible quality of the act. He has selected, and that indicates a plan and consti-tutes a presumption of sanity. There has been, so to speak, a method in M. Edmond de Goncourt's madness. I use the term madness because it so conveniently covers most of the ground. How else indeed should one express it when a man of talent defaces with his own hand not only the image of himself that public opinion has erected on the highway of literature but also the image of a loved and lost partner who can raise no protest and offer no explanation? If instead of publishing his *Journal* M. de Goncourt had burnt it up we should have been deprived of a very curious and entertaining book; but even with that consciousness we should have remembered that it would have been impertinent to expect him to do anything else. Barely conceivable would it have been had he withheld the copious record from the flames for the perusal of a posterity who would pass judgement on it when he himself should be dust. That would have been an act of high humility—the sacrifice of the finer part of one's reputation; but after all a man can commit suicide only in his lifetime, and the example would have had its distinction on the part of a curious mind moved by sympathy with the curiosity of a coming age.

If I suggest that if it were possible for us to hear Jules de Goncourt's voice to-day it might convey an explanation, this perhaps represents an explanation as more possible than we see it as yet. Certainly it is difficult to see it as graceful or as conciliatory. There is scarcely any account we can give of the motive of the act that doesn't make it almost less an occasion for complacency than the act itself. (I still refer, of course, to the publication, not to the composition, of the

Journal. The composition, for nervous, irritated, exasperated characters, may have been a relief—though even in this light its operation
appears to have been slow and imperfect. Indeed it occurs to one that
M. Edmond de Goncourt may have felt the whimsical impulse to
expose the fond remedy as ineffectual.) If the motive was not humility,
not mortification, it was something else—something that we can
properly appreciate only by remembering that it is not enough to be
proud and that the question inevitably comes up of what one's pride
is about. If MM. de Goncourt were two almost furious *névrosés*, if the
infinite vibration of their nerves and the soreness of their sentient parts
were the condition on which they produced many interesting books.
the fact was pathetic and the misfortune great, but the legitimacy of
the whole thing was incontestable. People are made as they are made,
and some are weak in one way and some in another. What passes our
comprehension is the state of mind in which their weakness appears
to them a source of glory, or even of dolorous general interest. It may
be an inevitable, or it may even for certain sorts of production be an
indispensable, thing to be a *névrosé*; but in what particular juncture is
it a communicable thing? M. de Goncourt not only communicates the
case, but insists upon it; he has done personally what M. Maxime du
Camp did a few years ago for Gustave Flaubert (in his *Souvenirs
Littéraires*) when he made known to the world that the author of
Madame Bovary had epileptic fits. The differences are great, however,
for if we are disposed to question M. du Camp's right to put another
person's secret into circulation we must admit that he does so with
compunction and mourning. M. de Goncourt, on the other hand,
waves the banner of the infirmity that his *collaborateur* shared with him
and invites all men to listen to the details. About his right, I hasten to
add, so far as he speaks for himself, there is nothing dubious, and this
puts us in a rare position for reading and enjoying his book. We are
not accomplices and our honour is safe. People are betrayed by their
friends, their enemies, their biographers, their critics, their editors,
their publishers, and so far as we give ear in these cases we are not quite
without guilt; but it is much plainer sailing when the burden of defence
rests on the very sufferers. What would have been thought of a
friend or an editor, what would have been thought even of an enemy,
who should have ventured to print the *Journal* of MM. de Goncourt?

The reason why it must always be asked in future, with regard to
any appreciation of these gentlemen, "Was it formed before the
Journal or after the *Journal?*" is simply that this publication has obtruded

into our sense of their literary performance the disturbance of a revelation of personal character. The scale on which the disturbance presents itself is our ground for surprise, and the nature of the character exhibited our warrant for regret. The complication is simply that if to-day we wish to judge the writings of the brothers De Goncourt freely, largely, historically, the feat is almost impossible. We have to reckon with a prejudice—a prejudice of our own. And that is why a critic may be sorry to have missed the occasion of testifying to a liberal comprehension before the prejudice was engendered. Almost impossible, I say, but fortunately not altogether; for is it not the very function of criticism and the sign of its intelligence to acquit itself honourably in embarrassing conditions and track the idea with patience just in proportion as it is elusive? The good method is always to sacrifice nothing. Let us therefore not regret too much either that MM. de Goncourt did not burn their *Journal* if they wished their novels to be liked, or that they did not burn their novels if they wished their *Journal* to be forgotten. The difficult point to deal with as regards this latter production is that it is a journal of pretensions; for is it not a sound generalization to say that when we speak of pretensions we always mean pretensions exaggerated? If the *Journal* sets them forth it is in the novels that we look to see them justified. If the justification is imperfect that will not disgust us, for what does the disparity do more than help to characterize our authors? The importance of their being characterized depends largely on their talent (for people engaged in the same general effort and interested in the same questions), and of a poverty of talent even the reader most struck with the unamiable way in which, as diarists, they for the most part use their powers, will surely not accuse MM. de Goncourt. They express, they represent, they give the sense of life; it is not always the life that such and such a one of their readers will find most interesting, but that is his affair and not theirs. Theirs is to vivify the picture. This art they unmistakably possess, and the *Journal* testifies to it still more than *Germinie Lacerteux* and *Manette Salomon*; infinitely more, I may add, than the novels published by M. Edmond de Goncourt since the death of his brother.

I do not pronounce for the moment either on the justice or the generosity of the portrait of Sainte-Beuve produced in the *Journal* by a thousand small touches, entries made from month to month and year to year and taking up so much place in the whole that the representation of that figure (with the Princess Mathilde, Gavarni, Théophile Gautier and Gustave Flaubert thrown in a little behind) may almost be said to be the main effect of the three volumes. What is incontestable is the intensity of the vision, the roundness of the conception, and the way that the innumerable little parts of the image hang together. The Sainte-Beuve of MM. de Goncourt may not be the real Sainte-Beuve, but he is a wonderfully possible and consistent personage. He is observed with detestation, but at least he is observed, and the faculty is welcome and rare. This is what we mean by talent—by having something fresh to contribute. Let us be grateful for anything at all fresh so long as our gratitude is not chilled—a case in which it has always the resource of being silent. It is obvious that this check is constantly at hand in our intercourse with MM. de Goncourt, for the simple reason that, with the greatest desire in the world to see all round, we cannot rid ourselves of the superstition that, when all is said and done, art is most in character when it most shows itself amiable. It is not amiable when it is narrow and exclusive and jealous, when it makes the deplorable confession that it has no secret for resisting exasperation. It is not the sign of a free intelligence or a rich life to be hysterical because somebody's work whom you don't like affirms itself in opposition to that of somebody else whom you do; but this condition is calculated particularly little to please when the excitement springs from a comparison more personal. It is almost a platitude to say that the artistic passion will ever most successfully assuage the popular suspicion that there is a latent cruelty in it when it succeeds in not appearing to be closely connected with egotism. The uncalculated trick played by our authors upon their reputation was to suppose that their name could bear such a strain. It is tolerably clear that it can't, and this is the mistake we should have to forgive them if we proposed to consider their productions as a whole. It doesn't cover all the ground to say that the injury of their mistake is only for themselves: it is really in some degree for those who take an interest in the art they practise. Such eccentrics, such passionate seekers may not, in England and America, be numerous, but even if they are a modest band their complaint is worth taking account of. No one can ever have been nearly so much interested in the work of Edmond and Jules de Goncourt as these gentlemen themselves; their deep absorption in it, defying all competition, is one of the honourable sides of their literary character. But the general brotherhood of men of letters may very well have felt humiliated by the disclosure of such wrath in celestial, that is, in analogous minds. It is in short rather a shock to find that artists who could make such a miniature of their Sainte-Beuve have not carried their delicacy a little further. It is always a pain to perceive that some of the qualities we prize don't imply the others.

What makes it important not to sacrifice the *Journal* (to speak for the present only of that) is this very illustration of the degree to which, for the indefatigable diarists, the things of literature and art are the great realities. If every genuine talent is for the critic a "case" constituted by the special mixture of elements and faculties, it is not difficult to put one's finger on the symptoms in which that of these unanimous brothers resides. It consists in their feeling life so exclusively as a theme for descriptive pictorial prose. Their exclusiveness is, so far as I know, unprecedented, for if we have encountered men of erudition, men of science as deeply buried in learning and in physics, we have never encountered a man of letters (our authors are really one in their duality), for whom his profession was such an exhaustion of his possibilities. Their friend and countryman Flaubert doubtless gave himself up to "art" with as few reservations, but our authors have over him exactly the superiority that the *Journal* gives them: it is a proof the more of their concentration, of their having drawn breath only in the world of subject and form. If they are not more representative they are at least more convenient to refer to. Their concentration comes in part from the fact that it is the meeting of two natures, but this also would have counted in favour of expansion, of leakage. "Collaboration" is always a mystery, and that of MM. de Goncourt was probably close beyond any other; but we have seen the process successful several times, so that the real wonder is not that in this case the parties to it should have been able to work together, to divide the task without dividing the effect, but rather that nature should have struck off a double copy of a rare original. An original is a conceivable thing, but a pair of originals who are original in exactly the same way is a phenomenon embodied so far as I know only in the authors of *Manette Salomon*. The relations borne by their feelings on the question of art and taste to their other feelings (which they assure us were very much less identical), this peculiar proportion constitutes their originality. In whom was ever the group of "other feelings" proportionately so small? In whom else did the critical vibration (in respect to the things cared for, limited in number, even very limited, I admit), represent so nearly the totality of emotion? The occasions left for MM. de Goncourt to vibrate differently were so few that they scarcely need be counted.

The manifestation of life that most appeals to them is the manifestation of Watteau, of Lancret, of Boucher, of Fragonard; they are primarily critics of pictorial art (with sympathies restricted very much to a period) whose form of expression happens to be literary, but whose sensibility is the sensibility of the painter and the sculptor, and whose attempt, allowing for the difference of the instrument, is to do what the painter and the sculptor do. The most general stricture to be made on their work is probably that they have not allowed enough for the difference of the instrument, have persisted in the effort to render impressions that the plastic artist renders better, neglecting too much those he is unable to render. From time to time they have put forth a volume which is really an instructive instance of misapplied ingenuity. In *Madame Gervaisais* for example, a picture of the visible, sketchable Rome of twenty-five years ago, we seem to hear the voice forced to sing in a register to which it doesn't belong, or rather (the comparison is more complete) to attempt effects of sound that are essentially not vocal. The novelist competes with the painter and the painter with the novelist, in the treatment of the aspect and figure of things; but what a happy tact each of them needs to keep his course straight, without poaching on the other's preserves! In England it is the painter who is apt to poach most and in France the writer. However this may be, no one probably has poached more than MM. de Goncourt.

Whether it be because there is something that touches us in pious persistence in error, or because even when it prevails there may on the part of a genuine talent be the happiest hits by the way, I will not pretend to declare; certain it is that the manner in which our authors abound in their own sense and make us feel that they would not for the world care for anything but what exactly they do care for raises the liveliest presumption in their favour. If literature is kept alive by a passion loyal even to narrowness, MM. de Goncourt have rendered real services. They may look for it on the one side in directions too few and on the other in regions thankless and barren; their *Journal* at all events is a signal proof of their good faith. Wonderful are such courage and patience and industry; fatigued, displeased, disappointed, they never intermit their chronicle nor falter in their task. We owe to this remarkable feat the vivid reflection of their life for twenty years, from the *coup d'état* which produced the second Empire to the death of the younger brother on the eve of the war with Germany; the history of their numerous books, their articles, their studies, on the social and artistic history of France during the latter half of the last century—on Mme de Pompadour, Mme du Barry and the other mistresses of Louis XV, on Marie Antoinette, on society and *la femme* during the Revolution and the Directory; the register moreover of their adventures and triumphs as collectors (collectors of the furniture, tapestries, drawings of the last century), of their observations of every kind in the direction in which their nature and their *milieu* prompt them to observe, of their talks, their visits, their dinners, their physical and intellectual states, their projects and visions, their ambitions and collapses, and above all of their likes and dislikes. Above all of their dislikes, perhaps I should say, for in this sort of testimony the *Journal* is exceedingly rich. The number of things and of people obnoxious to their taste is extremely large, especially when we consider the absence of variety, as the English reader judges variety, in their personal experience. What strikes an English reader curious about a society in which acuteness has a high development and thankful for a picture of it is the small surface over which the career of MM. de Goncourt is distributed. It seems all to take place in a little ring, a coterie of a dozen people. Movement, exercise, travel, other countries, play no part in it; the same persons, the same places, names and occasions perpetually recur; there is scarcely any change of scene or any enlargement of horizon. The authors rarely go into the country and when they do they hate it, for they find it *bête*. To the English mind that item probably describes them better than anything else. We end with the sensation of a closed room, of a want of ventilation; we long to open a window or two and let in the air of the world. The *Journal* of MM. de Goncourt is mainly a record of resentment and suffering, and to this circumstance they attribute many causes; but we suspect at last that the real cause is for them too the inconvenience from which we suffer as readers—simply the want of space and air.

Though the surface of the life represented is, as I have said, small, it is large enough to contain a great deal of violent reaction, an extraordinary quantity of animadversion, indignation, denunciation. Indeed as I have intimated, the simplest way to sketch the relation of disagreement of our accomplished diarists would be to mention the handful of persons and things expected from it. They are "down" absolutely on Sainte-Beuve and strongly on MM. Taine and Schérer. But I am taking the wrong course. The great exceptions then, in addition to the half-dozen friends I have mentioned (the Princess, Gavarni, Théophile Gautier, Flaubert and Paul de Saint-Victor, though the two last-named with restrictions which finally become in the one case considerable and in the other very marked), are the artistic production of the reign of Louis XV, and some of the literary, notably that of Diderot, which they

oppose with a good deal of acrimony to that of Voltaire. They have
also no quarrel with the wonderful figure of Marie Antoinette, unique
in its evocation of luxury and misery, as is proved by the elaborate
monograph which they published in 1858. This list may appear
meagre, but I think it really exhausts their positive sympathies, so far
as the *Journal* enlightens us. That is precisely the interesting point and
the fact that arrests us, that the *Journal*, copious as a memorandum of
the artistic life, is in so abnormally small a degree a picture of enjoyment. Such a fact suggests all sorts of reflections, and in particular an
almost anxious one as to whether the passionate artistic life necessarily
excludes enjoyment. I say the passionate because this makes the example better: it is only passion that gives us revelations and notes. If
the artist is necessarily sensitive does that sensitiveness form in its
essence a state constantly liable to shade off into the morbid? Does this
liability moreover increase in proportion as the effort is great and the
ambition intense? MM. de Goncourt have this ground for expecting
us to cite their experience in the affirmative, that it is an experience
abounding in revelations. I don't mean to say that they are all, but only
that they are preponderantly, revelations of suffering. In the month
of March 1859, in allusion to their occupations and projects, they make
the excellent remark, the fruit of acquired wisdom, that, "In this world
one must do a great deal, one must intend a great deal." That is refreshing, that is a breath of air. But as a general thing what they
commemorate as workers is the simple break-down of joy.

"Tell us," they would probably say, "where you will find an analysis
equally close of the cheerfulness of creation, and then we will admit
that our testimony is superficial. Many a record of a happy personal
life, yes; but that is not to the point. The question is how many
windows are opened, how many little holes are pierced, into the consciousness of the artist. Our contention would be that we have pierced
more little holes than any other gimlet has achieved. Doubtless there
are many people who are not curious about the consciousness of the
artist and who would look into our little holes—if the sense of a kind
of indelicacy, even, of indecency in the proceeding were not too much
for them—mainly with some ulterior view of making fun of them. Of
course the better economy for such people is to let us alone. But if
you *are* curious (there are a few who happen to be), where will you
get to the same degree as in these patient pages the particular sensation
of having your curiosity stimulated and fed? Will you get it in the
long biography of Scott, in that of Dickens, in the autobiography of

Trollope, in the letters of Thackeray? An intimation has reached us that in reading the letters of Thackeray you are moved on the contrary to wonder by what trick certain natural little betrayals of the consciousness of the artist have been conjured away. Very likely (we see you mean it), such betrayals are 'natural' only when people have a sense of responsibility. This sense may very well be a fault, but it is a fault to which the world owes some valuable information. Ah! of course if you don't think our information valuable there is no use talking." The most convenient answer to this little address would probably be the remark that valuable information is supplied by the artist in more ways than one and that we must look for it in his finished pieces as well as in his notebooks. If we should see a flaw in this supposititious plea of our contentious friends it would be after turning back to *Germinie Lacerteux* and *Manette Salomon*. Distinguished and suggestive as these performances are, they do not illustrate the artistic view so very much more than the works of those writers whose neglect of the practice of keeping a diary of protest lays them open to the imputation of levity.

In reading the three volumes pencil in hand I have marked page after page as strongly characteristic, but I find in turning them over that it would be difficult to quote from them without some principle of selection. The striking passages or pages range themselves under three or four heads—the observation of persons, the observation of places and things (works of art, largely), the report of conversations and the general chapter of the subjective, which, as I have hinted, is the general chapter of the *saignant*. "During dinner," I read in the second volume, "*nous avons l'agacement* of hearing Sainte-Beuve the fine talker, the fine connoisseur in letters, talk art in a muddled manner, praise Eugène Delacroix as a philosophical painter," etc. These words, *nous avons l'agacement*, might stand as the epigraph of the *Journal* at large, so exact a translation would they be of the emotion apparently most frequent with the authors. On every possible and impossible occasion they have the annoyance. I hasten to add that I can easily imagine it to have been an annoyance to hear the historian of Port Royal talk, and talk badly, about Eugène Delacroix. But on whatever subject he expressed himself he seems to have been to the historians of Manette Salomon even as a red rag to a bull. The aversion they entertained for him, a plant watered by frequent intercourse and protected by punctual notes, has brought them good luck; in this sense, I mean, that they have made a more living figure of him than of any name in their work.

The taste of the whole evocation is, to my mind and speaking crudely, atrocious; there is only one other case (the portrait of Mme de Païva) in which it is more difficult to imagine the justification of so great a licence. Nothing of all this is quotable by a cordial admirer of Sainte-Beuve, who, however, would resent the treachery of it even more than he does if he were not careful to remember that the scandalized reader has always the resource of opening the *Causeries du Lundi*. MM. de Goncourt write too much as if they had forgotten that. The thirty volumes of that wonderful work contain a sufficiently substantial answer to their account of the figure he cut when they dined with him as his invited guests or as fellow-members of a brilliant club. Impression for impression, we have that of the *Causeries* to set against that of the *Journal*, and it takes the larger hold of us. The reason is that it belongs to the finer part of Sainte-Beuve; whereas the picture from the Goncourt gallery (representing him for instance as a *petit mercier de province en partie fine*), deals only with his personal features. These are important, and they were unfortunately anything but superior; but they were not so important as MM. Goncourt's love of art for art makes them nor so odious surely when they were seen in conjunction with the nature of his extraordinary mind. Upon the nature of his extraordinary mind our authors throw no more light than his washer-woman or his shoemaker might have done. They may very well have said of course that this was not their business and that the fault was the eminent critic's if his small and ugly sides were what showed most in his conversation. Their business, they may contend, was simply to report that conversation and its accompaniment of little compromising personal facts as minutely and vividly as possible; to attempt to reproduce for others the image that moved before them with such infirmities and limitations. Why for others? the reader of these volumes may well ask himself in this connection as well as in many another; so clear does it appear to him that *he* must have been out of the question of Sainte-Beuve's private relations—just as he feels that he was never included in that of Mme de Païva's or the Princess Mathilde's. We are confronted afresh with the whole subject of critical discretion, the responsibility of exposure and the strange literary manners of our day. The *Journal* of MM. de Goncourt will have rendered at least the service of fortifying the blessed cause of occasional silence. If their ambition was to make Sainte-Beuve odious it has suffered the injury that we are really more disagreeably affected by the character of the attack. That is more odious even than the want of private dignity of a demoralized investigator. And in this case the question the reader further asks is, Why even for themselves? and what superior interest was served by the elaboration week by week of this minute record of an implacable animosity? Keeping so patiently-written, so crossed and dotted and dated a register of hatred is a practice that gives the queerest account of your own nature, and indeed there are strange lights thrown through-out these pages on that of MM. de Goncourt. There is a kind of ferocity in the way the reporter that abides in them (how could they have abstained from kicking him out of doors with a "You're very clever, but you're really a bird of night"?) pursues the decomposing *causeur* to the end, seeking effects of grotesqueness in the aspects of his person and the misery of his disease.

All this is most unholy, especially on the part of a pair of *délicats*. MM. de Goncourt, I know, profess a perfect readiness to relinquish this title in certain conditions; they consider that there is a large deli-cacy and a small one and they remind us of the fact that they could never have written *Germinie Lacerteux* if they had been afraid of being called coarse. In fact they imply, I think, that for people of masculine observation the term has no relevancy at all; it is simply non-observant in its associations and exists for the convenience of the ladies—a re-spectable function, but one of which the importance should not be overrated. This idea is luminous, but it will probably never go far without plumping against another, namely, that there is a reality in the danger of *feeling* coarsely, that the epithet represents also a state of perception. Does it come about, the danger in question, in con-sequence of too prolonged a study, however disinterested, of the ugli-nesses and uncleannesses of life? It may occur in that fashion and it may occur in others; the point is that we recognize its ravages when we encounter them and that they are a much more serious matter than the accident—the source of some silly reproach to our authors—of having narrated the history of an hysterical servant-girl. That is a detail (*Germinie Lacerteux* is a very brilliant experiment), whereas the catastrophe I speak of is of the very essence. We know it has taken place when we begin to notice that the artist's instrument has parted with the quality which is supposed to make it most precious—the fineness to which it owed its sureness, its exemption from mistakes. The spectator's disappointment is great of course in proportion as his con-fidence was high. The fine temper of MM. de Goncourt had inspired us with the highest; their whole attitude had been a protest against vulgarity. Mere prettiness of subject—we were aware of the very

relative place they give to that; but on the other hand had they not
mastered the whole gamut of the shades of the aristocratic sense?
Was not a part of the charm of execution of *Germinie Lacerteux* the
glimpse of the taper fingers that wielded the brush? It was not perhaps
the brush of Vandyke, but might Vandyke not have painted the white
hand that held it? It is no white hand that holds, alas, this uncontrollably querulous and systematically treacherous pen. *Mémoires de la
Vie Littéraire* is the sub-title of their *Journal*; but what sort of a life
will posterity credit us with having led and for what sort of chroniclers
will they take the two gentlemen who were assiduous attendants at
the Diner Magny only to the end that they might smuggle in, as it
were, the uninvited (that is you and me who read), and entertain them
at the expense of their colleagues and comrades? The Diner Magny
was a club, the club is a high expression of the civilization of our time;
but the way in which MM. de Goncourt interpret the institution makes
them singular participants of that civilization. It is a strange performance, when one thinks of the performers—celebrated representatives
of the refinement of their age. "If this was the best society," our
grandchildren may say, "what could have been the *procédés* in that
which was not so good?"

It is the firm conviction of many persons that literature is not doing
well, that it is even distinctly on the wane, and that before many years
it will have ceased to exist in any agreeable form, so that those living
at that period will have to look far back for any happy example of it.
May it not occur to us that if they look back to the phase lately embodied by MM. de Goncourt it will perhaps strike them that their loss
is not cruel, since the vanished boon was after all so far from guarantee-
ing the amenities of things? May the moral not appear pointed by the
authors of the *Journal* rather than by the *confrères* they have sacrificed?
We of the English tongue move here already now in a region of uncertain light, where our proper traditions and canons cease to guide
our steps. The portions of the work before us that refer to Mme de
Païva, to the Princess Mathilde Bonaparte, leave us absolutely without a
principle of appreciation. If it be correct according to the society in
which they live we have only to learn the lesson that we have no
equivalent for some of the ideas and standards of that society. We read
on one page that our authors were personal friends of Mme de Païva,
her guests, her interlocutors, recipients of her confidence, partakers of
her hospitality, spectators of her splendour. On the next we see her
treated like the last of the last, with not only her character but her

person held up to our irreverent inspection and the declaration that "elle s'est toute crachée" in a phrase which showed one day that she was purse-proud. Is it because the lady owed her great wealth to the favours of which she had been lavish that MM. de Goncourt hold themselves free to turn her friendship to this sort of profit? If Madame de Païva was good enough to dine, or anything else, she was good enough either to speak of without brutality or to speak of not at all. Does not this misdemeanour of MM. de Goncourt perhaps represent, where women are concerned, a national as well as a personal tendency—a tendency which introduces the strangest of complications into the French theory of gallantry? Our Anglo-Saxon theory has only one face, while the French appears to have two; with "Make love to her", as it were, on one side and "Tue-la" on the other. The French theory, in a word, involves a great deal of killing, and the ladies who are the subject of it must often ask themselves whether they do not pay dearly for this advantage of being made love to. By "killing" I allude to the exploits of the pen as well as to those of the directer weapons so ardently advocated by M. Dumas the younger. On what theory has M. Edmond de Goncourt handed over to publicity the whole record of his relations with the Princess Mathilde? He stays in her house for days, for weeks together, and then portrays for our entertainment her person, her clothes, her gestures and her *salon*, repeating her words, reproducing her language, relating anecdotes at her expense, describing the freedom of speech used towards her by her *convives*, the racy expressions that passed her own lips. In one place he narrates (or is it his brother?) how the Princess was unable to resist the impulse to place a kiss upon his brow. The liberty taken is immense and the idea of gallantry here has undergone a transmutation which lifts it quite out of measurement by any scale or scruple of ours. I repeat that the plea is surely idle that the brothers are accomplished reporters to whom an enterprising newspaper would have found it worth while to pay a high salary; for that cleverness, that intelligence are simply the very standard by which we judge them. The betrayal of the Princess is altogether beyond us.

Would Théophile Gautier feel that he is betrayed? Probably not, for Théophile Gautier's feelings, as represented by MM. de Goncourt, were nothing if not eccentric, his judgment nothing if not perverse. His two friends say somewhere that the sign of his conversation was *l'énormité dans le paradoxe*. He certainly then would have risen to the occasion if it were a question of maintaining that his friends had rendered a service to his reputation. This to my mind is contestable, though their intention (at least in publishing their notes on him) was evidently to do so, for the greater part of his talk, as they repeat it, owes most of its relief to its obscenity. That is not fair to a man really clever—they should have given some other examples. But what strongly strikes us, however the service to Gautier may be estimated, is that they have rendered a questionable service to themselves. He is the finest mind in their pages, he is ever the object of their sympathy and applause. That is very graceful, but it enlightens us as to their intellectual perspective, and I say this with a full recollection of all that can be urged on Gautier's behalf. He was a charming genius, he was an admirable, a delightful writer. His vision was all his own and his brush was worthy of his vision. He knew the French colour-box as well as if he had ground the pigments, and it may really be said of him that he did grind a great many of them. And yet with all this he is not one of the first, for his poverty of ideas was great. *Le sultan de l'épithéte* our authors call him, but he was not the emperor of thought. To be light is not necessarily a damning limitation. Who was lighter than Charles Lamb for instance, and yet who was wiser for our immediate needs? Gautier's defect is that he had veritably but one idea: he never got beyond the superstition that real literary greatness is to bewilder the *bourgeois*. Flaubert sat, intellectually, in the same everlasting twilight, and the misfortune is even greater for him, for his was the greater spirit. Gautier had other misfortunes as well, the struggle that never came to success, the want of margin, of time to do the best work, the conflict, in a hand-to-mouth, hackneyed literary career between splendid images and peculiarly sordid realities. Moreover his paradoxes were usually genial and his pessimism was amiable—in the poetic glow of many of his verses and sketches you can scarcely tell it from optimism. All this makes us tender to his memory, but it does not blind us to the fact that MM. de Goncourt classify themselves when they show us that in the literary circle of their time they find him the most typical figure. He has the supreme importance, he looms largest and covers most ground. This leaves Gautier very much where he was, but it tickets his fastidious friends.

"Théophile Gautier, who is here for some days, talks opera-dancers," they note in the summer of 1868. "He describes the white satin shoe which, for each of them, is strengthened by a little cushion of silk in the places where the dancer feels that she bears and presses most: a cushion which would indicate to an expert the name of the dancer.

And observe that this work is always done by the dancer herself."
I scarcely know why, but there is something singularly characteristic
in this last injunction of MM. de Goncourt, or of MM. de Goncourt and
Théophile Gautier combined: "Et remarquez——!" The circumstance
that a ballet-girl cobbles her shoes in a certain way has indeed an extreme significance. "Gautier begins to rejudge *The Misanthrope*, a
comedy for a Jesuit college on the return from the holidays. Ah! the
pig—what a language! it *is* ill-written!" And Gautier adds that he
can't say this in print; people would abuse him and it would take the
bread out of his mouth. And then he falls foul of Louis XIV. "A hog,
pockmarked like a colander, and short! He was not five feet high,
the great king. Always eating and——" My quotation is nipped in
the bud: an attempt to reproduce Gautier's conversation in English
encounters obstacles on the threshold. In this case we must burn pastilles
even to read the rest of the sketch and we cannot translate it at all.
"*Les bourgeois*—why, the most enormous things go on *chez les bourgeois*,"
he remarks on another occasion. "I have had a glimpse of a few in-
teriors. It is the sort of thing to make you veil your face." But again
I must stop. M. Taine on this occasion courageously undertakes the
defence of the *bourgeois*, of their decency, but M. Paul de Saint-Victor
comes to Gautier's support with an allusion impossible even to para-
phrase, which apparently leaves those gentlemen in possession of the
field. The effort of our time has been, as we know, to disinter the details
of history, to see the celebrities of the past, and even the obscure persons, in the small facts as well as in the big facts of their lives. In his
realistic evocation of Louis XIV, Gautier was in agreement with this
fashion; the historic imagination operated in him by the light of the
rest of his mind. But it is through the nose even more than through
the eyes that it appears to have operated, and these flowers of his
conversation suggest that, though he was certainly an animated talker,
our wonder at such an anomaly as that MM. de Goncourt should
apparently have sacrificed almost every one else to their estimate of
him is not without its reasons.

There are lights upon Flaubert's conversation which are somewhat
of the same character (though not in every case) as those projected
upon Gautier's. Gautier himself furnishes one of the most interesting
of them when he mentions that the author of *Madame Bovary* had said
to him of a new book: "It is finished; I have a dozen more pages to
write, but I have the fall of every phrase." Flaubert had the religion
of rhythm, and when he had caught the final cadence of each sentence

—something that might correspond, in prose, to the rhyme—he filled
in the beginning and middle. But Gautier makes the distinction that
his rhythms were addressed above all to the ear (they were "mouthers",
as the author of *Le Capitaine Fracasse* happily says), whereas those that
he himself sought were ocular, not intended to be read aloud. There
was no style worth speaking of for Flaubert but the style that required reading aloud to give out its value; he *mouthed* his passages to
himself. This was not in the least the sort of prose that MM. de Goncourt themselves cultivated. The reader of their novels will perceive
that harmonies and cadences are nothing to them and that their
rhythms are with a few rare exceptions neither to be sounded nor to
be seen. A page of *Madame Gervaisais* for instance is an almost impossible thing to read aloud. Perhaps this is why poor Flaubert ended
by giving on their nerves when on a certain occasion he invited them
to come and listen to a manuscript. They could endure the structure
of his phrase no longer and they alleviate themselves in their diary. It
accounts for the great difference between their treatment of him and
their treatment of Gautier: they accept the latter to the end, while
with the author of *Salammbô* at a given moment they break down.

It may appear that we *have* sacrificed MM. de Goncourt's *Journal* in
contradiction to the spirit professed at the beginning of these remarks;
so that we must not neglect to give back with the other hand something
presentable as the equivalent of what we have taken away. The truth
is our authors are, in a very particular degree, specialists, and the element
of which, as they would say, *nous avons l'agacement* in this autobiographic publication is largely the result of a disastrous attempt, undertaken under the circumstances with a strangely good conscience, to be
more general than nature intended them. Constituted in a remarkable
manner for receiving impressions of the external and resolving them
into pictures in which each touch looks fidgety but produces none the
less its effect—for conveying the suggestion (in many cases, perhaps in
most, the derisive or the invidious suggestion), of scenes, places, faces,
figures, objects, they have not been able to deny themselves in the
page directly before us the indulgence of a certain yearning for the
abstract, for conceptions and ideas. In this direction they are not happy,
not general and serene; they have a way of making large questions
small, of thrusting in their petulance, of belittling even the religion
of literature. *Je vomis mes contemporains*, one of them somewhere says,
and there is always danger for them that an impression will act as an
emetic. But when we meet them on their own ground, that of the

perception of feature and expression, that of translation of the printed and published text of life, they are altogether admirable. It is mainly on this ground that we meet them in their novels, and the best pages of the *Journal* are those in which they return to it. There are in fact very few of these that do not contain some striking illustration of the way in which every combination of objects about them makes a picture for them, and a picture that testifies vividly to the life led in the midst of it. In the year 1853 they were legally prosecuted as authors of a so-called indecent article in a foolish little newspaper; the prosecution was puerile and their acquittal was a matter of course. But they had to select a defender, and they called upon a barrister who had been recommended to them as "safe". "In his drawing-room he had a flower-stand of which the foot consisted of a serpent in varnished wood climbing in a spiral up to a bird's nest. When I saw this flower-stand I felt a chill in my back. I guessed the sort of advocate that was to be our lot." The object, rare or common, has on every occasion the highest importance for them; when it is rare it gives them their deepest pleasure, but when it is common it represents and signifies, and it is ever the thing that signifies most.

Théophile Gautier's phrase about his own talent has attained a certain celebrity ("Critics have been so good as to reason about me overmuch—I am simply a man for whom the visible world exists"), but MM. de Goncourt would have had every bit as good a right to utter it. People for whom the visible world doesn't "exist" are people with whom they have no manner of patience, and their conception of literature is a conception of something in which such people have no part. Moreover oddly enough, even as specialists they pay for their intensity by stopping short in certain directions; the country is a considerable part of the visible world, but their *Journal* is full of little expressions of annoyance and disgust with it. What they like is the things they can do something with, and they can do nothing with woods and fields, nothing with skies that are not the ceiling of crooked streets or the "glimmering square" of windows. However, we must of course take men for what they have, not for what they have not, and the good faith of the two brothers is immensely fruitful when they project it upon their own little plot. What an amount of it they have needed, we exclaim as we read, to sustain them in such an attempt as *Madame Gervaisais*—an attempt to trace the conversion of a spirit from scepticism to Catholicism through contact with the old marbles and frescoes, the various ecclesiastical bric-à-brac of Rome. Nothing could show

less the expert, the habitual explorer of the soul, than the purely
pictorial plane of the demonstration. Of the attitude of the soul itself,
of the combinations, the agitations of which it was traceably the scene,
there are no picture and no notation at all. When the great spiritual
change takes place for their heroine, the way in which it seems to the
authors most to the purpose to represent it is by a wonderful description of the confessional, at the Gesù, to which she goes for the first time
to kneel. A deep Christian mystery has been wrought within her, but
the account of it in the novel is that

> The confessional is beneath the mosaic of the choir, held and confined
> between the two supports carried by the heads of angels, with the shadow of
> the choir upon its brown wood, its little columns, its escutcheoned front,
> the hollow of its blackness detaching itself dark from the yellow marble of
> the pilasters, from the white marble of the wainscot. It has two steps on the
> side for the knees of the penitent; at the height for leaning a little square of
> copper trellis-work, in the middle of which the whisper of lips and the breath
> of sins has made a soiled, rusty circle; and above this, in a poor black frame,
> a meagre print, under which is stamped *Gesù muore in croce*, and the glass of
> which receives a sort of gleam of blood from the flickering fire of a lamp
> suspended in the chapel beside it.

The weakness of such an effort as *Madame Gervaisais* is that it has so
much less authority as the history of a life than as the exhibition of a
palette. On the other hand it expresses some of the aspects of the most
interesting city in the world with an art altogether peculiar, an art
which is too much, in places, an appeal to our patience, but which says
a hundred things to us about the Rome of our senses a hundred times
better than we could have said them for ourselves. At the risk of
seeming to attempt to make characterization an affair of as many combined and repeated touches as MM. de Goncourt themselves, or as the
cumulative Sainte-Beuve, master of aggravation, I must add that their
success, even where it is great, is greatest for those readers who are
submissive to description and even to enumeration. The process, I say,
is an appeal to our patience, and I have already hinted that the image,
the evocation, is not immediate, as it is for instance with Guy de
Maupassant: our painters believe above all in shades, deal essentially
with shades, have a horror of anything like rough delineation. They
arrive at the exact, the particular, but it is above all on a second reading
that we see them arrive, so that they perhaps suffer a certain injustice
from those who are unwilling to give more than a first. They select,
but they see so much in things that even their selection contains a

multiplicity of items. The *Journal*, none the less, is full of aspects caught in the fact. In 1867 they make a stay in Auvergne, and their notes are perhaps precisely the more illustrative from the circumstance that they find everything odious.

> Return to Clermont. We go up and down the town. Scarcely a passer. The flat Sabbatical gloom of *la province*, to which is added here the mourning of the horrible stone of the country, the slate-stone of the Volvic, which resembles the stones of dungeons in the fifth act of popular melodramas. Here and there a *campo* which urges suicide, a little square with little pointed paving-stones and the grass of the court of a seminary growing between them, where the dogs yawn as they pass. A church, the cathedral of colliers, black without, black within, a law-court, a black temple of justice, an Odeon-theatre of the law, academically funereal, from which one drops into a public walk where the trees are so bored that they grow thin in the wide mouldy shade. Always and everywhere the windows and doors bordered with black, like circulars conveying information of a demise. And sempiternally, on the horizon, that eternal Puy de Dome, whose blueish cone reminds one so, grocer-fashion, of a sugar-loaf wrapped in its paper.

A complete account of MM. de Goncourt would not close without some consideration on the whole question of, I will not say the legitimacy, but the discretion of the attempt on the part of an artist whose vehicle is only collocations of words to be nothing if not plastic, to do the same things and achieve the same effects as the painter. Our authors offer an excellent text for a discourse on that theme, but I may not pronounce it, as I have not in these limits pretended to do more than glance in the direction of that activity in fiction on which they appear mainly to take their stand. The value of the endeavour I speak of will be differently rated according as people like to "see" as they read and according as in their particular case MM. de Goncourt will appear to have justified by success a manner of which it is on every occasion to be said that it was handicapped at the start. My own idea would be that they have given this manner unmistakable life. They have had an observation of their own, which is a great thing, and it has made them use language in a light of their own. They have attempted an almost impossible feat of translation, but there are not many passages they have altogether missed. Those who feel the spectacle as they feel it will always understand them enough, and any writer—even those who risk less—may be misunderstood by readers who have not that sympathy. Of course the general truth remains that if you wish to compete with the painter prose is a roundabout vehicle and it is simpler to adopt the painter's tools. To this MM. de Goncourt would doubtless have replied that there is *no* use of words that is not an endeavour to "render", that lines of division are arrogant and arbitrary, that the point at which the pen should give way to the brush is a matter of appreciation, that the only way to see what it can do, in certain directions of ingenuity, is to try, and that they themselves have the merit of having tried and found out. What they have found out, what they show us, is not certainly of the importance that all the irritation, all the envy and uncharitableness of their *Journal* would seem to announce for compositions brought forth in such throes; but the fact that they themselves make too much of their genius should not lead us to make too little. Artists will find it difficult to forgive them for introducing such a confusion between æsthetics and ill-humour. That is compromising to the cause, for it tends to make the artistic spirit synonymous with the ungenerous. When one has the better thoughts one doesn't print the worse. We had never been ignorant of the fact that talent may be considerable even when character is peevish; that is a mystery which we have had to accept. It is a poor reward for our philosophy that providence should appoint MM. de Goncourt to insist upon the converse of the proposition during three substantial volumes.

12

CRITICISM

1891

If literary criticism may be said to flourish among us at all, it certainly flourishes immensely, for it flows through the periodical press like a river that has burst its dykes. The quantity of it is prodigious, and it is a commodity of which, however the demand may be estimated, the supply will be sure to be in any supposable extremity the last thing to fail us. What strikes the observer above all, in such an affluence, is the unexpected proportion the discourse uttered bears to the objects discoursed of—the paucity of examples, of illustrations and productions, and the deluge of doctrine suspended in the void, the profusion of talk and the contraction of experiment, of what one may call literary conduct. This indeed ceases to be an anomaly as soon as we look at the conditions of contemporary journalism. Then we see that these conditions have engendered the practice of "reviewing"—a practice that in general has nothing in common with the art of criticism. Periodical literature is a huge open mouth which has to be fed—a vessel of immense capacity which has to be filled. It is like a regular train which starts at an advertised hour, but which is free to start only if every seat be occupied. The seats are many, the train is ponderously long, and hence the manufacture of dummies for the seasons when there are not passengers enough. A stuffed manikin is thrust into the empty seat, where it makes a creditable figure till the end of the journey. It looks sufficiently like a passenger, and you know it is not one only when you perceive that it neither says anything nor gets out. The guard attends to it when the train is shunted, blows the cinders from its wooden face and gives a different crook to its elbow, so that it may serve for another run. In this way, in a well-conducted periodical, the blocks of *remplissage* are the dummies of criticism—the recurrent, regulated breakers in the tide of talk. They have a reason for being, and the situation is simpler when we perceive it. It helps to explain the disproportion I just mentioned, as well, in many a case, as the quality of the particular discourse. It helps us to understand that the "organs of public opinion" must be no less copious than punctual, that publicity must maintain its high standard, that ladies and gentlemen may turn an honest penny by the free expenditure of ink. It gives us a glimpse

133

of the high figure presumably reached by all the honest pennies accumulated in the cause, and throws us quite into a glow over the march of civilization and the way we have organized our conveniences. From this point of view it might indeed go far towards making us enthusiastic about our age. What is more calculated to inspire us with a just complacency than the sight of a new and flourishing industry, a fine economy of production? The great business of reviewing has, in its roaring routine, many of the signs of blooming health, many of the features which beguile one into rendering an involuntary homage to successful enterprise.

Yet it is not to be denied that certain captious persons are to be met who are not carried away by the spectacle, who look at it much askance, who see but dimly whither it tends and who find no aid to vision even in the great light (about itself, its spirit and its purposes, among other things) that it might have been expected to diffuse. "Is there any such great light at all?" we may imagine the most restless of the sceptics to inquire, "and isn't the effect rather one of a kind of pretentious and unprofitable gloom?" The vulgarity, the crudity, the stupidity which this cherished combination of the offhand review and of our wonderful system of publicity has put into circulation on so vast a scale may be represented, in such a mood, as an unprecedented invention for darkening counsel. The bewildered spirit may ask itself, without speedy answer, What is the function in the life of man of such a periodicity of platitude and irrelevance? Such a spirit will wonder how the life of man survives it, and above all, what is much more important, how literature resists it; whether indeed literature does resist it and is not speedily going down beneath it. The signs of this catastrophe will not in the case we suppose be found too subtle to be pointed out—the failure of distinction, the failure of style, the failure of knowledge, the failure of thought. The case is therefore one for recognizing with dismay that we are paying a tremendous price for the diffusion of penmanship and opportunity, that the multiplication of endowments for chatter may be as fatal as an infectious disease, that literature lives essentially, in the sacred depths of its being, upon example, upon perfection wrought, that, like other sensitive organisms, it is highly susceptible of demoralization, and that nothing is better calculated than irresponsible pedagogy to make it close its ears and lips. To be puerile and untutored about it is to deprive it of air and light, and the consequence of its keeping bad company is that it loses all heart. We may of course continue to talk about it long after it has bored itself to death, and there is every appearance that this is mainly the way in which our descendants will hear of it. They will however acquiesce in its extinction.

This, I am aware, is a dismal conviction, and I do not pretend to state the case gaily. The most I can say is that there are times and places in which it strikes one as less desperate than at others. One of the places is Paris, and one of the times is some comfortable occasion of being there. The custom of rough and ready reviewing is, among the French, much less rooted than with us, and the dignity of criticism is, to my perception, in consequence much higher. The art is felt to be one of the most difficult, the most delicate, the most occasional; and the material on which it is exercised is subject to selection, to restriction. That is, whether or no the French are always right as to what they do notice, they strike me as infallible as to what they don't. They publish hundreds of books which are never noticed at all, and yet they are much neater book-makers than we. It is recognized that such volumes have nothing to say to the critical sense, that they do not belong to literature and that the possession of the critical sense is exactly what makes it impossible to read them and dreary to discuss them—places them, as a part of critical experience, out of the question. The critical sense, in France, *ne se dérange pas*, as the phrase is, for so little. No one would deny on the other hand that when it does set itself in motion it goes further than with us. It handles the subject in general with finer finger-tips. The bluntness of ours, as tactile implements addressed to an exquisite process, is still sometimes surprising, even after frequent exhibition. We blunder in and out of the affair as if it were a railway station—the easiest and most public of the arts. It is in reality the most complicated and the most particular. The critical sense is so far from frequent that it is absolutely rare and that the possession of the cluster of qualities that minister to it is one of the highest distinctions. It is a gift inestimably precious and beautiful; therefore, so far from thinking that it passes overmuch from hand to hand, one knows that one has only to stand by the counter an hour to see that business is done with baser coin. We have too many small schoolmasters; yet not only do I not question in literature the high utility of criticism, but I should be tempted to say that the part it plays may be the supremely beneficent one when it proceeds from deep sources, from the efficient combination of experience and perception. In this light one sees the critic as the real helper of the artist, a torch-bearing outrider, the interpreter, the brother. The more the tune is noted and the direction observed the more we shall enjoy the convenience of a critical literature. When one thinks of the outfit required for free work in this spirit one is ready to pay almost any homage to the intelligence that has put it on; and when one considers the noble figure completely equipped—armed *cap-à-pie* in curiosity and sympathy—one falls in love with the apparition. It certainly represents the knight who has knelt through his long vigil and who has the piety of his office. For there is something sacrificial in his function, inasmuch as he offers himself as a general touchstone. To lend himself, to project himself and steep himself, to feel and feel till he understands and to understand so well that he can say, to have perception at the pitch of passion and expression as embracing as the air, to be infinitely curious and incorrigibly patient, and yet plastic and inflammable and determinable, stooping to conquer and serving to direct—these are fine chances for an active mind, chances to add the idea of independent beauty to the conception of success. Just in proportion as he is sentient and restless, just in proportion as he reacts and reciprocates and penetrates, is the critic a valuable instrument; for in literature assuredly criticism *is* the critic, just as art is the artist; it being assuredly the artist who invented art and the critic who invented criticism, and not the other way round.

And it is with the kinds of criticism exactly as it is with the kinds of art—the best kind, the only kind worth speaking of, is the kind that springs from the liveliest experience. There are a hundred labels and tickets, in all this matter, that have been pasted on from the outside and appear to exist for the convenience of passers-by; but the critic who lives *in* the house, ranging through its innumerable chambers, knows nothing about the bills on the front. He only knows that the more impressions he has the more he is able to record, and that the more he is saturated, poor fellow, the more he can give out. His life, at this rate, is heroic, for it is immensely vicarious. He has to understand for others, to answer for them; he is always under arms. He knows that the whole honour of the matter, for him, besides the success in his own eyes, depends upon his being indefatigably supple, and that is a formidable order. Let me not speak, however, as if his work were a conscious grind, for the sense of effort is easily lost in the enthusiasm of curiosity. Any vocation has its hours of intensity that is so closely connected with life. That of the critic, in literature, is connected doubly, for he deals with life at second-hand as well as at first; that is he deals with the experience of others, which he resolves into his own, and not of those invented and selected others with whom the novelist makes comfortable terms, but with the uncompromising swarm of authors, the clamorous children of history. He has to make them as vivid and as free as the novelist makes *his* puppets, and yet he has, as the phrase is, to take them as they come. We must be easy with him if the picture, even when the aim has really been to penetrate, is sometimes confused, for there are baffling and there are thankless subjects; and we make everything up to him by the peculiar purity of our esteem when the portrait is really, like the happy portraits of the other art, a text preserved by translation.

13

GUSTAVE FLAUBERT[1]

1893

IN the year 1877 Gustave Flaubert wrote to a friend: "You speak of Balzac's letters. I read them when they appeared, but with very little enthusiasm. The man gains from them, but not the artist. He was too much taken up with business. You never meet a general idea, a sign of his caring for anything beyond his material interests. . . . What a lamentable life!" At the time the volumes appeared (the year before), he had written to Edmond de Goncourt: "What a preoccupation with money and how little love of art! Have you noticed that he never *once* speaks of it? He strove for glory, but not for beauty."

The reader of Flaubert's own correspondence,[2] lately given to the world by his niece Mme Commanville and which in the fourth volume is brought to the eve of his death—the student of so much vivid and violent testimony to an intensely exclusive passion is moved to quote these words for the sake of contrast. It will not be said of the writer that he himself never once speaks of art; it will be said of him with a near approach to truth that he almost never once speaks of anything else. The effect of contrast is indeed strong everywhere in this singular publication, from which Flaubert's memory receives an assault likely to deepen the air of felicity missed that seemed destined henceforth to hang over his personal life. "May I be skinned alive," he writes in 1854, "before I ever turn my private feelings to literary account." His constant refrain in his letters is the impersonality, as he calls it, of the artist, whose work should consist exclusively of his subject and his style, without an emotion, an idiosyncrasy that is not utterly transmuted. Quotation does but scanty justice to his rage for this idea; almost all his feelings were such a rage that we wonder what form they would have borrowed from a prevision of such posthumous betrayal. "It's one of my principles that one must never write down *one's self*. The artist must be present in his work like God in Creation, invisible and almighty, everywhere felt but nowhere seen." Such was the part he allotted to form, to that rounded detachment which enables the perfect work to live by its own life, that he regarded as indecent and

---

[1] For a further essay on Flaubert, see p. 212.
[2] *Correspondance de Gustave Flaubert.* Quatrième Série. Paris, 1893.

dishonourable the production of any impression that was not intensely calculated. "Feelings" were necessarily crude because they were inevitably unselected, and selection (for the picture's sake) was Flaubert's highest morality.

This principle has been absent from the counsels of the editor of his letters, which have been given to the world, so far as they were procurable, without attenuation and without scruple. There are many of course that circumstances have rendered inaccessible, but in spite of visible gaps the revelation is full enough and remarkable enough. These communications would of course not have been matter for Flaubert's highest literary conscience; but the fact remains that in our merciless age ineluctable fate has overtaken the man in the world whom we most imagine gnashing his teeth under it. His ideal of dignity, of honour and renown, was that nothing should be known of him but that he had been an impeccable writer. "I feel all the same," he wrote in 1852, "that I shall not die before I've set a-roaring somewhere (*sans avoir fait rugir quelque part*) such a style as hums in my head and which may very well overpower the sound of the parrots and grasshoppers." This is a grievous accident for one who could write that "The worship of art contributes to pride, and of pride one has never too much". Sedentary, cloistered, passionate, cynical, tormented, in his love of magnificent expression, of subjects remote and arduous, with an unattainable ideal, he kept clear all his life of vulgarity and publicity and newspaperism only to be dragged after death into the middle of the market-place, where the electric light beats fiercest. Mme Commanville's publication hands him over to the Philistines with every weakness exposed, every mystery dispelled, every secret betrayed. Almost the whole of her second volume, to say nothing of a large part of her first, consists of his love-letters to the only woman he appears to have addressed in the accents of passion. His private style moreover was as unchastened as his final form was faultless. The result happens to be deeply interesting to the student of the famous "artistic temperament"; it can scarcely be so for a reader less disposed, I think, for Flaubert was a writers' writer as much as Shelley was a "poets' poet"; but we may ask ourselves if the time has not come when it may well cease to be a leading feature of our homage to a distinguished man that we shall sacrifice him with sanguinary rites on the altar of our curiosity. Flaubert's letters indeed bring up with singular intensity the whole question of the rights and duties, the decencies and discretions of the insurmountable desire to *know*. To lay down a general code is perhaps as yet impossible, for there is no doubt that to know is good, or to want to know, at any rate, supremely natural. Some day or other surely we shall all agree that everything is relative, that facts themselves are often falsifying and that we pay more for some kinds of knowledge than those particular kinds are worth. Then we shall perhaps be sorry to have had it drummed into us that the author of calm, firm masterpieces, of *Madame Bovary*, of *Salammbô*, of *Saint-Julien l'Hospitalier*, was narrow and noisy and had not personally and morally, as it were, the great dignity of his literary ideal.

When such revelations are made, however, they are made, and the generous attitude is doubtless at that stage to catch them in sensitive hands. Poor Flaubert has been turned inside out for the lesson, but it has been given to him to constitute practically—on the demonstrator's table with an attentive circle round—an extraordinary, a magnificent "case". Never certainly in literature was the distinctively literary idea, the fury of execution, more passionately and visibly manifested. This rare visibility is probably the excuse that the responsible hand will point to. The letters enable us to note it, to follow it from phase to phase, from one wild attitude to another, through all the contortions and objurgations, all the exaltations and despairs, tensions and collapses, the mingled pieties and profanities of Flaubert's simplified yet intemperate life. Their great interest is that they exhibit an extraordinary singleness of aim, show us the artist not only disinterested but absolutely dishumanized. They help us to perceive what Flaubert missed almost more than what he gained, and if there are many questions in regard to such a point of view that they certainly fail to settle, they at least cause us to turn them over as we have seldom turned them before. It was the lifelong discomfort of this particular fanatic, but it is our own extreme advantage, that he was almost insanely excessive. "In literature," he wrote in 1861, "the best chance one has is by following out one's temperament and exaggerating it." His own he could scarcely exaggerate; but it carried him so far that we seem to see on distant heights his agitations outlined against the sky. "Impersonal" as he wished his work to be, it was his strange fortune to be the most expressive, the most vociferous, the most spontaneous of men. The record of his temperament is therefore complete, and if his ambiguities make the illuminating word difficult to utter, it is not because the picture is colourless.

Why was such a passion, in proportion to its strength, after all so sterile? There is life, there is blood in a considerable measure in

Madame Bovary, but the last word about its successors can only be, it seems to me, that they are splendidly and infinitely curious. Why may, why *must* indeed in certain cases, the effort of expression spend itself, and spend itself in success, without completing the circle, without coming round again to the joy of evocation? How can art be so genuine and yet so unconsoled, so unhumorous, so unsociable? When it is a religion, and therefore an authority, why should it not be, like other authorities, a guarantee? How can it be such a curse without being also a blessing? What germ of treachery lurks in it to make it, not necessarily but so easily that there is but a hair-line to cross, delusive for personal happiness? Why in short when the struggle is success should the success not be at last serenity? These mysteries and many others pass before us as we listen to Flaubert's loud plaint, which is precisely the profit we derive from his not having with his correspondents struck, like Balzac, only the commercial note. Nothing in his agitated and limited life, which began at Rouen in 1821, is more striking than the prompt, straightforward way his destiny picked him out and his conscience handed him over. As most young men have to contend with some domestic disapproval of the muse, so this one had rather to hang back on the easy incline and to turn away his face from the formidable omens. It was only too evident that he would be free to break his heart, to *gueuler*, as he fondly calls it, to spout, to mouth and thresh about, to that heart's content. No career was ever more taken for granted in its intensity, nor any series of tribulations more confidently invited. It was recognized from the first that the tall and splendid youth, green-eyed and sonorous (his stature and aspect were distinguished), was born to *gueuler*, and especially his own large cadences.

His father, a distinguished surgeon, who died early, had purchased near Rouen, on the Seine, the small but picturesque property of Croisset; and it was in a large five-windowed corner room of this quiet old house, his study for forty years, that his life was virtually spent. It was marked by two great events; his journey to the East and return through the south of Europe with Maxime Du Camp in 1849, and the publication of *Madame Bovary* (followed by a train of consequences) in 1857. He made a second long journey (to Algeria, Tunis and the site of Carthage) while engaged in writing *Salammbô;* he had before his father's death taken part in a scanted family pilgrimage to the north of Italy, and he appears once to have spent a few weeks on the Righi and at another time a few days in London, an episode, oddly enough, of which there is but the faintest, scarcely a recognizable, echo in his correspondence. For the rest, and save for an occasional interlarding of Paris, his years were spent at his patient table in the room by the rural Seine. If success in life (and it is the definition open perhaps to fewest objections), consists of achieving in maturity the dreams of one's prime, Flaubert's measure may be said to have been full. M. Maxime Du Camp, in those two curious volumes of *Impressions Littéraires* which in 1882 treated a surprised world and a scandalized circle to the physiological explanation of his old friend's idiosyncrasies, declares that exactly as that friend was with intensity at the beginning, so was he with intensity in the middle and at the end, and that no life was ever simpler or straighter in the sense of being a case of growth without change. Doubtful indeed were the urgency of M. Du Camp's revelation and the apparent validity of his evidence; but whether or no Flaubert was an epileptic subject, and whether or no there was danger in our unconsciousness of the question (danger to any one but M. Maxime Du Camp), the impression of the reader of the letters is in complete conformity with the pronouncement to which I allude. The Flaubert of fifty differs from the Flaubert of twenty only in size. The difference between *Bouvard et Pécuchet* and *Madame Bovary* is not a difference of spirit; and it is a proof of the author's essential continuity that his first published work, appearing when he had touched middle life and on which his reputation mainly rests, had been planned as long in advance as if it had been a new religion.

Madame Bovary was five years in the writing, and the *Tentation de Saint-Antoine*, which saw the light in 1874, but the consummation of an idea entertained in his boyhood. *Bouvard et Pécuchet*, the intended epos of the blatancy, the comprehensive *bêtise* of mankind, was in like manner the working-out at the end of his days of his earliest generalization. It had literally been his life-long dream to crown his career with a panorama of human ineptitude. Everything in his literary life had been planned and plotted and prepared. One moves in it through an atmosphere of the darkest, though the most innocent, conspiracy. He was perpetually laying a train, a train of which the inflammable substance was "style". His great originality was that the long siege of his youth was successful. I can recall no second case in which poetic justice has interfered so gracefully. He began *Madame Bovary* from afar off, not as an amusement or a profit or a clever novel or even a work of art or a *morceau de vie*, as his successors say to-day, not even, either, as the best thing he could make it; but as a premeditated classic, a masterpiece pure and simple, a thing of conscious perfection and a contribution of the first magnitude to the literature of his country. There would have been every congruity in his encountering proportionate failure and the full face of that irony in things of which he was so inveterate a student. A writer of tales who should have taken the extravagance of his design for the subject of a sad "novelette" could never have permitted himself any termination of such a story but an effective anti-climax. The masterpiece at the end of years would inevitably fall very flat and the overweening spirit be left somehow to its illusions. The solution in fact was very different, and as Flaubert had deliberately sown so exactly and magnificently did he reap. The perfection of *Madame Bovary* is one of the commonplaces of criticism, the position of it one of the highest a man of letters dare dream of, the possession of it one of the glories of France. No calculation was ever better fulfilled, nor any train more successfully laid. It is a sign of the indefeasible bitterness to which Flaubert's temperament condemned him and the expression of which, so oddly, is yet as obstreperous and boyish as that of the happiness arising from animal spirits—it is a mark of his amusing pessimism that so honourable a first step should not have done more to reconcile him to life. But he was a creature of transcendent dreams and unfathomable perversities of taste, and it was in his nature to be more conscious of one broken spring in the couch of fame, more wounded by a pin-prick, more worried by an assonance, than he could ever be warmed or pacified from within. Literature and life were a single business to him, and the "torment of style" that might occasionally intermit in one place was sufficiently sure to break out in another. We may polish our periods till they shine again, but over the style of life our control is necessarily more limited.

To such limitations Flaubert resigned himself with the worst possible grace. He polished ferociously, but there was a side of the matter that his process could never touch. Some other process might have been of use; some patience more organized, some formula more elastic, or simply perhaps some happier trick of good-humour; at the same time it must be admitted that in his deepening vision of the imbecility of the world any remedy would have deprived him of his prime, or rather of his sole, amusement. The *bêtise* of mankind was a colossal comedy, calling aloud to heaven for an Aristophanes to match, and Flaubert's nearest approach to joy was in noting the opportunities of such an observer and feeling within himself the stirrings of such a genius. Towards the end he found himself vibrating at every turn to this ideal, and if he knew to the full the tribulation of proper speech no one ever suffered less from that of proper silence. He broke it in his letters, on a thousand queer occasions, with all the luxury of relief. He was blessed with a series of correspondents with whom he was free to leave nothing unsaid; many of them ladies too, so that he had in their company all the inspiration of gallantry without its incidental sacrifices. The most interesting of his letters are those addressed between 1866 and 1876 to Madame George Sand, which, originally collected in 1884, have been re-embodied in Mme Commanville's publication. They are more interesting than ever when read, as we are now able to read them, in connection with Mme Sand's equally personal and much more luminous answers, accessible in the fifth and sixth volumes of her own copious and strikingly honourable *Correspondance*. No opposition could have been more of a nature to keep the ball rolling than that of the parties to this candid commerce, who were as united by affection and by common interests as they were divided by temper and their way of feeling about those interests. Living each of them, for literature (though Mme Sand, in spite of her immense production, very much less exclusively for it than her independent and fastidious friend), their comparison of most of the impressions connected with it could yet only be a lively contrast of temperaments. Flaubert, whose bark indeed (it is the rule) was much worse than his bite, spent his life, especially the later part of it, in a state of acute exasperation; but her inalterable serenity was one of the few irritants that were tolerable to him.

Their letters are a striking lesson in the difference between good-humour and bad, and seem to point the moral that either form has only to be cultivated to become our particular kind of intelligence. They compared conditions at any rate, her expansion with his hard contraction, and he had the advantage of finding in a person who had sought wisdom in ways so many and so devious one of the few objects within his ken that really represented virtue and that he could respect. It gives us the pattern of his experience that Mme Sand should have stood to him for so much of the ideal, and we may say this even under the impression produced by a reperusal of her total correspondence, a monument to her generosity and variety. Poor Flaubert appears to us to-day almost exactly by so much less frustrated as he was beguiled by this happy relation, the largest he ever knew. His interlocutress, who in the evening of an arduous life accepted refreshment wherever she found it and who could still give as freely as she took, for immemorial habit had only added to each faculty; his correspondent, for all her love of well-earned peace, offered her breast to his aggressive pessi-

mism, had motherly, reasoning, coaxing hands for it, made in short
such sacrifices that she often came to Paris to go to brawling Magny
dinners to meet him and wear, to please him, as I have heard one of the
diners say, unaccustomed peach-blossom dresses. It contributes to our
sense of what there was lovable at the core of his effort to select and his
need to execrate that he should have been able to read and enjoy so freely
a writer so fluid; and it also reminds us that imagination is after all, for
the heart, the safest quality. Flaubert had excellent honest inconsisten-
cies, crude lapses from purity in which he could like the books of his
friends. He was susceptible of painless amusement (a rare emotion
with him) when his imagination was touched, as it was infallibly and
powerfully, by affection. To make a hard rule never to be corrupted,
and then to make a special exception for fondness, is of course the right
attitude.

He had several admirations, and it might always be said of him that
he would have admired if he could, for he could like a thing if he could
be proud of it, and the act adapted itself to his love of magnificence.
He could like indeed almost any one he could say great coloured things
about: the ancients, almost promiscuously, for they never wrote in
newspapers, and Shakespeare (of whom he could not say fine things
enough), and Rabelais, and Montaigne, and Goethe, and Victor Hugo
(his biggest modern enthusiasm), and Leconte de Lisle, and Renan, and
Théophile Gautier. He did scant justice to Balzac and even less to
Alfred de Musset. On the other hand he had an odd and interesting
indulgence for Boileau. Balzac and Musset were not, by his measure,
"writers", and he maintains that be it in verse, be it in prose, it is only
so far as they "write" that authors live; between the two categories he
makes a fundamental distinction. The latter indeed, the mere authors,
simply did not exist for him, and with Mr. Besant's Incorporated
Society he would have had nothing whatever to do. He declares somewhere that it is only the writer who survives in the poet. In spite of
his patience with the "muse" to whom the majority of the letters in the
earlier of the volumes before us were addressed, and of the great
invidious *coup de chapeau* with which he could here and there render
homage to versification, his relish for poetry as poetry was moderate.
Far higher was his estimate of prose as prose, which he held to be
much the more difficult art of the two, with more maddening problems and subtler rhythms, and on whose behalf he found it difficult to
forgive the "proud sister" attitude of verse. No man at any rate, to
make up for scanty preferences, can have had a larger list of literary

aversions, His eye swept the field in vain for specimens untainted with the "modern infection", the plague which had killed Théophile Gautier and to which he considered that he himself had already succumbed. If he glanced at a *feuilleton* he saw that Mme Sarah Bernhardt was "a social expression", and his resentment of this easy wisdom resounded disproportionately through all the air he lived in. One has always a kindness for people who detest the contemporary tone if they have done something fine; but the baffling thing in Flaubert was the extent of his suffering and the inelasticity of his humour. The jargon of the newspapers, the slovenliness of the novelists, the fatuity of Octave Feuillet, to whom he was exceedingly unjust for that writer's love of magnificence was not inferior to his critic's, all work upon him with an intensity only to be explained by the primary defect of his mind, his want of a general sense of proportion. That sense stopped apparently when he had settled the relation of the parts of a phrase, as to which it was exquisite.

Fortunately he had confidants to whom he could cry out when he was hurt and whose position, as he took life for the most part as men take a violent toothache, was assuredly no sinecure. To more than one intense friendship were his younger and middle years devoted; so close was his union with Louis Bouilhet, the poet and dramatist, that he could say in 1870: "I feel no longer the need to write, because I wrote especially for a being who is no more. There's no taste in it now—the impulse has gone." As he wrote for Bouilhet, so Bouilhet wrote for him. "There are so few people who like what I like or have an idea of what I care for." That was the indispensable thing for him in a social, a personal relation, the existence in another mind of a love of literature sufficiently demonstrated to relieve the individual from the great and damning charge, the charge perpetually on Flaubert's lips in regard to his contemporaries, the accusation of malignantly hating it. This universal conspiracy he perceived, in his own country, in every feature of manners, and to a degree which may well make us wonder how high he would have piled the indictment if he had extended the inquiry to the manners of ours. We draw a breath of relief when we think to what speedier suffocation he would have yielded had he been materially acquainted with the great English-speaking peoples. When he declared, naturally enough, that liking what he liked was a condition of intercourse, his vision of this community was almost destined, in the nature of things, to remain unachievable; for it may really be said that no one in the world ever liked anything so much as

Flaubert liked beauty of style. The mortal indifference to it of empires
and republics was the essence of that "modern infection" from which
the only escape would have been to *ne faire que de l'art*. Mankind, for
him, was made up of the three or four persons, Ivan Turgénieff in the
number, who perceived what he was trying for, and of the innumerable
millions who didn't. Poor M. Maxime Du Camp, in spite of many of
the leading characteristics of a friend, was one of this multitude, and he
pays terribly in the pages before us for his position. He pays, to my
sense, excessively, for surely he had paid enough and exactly in the
just and appropriate measure, when, in the introduction contributed to
the "definitive" edition of *Madame Bovary*, M. Guy de Maupassant,
avenging his master by an exquisite stroke, made public the letter of
advice and remonstrance addressed to Flaubert by M. Du Camp, then
editor of the *Revue de Paris*, on the eve of the serial appearance of the
former's first novel in that periodical. This incomparable effusion, with
its amazing reference to excisions and its suggestion that the work be
placed in the hands of an expert and inexpensive corrector who will
prepare it for publication, this priceless gem will twinkle for ever in the
setting M. de Maupassant has given it, or we may perhaps still more
figuratively say in the forehead of the masterpiece it discusses. But
there was surely a nervous and individual ferocity in such a vindictive
giving to the world of every passage of every letter in which the author
of that masterpiece has occasion to allude to his friend's want of tact.
It naturally made their friendship unsuccessful that Flaubert disliked
M. Du Camp, but it is a monstrous imputation on his character to
assume that he was small enough never to have forgiven and forgotten
the other's mistake. Great people never should be avenged; it dimin-
ishes their privilege. What M. Du Camp, so far as an outsider may
judge, had to be punished for was the tone of his reminiscences. But
the tone is unmistakably the tone of affection. He may have felt but
dimly what his old comrade was trying for, and even the latent richness
of *L'Education Sentimentale*, but he renders full justice to Flaubert's
noble independence. The tone of Flaubert's own allusions is a different
thing altogether. It is not unfair to say that all this disproportionate
tit-for-tat renders the episode one of the ugliest little dramas of recent
literary history. The irony of a friend's learning after long years and
through the agency of the press how unsuspectedly another friend was
in the habit of talking of him, is an irony too cruel for impartial
minds. The disaster is absolute, and our compassion goes straight
to the survivor. There are other survivors who will have but little

more reason to think that the decencies have presided over such a publication.

It is only a reader here and there in all the wide world who understands to-day, or who ever understood, what Gustave Flaubert tried for; and it is only when such a reader is also a writer, and a tolerably tormented one, that he particularly cares. Poor Flaubert's great revenge, however, far beyond that of any editorial treachery, is that when this occasional witness does care he cares very peculiarly and very tenderly and much more than he may be able successfully to say. Then the great irritated style-seeker becomes, in the embracing mind, an object of interest and honour; not so much for what he altogether achieved as for the way he strove and for the inspiring image that he presents. There is no reasoning about him; the more we take him as he is the more he has a special authority. *Salammbô*, in which we breathe the air of pure æsthetics, is as hard as stone; *L'Education*, for the same reason, is as cold as death; *Saint-Antoine* is a medley of wonderful bristling metals and polished agates, and the drollery of *Bouvard et Pécuchet* (a work as sad as something perverse and puerile done for a wager), about as contagious as the smile of a keeper showing you through the ward of a madhouse. In *Madame Bovary* alone emotion is just sufficiently present to take off the chill. This truly is a qualified report, yet it leaves Flaubert untouched at the points where he is most himself, leaves him master of a province in which, for many of us, it will never be an idle errand to visit him. The way to care for him is to test the virtue of his particular exaggeration, to accept for the sake of his æsthetic influence the idiosyncrasies now revealed to us, his wild gesticulation, his plaintive, childish side, the side as to which one asks one's self what has become of ultimate good-humour, of human patience, of the enduring *man*. He pays and pays heavily for his development in a single direction, for it is probable that no literary effort so great, accompanied with an equal literary talent, ever failed on so large a scale to be convincing. It convinces only those who are converted, and the number of such is very small. It is an appeal so technical that we may say of him still, but with more resignation, what he personally wailed over, that nobody takes his great question seriously. This is indeed why there may be for each of the loyal minority a certain fine scruple against insistence. If he had had in his nature a contradiction the less, if his indifference had been more forgiving, this is surely the way in which he would have desired most to be preserved.

To no one at any rate need it be denied to say that the best way to appreciate him is, abstaining from the clumsy process of an appeal and the vulgar process of an advertisement, exclusively to *use* him, to feel him, to be privately glad of his message. In proportion as we swallow him whole and cherish him as a perfect example, his weaknesses fall into their place as the conditions about which, in estimating a man who has been original, there is a want of tact in crying out. There is of course always the answer that the critic is to be suborned only by originalities that fertilize; the rejoinder to which, of equal necessity, must ever be that even to the critics of unborn generations poor Flaubert will doubtless yield a fund of amusement. To the end of time there will be something flippant, something perhaps even "clever" to be said of his immense ado about nothing. Those for some of whose moments, on the contrary, this ado will be as stirring as music, will belong to the group that has dabbled in the same material and striven with the same striving. The interest he presents, in truth, can only be a real interest for fellowship, for initiation of the practical kind; and in that case it becomes a sentiment, a sort of mystical absorption or fruitful secret. The sweetest things in the world of art or the life of letters are the irresponsible sympathies that seem to rest on divination. Flaubert's hardness was only the act of holding his breath in the reverence of his search for beauty; his universal renunciation, the long spasm of his too-fixed attention, was only one of the absurdest sincerities of art. To the participating eye these things are but details in the little square picture made at this distance of time by his forty years at the battered table at Croisset. Everything lives in this inward vision of the wide room on the river, almost the cell of a monomaniac, but consecrated ground to the faithful, which, as he tried and tried again, must so often have resounded with the pomp of a syntax addressed, in his code, peremptorily to the ear. If there is something tragi-comic in the scene, as of a tenacity in the void of a life laid down for grammar, the impression passes when we turn from the painful process to the sharp and splendid result. Then, since if we like people very much we end by liking their circumstances, the eternal chamber and the dry Benedictine years have a sufficiently palpable offset in the *repoussé* bronze of the books.

An incorruptible celibate and *dédaigneux des femmes* (as, in spite of the hundred and forty letters addressed to Mme Louise Colet, M. de Maupassant styles him and, in writing to Mme Sand, he confesses himself), it was his own view of his career that, as art was the only thing worth living for, he had made immense sacrifices to application— sacrificed passions, joys, affections, curiosities and opportunities. He says that he shut his passions up in cages and only at long intervals, for amusement, had a look at them. The *orgie de littérature*, in short, had been his sole form of excess. He knew best of course, but his imaginations about himself (as about other matters) were, however, justly, rich, and to the observer at this distance he appears truly to have been made of the very stuff of a Benedictine. He compared himself to the camel, who can neither be stopped when he is going nor moved when he is resting. He was so sedentary, so averse to physical exercise, which he speaks of somewhere as an *occupation funeste*, that his main alternative to the chair was, even by day, the bed, and so omnivorous in research that the act of composition, with him, was still more impeded by knowledge than by taste. "I have in me," he writes to the imperturbable Mme Sand, "a *fond d'ecclésiastique* that people don't know"—the clerical basis of the Catholic clergy. "We shall talk of it," he adds, "much better *vivâ voce* than by letter"; and we can easily imagine the thoroughness with which between the unfettered pair, when opportunity favoured, the interesting subject was treated. At another time indeed, to the same correspondent, who had given him a glimpse of the happiness of being a grandmother, he refers with touching sincerity to the poignancy of solitude to which the "radical absence of the feminine element" in his life had condemned him. "Yet I was born with every capacity for tenderness. One doesn't shape one's destiny, one undergoes it. I was pusillanimous in my youth—I was *afraid* of life. We pay for everything." Besides, it was his theory that a "man of style" should never stoop to action. If he had been afraid of life in fact, I must add, he was preserved from the fear of it in imagination by that great "historic start", the sensibility to the *frisson historique*, which dictates the curious and beautiful outburst, addressed to Mme Colet, when he asks why it had not been his lot to live in the age of Nero. "How I would have talked with the Greek rhetors, travelled in the great chariots on the Roman roads, and, in the evening in the hostelries, turned in with the vagabond priests of Cybele! . . . I *have* lived, all over, in those directions; doubtless in some prior state of being. I'm sure I've been, under the Roman empire, manager of some troop of strolling players, one of the rascals who used to go to Sicily to buy women to make actresses, and who were at once professors, panders and artists. These scoundrels have wonderful 'mugs' in the comedies of Plautus, in reading which I seem to myself to remember things."

He was an extreme admirer of Apuleius, and his florid inexperience helps doubtless somewhat to explain those extreme sophistications of taste of which *La Tentation de Saint-Antoine* is so elaborate an example. Far and strange are the refuges in which such an imagination seeks oblivion of the immediate and the ugly. His life was that of a pearl-diver, breathless in the thick element while he groped for the priceless word, and condemned to plunge again and again. He passed it in re-constructing sentences, exterminating repetitions, calculating and comparing cadences, harmonious *chutes de phrase*, and beating about the bush to deal death to the abominable assonance. Putting aside the particular ideal of style which made a pitfall of the familiar, few men surely have ever found it so difficult to deal with the members of a phrase. He loathed the smug face of facility as much as he suffered from the nightmare of toil; but if he had been marked in the cradle for literature it may be said without paradox that this was not on account of any native disposition to write, to write at least as he aspired and as he understood the term. He took long years to finish his books, and terrible months and weeks to deliver himself of his chapters and his pages. Nothing could exceed his endeavour to make them all rich and round, just as nothing could exceed the unetherized anguish in which his successive children were born. His letters, in which, inconsequently for one who had so little faith in any rigour of taste or purity of per-ception save his own, he takes everybody into his most intimate literary confidence, the pages of the publication before us are the record of everything that retarded him. The abyss of reading answered to the abyss of writing; with the partial exception of *Madame Bovary* every subject that he treated required a rising flood of information. There are libraries of books behind his most innocent sentences. The question of "art" for him was so furiously the question of form, and the question of form was so intensely the question of rhythm, that from the beginning to the end of his correspondence we scarcely ever encounter a mention of any beauty but verbal beauty. He quotes Goethe fondly as to the supreme importance of the "conception", but the conception remains for him essentially the plastic one.

There are moments when his restless passion for form strikes us as leaving the subject out of account altogether, as if he has taken it up arbitrarily, blindly, preparing himself the years of misery in which he is to denounce the grotesqueness, the insanity of his choice. Four times, with his *orgueil*, his love of magnificence, he condemned himself in-congruously to the modern and familiar, groaning at every step over the horrible difficulty of reconciling "style" in such cases with truth and dialogue with surface. He wanted to do the battle of Thermopylæ, and he found himself doing *Bouvard et Pécuchet*. One of the sides by which he interests us, one of the sides that will always endear him to the student, is his extraordinary ingenuity in lifting without falsifying, finding a middle way into grandeur and edging off from the literal without forsaking truth. This way was open to him from the moment he could look down upon his theme from the position of *une blague supérieure*, as he calls it, the amused freedom of an observer as irreverent as a creator. But if subjects were made for style (as to which Flaubert had a rigid theory: the idea was good enough if the expression was), so style was made for the ear, the last court of appeal, the supreme touchstone of perfection. He was perpetually demolishing his periods in the light of his merciless *gueulades*. He tried them on every one; his *gueulades* could make him sociable. The horror, in particular, that haunted all his years was the horror of the *cliché*, the stereotyped, the thing usually said and the way it was usually said, the current phrase that passed muster. Nothing, in his view, passed muster but freshness, that which came into the world, with all the honours, for the occasion. To use the ready-made was as disgraceful as for a self-respecting cook to buy a tinned soup or a sauce in a bottle. Flaubert considered that the dispenser of such wares was indeed the grocer, and, producing his ingredients exclusively at home, he would have stabbed himself for shame like Vatel. This touches on the strange weakness of his mind, his puerile dread of the grocer, the *bourgeois*, the sentiment that in his generation and the preceding misplaced, as it were, the spirit of adventure and the sense of honour, and sterilized a whole province of French literature. The worthy citizen ought never to have kept a poet from dreaming.

He had for his delectation and for satiric purposes a large collection of those second-hand and approximate expressions which begged the whole literary question. To light upon a perfect example was his nearest approach to natural bliss. *Bouvard et Pécuchet* is a museum of such examples, the cream of that *Dictionnaire des Idées Reçues* for which all his life he had taken notes and which eventually resolved itself into the encyclopædic exactitude and the lugubrious humour of the novel. Just as subjects were meant for style, so style was meant for images; therefore as his own were numerous and admirable he would have contended, coming back to the source that he was one of the writers to whom the significance of a work had ever been most present. This significance was measured by the amount of style and the quantity of metaphor thrown up. Poor subjects threw up a little, fine subjects

threw up much, and the finish of his prose was the proof of his pro-
fundity. If you pushed far enough into language you found yourself
in the embrace of thought. There are doubtless many persons whom
this account of the matter will fail to satisfy, and there will indeed be
no particular zeal to put it forward even on the part of those for whom
as a writer, Flaubert most vividly exists. He is a strong taste, like any
other that is strong, and he exists only for those who have a constitutional need to feel in some direction the particular æsthetic
confidence that he inspires. That confidence rests on the simple fact
that he carried execution so far and nailed it so fast. No one will care
for him at all who does not care for his metaphors, and those moreover
who care most for these will be discreet enough to admit that even
a style rich in similes is limited when it renders only the visible. The
invisible Flaubert scarcely touches; his vocabulary and all his methods
were unadjusted and alien to it. He could not read his French Wordsworth, M. Sully-Prudhomme; he had no faith in the power of the
moral to offer a surface. He himself offers such a flawless one that this
hard concretion is success. If he is impossible as a companion he is
deeply refreshing as a reference; and all that his reputation asks of you
is an occasional tap of the knuckle at those firm thin plates of gold
which constitute the leaves of his books. This passing tribute will
yield the best results when you have been prompted to it by some
other purpose.

In other words, with all his want of *portée*, as the psychological
critics of his own country would say of him, poor Flaubert is one of
the artists to whom an artist will always go back. And if such a pilgrim,
in the very act of acknowledgment, drops for an instant into the tenderness of compassion, it is a compassion singularly untainted with
patronage or with contempt; full moreover of mystifications and
wonderments, questions unanswered and speculations vain. Why was
he so unhappy if he was so active; why was he so intolerant if he was so
strong? Why should he not have accepted the circumstance that M.
de Lamartine also wrote as his nature impelled, and that M. Louis
Enault embraced a convenient opportunity to go to the East? The
East, if we listen to him, should have been closed to one of these
gentlemen and literature forbidden to the other. Why does the inevitable perpetually infuriate him, and why does he inveterately resent
the ephemeral? Why does he, above all, in his private, in other words
his continuous epistolary, despair, assault his correspondents with malodorous comparisons? The bad smell of the age was the main thing he

knew it by. Naturally therefore he found life a *chose hideuse*. If it was his great merit and the thing we hold on to him for that the artist and the man were welded together, what becomes, in the proof, of a merit that is so little illuminating for life? What becomes of the virtue of the beauty that pretends to be worth living for? Why feel, and feel genuinely, so much about "art", in order to feel so little about its privilege? Why proclaim it on the one hand the holy of holies, only to let your behaviour confess it on the other a temple open to the winds? Why be angry that so few people care for the real thing, since this aversion of the many leaves a luxury of space? The answer to these too numerous questions is the final perception that the subject of our observations failed of happiness, failed of temperance, not through his excesses, but absolutely through his barriers. He passed his life in strange oblivion of the circumstance that, however incumbent it may be on most of us to do our duty, there is, in spite of a thousand narrow dogmatisms, nothing in the world that any one is under the least obligation to *like*—not even (one braces one's self to risk the declaration), a particular kind of writing. Particular kinds of writing may sometimes, for their producers, have the good fortune to please; but these things are windfalls, pure luxuries, not resident even in the cleverest of us as natural rights. Let Flaubert always be cited as one of the devotees and even, when people are fond of the word, as one of the martyrs of the plastic idea; but let him be still more considerately preserved and more fully presented as one of the most conspicuous of the faithless. For it was not that he went too far, it was on the contrary that he stopped too short. He hovered for ever at the public door, in the outer court, the splendour of which very properly beguiled him, and in which he seems still to stand as upright as a sentinel and as shapely as a statue. But that immobility and even that erectness were paid too dear. The shining arms were meant to carry further, the other doors were meant to open. He should at least have listened at the chamber of the soul. This would have floated him on a deeper tide; above all it would have calmed his nerves.

14

GEORGE SAND

1897

I HAVE been reading in the *Revue de Paris* for November 1st, 1896, some fifty pages, of an extraordinary interest, which have had in respect to an old admiration a remarkable effect. Undoubtedly for other admirers too who have come to fifty-year—admirers, I mean, once eager, of the distinguished woman involved—the perusal of the letters addressed by George Sand to Alfred de Musset in the course of a famous friendship will have stirred in an odd fashion the ashes of an early ardour. I speak of ashes because early ardours for the most part burn themselves out, while the place they hold in our lives varies, I think, mainly according to the degree of tenderness with which we gather up and preserve their dust; and I speak of oddity because in the present case it is difficult to say whether the agitation of the embers results at last in a returning glow or in a yet more sensible chill. That indeed is perhaps a small question compared with the simple pleasure of the reviving emotion. One reads and wonders and enjoys again, just for the sake of the renewal. The small fry of the hour submit to further shrinkage, and we revert with a sigh of relief to the free genius and large life of one of the greatest of all masters of expression. Do people still handle the works of this master—people other than young ladies studying French with *La Mare au Diable* and a dictionary? Are there persons who still read *Valentine*? Are there others capable of losing themselves in *Mauprat*? Has *André*, the exquisite, dropped out of knowledge, and is anyone left who remembers *Teverino*? I ask these questions for the mere sweet sound of them, without the least expectation of an answer. I remember asking them twenty years ago, after Mme Sand's death, and not then being hopeful of the answer of the future. But the only response that matters to us perhaps is our own, even if it be after all somewhat ambiguous. *André* and *Valentine* then are rather on our shelves than in our hands, but in the light of what is given us in the *Revue de Paris* who shall say that we do not, and with avidity, "read" George Sand? She died in 1876, but she lives again intensely in these singular pages, both as to what in her spirit was most attaching and what most disconcerting. We are vague as to what they may represent for the generation that has come to the front since her death; nothing, I dare say, very imposing or even very pleasing. But they give out a great deal to a reader for whom thirty years ago—the best time to have taken her as a whole—she was a high clear figure, a great familiar magician. This impression is a strange mixture, but perhaps not quite incommunicable; and we are steeped as we receive it in one of the most curious episodes in the annals of the literary race.

I

It is the great interest of such an episode that, apart from its proportionate place in the unfolding of a personal life it has a wonderful deal to say on the relation between experience and art at large. It constitutes an eminent special case, in which the workings of that relation are more or less uncovered; a case too of which one of the most striking notes is that we are in possession of it almost exclusively by the act of one of the persons concerned. Mme Sand at least, as we see to-day, was eager to leave nothing undone that could make us further acquainted than we were before with one of the liveliest chapters of her personal history. We cannot, doubtless, be sure that her conscious purpose in the production of *Elle et Lui* was to show us the process by which private ecstasies and pains find themselves transmuted in the artist's workshop into promising literary material—any more than we can be certain of her motive for making towards the end of her life earnest and complete arrangements for the ultimate publication of the letters in which the passion is recorded and in which we can remount to the origin of the volume. If *Elle et Lui* had been the inevitable picture, postponed and retouched, of the great adventure of her youth, so the letters show us the crude primary stuff from which the moral detachment of the book was distilled. Were they to be given to the world for the encouragement of the artist-nature—as a contribution to the view that no suffering is great enough, no emotion tragic enough to exclude the hope that such pangs may sooner or later be æsthetically assimilated? Was the whole proceeding, in intention, a frank plea for the intellectual and in some degree even the commercial profit, to a robust organism, of a store of erotic reminiscence? Whatever the reasons behind the matter, that is to a certain extent the moral of the strange story. It may be objected that this moral is qualified to come home to us only when the relation between art and experience really proves a happier one than it may be held to have proved in the combination before us. The element in danger of being most absent from the process is the element of dignity, and its presence, so far as that may ever at all be hoped for in an appeal from a personal quarrel, is assured only in proportion as the æsthetic event, standing on its own feet, represents a noble gift. It was vain, the objector may say, for our author to pretend to justify by so slight a performance as *Elle et Lui* that sacrifice of all delicacy which has culminated in this supreme surrender. "If you sacrifice all delicacy," I hear such a critic contend, "show at least that you were right by giving us a masterpiece. The novel in question is no more a masterpiece," I even hear him proceed, "than any other of the loose liquid lucid works of its author. By your supposition of a great intention you give much too fine an account on the one hand of a personal habit of incontinence and on the other of a literary habit of egotism. Mme Sand, in writing her tale and in publishing her love-letters, obeyed no prompting more exalted than that of exhibiting her personal (in which I include her verbal) facility, and of doing so at the cost of whatever other persons might be concerned; and you are therefore—and you might as well immediately confess it—thrown back for the element of interest on the attraction of her general eloquence, the plausibility of her general manner and the great number of her particular confidences. You are thrown back on your mere curiosity or sympathy—thrown back from any question of service rendered to 'art'." One might be thrown back doubtless still further even than such remarks would represent if one were not quite prepared with the confession they propose. It is only because such a figure is interesting—in every manifestation—that its course is marked for us by vivid footprints and possible lessons. And to enable us to find these it scarcely need have aimed after all so extravagantly high. George Sand lived her remarkable life and drove her perpetual pen, but the illustration that I began by speaking of is for ourselves to gather—if we can.

I remember hearing many years ago in Paris an anecdote for the truth of which I am far from vouching, though it professed to come direct—an anecdote that has recurred to me more than once in turning over the revelations of the *Revue de Paris*, and without the need for the special reminder (in the shape of an allusion to her intimacy with the hero of the story) contained in those letters to Sainte-Beuve which are published in the number of November 15th. Prosper Mérimée was said to have related—in a reprehensible spirit—that during a term of association with the author of *Lélia* he once opened his eyes, in the raw winter dawn, to see his companion, in a dressing-gown, on her knees before the domestic hearth, a candlestick beside her and a red *madras* round her head, making bravely, with her own hands, the fire that was to enable her to sit down betimes to urgent pen and paper. The story represents him as having felt that the spectacle chilled his ardour and tried his taste; her appearance was unfortunate, her occupation an inconsequence and her industry a reproof—the result of all of which was a lively irritation and an early rupture. To the firm admirer of Mme Sand's prose the little sketch has a very different value, for it presents her in an attitude which is the very key to the enigma, the answer to most of the questions with which her character confronts us. She rose early because she was pressed to write, and she was pressed to write because she had the greatest instinct of expression ever conferred on a woman; a faculty that put a premium on all passion, on all pain, on all experience and all exposure, on the greatest variety of ties and the smallest reserve about them. The really interesting thing in these posthumous *laideurs* is the way the gift, the voice, carries its possessor through them and lifts her on the whole above them. It gave her, it may be confessed at the outset and in spite of all magnanimities in the use of it, an unfair advantage in every connection. So at least we must continue to feel till—for our appreciation of this particular one—we have Alfred de Musset's share of the correspondence. For we shall have it at last, in whatever faded fury or beauty it may still possess— to that we may make up our minds. Let the galled jade wince, it is only a question of time. The greatest of literary quarrels will in short, on the general ground, once more come up—the quarrel beside which all others are mild and arrangeable, the eternal dispute between the public and the private, between curiosity and delicacy.

This discussion is precisely all the sharper because it takes place for each of us within as well as without. When we wish to know at all we wish to know everything; yet there happen to be certain things of which no better description can be given than that they are simply none of our business. "What *is* then forsooth of our business?" the genuine analyst may always ask; and he may easily challenge us to produce any rule of general application by which we shall know when to push in and when to back out. "In the first place," he may continue, "half the 'interesting' people in the world have at one time or another set themselves to drag us in with all their might; and what in the world in such a relation is the observer that he should absurdly pretend to be in more of a flutter than the object observed? The manikin, in all schools, is at an early stage of study of the human form inexorably superseded by the man. Say that we are to give up the attempt to understand: it might certainly be better so, and there would be a delightful side to the new arrangement. But in the name of common sense don't say that the continuity of life is not to have some equivalent in the continuity of pursuit, the renewal of phenomena in the renewal of notation. There is not a door you can lock here against the critic or the painter, not a cry you can raise or a long face you can pull at him, that are not quite arbitrary things. The only thing that makes the observer competent is that he is neither afraid nor ashamed; the only thing that makes him decent—just think!—is that he is not superficial." All this is very well, but somehow we all equally feel that there is clean linen and soiled and that life would be intolerable without some acknowledgment even by the pushing of such a thing as forbidden ground. M. Émile Zola, at the moment I write, gives to the world his reasons for rejoicing in the publication of the physiological *enquête* of Dr. Toulouse—a marvellous catalogue or handbook of M. Zola's outward and inward parts, which leaves him not an inch of privacy, so to speak, to stand on, leaves him nothing about himself that is *for* himself for his friends, his relatives, his intimates, his lovers, for discovery, for emulation, for fond conjecture or flattering deluded envy. It is enough for M. Zola that everything is for the public and no sacrifice worth thinking of when it is a question of presenting to the open mouth of that apparently gorged but still gaping monster the smallest spoonful of truth. The truth, to his view, is never either ridiculous or unclean, and the way to a better life lies through telling it, so far as possible, about everything and about everyone.

There would probably be no difficulty in agreeing to this if it didn't seem on the part of the speaker the result of a rare confusion between give and take, between "truth" and information. The true thing that most matters to us is the true thing we have most use for, and there are surely many occasions on which the truest thing of all is the necessity of the mind, its simple necessity of feeling. Whether it feels in order to learn or learns in order to feel, the event is the same: the side on which it shall most feel will be the side to which it will most incline. If it feels more about a Zola functionally undeciphered it will be governed more by that particular truth than by the truth about his digestive idiosyncrasies, or even about his "olfactive perceptions" and his "arithomania or impulse to count". An affirmation of our "mere taste" may very supposably be our individual contribution to the general clear-up. Nothing often is less superficial than to ignore and overlook, or more constructive (for living and feeling at all) than to want impatiently to choose. If we are aware that in the same way as about a Zola undeciphered we should have felt more about a George Sand unexposed, the true thing we have gained becomes a poor substitute for the one we have lost; and I scarce see what difference it makes that the view of the elder novelist appears in this matter quite to march with that of the younger. I hasten to add that as to being of course asked why in the world with such a leaning we have given time either to M. Zola's physician or to Musset's correspondent, this is only another illustration of the bewildering state of the subject.

When we meet on the broad highway the rueful denuded figure we need some presence of mind to decide whether to cut it dead or to lead it gently home, and meanwhile the fatal complication easily occurs. We have *seen*, in a flash of our own wit, and mystery has fled with a shriek. These encounters are indeed accidents which may at any time take place, and the general guarantee in a noisy world lies, I judge, not so much in any hope of really averting them as in a regular organization of the struggle. The reporter and the reported have duly and equally to understand that they carry their life in their hands. There are secrets for privacy and silence; let them only be cultivated on the part of the hunted creature with even half the method with which the love of sport—or call it the historic sense—is cultivated on the part of the investigator. They have been left too much to the natural, the instinctive man; but they will be twice as effective after it begins to be observed that they may take their place among the triumphs of civilization. Then at last the game will be fair and the two forces face to face; it will be "pull devil, pull tailor", and the hardest pull will doubtless provide the happiest result. Then the cunning of the inquirer, envenomed with resistance, will exceed in subtlety and ferocity anything we to-day conceive, and the pale fore-warned victim, with every track covered, every paper burnt and every letter unanswered, will, in the tower of art, the invulnerable granite, stand, without a sally, the siege of all the years.

II

It was not in the tower of art that George Sand ever shut herself up; but I come back to a point already made in saying that it is in the citadel of style that, notwithstanding rash *sorties*, she continues to hold out. The outline of the complicated story that was to cause so much ink to flow gives, even with the omission of a hundred features, a direct measure of the strain to which her astonishing faculty was exposed. In the summer of 1833, as a woman of nearly thirty, she encountered Alfred de Musset, who was six years her junior. In spite of their youth they were already somewhat bowed by the weight of a troubled past. Musset, at twenty-three, had that of his confirmed libertinism—so Mme Arvède Barine, who has had access to materials, tells us in the admirable short biography of the poet contributed to the rather markedly unequal but very interesting series of Hachette's Grands Ecrivains Français. Mme Sand had a husband, a son and a daughter, and the impress of that succession of lovers—Jules Sandeau had been one, Prosper Mérimée another—to which she so freely alludes in the letters to Sainte-Beuve, a friend more disinterested than these and qualified to give much counsel in exchange for much confidence. It cannot be said that the situation of either of our young persons was of good omen for a happy relation, but they appear to have burnt their ships with much promptitude and a great blaze, and in the December of that year they started together for Italy. The following month saw them settled, on a frail basis, in Venice, where the elder companion remained till late in the summer of 1834 and where she wrote, in part, *Jacques* and the *Lettres d'un Voyageur*, as well as *André* and *Léone-Léoni*, and gathered the impressions to be embodied later in half-a-dozen stories with Italian titles—notably in the delightful *Consuelo*. The journey, the Italian climate, the Venetian winter at first agreed with neither of the friends; they were both taken ill—the young man very gravely—and after a stay of three months Musset returned, alone and much ravaged, to Paris.

In the meantime a great deal had happened, for their union had been stormy and their security small. Mme Sand had nursed her companion in illness (a matter-of-course office, it must be owned) and her companion had railed at his nurse in health. A young physician, called in, had become a close friend of both parties, but more particularly a close friend of the lady, and it was to his tender care that on quitting the scene Musset solemnly committed her. She took up life with Pietro Pagello—the transition is startling—for the rest of her stay, and on her journey back to France he was no inconsiderable part of her luggage. He was simple, robust and kind—not a man of genius. He remained, however, but a short time in Paris; in the autumn of 1834 he returned to Italy, to live on till our own day but never again, so far as we know, to meet his illustrious mistress. Her intercourse with her poet was, in all its intensity, one may almost say its ferocity, promptly renewed, and was sustained in that key for several months more. The effect of this strange and tormented passion on the mere student of its records is simply to make him ask himself what on earth is the matter with the subjects of it. Nothing is more easy than to say, as I have intimated, that it has no need of records and no need of students; but this leaves out of account the thick medium of genius in which it was foredoomed to disport itself. It was self-registering, as the phrase is, for the genius on both sides happened to be the genius of eloquence. It is all rapture and all rage and all literature. The *Lettres d'un Voyageur* spring from the thick of the fight; *La Confession d'un Enfant du Siècle* and *Les Nuits* are immediate echoes of the concert. The lovers are naked in the market-place and perform for the benefit of society. The matter with them, to the perception of the stupefied spectator, is that they entertained for each other every feeling in life but the feeling of respect. What the absence of that article may do for the passion of hate is apparently nothing to what it may do for the passion of love.

By our unhappy pair at any rate the luxury in question—the little luxury of plainer folk—was not to be purchased, and in the comedy of their despair and the tragedy of their recovery nothing is more striking than their convulsive effort either to reach up to it or to do without it. They would have given for it all else they possessed, but they only meet in their struggle the inexorable *never*. They strain and pant and gasp, they beat the air in vain for the cup of cold water of their hell. They missed it in a way for which none of their superiorities could make up. Their great affliction was that each found in the life of the other an armoury of weapons to wound. Young as they were, young as Musset was in particular, they appeared to have afforded each other in that direction the most extraordinary facilities; and nothing in the matter of the mutual consideration that failed them is more sad and strange than that even in later years, when their rage, very quickly, had cooled, they never arrived at simple silence. For Mme Sand, in her so much longer life, there was no hush, no letting alone; though it would be difficult indeed to exaggerate the depth of relative indifference from which, a few years after Musset's death, such a production as *Elle et Lui* could spring. Of course there had been floods of tenderness, of forgiveness; but those, for all their beauty of expression, are quite another matter. It is just the fact of our sense of the ugliness of so much of the episode that makes a wonder and a force of the fine

style, all round, in which it is offered us. That force is in its turn a sort
of clue to guide, or perhaps rather a sign to stay, our feet in paths after
all not the most edifying. It gives a degree of importance to the somewhat squalid and the somewhat ridiculous story, and, for the old
George-Sandist at least, lends a positive spell to the smeared and
yellowed paper, the blotted and faded ink. In this twilight of association we seem to find a reply to our own challenge and to be able to
tell ourselves why we meddle with such old dead squabbles and waste
our time with such grimacing ghosts. If we were superior to the weakness, moreover, how should we make our point (which we must really
make at any cost) as to the so valuable vivid proof that a great talent
is the best guarantee—that it may really carry off almost anything?

The rather sorry ghost that beckons us on furthest is the rare personality of Mme Sand. Under its influence—or that of old memories
from which it is indistinguishable—we pick our steps among the
laideurs aforesaid: the misery, the levity, the brevity of it all, the
greatest ugliness in particular that this life shows us, the way the
devotions and passions that we see heaven and earth called to witness
are over before we can turn round. It may be said that, for what it was,
the intercourse of these unfortunates surely lasted long enough; but
the answer to that is that if it had only lasted longer it wouldn't have
been what it was. It was not only preceded and followed by intimacies,
on one side and the other, as unadorned by the stouter sincerity, but
was mixed up with them in a manner that would seem to us dreadful if
it didn't still more seem to us droll, or rather perhaps if it didn't refuse
altogether to come home to us with the crudity of contemporary
things. It is antediluvian history, a queer vanished world—another
Venice from the actually, the deplorably familiarized, a Paris of
greater bonhomie, an inconceivable impossible Nohant. This relegates
it to an order agreeable somehow to the imagination of the fond
quinquagenarian, the reader with a fund of reminiscence. The vanished
world, the Venice unrestored, the Paris unextended, is a bribe to his
judgment; he has even a glance of complacency for the lady's liberal
foyer. Liszt, one lovely year at Nohant, "jouait du piano au rez-de-
chaussée, et les rossignols, ivres de musique et de soleil, s'égosillaient
avec rage sur les lilas environnants". The beautiful manner confounds
itself with the conditions in which it was exercised, the large liberty
and variety overflow into admirable prose, and the whole thing makes
a charming faded medium in which Chopin gives a hand to Consuelo
and the small Fadette has her elbows on the table of Flaubert.

There is a terrible letter of the autumn of 1834 in which our heroine has recourse to Alfred Tattet on a dispute with the bewildered Pagello —a disagreeable matter that involved a question of money. "À Venise il comprenait," she somewhere says, "à Paris il ne comprend plus." It was a proof of remarkable intelligence that he did understand in Venice, where he had become a lover in the presence and with the exalted approval of an immediate predecessor—an alternate representative of the part, whose turn had now, on the removal to Paris, come round again and in whose resumption of office it was looked to him to concur. This attachment—to Pagello—had lasted but a few months; yet already it was the prey of complication and change, and its sun appears to have set in no very graceful fashion. We are not here in truth among very graceful things, in spite of superhuman attitudes and great romantic flights. As to these forced notes Mme Arvède Barine judiciously says that the picture of them contained in the letters to which she had had access, and some of which are before us, "presents an example extra-ordinary and unmatched of what the romantic spirit could do with beings who had become its prey". She adds that she regards the records in question, "in which we follow step by step the ravages of the monster", as "one of the most precious psychological documents of the first half of the century". That puts the story on its true footing, though we may regret that it should not divide these documentary honours more equally with some other story in which the monster has not quite so much the best of it. But it is the misfortune of the compara-tively short and simple annals of conduct and character that they should ever seem to us somehow to cut less deep. Scarce—to quote again his best biographer—had Musset, at Venice, begun to recover from his illness than the two lovers were seized afresh by *le vertige du sublime et de l'impossible*. "Ils imaginèrent les déviations de sentiment les plus bizarres, et leur intérieur fut le théâtre de scènes qui égalaient en étrangeté les fantaisies les plus audacieuses de la littérature contem-poraine"; that is of the literature of their own day. The register of virtue contains no such lively items—save indeed in so far as these contortions and convulsions were a conscious tribute to virtue.

Ten weeks after Musset has left her in Venice his relinquished but not dissevered mistress writes to him in Paris: "God keep you, my friend, in your present disposition of heart and mind. Love is a temple built by the lover to an object more or less worthy of his worship, and what is grand in the thing is not so much the god as the altar. Why should you be afraid of the risk?"—of a new mistress she means.

There would seem to be reasons enough why he should have been afraid, but nothing is more characteristic than her eagerness to push him into the arms of another woman—more characteristic either of her whole philosophy in these matters or of their tremendous, though somewhat conflicting, effort to be good. She is to be good by showing herself so superior to jealousy as to stir up in him a new appetite for a new object, and he is to be so by satisfying it to the full. It appears not to occur to either one that in such an arrangement his own honesty is rather sacrificed. Or is it indeed because he has scruples—or even a sense of humour—that she insists with such ingenuity and such eloquence? "Let the idol stand long or let it soon break, you will in either case have built a beautiful shrine. Your soul will have lived in it, have filled it with divine incense, and a soul like yours must produce great works. The god will change perhaps, the temple will last as long as yourself." "Perhaps", under the circumstances, was charming. The letter goes on with the ample flow that was always at the author's command—an ease of suggestion and generosity, of beautiful melancholy acceptance, in which we foresee, on her own horizon, the dawn of new suns. Her simplifications are delightful—they remained so to the end; her touch is a wondrous sleight-of-hand. The whole of this letter in short is a splendid utterance and a masterpiece of the shade of sympathy, not perhaps the clearest, which consists of wishing another to feel as you feel yourself. To feel as George Sand felt, however, one had to be, like George Sand, of the true male inwardness; which poor Musset was far from being. This, we surmise, was the case with most of her lovers, and the truth that makes the idea of her *liaison* with Mérimée, who *was* of a consistent virility, sound almost like a union against nature. She repeats to her correspondent, on grounds admirably stated, the injunction that he is to give himself up, to let himself go, to take his chance. That he took it we all know—he followed her advice only too well. It is indeed not long before his manner of doing so draws from her a cry of distress. "Ta conduite est déplorable, impossible. Mon Dieu, à quelle vie vais-je te laisser? l'ivresse, le vin, les filles, et encore et toujours!" But apprehensions were now too late; they would have been too late at the very earliest stage of this celebrated connection.

III

The great difficulty was that, though they were sublime, the couple were really not serious. But on the other hand if on a lady's part in

such a relation the want of sincerity or of constancy is a grave reproach
the matter is a good deal modified when the lady, as I have mentioned,
happens to be—I may not go so far as to say a gentleman. That George
Sand just fell short of this character was the greatest difficulty of all;
because if a woman, in a love affair, may be—for all she is to gain or to
lose—what she likes, there is only one thing that, to carry it off with
any degree of credit, a man may be. Mme Sand forgot this on the
day she published *Elle et Lui*; she forgot it again more gravely when
she bequeathed to the great snickering public these present shreds and
relics of unutterably personal things. The aberration refers itself to the
strange lapses of still other occasions—notably to the extraordinary
absence of scruples with which she in the delightful *Histoire de ma Vie*
gives away, as we say, the character of her remarkable mother. The
picture is admirable for vividness, for breadth of touch; it would be
perfect from any hand not a daughter's, and we ask ourselves wonderingly how through all the years, to make her capable of it, a long perversion must have worked and the filial fibre—or rather the general
flower of sensibility—have been battered. Not this particular anomaly,
however, but many another, yields to the reflection that as just after her
death a very perceptive person who had known her well put it to the
author of these remarks, she was a woman quite by accident. Her
immense plausibility was almost the only sign of her sex. She needed
always to prove that she had been in the right; as how indeed could a
person fail to who, thanks to the special equipment I have named,
might prove it so brilliantly? It is not too much to say of her gift of
expression—and I have already in effect said so—that from beginning
to end it floated her over the real as a high tide floats a ship over the
bar. She was never left awkwardly straddling on the sandbank of fact.

For the rest, in any case, with her free experience and her free use of
it, her literary style, her love of ideas and questions of science and
philosophy, her comradeship, her boundless tolerance, her intellectual
patience, her personal good humour and perpetual tobacco (she
smoked long before women at large felt the cruel obligation), with all
these things and many I don't mention she had more of the inward and
outward of the other sex than of her own. She had above all the mark
that, to speak at this time of day with a freedom for which her action
in the matter of publicity gives us warrant, the history of her personal
passions reads singularly like a chronicle of the ravages of some male
celebrity. Her relations with men closely resembled those relations
with women that, from the age of Pericles or that of Petrarch, have

been complacently commemorated as stages in the unfolding of the great statesman and the great poet. It is very much the same large list, the same story of free appropriation and consumption. She appeared in short to have lived through a succession of such ties exactly in the manner of a Goethe, a Byron or a Napoleon; and if millions of women, of course, of every condition, had had more lovers, it was probable that no woman independently so occupied and so diligent had had, as might be said, more unions. Her fashion was quite her own of extracting from this sort of experience all that it had to give her and being withal only the more just and bright and true, the more sane and superior, improved and improving. She strikes us as in the benignity of such an intercourse even more than maternal: not so much of the mere fond mother as the supersensuous grandmother of the wonderful affair. Is not that practically the character in which Thérèse Jacques studies to present herself to Laurent de Fauvel? the light in which *Lucrezia Floriani* (a memento of a friendship for Chopin, for Liszt) shows the heroine as affected towards Prince Karol and his friend? George Sand is too inveterately moral, too preoccupied with that need to do good which is in art often the enemy of doing well; but in all her work the story-part, as children call it, has the freshness and good faith of a monastic legend. It is just possible indeed that the moral idea was the real mainspring of her course—I mean a sense of the duty of avenging on the unscrupulous race of men their immemorial selfish success with the plastic race of women. Did she wish above all to turn the tables—to show how the sex that had always ground the other in the volitional mill was on occasion capable of being ground?

However this may be, nothing is more striking than the inward impunity with which she gave herself to conditions that are usually held to denote or to involve a state of demoralization. This impunity (to speak only of consequences or features that concern us) was not, I admit, complete, but it was sufficiently so to warrant us in saying that no one was ever less demoralized. She presents a case prodigiously discouraging to the usual view—the view that there is no surrender to "unconsecrated" passion that we escape paying for in one way or another. It is frankly difficult to see where this eminent woman conspicuously paid. She positively got off from paying—and in a cloud of fluency and dignity, benevolence, competence, intelligence. She sacrificed, it is true, a handful of minor coin—suffered by failing wholly to grasp in her picture of life certain shades and certain delicacies. What she paid was this irrecoverable loss of her touch for them. That is undoubtedly one of the reasons why to-day the picture in question has perceptibly faded, why there are persons who would perhaps even go so far as to say that it has really a comic side. She doesn't know, according to such persons, her right hand from her left, the crooked from the straight and the clean from the unclean: it was a sense she lacked or a tact she rubbed off, and her great work is by the fatal twist quite as lopsided a monument as the leaning tower of Pisa. Some readers may charge her with a graver confusion still—the incapacity to distinguish between fiction and fact, the truth straight from the well and the truth curling in steam from the kettle and preparing the comfortable tea. There is no word oftener on her pen, they will remind us, than the verb to "arrange". She arranged constantly, she arranged beautifully; but from this point of view, that of a general suspicion of arrangements, she always proved too much. Turned over in the light of it the story of *Elle et Lui* for instance is an attempt to prove that the mistress of Laurent de Fauvel was little less than a prodigy of virtue. What is there not, the intemperate admirer may be challenged to tell us, an attempt to prove in *L'Histoire de ma Vie?*—a work from which we gather every delightful impression but the impression of an impeccable veracity.

These reservations may, however, all be sufficiently just without affecting our author's peculiar air of having eaten her cake and had it, been equally initiated in directions the most opposed. Of how much cake she partook the letters to Musset and Sainte-Beuve well show us, and yet they fall in at the same time, on other sides, with all that was noble in her mind, all that is beautiful in the books just mentioned and in the six volumes of the general *Correspondance: 1812–1876*, out of which Mme Sand comes so immensely to her advantage. She had, as liberty, all the adventures of which the dots are so put on the i's by the documents lately published, and then she had, as law, as honour and serenity, all her fine reflections on them and all her splendid busy literary use of them. Nothing perhaps gives more relief to her masculine stamp than the rare art and success with which she cultivated an equilibrium. She made from beginning to end a masterly study of composure, absolutely refusing to be upset, closing her door at last against the very approach of irritation and surprise. She had arrived at her quiet elastic synthesis—a good humour, an indulgence that were an armour of proof. The great felicity of all this was that it was neither indifference nor renunciation, but on the contrary an intense partaking; imagination, affection, sympathy and life, the way she had found for

herself of living most and living longest. However well it all agreed
with her happiness and her manners, it agrees still better with her style,
as to which we come back with her to the sense that this was really
her *point d'appui* or sustaining force. Most people have to say, especially
about themselves, only what they can; but she said—and we nowhere
see it better than in the letters to Musset—everything in life that she
wanted. We can well imagine the effect of that consciousness on the
nerves of this particular correspondent, his own poor gift of occasional
song (to be so early spent) reduced to nothing by so unequalled a
command of the last word. We feel it, I hasten to add, this last word,
in all her letters: the occasion, no matter which, gathered it from her
as the breeze gathers the scent from the garden. It is always the last
word of sympathy and sense, and we meet it on every page of the
voluminous *Correspondance*. These pages are not so "clever" as those, in
the same order, of some other famous hands—the writer always denied,
justly enough, that she had either wit or presence of mind—and they
are not a product of high spirits or of a marked avidity for gossip. But
they have admirable ease, breadth and generosity; they are the clear
quiet overflow of a very full cup. They speak above all for the author's
great gift, her eye for the inward drama. Her hand is always on the
fiddle-string, her ear is always at the heart. It was in the soul, in a
word, that she saw the drama begin, and to the soul that, after whatever outward flourishes, she saw it confidently come back. She herself
lived with all her perceptions and in all her chambers—not merely in
the showroom of the shop. This brings us once more to the question
of the instrument and the tone, and to our idea that the tone, when you
are so lucky as to possess it, may be of itself a solution.

By a solution I mean a secret for saving not only your reputation but
your life—that of your soul; an antidote to dangers which the unendowed can hope to escape by no process less uncomfortable or less
inglorious than that of prudence and precautions. The unendowed
must go round about, the others may go straight through the wood.
Their weaknesses, those of the others, shall be as well redeemed as their
books shall be well preserved; it may almost indeed be said that they
are made wise in spite of themselves. If you have never in all your days
had a weakness worth mentioning, you can be after all no more, at the
very most, than large and cheerful and imperturbable. All these things
Mme Sand managed to be on just the terms she had found, as we see,
most convenient. So much, I repeat, does there appear to be in a tone.
But if the perfect possession of one made her, as it well might, an

optimist, the action of it is perhaps more consistently happy in her letters and her personal records than in her "creative" work. Her novels to-day have turned rather pale and faint, as if the image projected—not intense, nor absolutely concrete—failed to reach completely the mind's eye. And the odd point is that the wonderful charm of expression is not really a remedy for this lack of intensity, but rather an aggravation of it through a sort of suffusion of the whole thing by the voice and speech of the author. These things set the subject, whatever it be, afloat in the upper air, where it takes a happy bath of brightness and vagueness or swims like a soap-bubble kept up by blowing. This is no drawback when she is on the ground of her own life, to which she is tied by a certain number of tangible threads; but to embark on one of her confessed fictions is to have—after all that has come and gone, in our time, in the trick of persuasion—a little too much the feeling of going up in a balloon. We are borne by a fresh cool current and the car delightfully dangles; but as we peep over the sides we see things—as we usually know them—at a dreadful drop beneath. Or perhaps a better way to express the sensation is to say what I have just been struck with in the reperusal of *Elle et Lui*; namely that this book, like others by the same hand, affects the reader—and the impression is of the oddest—not as a first but as a second echo or edition of the immediate real, or in other words of the subject. The tale may in this particular be taken as typical of the author's manner; beautifully told, but told, as if on a last remove from the facts, by some one repeating what he has read or what he has had from another and thereby inevitably becoming more general and superficial, missing or forgetting the "hard" parts and slurring them over and making them up. Of everything but feelings the presentation is dim. We recognize that we shall never know the original narrator and that the actual introducer is the only one we can deal with. But we sigh perhaps as we reflect that we may never confront her with her own informant.

To that, however, we must resign ourselves; for I remember in time that the volume from which I take occasion to speak with this levity is the work that I began by pronouncing a precious illustration. With the aid of the disclosures of the *Revue de Paris* it was, as I hinted, to show us that no mistakes and no pains are too great to be, in the air of art, triumphantly convertible. Has it really performed this function? I thumb again my copy of the limp little novel and wonder what, alas, I shall reply. The case is extreme, for it was the case of a suggestive experience particularly dire, and the literary flower that has bloomed upon it is not quite the full-blown rose. "Œuvre de rancune," Arvède Barine pronounces it, and if we take it as that we admit that the artist's distinctness from her material was not ideally complete. Shall I not better the question by saying that it strikes me less as a work of rancour than—in a peculiar degree—as a work of egotism? It becomes in that light at any rate a sufficiently happy affirmation of the author's infallible form. This form was never a more successful vehicle for the conveyance of sweet reasonableness. It is all superlatively calm and clear; there never was a kinder, balmier last word. Whatever the measure of justice of the particular representation, moreover, the picture has only to be put beside the recent documents, the "study", as I may call them, to illustrate the general phenomenon. Even if *Elle et Lui* is not the full-blown rose we have enough here to place in due relief an irrepressible tendency to bloom. In fact I seem already to discern that tendency in the very midst of the storm; the "tone" in the letters too has its own way and performs on its own account—which is but another manner of saying that the literary instinct, in the worst shipwreck, is never out of its depth. The worker observed at the fire by Mérimée could be drowned but in an ocean of ink. Is that a sufficient account of what I have called the laying bare of the relation between experience and art? With the two elements, the life and the genius, face to face—the smutches and quarrels at one end of the chain and the high luminosity at the other—does some essential link still appear to be missing? How do the graceless facts after all confound themselves with the beautiful spirit? They do so, incontestably, before our eyes, and the mystification remains. We try to trace the process, but before we break down we had better perhaps hasten to grant that—so far at least as George Sand is concerned—some of its steps are impenetrable secrets of the grand manner.

LONDON NOTES

I—The Diamond Jubilee, 1897[1]

I AM afraid there are at this moment only two notes for a communication from London to strike. One is that of the plunge into the deep
and turbid waters of the Jubilee; the other is that of the inevitable
retreat from them—the backward scramble up the bank and scurry
over its crest and out of sight. London is in a sorry state; nevertheless
I judge that the number of persons about to arrive undaunted will not
fall substantially short of the number of horror-stricken fugitives. Not
to depart is practically to arrive; for there is little difference in the two
kinds of violence, the shock you await or the shock that awaits you.
Let me hasten, however, to declare that—to speak for the present only
of the former of these—the prospect is full of suggestion, the affair
promises a rare sort of interest. It began a fortnight since to be clear—
and the certitude grows each day—that we are to be treated to a
revelation really precious, the domestic or familiar vision, as it were,
the back-stairs or underside view, of a situation that will rank as
celebrated. Balzac's image of *l'envers de l'histoire contemporaine* is in
fact already under our nose, already offered us in a big bouncing unmistakable case. We brush with an irreverent hand the back of the
tapestry—we crawl on unabashed knees under the tent of the circus.
The commemoration of the completed sixtieth year of her Majesty's
reign will figure to the end of time in the roll of English wonders and
can scarcely fail to hold its own as an occasion unparalleled. And yet
we touch it as we come and go—we feel it mainly as a great incom-
modity. It has already so intimate, so ugly, so measurable a side that
these impressions begin to fall into their place with a kind of representative force, to figure as a symbol of the general truth that the
principal pomps and circumstances of the historic page have had their
most intense existence as material and social arrangements, disagreeable
or amusing accidents, affecting the few momentary mortals at that time
in the neighbourhood. The gross defacement of London, the up-
roarious traffic in seats, the miles of unsightly scaffolding between
the West End and the City, the screaming advertisements, the sordid

[1] London Notes, June 1897, in *Harper's Weekly*, and later in *Notes on
Novelists*, 1914.

struggle, the individual questions—"Haven't we been cheated by the plausible wretch?" or, "How the devil shall we get *to* our seats after paying such a lot, hey?"—these things are actually the historic page. If we are writing that page every hour let us at any rate commend ourselves for having begun betimes, even though this early diligence be attended with extraordinary effects. The great day was a week ago still a month off, but what we even then had full in view, was, for the coming stretch of time, a London reduced to such disfigurement as might much better seem to consort with some great national penance or mourning. The show, when the show comes off, is to last but a couple of hours; and nothing so odd surely ever occurred in such a connection as so huge a disproportion between the discipline and the joy. If this be honour, the simple may well say, give us, merciful powers, the rigour of indifference! From Hyde Park Corner to the heart of the City and over the water to the solid south the long line of thoroughfares is masked by a forest of timber and smothered in swaggering posts and catchpenny bids, with all of which and with the vociferous air that enfolds them we are to spend these next weeks in such comfort as we may. The splendour will have of course to be great to wash down the vulgarity—and infinitely dazzling no doubt it will be; yet even if it fall short I shall still feel that, let the quantity of shock, as I have ventured to call it, be what it must, it will on the whole be exceeded by what I have ventured to call the quantity of suggestion. This, to be frank, has even now rolled up at such a rate that to deal with it I should scarce know where to take it first. Let me not therefore pretend to deal, but only glance and pass.

The foremost, the immense impression is of course the constant, the permanent, the ever-supreme—the impression of that greatest glory of our race, its passionate feeling for trade. I doubt if the commercial instinct be not, as London now feels it throb and glow, quite as striking as any conceivable projection of it that even our American pressure of the pump might, at the highest, produce. That is the real tent of the circus—that is the real back of the tapestry. There have long, I know, been persons ready to prove by book that the explanation of the "historical event" has always been somebody's desire to make money; never, at all events, from the near view, will that explanation have covered so much of the ground. No result of the fact that the Queen has reigned sixty years—no sort of sentimental or other association with it—begins to have the air of coming home to the London conscience like this happy consequence of the chance in it to sell something dear. As yet that chance is the one sound that fills the air, and will probably be the only note audibly stuck till the plaudits of the day itself begin to substitute, none too soon, a more mellifluous one. When the people are all at the windows, and in the trees and on the water-spouts, house-tops, scaffolds and other ledges and coigns of vantage set as traps for them by the motive power, *then* doubtless there will be another aspect to reckon with—then we shall see, of the grand occasion, nothing but what is decently and presentably historic. All I mean is that, pending the apotheosis, London has found in this particular chapter of the career of its aged sovereign only an enormous selfish advertisement. It came to me the other day in a quoted epigram that the advertisement shows as far off as across the Channel and all the way to Paris, where one of the reflections it has suggested—as it must inevitably suggest many—appears to be that, in contrast, when, a year ago, the Russian sovereigns were about to arrive no good Parisian thought for a moment of anything but how he could most work for the adornment of his town. I dare say that in fact from a good Parisian or two a window or a tree was to be hired; but the echo is at least interesting *as* an echo, not less than as a reminder of how we still wait here for the outbreak of the kind of enthusiasm that shall take the decorative form. The graceful tip of its nose has, it must be admitted, yet to show. But there are other sides still, and one of them immense—the light we may take as flooding, I mean, the whole question of the solidity of the throne. It is impossible to live long in England without feeling that the monarchy is—below-ground, so to speak, in particular—a rock; but it was reserved for these days to accentuate the immobility of even that portion of the rock which protrudes above the surface. It is being tested in a manner by fire, and it resists with a vitality nothing short of prophetic. The commercial instinct, as I say, perches upon it with a security and a success that banish a rival from the field. It is the biggest of all draws for the biggest of all circuses; it will bring more money to more doors than anything that can be imagined in its place. It will march through the ages unshaken. The coronation of a new sovereign is an event, at the worst, well within the compass of the mind, and what will that bring with it so much as a fresh lively market and miles of new posters and new carpentry? Then, who knows?—coronations will, for a stretch and a change perhaps, be more frequent than anniversaries; and the bargains struck over the last will, again at the worst, carry an hilarious country well on to the next. Has not the monarchy moreover—

besides thus periodically making trade roar—the lively merit, for such an observer as I fancy considering these things, of helping more than anything else the answers to the questions into which our actual curiosity most overflows; the question for instance of whether in the case before us the triumph of vulgarity be not precisely the flushed but muscular triumph of the inevitable? If vulgarity thrones now on the house-tops, "blown" and red in the face, is it not because it has been pushed aloft by deep forces and is really after all itself the show? The picturesque at any rate has to meet the conditions. We miss, we regret the old "style" of history; but the style would, I think, be there if we let it: the age has a manner of its own that disconcerts, that swamps it. The age is the loudest thing of all. What has altered is simply the conditions. Poor history has to meet them, these conditions; she must accommodate herself. She must accept vulgarity or perish. Some day doubtless she *will* perish, but for a little while longer she remembers and struggles. She becomes indeed, as we look up Piccadilly in the light of this image, perhaps rather more dramatic than ever—at any rate more pathetic, more noble in her choked humiliation. Then even as we pity her we try perhaps to bring her round, to make her understand a little better. We try to explain that if we are dreadful to deal with it is only, really, a good deal because we so detestably grow and grow. There is so horribly much of us—that's where *our* style breaks down. Small crows and paltry bargains didn't matter, and a little vulgarity—just a very little—could in other times manage to pass. Our shame, alas, is our quantity.

I have no sooner, none the less, qualified it so ungraciously than I ask myself what after all we should do without it. If we have opened the floodgates we have at least opened them wide, and it is our very quantity that perhaps in the last resort will save us. It cuts both ways, as the phrase is—it covers all the ground; it helps the escape as well as produces the assault. If retreat for instance at the present juncture is, as I began by hinting, urgently imposed, it is thanks to our having so much of everything that we find a bridge for our feet. We hope to get off in time, but meanwhile even on the spot there are blessed alternatives and reliefs. I have been trying a number very hard, but have expatiated so on the complaint that I have left little room for the remedy. London reminds one of nothing so often as of the help she gives one to forget her. One of the forms actually taken by this happy habit is the ingenious little exhibition, at the Grafton Galleries, of so-called Dramatic and Musical Art. . . .

16

LONDON NOTES

II—The Classical Spirit, 1897[1]

I SHRINK at this day from any air of relapsing into reference to those
Victorian saturnalia of which the force may now be taken as pretty
well spent; and if I remount the stream for an instant it is but with the
innocent intention of plucking the one little flower of literature that,
while the current roared, happened—so far at least as I could observe—
to sprout by the bank. If it was sole of its kind moreover it was, I
hasten to add, a mere accident of the Jubilee and as little a prominent
as a preconcerted feature. What it comes to therefore is that if I
gathered at the supreme moment a literary impression, the literary impression had yet nothing to do with the affair; nothing, that is, beyond
the casual connection given by a somewhat acrid aftertaste, the vision
of the London of the morrow as I met this experience in a woeful
squeeze through the town the day after the fair. It was the singular fate
of M. Paul Bourget, invited to lecture at Oxford under university
patronage and with Gustave Flaubert for his subject, to have found his
appearance arranged for June 23. I express this untowardness but
feebly, I know, for those at a distance from the edge of the whirlpool,
the vast concentric eddies that suck down all other life.

I found, on the morrow in question—the great day had been the
22nd—the main suggestion of a journey from the south of England
up to Waterloo and across from Waterloo to Paddington to be that
of one of those deep gasps or wild staggers, losses of wind and of
balance, that follow some tremendous effort or some violent concussion. The weather was splendid and torrid and London a huge
dusty cabless confusion of timber already tottering, of decorations
already stale, of *badauds* already bored. The banquet-hall was by no
means deserted, but it was choked with mere echoes and candle-ends;
one had heard often enough of a "great national awakening", and this
was the greatest it would have been possible to imagine. Millions of
eyes, opening to dust and glare from the scenery of dreams, seemed
slowly to stare and to try to recollect. Certainly at that distance the
omens were poor for such concentration as a French critic might have

[1] London Notes, June 1897, in *Harper's Weekly;* and later in *Notes on
Novelists*, 1914.

been moved to count upon, and even on reaching Oxford I was met by the sense that the spirit of that seat of learning, though accustomed to intellectual strain, had before the afternoon but little of a margin for pulling itself together. Let me say at once that it made the most of the scant interval and that when five o'clock came the bare scholastic room at the Taylorian offered M. Bourget's reputation and topic, in the hot dead Oxford air, an attention as deep and as many-headed as the combination could ever have hoped to command.

For one auditor of whom I can speak, at all events, the occasion had an intensity of interest transcending even that of Flaubert's strange personal story—which was part of M. Bourget's theme—and of the new and deep meanings that the lecturer read into it. Just the fact of the occasion itself struck me as having well-nigh most to say, and at any rate fed most the all but bottomless sense that constitutes to-day my chief receptacle of impressions; a sense which at the same time I fear I cannot better describe than as that of the way we are markedly going. No undue eagerness to determine whether this be well or ill attaches to the particular consciousness I speak of, and I can only give it frankly for what, on the whole, it most, for beguilement, for amusement, for the sweet thrill of perception, represents and achieves—the quickened notation of our "modernity". I feel that I can pay this last-named lively influence no greater tribute than by candidly accepting as an aid to expression its convenient name. To do that doubtless is to accept with the name a host of other things. From the moment, at any rate, the quickening I speak of sets in it is wonderful how many of these other things play, by every circumstance, into the picture.

That the day should have come for M. Bourget to lecture at Oxford, and should have come by the same stroke for Gustave Flaubert to be lectured about, filled the mind to a degree, and left it in an agitation of violence, which almost excluded the question of what in especial one of these spirits was to give and the other to gain. It was enough of an emotion, for the occasion, to live in the circumstance that the author of *Madame Bovary* could receive in England a public baptism of such peculiar solemnity. With the vision of that, one could bring in all the light and colour of all the rest of the picture and absolutely see, for the instant, something momentous in the very act of happening, something certainly that might easily become momentous with a little interpretation. Such are the happy chances of the critical spirit, always yearning to interpret, but not always in presence of the right mystery.

There was a degree of poetic justice, or at least poetic generosity, in the introduction of Flaubert to a scene, to conditions of credit and honour, so little to have been by himself ever apprehended or estimated: it was impossible not to feel that no setting or stage for the crowning of his bust could less have appeared familiar to him, and that he wouldn't have failed to wonder into what strangely alien air his glory had strayed. So it is that, as I say, the whole affair was a little miracle of our breathless pace, and no corner from which another member of the craft could watch it was so quiet as to attenuate the small magnificence of the hour. No novelist, in a word, worth his salt could fail of a consciousness, under the impression, of his becoming rather more of a novelist than before. Was it not, on the whole, just the essence of the matter that had for the moment there its official recognition? Were not the best mystery and art ushered forward in a more expectant and consecrating hush than had ever yet been known to wait upon them?

One may perhaps take these things too hard and read into them foolish fancies; but the hush in question was filled to my imagination —quite apart from the listening faces, of which there would be special things to say that I wouldn't for the world risk—with the great picture of all the old grey quads and old green gardens, of all the so totally different traditions and processions that were content at last, if only for the drowsy end of a summer afternoon, to range themselves round and play at hospitality. What it appeared possible to make out was a certain faint convergence: that was the idea of which, during the whole process, I felt the agreeable obsession. From the moment it brushed the mind certainly the impulse was to clutch and detain it: too doleful would it have been to entertain for an instant the fear that M. Bourget's lecture could leave the two elements of his case facing each other only at the same distance at which it had found them. No, no; there was nothing for it but to assume and insist that with each tick of the clock they moved a little nearer together. That was the process, as I have called it, and none the less interesting to the observer that it may not have been, and may not yet be, rapid, full, complete, quite easy or clear or successful. It was the seed of contact that assuredly was sown; it was the friendly beginning that in a manner was made. The situation was handled and modified—the day was a date. I shall perhaps remain obscure unless I say more expressly and literally that the particular thing into which, for the perfect outsider, the occasion most worked, was a lively interest—so far as an outsider could feel it—in the whole odd phenomenon and spectacle of a certain usual

LONDON NOTES (THE CLASSICAL SPIRIT)   179

positive *want* of convergence, want of communication between what
the seat and habit of the classics, the famous frequentation and discipline, do for their victims in one direction and what they do not do
for them in another. Was the invitation to M. Bourget not a dim
symptom of a bridging of this queerest of all chasms? I can only so
denominate—as a most anomalous gap—the class of possibilities to
which we owe its so often coming over us in England that the light
kindled by the immense academic privilege is apt suddenly to turn to
thick smoke in the air of contemporary letters.

There are movements of the classic torch round modern objects—
strange drips and drops and wondrous waverings—that have the effect
of putting it straight out. The range of reference that I allude to and
that is most the fashion draws its credit from being an education of the
taste, and it doubtless makes on the prescribed lines and in the close
company of the ancients tremendous tests and triumphs for that
principle. Nothing, however, is so singular as to see what again and
again becomes of it in the presence of examples for which prescription
and association are of no avail. I am speaking here of course not of
unexpected reserves, but of unexpected raptures, bewildering revelations of a failure of the sense of perspective. This leads at times to queer
conjunctions, strange collocations in which Euripides gives an arm to
Sarah Grand and Octave Feuillet harks back to Vergil. It is the breath
of a madness in which one gropes for a method—probes in vain the
hiatus and sighs for the missing link. I am far from meaning to say
that all this will find itself amended by the discreet dose administered
the other day at the Taylorian of even so great an antidote as Flaubert;
but I come back to my theory that there is after all hope for a world
still so accessible to salutary shocks. That was apparent indeed some
years ago. Was it not at the Taylorian that Taine and Renan successively lectured? Oxford, wherever it was, heard them even then to
the end. It is for the Taines, Renans and Bourgets very much the
salting of the tail of the bird: there must be more than one try.

17

THE FUTURE OF THE NOVEL

1899

BEGINNINGS, as we all know, are usually small things, but continuations are not always strikingly great ones, and the place occupied in the world by the prolonged prose fable has become, in our time, among the incidents of literature, the most surprising example to be named of swift and extravagant growth, a development beyond the measure of every early appearance. It is a form that has had a fortune so little to have been foretold at its cradle. The germ of the comprehensive epic was more recognizable in the first barbaric chant than that of the novel as we know it to-day in the first anecdote retailed to amuse. It arrived, in truth, the novel, late at self-consciousness; but it has done its utmost ever since to make up for lost opportunities. The flood at present swells and swells, threatening the whole field of letters, as would often seem, with submersion. It plays, in what may be called the passive consciousness of many persons, a part that directly marches with the rapid increase of the multitude able to possess itself in one way and another of the *book*. The book, in the Anglo-Saxon world, is almost everywhere, and it is in the form of the voluminous prose fable that we see it penetrate easiest and farthest. Penetration appears really to be directly aided by mere mass and bulk. There is an immense public, if public be the name, inarticulate, but abysmally absorbent, for which, at its hours of ease, the printed volume has no other association. This public—the public that subscribes, borrows, lends, that picks up in one way and another, sometimes even by purchase—grows and grows each year, and nothing is thus more apparent than that of all the recruits it brings to the book the most numerous by far are those that it brings to the "story".

This number has gained, in our time, an augmentation from three sources in particular, the first of which, indeed, is perhaps but a comprehensive name for the two others. The diffusion of the rudiments, the multiplication of common schools, has had more and more the effect of making readers of women and of the very young. Nothing is so striking in a survey of this field, and nothing to be so much borne in mind, as that the larger part of the great multitude that sustains the teller and the publisher of tales is constituted by boys and girls; by girls in especial, if we apply the term to the later stages of the life of the innumerable women who, under modern arrangements, increasingly fail to marry—fail, apparently, even, largely, to desire to. It is not too much to say of many of these that they live in a great measure by the immediate aid of the novel—confining the question, for the moment, to the fact of consumption alone. The literature, as it may be called for convenience, of children is an industry that occupies by itself a very considerable quarter of the scene. Great fortunes, if not great reputations, are made, we learn, by writing for schoolboys, and the period during which they consume the compound artfully prepared for them appears—as they begin earlier and continue later—to add to itself at both ends. This helps to account for the fact that public libraries, especially those that are private and money-making enterprises, put into circulation more volumes of "stories" than of all other things together of which volumes can be made. The published statistics are extraordinary, and of a sort to engender many kinds of uneasiness. The sort of taste that used to be called "good" has nothing to do with the matter: we are so demonstrably in presence of millions for whom taste is but an obscure, confused, immediate instinct. In the flare of railway bookstalls, in the shop-fronts of most booksellers, especially the provincial, in the advertisements of the weekly newspapers, and in fifty places besides, this testimony to the general preference triumphs, yielding a good-natured corner at most to a bunch of treatises on athletics or sport, or a patch of theology old and new.

The case is so marked, however, that illustrations easily overflow, and there is no need of forcing doors that stand wide open. What remains is the interesting oddity or mystery—the anomaly that fairly dignifies the whole circumstance with its strangeness: the wonder in short, that men, women, and children *should* have so much attention to spare for improvisations mainly so arbitrary and frequently so loose. That, at the first blush, fairly leaves us gaping. This great fortune then, since fortune it seems, has been reserved for mere unsupported and unguaranteed history, the *inexpensive* thing, written in the air, the record of what, in any particular case, has *not* been, the account that remains responsible, at best, to "documents" with which we are practically unable to collate it. This is the side of the whole business of fiction on which it can always be challenged, and to that degree that if the general venture had not become in such a manner the admiration of the world it might but too easily have become the derision. It has in truth, I think, never philosophically met the challenge, never found a formula to inscribe on its shield, never defended its position by any better argument than the frank, straight blow: "Why am I not so unprofitable as to be preposterous? Because I can do *that*. There!" And it throws up from time to time some purely practical masterpiece. There is nevertheless an admirable minority of intelligent persons who care not even for the masterpieces, nor see any pressing point in them, for whom the very form itself has, equally at its best and at its worst, been ever a vanity and a mockery. This class, it should be added, is beginning to be visibly augmented by a different circle altogether, the group of the formerly subject, but now estranged, the deceived and bored, those for whom the whole movement too decidedly fails to live up to its possibilities. There are people who have loved the novel, but who actually find themselves drowned in its verbiage, and for whom, even in some of its approved manifestations, it has become a terror they exert every ingenuity, every hypocrisy, to evade. The indifferent and the alienated testify, at any rate, almost as much as the omnivorous, to the reign of the great ambiguity, the enjoyment of which rests, evidently, on a primary need of the mind. The novelist can only fall back on that—on his recognition that man's constant demand for what he has to offer is simply man's general appetite for a *picture*. The novel is of all pictures the most comprehensive and the most elastic. It will stretch anywhere—it will take in absolutely anything. All it needs is a subject and a painter. But for its subject, magnificently, it has the whole human consciousness. And if we are pushed a step farther backward, and asked why the representation should be required when the object represented is itself mostly so accessible, the answer to that appears to be that man combines with his eternal desire for more experience an infinite cunning as to getting his experience as cheaply as possible. He will steal it whenever he can. He likes to live the life of others, yet is well aware of the points at which it may too intolerably resemble his own. The vivid fable, more than anything else, gives him this satisfaction on easy terms, gives him knowledge abundant yet vicarious. It enables him to select, to take and to leave; so that to feel he can afford to neglect it he must have a rare faculty, or great opportunities, for the extension of experience—by thought, by emotion, by energy—at first hand.

Yet it is doubtless not this cause alone that contributes to the contemporary deluge; other circumstances operate, and one of them is probably, in truth, if looked into, something of an abatement of the great fortune we have been called upon to admire. The high prosperity of fiction has marched, very directly, with another "sign of the times", the demoralization, the vulgarization of literature in general, the increasing familiarity of all such methods of communication, the making itself supremely felt, as it were, of the presence of the ladies and children—by whom I mean, in other words, the reader irreflective and uncritical. If the novel, in fine, has found itself, socially speaking, at such a rate, the book *par excellence*, so on the other hand the book has in the same degree found itself a thing of small ceremony. So many ways of producing it easily have been discovered that it is by no means the occasional prodigy, for good or for evil, that it was taken for in simpler days, and has therefore suffered a proportionate discredit. Almost any variety is thrown off and taken up, handled, admired, ignored by too many people, and this, precisely, is the point at which the question of its future becomes one with that of the future of the total swarm. How are the generations to face, at all, the monstrous multiplications? Any speculation on the further development of a particular variety is subject to the reserve that the generations may at no distant day be obliged formally to decree, and to execute, great clearings of the deck, great periodical effacements and destructions. It fills, in fact, at moments the expectant ear, as we watch the progress of the ship of civilization—the huge splash that must mark the response to many an imperative, unanimous "Overboard!" What at least is already very plain is that practically the great majority of volumes printed within a year cease to exist as the hour passes, and give up by that circumstance all claim to a career, to being accounted or provided for. In speaking of the future of the novel we must of course, therefore, be taken as limiting the inquiry to those types that have, for criticism, a present and a past. And it is only superficially that confusion seems here to reign. The fact that in England and in the United States every specimen that sees the light may look for a "review" testifies merely to the point which, in these countries, literary criticism has sunk. The review is in nine cases out of ten an effort of intelligence as undeveloped as the ineptitude over which it fumbles, and the critical spirit, which knows where it is concerned and where not, is not touched, is still less compromised, by the incident. There are too many reasons why newspapers must live.

So, as regards the tangible type, the end is that in its undefended, its positively exposed state, we continue to accept it, conscious even of a peculiar beauty in an appeal made from a footing so precarious. It throws itself wholly on our generosity, and very often indeed gives us, by the reception it meets, a useful measure of the quality, of the delicacy, of many minds. There is to my sense no work of literary, or of any other, art, that any human being is under the smallest positive obligation to "like". There is no woman—no matter of what loveliness—in the presence of whom it is anything but a man's unchallengeably *own* affair that he is "in love" or out of it. It is not a question of manners; vast is the margin left to individual freedom; and the trap set by the artist occupies no different ground—Robert Louis Stevenson had admirably expressed the analogy—from the offer of her charms by the lady. There only remain infatuations that we envy and emulate. When we do respond to the appeal, when we *are* caught in the trap, we are held and played upon; so that how in the world can there *not* still be a future, however late in the day, for a contrivance possessed of this precious secret? The more we consider it the more we feel that the prose picture can never be at the end of its tether until it loses the sense of what it can do. It can do simply everything, and that is its strength and its life. Its plasticity, its elasticity are infinite; there is no colour, no extension it may not take from the nature of its subject or the temper of its craftsman. It has the extraordinary advantage— a piece of luck scarcely credible—that, while capable of giving an impression of the highest perfection and the rarest finish, it moves in a luxurious independence of rules and restrictions. Think as we may there is nothing we can mention as a consideration outside itself with which it must square, nothing we can name as one of its peculiar obligations or interdictions. It must, of course, hold our attention and reward it, it must not appeal on false pretences; but these necessities, with which, obviously, disgust and displeasure interfere, are not peculiar to it—all works of art have them in common. For the rest it has so clear a field that if it perishes this will surely be by its fault—by its superficiality, in other words, or its timidity. One almost, for the very love of it, likes to think of its appearing threatened with some such fate, in order to figure the dramatic stroke of its revival under the touch of a life-giving master. The temperament of the artist can do so much for it that our desire for some exemplary felicity fairly demands even the vision of that supreme proof. If we were to linger on this vision long enough, we should doubtless, in fact, be brought to wondering —and still for very loyalty to the form itself—whether our own prospective conditions may not before too long appear to many critics to call for some such happy *coup* on the part of a great artist yet to come.

There would at least be this excuse for such a reverie: that speculation

is vain unless we confine it, and that for ourselves the most convenient
branch of the question is the state of the industry that makes its appeal
to readers of English. From any attempt to measure the career still
open to the novel in France I may be excused, in so narrow a compass,
for shrinking. The French, as a result of having ridden their horse
much harder than we, are at a different stage of the journey, and we
have doubtless many of their stretches and baiting-places yet to traverse.
But if the range grows shorter from the moment we drop to inductions
drawn only from English and American material, I am not sure that
the answer comes sooner. I should have at all events—a formidably
large order—to plunge into the particulars of the question of the present.
If the day *is* approaching when the respite of execution for almost any
book is but a matter of mercy, does the English novel of commerce
tend to strike us as a production more and more equipped by its high
qualities for braving the danger? It would be impossible, I think, to
make one's attempt at an answer to that riddle really interesting without bringing into the field many illustrations drawn from individuals
—without pointing the moral with names both conspicuous and
obscure. Such a freedom would carry us, here, quite too far, and would
moreover only encumber the path. There is nothing to prevent our
taking for granted all sorts of happy symptoms and splendid promises
—so long, of course, I mean, as we keep before us the general truth
that the future of fiction is intimately bound up with the future of the
society that produces and consumes it. In a society with a great and
diffused literary sense the talent at play can only be a less negligible
thing than in a society with a literary sense barely discernible. In a
world in which criticism is acute and mature such talent will find itself
trained, in order successfully to assert itself, to many more kinds of
precautionary expertness than in a society in which the art I have
named holds an inferior place or makes a sorry figure. A community
addicted to reflection and fond of ideas will try experiments with the
"story" that will be left untried in a community mainly devoted to
travelling and shooting, to pushing trade and playing football. There
are many judges, doubtless, who hold that experiments—queer and
uncanny things at best—are not necessary to it, that its face has been,
once for all, turned in one way, and that it has only to go straight
before it. If that is what it is actually doing in England and America
the main thing to say about its future would appear to be that this
future will in very truth more and more define itself as negligible. For
all the while the immense variety of life will stretch away to right and

to left, and all the while there may be, on such lines, perpetuation of its great mistake of failing of intelligence. That mistake will be, ever, for the admirable art, the only one really inexcusable, because of being a mistake about, as we may say, its own soul. The form of novel that is stupid on the general question of its freedom is the single form that may, *a priori*, be unhesitatingly pronounced wrong.

The most interesting thing to-day, therefore, among ourselves is the degree in which we may count on seeing a sense of that freedom cultivated and bearing fruit. What else is this, indeed, but one of the most attaching elements in the great drama of our wide English-speaking life! As the novel is at any moment the most immediate and, as it were, admirably *treacherous* picture of actual manners—indirectly as well as directly, and by what it does not touch as well as by what it does—so its present situation, where we are most concerned with it, is exactly a reflection of our social changes and chances, of the signs and portents that lay most traps for most observers, and make up in general what is most "amusing" in the spectacle we offer. Nothing, I may say, for instance, strikes me more as meeting this description than the predicament finally arrived at, for the fictive energy, in consequence of our long and most respectable tradition of making it defer supremely, in the treatment, say, of a delicate case, to the in-experience of the young. The particular knot the coming novelist, who shall prefer not simply to beg the question, will have here to untie may represent assuredly the essence of his outlook. By what it shall decide to do in respect to the "young" the great prose fable will, from any serious point of view, practically see itself stand or fall. What is clear is that it has, among us, veritably never chosen—it has, mainly, always obeyed an unreasoning instinct of avoidance in which there has often been much that was felicitous. While society was frank, was free about the incidents and accidents of the human constitution, the novel took the same robust ease as society. The young then were so very young that they were not table-high. But they began to grow and from the moment their little chins rested on the mahogany, Richardson and Fielding began to go under it. There came into being a mistrust of any but the most guarded treatment of the great relation between men and women, the constant world-renewal, which was the conspicuous sign that whatever the prose picture of life was prepared to take upon itself, it was not prepared to take upon itself not to be superficial. Its position became very much: "There are other things, don't you know? For heaven's sake let *that* one pass!" And to this wonderful propriety of letting it pass the business has been for these so many years—with the consequences we see to-day—largely devoted. These consequences are of many sorts, not a few altogether charming. One of them has been that there is an immense omission in our fiction—which, though many critics will always judge that it has vitiated the whole, others will continue to speak of as signifying but a trifle. One can only talk for one's self, and of the English and American novelists of whom I am fond, I am so superlatively fond that I positively prefer to take them as they are. I cannot so much as imagine Dickens and Scott *without* the "love-making" left, as the phrase is, out. They were, to my perception, absolutely right—from the moment their attention to it could only be perfunctory—practically not to deal with it. In all their work it is, in spite of the number of pleasant sketches of affection gratified or crossed, the element that matters least. Why not therefore assume, it may accordingly be asked, that discriminations which have served their purpose so well in the past will continue not less successfully to meet the case? What will you have better than Scott and Dickens?

Nothing certainly *can* be, it may at least as promptly be replied, and I can imagine no more comfortable prospect than jogging along perpetually with a renewal of such blessings. The difficulty lies in the fact that two of the great conditions have changed. The novel is older, and so are the young. It would seem that everything the young can possibly do for us in the matter has been successfully done. They have kept out one thing after the other, yet there is still a certain completeness we lack, and the curious thing is that it appears to be they themselves who are making the grave discovery. "You have kindly taken," they seem to say to the fiction-mongers, "our education off the hands of our parents and pastors, and that, doubtless, has been very convenient for *them*, and left them free to amuse themselves. But what, all the while, pray, if it is a question of education, have you done with your own? These are directions in which you seem dreadfully untrained, and in which *can* it be as vain as it appears to apply to you for information?" The point is whether, from the moment it is a question of averting discredit, the novel can afford to take things quite so easily as it has, for a good while now, settled down into the way of doing. There are too many sources of interest neglected—whole categories of manners, whole corpuscular classes and provinces, museums of character and condition, unvisited; while it is on the other hand mistakenly taken for granted that safety lies in all the loose and thin material that keeps reappearing in forms at once ready-made and sadly worse for wear. The simple themselves may finally turn against our simplifications; so that we need not, after all, be more royalist than the king or more childish than the children. It is certain that there is no real health for any art—I am not speaking. of course, of any mere industry —that does not move a step in advance of its farthest follower. It would be curious—really a great comedy—if the renewal were to spring just from the satiety of the very readers for whom the sacrifices have hitherto been supposed to be made. It bears on this that as nothing is more salient in English life to-day, to fresh eyes, than the revolution taking place in the position and outlook of women—and taking place much more deeply in the quiet than even the noise on the surface demonstrates—so we may very well yet see the female elbow itself, kept in increasing activity by the play of the pen, smash with final resonance the window all this time most superstitiously closed. The particular draught that has been most deprecated will in that case take care of the question of freshness. It is the opinion of some observers that when women do obtain a free hand they will not repay their long debt to the precautionary attitude of men by unlimited consideration for the natural delicacy of the latter.

To admit, then, that the great anodyne can ever totally fail to work, is to imply, in short, that this will only be by some grave fault in some high quarter. Man rejoices in an incomparable faculty for presently mutilating and disfiguring any plaything that has helped create for him the illusion of leisure; nevertheless, so long as life retains its power of projecting itself upon his imagination, he will find the novel work off the impression better than anything he knows. Anything better for the purpose has assuredly yet to be discovered. He will give it up only when life itself too thoroughly disagrees with him. Even then, indeed. may fiction not find a second wind, or a fiftieth, in the very portrayal of that collapse? Till the world is an unpeopled void there will be an image in the mirror. What need more immediately concern us, therefore, is the care of seeing that the image shall continue various and vivid. There is much, frankly, to be said for those who, in spite of all brave pleas, feel it to be considerably menaced, for very little reflection will help to show us how the prospect strikes them. They see the whole business too divorced on the one side from observation and perception, and on the other from the art and taste. They get too little of the first-hand impression, the effort to penetrate—that effort for which the French have the admirable expression to *fouiller*—and still less, if possible, of any science of composition, any architecture, distribution, proportion. It is not a trifle, though indeed it is the concomitant of an edged force, that "mystery" should, to so many of the sharper eyes, have disappeared from the craft, and a facile flatness be, in place of it, in acclaimed possession. But these are, at the worst, even for such of the disconcerted, signs that the novelist, not that the novel, has dropped. So long as there is a subject to be treated, so long will it depend wholly on the treatment to rekindle the fire. Only the ministrant must really approach the altar; for if the novel *is* the treatment, it is the treatment that is essentially what I have called the anodyne.

[18]

HONORÉ DE BALZAC

1902

I

STRONGER than ever, even under the spell of first acquaintance and of the early time, is the sense—thanks to a renewal of intimacy and, I am tempted to say of loyalty—that Balzac stands signally apart, that he is the first and foremost member of his craft, and that above all the Balzac-lover is in no position till he has cleared the ground by saying so. The Balzac-lover alone, for that matter, is worthy to have his word on so happy an occasion as this[1] about the author of *La Comédie humaine*, and it is indeed not easy to see how the amount of attention so inevitably induced could at the worst have failed to find itself turning to an act of homage. I have been deeply affected, to be frank, by the mere refreshment of memory, which has brought in its train moreover consequences critical and sentimental too numerous to figure here in their completeness. The authors and the books that have, as we say, done something for us, become part of the answer to our curiosity when our curiosity had the freshness of youth, these particular agents exist for us, with the lapse of time, as the substance itself of knowledge: they have been intellectually so swallowed, digested and assimilated that we take their general use and suggestion for granted, cease to be aware of them because they have passed out of sight. But they have passed out of sight simply by having passed into our lives. They have become a part of our personal history, a part of ourselves, very often, so far as we may have succeeded in best expressing ourselves. Endless, however, are the uses of great persons and great things, and it may easily happen in these cases that the connection, even as an "excitement" —the form mainly of the connections of youth—is never really broken. We have largely been living on our benefactor—which is the highest acknowledgment one can make; only, thanks to a blest law that operates in the long run to rekindle excitement, we are accessible to the sense of having neglected him. Even when we may not constantly have read him over the neglect is quite an illusion, but the illusion perhaps prepares us for the finest emotion we are to have owed to the

[1] The appearance of a translation of the *Deux Jeunes Mariées* in *A Century of French Romance*.

190

acquaintance. Without having abandoned or denied our author we yet come expressly back to him, and if not quite in tatters and in penitence like the Prodigal Son, with something at all events of the tenderness with which we revert to the parental threshold and hearth-stone, if not, more fortunately, to the parental presence. The beauty of this adventure, that of seeing the dust blown off a relation that had been put away as on a shelf, almost out of reach, at the back of one's mind, consists in finding the precious object not only fresh and intact, but with its firm lacquer still further figured, gilded and enriched. It is all overscored with traces and impressions—vivid, definite, almost as valuable as itself—of the recognitions and agitations it originally produced in us. Our old—that is our young—feelings are very nearly what page after page most gives us. The case has become a case of authority *plus* association. If Balzac in himself is indubitably wanting in the sufficiently common felicity we know as charm, it is this associ-ation that may on occasion contribute the grace.

The impression then, confirmed and brightened, is of the mass and weight of the figure and of the extent of ground it occupies; a tract on which we might all of us together quite pitch our little tents, open our little booths, deal in our little wares, and not materially either diminish the area or impede the circulation of the occupant. I seem to see him in such an image moving about as Gulliver among the pigmies, and not less good-natured than Gulliver for the exercise of any function, without exception, that can illustrate his larger life. The first and the last word about the author of *Les Contes drolatiques* is that of all novelists he is the most serious—by which I am far from meaning that in the human comedy as he shows it the comic is an absent quantity. His sense of the comic was on the scale of his extra-ordinary senses in general, though his expression of it suffers perhaps exceptionally from that odd want of elbow-room—the penalty some-how of his close-packed, pressed-down contents—which reminds us of some designedly beautiful thing but half-disengaged from the clay or the marble. It is the scheme and the scope that are supreme in him, applying this moreover not to mere great intention, but to the concrete form, the proved case, in which we possess them. We most of us aspire to achieve at the best but a patch here and there, to pluck a sprig or a single branch, to break ground in a corner of the great garden of life. Balzac's plan was simply to do everything that could be done. He proposed to himself to "turn over" the great garden from north to south and from east to west; a task—immense, heroic, to this day

immeasurable—that he bequeathed us the partial performance of, a prodigious ragged clod, in the twenty monstrous years representing his
productive career, years of concentration and sacrifice the vision of
which still makes us ache. He had indeed a striking good fortune, the
only one he was to enjoy as an harassed and exasperated worker: the
great garden of life presented itself to him absolutely and exactly in the
guise of the great garden of France, a subject vast and comprehensive
enough, yet with definite edges and corners. This identity of his universal with his local and national vision is the particular thing we should
doubtless call his greatest strength were we preparing agreeably to
speak of it also as his visible weakness. Of Balzac's weaknesses, however, it takes some assurance to talk; there is always plenty of time for
them; they are the last signs we know him by—such things truly as
in other painters of manners often come under the head of mere exuberance of energy. So little in short do they earn the invidious name
even when we feel them as defects.

What he did above all was to read the universe, as hard and as loud
as he could, *into* the France of his time; his own eyes regarding his
work as at once the drama of man and a mirror of the mass of social
phenomena the most rounded and registered, most organized and
administered, and thereby most exposed to systematic observation
and portrayal, that the world had seen. There are happily other interesting societies, but these are for schemes of such an order comparatively loose and incoherent, with more extent and perhaps more
variety, but with less of the great enclosed and exhibited quality, less
neatness and sharpness of arrangement, fewer categories, subdivisions,
juxtapositions. Balzac's France was both inspiring enough for an immense prose epic and reducible enough for a report or a chart. To
allow his achievement all its dignity we should doubtless say also
treatable enough for a history, since it was as a patient historian, a
Benedictine of the actual, the living painter of his living time, that he
regarded himself and handled his material. All painters of manners
and fashions, if we will, are historians, even when they least don the
uniform: Fielding, Dickens, Thackeray, George Eliot, Hawthorne
among ourselves. But the great difference between the great Frenchman and the eminent others is that, with an imagination of the highest
power, an unequalled intensity of vision, he saw his subject in the
light of science as well, in the light of the bearing of all its parts on
each other, and under pressure of a passion for exactitude, an appetite,
the appetite of an ogre, for *all* the kinds of facts. We find I think in

the union here suggested something like the truth about his genius, the nearest approach to a final account of him. Of imagination on one side all compact, he was on the other an insatiable reporter of the immediate, the material, the current combination, and perpetually moved by the historian's impulse to fix, preserve and explain them. One asks one's self as one reads him what concern the poet has with so much arithmetic and so much criticism, so many statistics and documents, what concern the critic and the economist have with so many passions, characters and adventures. The contradiction is always before us; it springs from the inordinate scale of the author's two faces; it explains more than anything else his eccentricities and difficulties. It accounts for his want of grace, his want of the lightness associated with an amusing literary form, his bristling surface, his closeness of texture, so rough with richness, yet so productive of the effect we have in mind when we speak of not being able to see the wood for the trees.

A thorough-paced votary, for that matter, can easily afford to declare at once that his confounding duality of character does more things still, or does at least the most important of all—introduces us without mercy (mercy for ourselves I mean) to the oddest truth we could have dreamed of meeting in such a connection. It was certainly *a priori* not to be expected we should feel it of him, but our hero is after all not in his magnificence totally an artist: which would be the strangest thing possible, one must hasten to add, were not the smallness of the practical difference so made even stranger. His endowment and his effect are each so great that the anomaly makes at the most a difference only by adding to his interest for the critic. The critic worth his salt is indiscreetly curious and wants ever to know how and why—whereby Balzac is thus a still rarer case for him, suggesting that exceptional curiosity may have exceptional rewards. The question of what makes the artist on a great scale is interesting enough; but we feel it in Balzac's company to be nothing to the question of what on an equal scale frustrates him. The scattered pieces, the *disjecta membra* of the character are here so numerous and so splendid that they prove misleading; we pile them together and the help assuredly is monumental; it forms an overtopping figure. The genius this figure stands for, none the less, is really such a lesson to the artist as perfection itself would be powerless to give; it carries him so much further into the special mystery. Where it carries him, at the same time, I must not in this scant space attempt to say—which would be a loss of the fine thread of my argument. I stick to our point in putting it, more concisely, that the artist of the *Comédie humaine* is half smothered by the historian. Yet it belongs as well to the matter also to meet the question of whether the historian himself may not be an artist—in which case Balzac's catastrophe would seem to lose its excuse. The answer of course is that the reporter, however philosophic, has one law, and the originator, however substantially fed, has another; so that the two laws can with no sort of harmony or congruity make, for the finer sense, a common household. Balzac's catastrophe—so to name it once again—was in this perpetual conflict and final impossibility, an impossibility that explains his defeat on the classic side and extends so far at times as to make us think of his work as, from the point of view of beauty, a tragic waste of effort.

What it would come to, we judge, is that the irreconcilability of the two kinds of law is, more simply expressed, but the irreconcilability of two different ways of composing one's effect. The principle of composition that his free imagination would have, or certainly might have, handsomely imposed on him is perpetually dislocated by the quite opposite principle of the earnest seeker, the inquirer to a useful end, in whom nothing is free but a born antipathy to his yokefellow. Such a production as *Le Curé de village*, the wonderful story of Mme Graslin, so nearly a masterpiece yet so ultimately not one, would be, in this connection, could I take due space for it, a perfect illustration. If, as I say, Mme Graslin's creator was confined by his doom to patches and pieces, no piece is finer than the first half of the book in question, the half in which the picture is determined by his unequalled power of putting people on their feet, planting them before us in their habit as they lived—a faculty nourished by observation as much as one will, but with the inner vision all the while wide-awake, the vision for which ideas are as living as facts and assume an equal intensity. This intensity, greatest indeed in the facts, has in Balzac a force all its own, to which none other in any novelist I know can be likened. His touch communicates on the spot to the object, the creature evoked, the hardness and permanence that certain substances, some sorts of stone, acquire by exposure to the air. The hardening medium, for the image soaked in it, is the air of his mind. It would take but little more to make the peopled world of fiction as we know it elsewhere affect us by contrast as a world of rather grey pulp. This mixture of the solid and the vivid is Balzac at his best, and it prevails without a break, without a note not admirably true, in *Le Curé de village*—since I have named that

instance—up to the point at which Mme Graslin moves out from
Limoges to Montégnac in her ardent passion of penitence, her determination to expiate her strange and undiscovered association with a
dark misdeed by living and working for others. Her drama is a particularly inward one, interesting, and in the highest degree, so long as
she herself, her nature, her behaviour, her personal history and the
relations in which they place her, control the picture and feed our
illusion. The firmness with which the author makes them play this
part, the whole constitution of the scene and of its developments from
the moment we cross the threshold of her dusky stuffy old-time birth-
house, is a rare delight, producing in the reader that sense of local and
material immersion which is one of Balzac's supreme secrets. What
characteristically befalls, however, is that the spell accompanies us but
part of the way—only until, at a given moment, his attention ruthlessly
transfers itself from inside to outside, from the centre of his subject to
its circumference.

This is Balzac caught in the very fact of his monstrous duality, caught
in his most complete self-expression. He is clearly quite unwitting
that in handing over his *data* to his twin-brother the impassioned
economist and surveyor, the insatiate general inquirer and reporter, he
is in any sort betraying our confidence, for his good conscience at such
times, the spirit of edification in him, is a lesson even to the best of us,
his rich robust temperament nowhere more striking, no more marked
anywhere the great push of the shoulder with which he makes his
theme move, overcharged though it may be like a carrier's van. It is
not therefore assuredly that he loses either sincerity or power in putting
before us to the last detail such a matter as, in this case, his heroine's
management of her property, her tenantry, her economic opportunities
and visions, for these are cases in which he never shrinks nor relents,
in which positively he stiffens and terribly towers—to remind us again
of M. Taine's simplifying word about his being an artist doubled with
a man of business. Balzac was indeed doubled if ever a writer was,
and to that extent that we almost as often, while we read, feel ourselves
thinking of him as a man of business doubled with an artist. Which-
ever way we turn it the oddity never fails, nor the wonder of the ease
with which either character bears the burden of the other. I use the
word burden because, as the fusion is never complete—witness in the
book before us the fatal break of "tone", the one unpardonable sin
for the novelist—we are beset by the conviction that but for this
strangest of dooms one or other of the two partners might, to our

relief, and to his own, have been disembarrassed. The disembarrass-
ment, for each, by a more insidious fusion, would probably have con-
duced to the mastership of interest proceeding from form, or at all
events to the search for it, that Balzac fails to embody. Perhaps the
possibility of an artist constructed on such strong lines is one of those
fine things that are not of this world, a mere dream of the fond critical
spirit. Let these speculations and condonations at least pass as the
amusement, as a result of the high spirits—if high spirits be the word
—of the reader feeling himself again in touch. It was not of our
author's difficulties—that is of his difficulty, the great one—that I proposed to speak, but of his immense clear action. Even that is not truly
an impression of ease, and it is strange and striking that we are in fact
so attached by his want of the unity that keeps surfaces smooth and
dangers down as scarce to feel sure at any moment that we shall not
come back to it with most curiosity. We are never so curious about
successes as about interesting failures. The more reason therefore to
speak promptly, and once for all, of the scale on which, in its own
quarter of his genius, success worked itself out for him.

It is to that I *should* come back—to the infinite reach in him of the
painter and the poet. We can never know what might have become of
him with less importunity in his consciousness of the machinery of
life, of its furniture and fittings, of all that, right and left, he causes to
assail us, sometimes almost to suffocation, under the general rubric of
things. Things, in this sense with him, are at once our delight and our
despair; we pass from being inordinately beguiled and convinced by
them to feeling that his universe fairly smells too much of them, that
the larger ether, the divine air, is in peril of finding among them scarce
room to circulate. His landscapes, his "local colour"—thick in his
pages at a time when it was found in his pages almost alone—his towns,
his streets, his houses, his Saumurs, Angoulêmes, Guérandes, his great
prose Turner-views of the land of the Loire, his rooms, shops, in-
teriors, details of domesticity and traffic, are a short list of the terms
into which he saw the real as clamouring to be rendered and into
which he rendered it with unequalled authority. It would be doubtless more to the point to make our profit of this consummation
than to try to reconstruct a Balzac planted more in the open. We
hardly, as the case stands, know most whether to admire in such an
example as the short tale of "La Grenadière" the exquisite feeling for
"natural objects" with which it overflows like a brimming wine-cup,
the energy of perception and description which so multiplies them for

beauty's sake and for the love of their beauty, or the general wealth of genius that can calculate, or at least count, so little and spend so joyously. The tale practically exists for the sake of the enchanting aspects involved—those of the embowered white house that nestles on its terraced hill above the great French river, and we can think frankly, of no one else with an equal amount of business on his hands who would either have so put himself out for aspects or made them almost by themselves a living subject. A born son of Touraine, it must be said, he pictures his province, on every pretext and occasion, with filial passion and extraordinary breadth. The prime aspect in his scene all the while, it must be added, is the money aspect. The general money question so loads him up and weighs him down that he moves through the human comedy, from beginning to end, very much in the fashion of a camel, the ship of the desert, surmounted with a cargo. "Things" for him are francs and centimes more than any others, and I give up as inscrutable, unfathomable, the nature, the peculiar avidity of his interest in them. It makes us wonder again and again what then is the use on Balzac's scale of the divine faculty. The imagination, as we all know, may be employed up to a certain point in inventing uses for money; but its office beyond that point is surely to make us forget that anything so odious exists. This is what Balzac never forgot; his universe goes on expressing itself for him, to its furthest reaches, on its finest sides, in the terms of the market. To say these things, however, is after all to come out where we want, to suggest his extraordinary scale and his terrible completeness. I am not sure that he does not see character too, see passion, motive, personality, as quite in the order of the "things" we have spoken of. He makes them no less concrete and palpable, handles them no less directly and freely. It is the whole business in fine—that grand total to which he proposed to himself to do high justice—that gives him his place apart, makes him, among the novelists, the largest weightiest presence. There are some of his obsessions—that of the material, that of the financial, that of the "social", that of the technical, political, civil—for which I feel myself unable to judge him, judgment losing itself unexpectedly in a particular shade of pity. The way to judge him is to try to walk all round him—on which we see how remarkably far we have to go. He is the only member of his order really monumental, the sturdiest-seated mass that rises in our path.

We recognize none the less that the finest consequence of these re-established relations is linked with just that appearance in him, that obsession of the actual under so many heads, that makes us look at him, as we would at some rare animal in captivity, between the bars of a cage. It amounts to a sort of suffered doom, since to be solicited by the world from all quarters at once, what is that for the spirit but a denial of escape? We feel his doom to be his want of a private door, and that he felt it, though more obscurely, himself. When we speak of his want of charm therefore we perhaps so surrender the question as but to show our own poverty. If charm, to cut it short, is what he lacks, how comes it that he so touches and holds us that—above all if we be actual or possible fellow-workers—we are uncomfortably conscious of the disloyalty of almost any shade of surrender? We are lodged perhaps by our excited sensibility in a dilemma of which one of the horns is a compassion that savours of patronage; but we must resign ourselves to that by reflecting that our partiality at least takes nothing away from him. It leaves him solidly where he is and only brings us near, brings us to a view of *all* his formidable parts and properties. The conception of the *Comédie humaine* represents them all, and represents them mostly in their felicity and their triumph—or at least the execution does: in spite of which we irresistibly find ourselves thinking of him, in reperusals, as most essentially the victim of a cruel joke. The joke is one of the jokes of fate, the fate that rode him for twenty years at so terrible a pace and with the whip so constantly applied. To have wanted to do so much, to have thought it possible, to have faced and in a manner resisted the effort, to have felt life poisoned and consumed by such a bravery of self-committal—these things form for us in him a face of trouble that, oddly enough, is not appeciably lighted by the fact of his success. It was the having wanted to do so much that was the trap, whatever possibilities of glory might accompany the good faith with which he fell into it. What accompanies *us* as we frequent him is a sense of the deepening ache of that good faith with the increase of his working consciousness, the merciless development of his huge subject and of the rigour of all the conditions. We see the whole thing quite as if Destiny had said to him:

'You want to "do" France, presumptuous, magnificent, miserable man —the France of revolutions, revivals, restorations, of Bonapartes, Bourbons, republics, of war and peace, of blood and romanticism, of violent

change and intimate continuity, the France of the first half of your century? Very well; you most distinctly *shall*, and you shall particularly let
me hear, even if the great groan of your labour do fill at moments the
temple of letters, how you like the job.'

We must of course not appear to deny the existence of a robust joy
in him, the joy of powers and creation, the joy of the observer and the
dreamer who finds a use for his observations and his dreams as fast as
they come. The *Contes drolatiques* would by themselves sufficiently
contradict us, and the savour of the *Contes drolatiques* is not confined
to these productions. His work at large tastes of the same kind of
humour, and we feel him again and again, like any other great healthy
producer of these matters, beguiled and carried along. He would have
been, I dare say, the last not to insist that the artist has pleasures for
ever indescribable; he lived in short in his human comedy with the
largest life we can attribute to the largest capacity. There are particular parts of his subject from which, with our sense of his enjoyment of
them, we have to check the impulse to call him away—frequently as
I confess in this relation that impulse arises.

The relation is with the special element of his spectacle from which
he never fully detaches himself, the element, to express it succinctly, of
the "old families" and the great ladies. Balzac frankly revelled in his
conception of an aristocracy—a conception that never succeeded in
becoming his happiest; whether, objectively, thanks to the facts
supplied him by the society he studied, or through one of the strangest
deviations of taste that the literary critic is in an important connection
likely to encounter. Nothing would in fact be more interesting than
to attempt a general measure of the part played in the total comedy,
to his imagination, by the old families; and one or two contributions
to such an attempt I must not fail presently to make. I glance at them
here, however, the delectable class, but as most representing on the
author's part free and amused creation; by which too I am far from
hinting that the amusement is at all at their expense. It is in their great
ladies that the old families most shine out for him, images of strange
colour and form, but "felt", as we say, to their finger-tips, and extraordinarily interesting as a mark of the high predominance—predominance of character, of cleverness, of will, of general "personality"
—that almost every scene of the Comedy attributes to women. It
attributes to them in fact a recognized, an uncontested supremacy; it is
through them that the hierarchy of old families most expresses itself;
and it is surrounded by them even as some magnificent indulgent pasha

by his overflowing seraglio that Balzac sits most at his ease. All of
which reaffirms—if it be needed—that his inspiration, and the sense of
it, were even greater than his task. And yet such betrayals of spon-
taneity in him make for an old friend at the end of the chapter no great
difference in respect to the pathos—since it amounts to that—of his
genius-ridden aspect. It comes to us as we go back to him that his
spirit had fairly made of itself a cage in which he was to turn round and
round, always unwinding his reel, much in the manner of a criminal
condemned to hard labour for life. The cage is simply the complicated
but dreadfully definite French world that built itself so solidly in and
roofed itself so impenetrably over him.

It is not that, caught there with him though we be, we ourselves
prematurely seek an issue: we throw ourselves back, on the contrary,
for the particular sense of it, into his ancient superseded comparatively
rococo and quite patriarchal France—patriarchal in spite of social and
political convulsions; into his old-time antediluvian Paris, all picturesque and all workable, full to the fancy, of an amenity that has
passed away; into his intensely differentiated sphere of *la province*,
evoked in each sharpest or faintest note of its difference, described
systematically as narrow and flat, and yet attaching us if only by the
contagion of the author's over-flowing sensibility. He feels in his vast
exhibition many things, but there is nothing he feels with the communicable shocks and vibrations, the sustained fury of perception—
not always a fierceness of judgment, which is another matter—that *la
province* excites in him. Half our interest in him springs still from our
own sense that, for all the convulsions, the revolutions and experiments
that have come and gone, the order he describes is the old order that
our sense of the past perversely recurs to as to something happy we
have irretrievably missed. His pages bristle with the revelation of the
lingering earlier world, the world in which places and people still had
their queerness, their strong marks, their sharp type, and in which, as
before the platitude that was to come, the observer with an appetite
for the salient could by way of precaution fill his lungs. Balzac's
appetite for the salient was voracious, yet he came, as it were, in time,
in spite of his so often speaking as if what he sees about him is but the
last desolation of the modern. His conservatism, the most entire, consistent and convinced that ever was—yet even at that much inclined
to whistling in the dark as if to the tune of "Oh how mediæval I *am*!"
—was doubtless the best point of view from which he could rake his
field. But if what he sniffed from afar in that position was the ex-

tremity of change, we in turn feel both subject and painter drenched
with the smell of the past. It is preserved in his work as nowhere else—
not vague nor faint nor delicate, but as strong to-day as when first
distilled.

It may seem odd to find a conscious melancholy in the fact that a
great worker succeeded in clasping his opportunity in such an embrace,
this being exactly our usual measure of the felicity of great workers.
I speak, I hasten to reassert, all in the name of sympathy—without
which it would have been detestable to speak at all; and the sentiment
puts its hand instinctively on the thing that makes it least futile. This
particular thing then is not in the least Balzac's own hold of his terrible
mass of matter; it is absolutely the convolutions of the serpent he had
with a magnificent courage invited to wind itself round him. We must
use the common image—he had created his Frankenstein monster. It
is the fellow-craftsman who can most feel for him—it being apparently
possible to read him from another point of view without getting really
into his presence. We undergo with him from book to book, from
picture to picture, the convolutions of the serpent, we especially whose
refined performances are given, as we know, but with the small common or garden snake. I stick to this to justify my image just above of
his having been "caged" by the intensity with which he saw his general
matter as a whole. To see it always as a whole is our wise, our virtuous
effort, the very condition, as we keep in mind, of superior art. Balzac
was in this connection then wise and virtuous to the most exemplary
degree; so that he doubtless ought logically but to prompt to complacent reflections. No painter ever saw his general matter nearly so
much as a whole. Why is it then that we hover about him, if we are
real Balzacians, not with cheerful chatter, but with a consideration
deeper in its reach than any mere moralizing? The reason is largely
that if you wish with absolute immaculate virtue to look at your matter
as a whole and yet remain a theme for cheerful chatter, you must be
careful to take some quantity that will not hug you to death. Balzac's
active intention was, to vary our simile, a beast with a hundred claws,
and the spectacle is in the hugging process of which, as energy against
energy, the beast was capable. Its victim died of the process at fifty,
and if what we see in the long gallery in which it is mirrored is not the
defeat, but the admirable resistance, we none the less never lose the
sense that the fighter is shut up with his fate. He has locked himself
in—it is doubtless his own fault—and thrown the key away. Most of
all perhaps the impression comes—the impression of the adventurer

committed and anxious, but with no retreat—from the so formidably concrete nature of his plastic stuff. When we work in the open, as it were, our material is not classed and catalogued, so that we have at hand a hundred ways of being loose, superficial, disingenuous, and yet passing, to our no small profit, for remarkable. Balzac had no "open"; he held that the great central normal fruitful country of his birth and race, overarched with its infinite social complexity, yielded a sufficiency of earth and sea and sky. We seem to see as his catastrophe that the sky, all the same, came down on him. He couldn't keep it up—in more senses than one. These are perhaps fine fancies for a critic to weave about a literary figure of whom he has undertaken to give a plain account; but I leave them so on the plea that there are relations in which, for the Balzacian, criticism simply drops out. That is not a liberty, I admit, ever to be much encouraged; critics in fact are the only people who have a right occasionally to take it. There is no such plain account of the *Comédie humaine* as that it makes us fold up our yard-measure and put away our note-book quite as we do with some extraordinary character, some mysterious and various stranger, who brings with him his own standards and his own air. There is a kind of eminent presence that abashes even the interviewer, moves him to respect and wonder, makes him, for consideration itself, not insist. This takes of course a personage sole of his kind. But such a personage precisely is Balzac.

III

By all of which have I none the less felt it but too clear that I must not pretend in this place to take apart the pieces of his immense complicated work, to number them or group them or dispose them about. The most we can do is to pick one up here and there and wonder, as we weigh it in our hand, at its close compact substance. That is all even M. Taine could do in the longest and most penetrating study of which our author has been the subject. Every piece we handle is so full of stuff, condensed like the edibles provided for campaigns and explorations, positively so charged with distilled life, that we find ourselves dropping it, in certain states of sensibility, as we drop an object unguardedly touched that startles us by being animate. We seem really scarce to want anything to *be* so animate. It would verily take Balzac to detail Balzac, and he has had in fact Balzacians nearly enough affiliated to affront the task with courage. The *Répertoire de la Comédie humaine* of MM. Anatole Cerfberr and Jules Christophe is a closely-printed octavo of 550 pages which constitutes in relation to his characters great and small an impeccable biographical dictionary. His votaries and expositors are so numerous that the Balzac library of comment and research must be, of its type, one of the most copious. M. de Lovenjoul has laboured all round the subject; his *Histoire des œuvres* alone is another crowded octavo of 400 pages; in connection with which I must mention Miss Wormeley, the devoted American translator, interpreter, worshipper, who in the course of her own studies has so often found occasion to differ from M. de Lovenjoul on matters of fact and questions of date and of appreciation. Miss Wormeley, M. Paul Bourget and many others are examples of the passionate piety that our author can inspire. As I turn over the encyclopedia of his characters I note that whereas such works usually commemorate but the ostensibly eminent of a race and time, every creature so much as named in the fictive swarm is in this case preserved to fame: so close is the implication that to have *been* named by such a dispenser of life and privilege is to be, as we say it of baronets and peers, created. He infinitely divided moreover, as we know, he subdivided, altered and multiplied his heads and categories—his "Vie Parisienne", his "Vie de province", his "Vie politique", his "Parents pauvres", his "Etudes philosophiques", his "Splendeurs et misères des courtisanes", his "Envers de l'histoire contemporaine" and all the rest; so that nominal reference to them becomes the more difficult. Yet without prejudice either to the energy of conception with which he mapped out his theme as with chalk on a huge blackboard, or to the prodigious patience with which he executed his plan, practically filling in with a wealth of illustration, from sources that to this day we fail to make out, every compartment of his table, M. de Lovenjoul draws up the list, year by year, from 1822 to 1848, of his mass of work, giving us thus the measure of the tension represented for him by almost any twelvemonth. It is wholly unequalled, considering the quality of Balzac's show, by any other eminent abundance.

I must be pardoned for coming back to it, for seeming unable to leave it; it enshrouds so interesting a mystery. How was so solidly systematic a literary attack on life to be conjoined with whatever workable minimum of needful intermission, of free observations, of personal experience? Some small possibility of personal experience and disinterested life must, at the worst, from deep within or far without, feed and fortify the strained productive machine. These things were luxuries that Balzac appears really never to have tasted on any appreciable scale. His published letters—the driest and most starved of those of any man of equal distinction—are with the exception of those to Mme de Hanska, whom he married shortly before his death, almost exclusively the audible wail of a galley-slave chained to the oar. M. Zola, in our time, among the novelists, has sacrificed to the huge plan in something of the same manner, yet with goodly modern differences that leave him a comparatively simple instance. His work assuredly has been more nearly dried up by the sacrifice than ever Balzac's was— so miraculously, given the conditions, was Balzac's to escape the anti-climax. Method and system, in the chronicle of the tribe of *Rougon-Macquart*, an economy in itself certainly of the rarest and most interesting, have spread so from centre to circumference that they have ended by being almost the only thing we feel. And then M. Zola has survived and triumphed in his lifetime, has continued and lasted, has piled up and, if the remark be not frivolous, enjoyed in all its *agréments* the reward for which Balzac toiled and sweated in vain. On top of which he will have had also his literary great-grandfather's heroic example to start from and profit by, the positive heritage of a *fils de famille* to enjoy, spend, save, waste. Balzac had frankly no heritage at all but his stiff subject, and by way of model not even in any direct or immediate manner that of the inner light and kindly admonition of his genius. Nothing adds more to the strangeness of his general performance than his having failed so long to find his inner light, groped for it almost ten years, missed it again and again, moved straight away from it, turned his back on it, lived in fine round about it, in a darkness still scarcely penetrable, a darkness into which we peep only half to make out the dreary little waste of his numerous *œuvres de jeunesse*. To M. Zola was vouchsafed the good fortune of settling down to the *Rougon-Macquart* with the happiest promptitude; it was as if time for one look about him—and I say it without disparagement to the reach of his look— had sufficiently served his purpose. Balzac moreover might have written five hundred novels without our feeling in him the faintest hint of the breath of doom, if he had only been comfortably capable of conceiving the short cut of the fashion practised by others under his eyes. As Alexandre Dumas and George Sand, illustrious contemporaries, cultivated a personal life and a disinterested consciousness by the bushel, having, for their easier duration, not too consistently known, as the true painter knows it, the obsession of the thing to be done, so Balzac was condemned by his constitution itself, by his inveterately seeing this "thing to be done" as part and parcel, as of the very essence, of his enterprise. The latter existed for him, as the process worked and hallucination settled, in the form, and the form only, of the thing done, and not in any hocus-pocus about doing. There was no kindly convenient escape for him by the little swinging back-door of the thing *not* done. He desired—no man more—to get out of his obsession, but only at the other end, that is by boring through it. "How then, thus deprived of the outer air almost as much as if he were gouging a passage for a railway through an Alp, *did* he live?" is the question that haunts us—with the consequence for the most part of promptly meeting its fairly tragic answer. He did *not* live—save in his imagination, or by other aid than he could find there; his imagination was all his experience; he had provably no time for the real thing. This brings us to the rich if simple truth that his imagination alone did the business, carried through both the conception and the execution—as large an effort and as proportionate a success, in all but the vulgar sense, as the faculty when equally handicapped was ever concerned in. Handicapped I say because this interesting fact about him, with the claim it makes, rests on the ground, the high distinction, that more than all the rest of us put together he went in, as we say, for detail, circumstance and specification, proposed to himself *all* the connections of every part of his matter and the full total of the parts. The whole thing, it is impossible not to keep repeating, was what he deemed treatable. One really knows in all imaginative literature no undertaking to compare with it for courage, good faith and sublimity. There, once more, was the necessity that rode him and that places him apart in our homage. It is no light thing to have been condemned to become provably sublime. And looking through, or trying to, at what is beneath and behind, we are left benevolently uncertain if the predominant quantity be audacity or innocence.

It is of course inevitable at this point to seem to hear the colder critic promptly take us up. He undertook the whole thing—oh exactly the ponderous person! But *did* he "do" the whole thing, if you please, any more than sundry others of fewer pretensions? The retort to this it can only be a positive joy to make, so high a note instantly sounds as an effect of the inquiry. Nothing is more interesting and amusing than to find one's self recognizing both that Balzac's pretensions were immense, portentous, and that yet, taking him—and taking *them*— altogether, they but minister in the long run to our fondness. They affect us not only as the endearing eccentricities of a person we greatly admire, but fairly as the very condition of his having become such a person. We take them thus in the first place for the very terms of his plan, and in the second for a part of that high robustness and that general richness of nature which made him in face of such a project believe in himself. One would really scarce have liked to see such a job as La Comédie humaine tackled without swagger. To think of the thing really as practicable *was* swagger, and of the very rarest order. So to think assuredly implied pretensions, pretensions that risked showing as monstrous should the enterprise fail to succeed. It is for the colder critic to take the trouble to make out that of the two parties to it the body of pretension remains greater than the success. One may put it moreover at the worst for him, may recognize that it is in the matter of opinion still more than in the matter of knowledge that Balzac offers himself as universally competent. He has flights of judgment—on subjects the most special as well as the most general—that are vertiginous and on his alighting from which we greet him with a special indulgence. We can easily imagine him to respond, confessing humorously—if he had only time—to such a benevolent understanding smile as would fain hold our own eyes a moment. Then it is that he would most show us his scheme and his necessities and how in operation they all hang together. *Naturally* everything about everything, though how he had time to learn it is the last thing he has time to tell us; which matters the less, moreover, as it is not over the question of his knowledge that we sociably invite him, as it were (and remembering the two augurs behind the altar) to wink at us for a sign. His convictions it is that are his great pardonable "swagger"; to them in particular I refer as his general operative condition, the constituted terms of his experiment, and not less as his consolation, his support, his amusement by the way. They embrace everything in the world—that is in his world of the so parti-coloured France of his age: religion, morals, politics, economics, physics, æsthetics, letters, art, science, sociology, every question of faith, every branch of research. They represent thus his equipment of ideas, those ideas of which it will never do for a man who aspires to constitute a State to be deprived. He must take them with him as an ambassador extraordinary takes with him secretaries, uniforms, stars and garters, a gilded coach and a high assurance. Balzac's opinions are his gilded coach, in which he is more amused than anything else to feel himself riding, but which is indispensably concerned in getting him over the ground. What more inevitable than that they should be intensely Catholic, intensely monarchical, intensely saturated with the real genius—as between 1830 and 1848 he believed it to be—of the French character and French institutions?

Nothing is happier for us than that he should have enjoyed his outlook before the first half of the century closed. He could then still treat his subject as comparatively homogeneous. Any country could have a Revolution—every country *had* had one. A Restoration was merely what a revolution involved, and the Empire had been for the French but a revolutionary incident, in addition to being by good luck for the novelist an immensely pictorial one. He was free therefore to arrange the background of the comedy in the manner that seemed to him best to suit anything so great; in the manner at the same time prescribed according to his contention by the noblest traditions. The church, the throne, the noblesse, the bourgeoisie, the people, the peasantry, all in their order and each solidly kept in it, these were precious things, things his superabundant insistence on the price of which is what I refer to as his exuberance of opinion. It was a luxury for more reasons than one, though one, presently to be mentioned, handsomely predominates. The meaning of that exchange of intelligencies in the rear of the oracle which I have figured for him with the perceptive friend bears simply on his pleading guilty to the purport of the friend's discrimination. The point the latter makes with him—a beautiful cordial critical point—is that he truly cares for nothing in the world, thank goodness, so much as for the passions and embroilments of men and women, the free play of character and the sharp revelation of type, all the real stuff of drama and the natural food of novelists. Religion, morals, politics, economics, æsthetics would be thus, as systematic matter, very well in their place, but quite secondary and subservient. Balzac's attitude is again and again that he cares for the adventures and emotions because, as his last word he cares for the good and the greatness of the State—which is where his swagger, with a whole society on his hands, comes in. What we on our side in a thousand places gratefully feel is that he cares for his monarchical and hierarchical and ecclesiastical society because it rounds itself for his mind into the most congruous and capacious theatre for the repertory of his innumerable comedians. It has above all, for a painter abhorrent of the superficial, the inestimable benefit of the accumulated, of strong marks and fine shades, contrasts and complications. There had certainly been since 1789 dispersals and confusions enough, but the thick tradition, no more at the most than half smothered, lay under them all. So the whole of his faith and no small part of his working omniscience were neither more nor less than that historic sense which I have spoken of as the spur of his invention and which he possessed as no other novelist has done. We immediately feel that to name it in connection with him is to answer every question he suggests and to account for each of his idiosyncrasies in turn. The novel, the tale, however brief, the passage, the sentence by itself, the situation, the person, the place, the motive exposed, the speech reported—these things were in his view history, with the absoluteness and the dignity of history. This is the source both of his weight and wealth. What is the historic sense after all but animated, but impassioned knowledge seeking to enlarge itself? I have said that his imagination did the whole thing, no other explanation—no reckoning of the possibilities of personal saturation—meeting the mysteries of the case. Therefore his imagination achieved the miracle of absolutely resolving itself into multifarious knowledge. Since history proceeds by documents he constructed, as he needed them, the documents too—fictive sources that imitated the actual to the life. It was of course a terrible business, but at least in the light of it his claims to creatorship are justified—which is what was to be shown.

IV

It is very well even in the sketchiest attempt at a portrait of his genius to try to take particulars in their order: one peeps over the shoulder of another at the moment we get a feature into focus. The loud appeal not to be left out prevails among them all, and certainly with the excuse that each as we fix it seems to fall most into the picture. I have so indulged myself as to his general air that I find a whole list of vivid contributive marks almost left on my hands. Such a list, in any study of Balzac, is delightful for intimate edification as well as for the fine humour of the thing; we proceed from one of the items of his breathing physiognomy to the other with quite the same sense of life, the same active curiosity, with which we push our way through the thick undergrowth of one of the novels. The difficulty is really that the special point for which we at the moment observe him melts into all the other points, is swallowed up before our eyes in the formidable mass. The French apply the happiest term to certain characters when they speak of them as *entiers* and if the word had been invented for Balzac it could scarce better have expressed him. He is "entire" as was never a man of his craft; he moves always in his mass; wherever we find him we find him in force; whatever touch he applies he applies it with his whole apparatus. He is like an army gathered to besiege a cottage equally with a city, and living voraciously in either case on all the country about. It may well be, at any rate, that his infatuation with the idea of the social, the practical primacy of "the sex" is the article at the top of one's list; there could certainly be no better occasion than this of a rich reissue of the *Deux Jeunes Mariées* for placing it there at a venture. Here indeed precisely we get a sharp example of the way in which, as I have just said, a capital illustration of one of his sides becomes, just as we take it up, a capital illustration of another. The correspondence of Louise de Chaulieu and Renée de Maucombe is in fact one of those cases that light up with a great golden glow all his parts at once. We needn't mean by this that such parts are themselves absolutely all golden—given the amount of tinsel for instance in his view, supereminent, transcendent here, of the old families and the great ladies. What do we convey, however, is that his creative temperament finds in such *data* as these one of its best occasions for shining out. Again we fondly recognize his splendid, his attaching swagger— that of a "bounder" of genius and of feeling; again we see how, with opportunity, its elements may vibrate into a perfect ecstasy of creation.

Why shouldn't a man swagger, he treats us to the diversion of asking ourselves, who has created from top to toe the most brilliant, the most historic, the most insolvent, above all the most detailed and discriminated of aristocracies? Balzac carried the uppermost class of his comedy, from the princes, dukes, and unspeakable duchesses down to his poor barons *de province*, about in his pocket as he might have carried a tolerably befingered pack of cards, to deal them about with a flourish of the highest authority whenever there was the chance of a game. He knew them up and down and in and out, their arms, infallibly supplied, their quarterings, pedigrees, services, intermarriages, relationships, ramifications and other enthralling attributes. This indeed is comparatively simple learning; the real wonder is rather when we linger on the ground of the patrician consciousness itself, the innermost, the esoteric, the spirit, temper, tone—tone above all—of the titled and the proud. The questions multiply for every scene of the comedy; there is no one who makes us walk in such a cloud of them. The clouds elsewhere, in comparison, are at best of questions not worth asking. *Was* the patrician consciousness that figured as our author's model so splendidly fatuous as he—almost without irony, often in fact with a certain poetic sympathy—everywhere represents it? His imagination

lives in it, breathes its scented air, swallows this element with the smack
of the lips of the connoisseur; but I feel that we never know, even to the
end, whether he be here directly historic or only quite misguidedly
romantic. The romantic side of him has the extent of all the others;
it represents in the oddest manner his escape from the walled and roofed
structure into which he had built himself—his longing for the vaguely-
felt outside and as much as might be of the rest of the globe. But it is
characteristic of him that the most he could do for this relief was to
bring the fantastic into the circle and fit it somehow to his conditions.
Was his tone for the duchess, the marquise but the imported fantastic,
one of those smashes of the window-pane of the real that reactions
sometimes produce even in the stubborn? or are we to take it as
observed, as really reported, as, for all its difference from our notion
of the natural—and, quite as much, of the artificial—in another and
happier strain of manners, substantially true? The whole episode, in
Les Illusions perdues, of Mme de Bargeton's "chucking" Lucien de
Rubempré, on reaching Paris with him, under pressure of Mme
d'Espard's shockability as to his coat and trousers and other such
matters, is either a magnificent lurid document or the baseless fabric
of a vision. The great wonder is that, as I rejoice to put it, we can never
really discover which, and that we feel as we read that we can't, and
that we suffer at the hands of no other author this particular helplessness
of immersion. It is *done*—we are always thrown back on that; we can't
get out of it; all we can do is to say that the true itself can't be more
than done and that if the false in this way equals it we must give up
looking for the difference. Alone among novelists Balzac has the secret
of an insistence that somehow makes the difference nought. He warms
his facts into life—as witness the certainty that the episode I just cited
has absolutely as much of that property as if perfect matching had been
achieved. If the great ladies in question *didn't* behave, wouldn't,
couldn't have behaved, like a pair of nervous snobs, why so much the
worse, we say to ourselves, for the great ladies in question. We *know*
them so—they owe their being to our so seeing them; whereas we
never can tell ourselves how we should otherwise have known them
or what quantity of being they would on a different footing have been
able to put forth.

The case is the same with Louise de Chaulieu, who besides coming
out of her convent school, as a quite young thing, with an amount of
sophistication that would have chilled the heart of a horse-dealer,
exhales—and to her familiar friend, a young person of a supposedly

equal breeding—an extravagance of complacency in her "social position" that makes us rub our eyes. Whereupon after a little the same phenomenon occurs; we swallow her bragging, against our better reason, or at any rate against our startled sense, under coercion of the total intensity. We do more than this, we cease to care for the question, which loses itself in the hot fusion of the whole picture. He has "gone for" his subject, in the vulgar phrase, with an avidity that makes the attack of his most eminent rivals affect us as the intercourse between introduced indifferences at a dull evening party. He squeezes it till it cries out, we hardly know whether for pleasure or pain. In the case before us for example—without wandering from book to book, impossible here, I make the most of the ground already broken—he has seen at once that the state of marriage itself, sounded to its depths, is, in the connection, his real theme. He sees it of course in the conditions that exist for him, but he weighs it to the last ounce, feels it in all its dimensions, as well as in all his own, and would scorn to take refuge in any engaging side-issue. He gets, for further intensity into the very skin of his *jeunes mariées*—into each alternately, as they are different enough; so that, to repeat again, any other mode of representing women, or of representing anybody, becomes, in juxtaposition, a thing so void of the active contortions of truth as to be comparatively wooden. He bears children with Mme de l'Estorade, knows intimately how she suffers for them, and not less intimately how her correspondent suffers, as well as enjoys, without them. Big as he is he makes himself small to be handled by her with young maternal passion and positively to handle her in turn with infantile innocence. These things are the very flourishes, the little technical amusements of his penetrating power. But it is doubtless in his hand for such matter as the jealous passion of Louise de Chaulieu, the free play of her intelligence and the almost beautiful good faith of her egotism, that he is most individual. It is one of the neatest examples of his extraordinary leading gift, his art— which is really moreover not an art—of working the exhibition of a given character up to intensity. I say it is not an art because it acts for us rather as a hunger on the part of his nature to take on in all freedom another nature—take it by a direct process of the senses. Art is for the mass of us who have only the process of art, comparatively so stiff. The thing amounts with him to a kind of shameless personal, physical, not merely intellectual, duality—the very spirit and secret of transmigration.

19

GUSTAVE FLAUBERT

1902

THE first thing I find to-day and on my very threshold to say about Gustave Flaubert is that he has been reported on by M. Emile Faguet in the series of Les Grands Ecrivains Français with such lucidity as may almost be taken to warn off a later critic. I desire to pay at the outset my tribute to M. Faguet's exhaustive study, which is really in its kind a model and a monument. Never can a critic have got closer to a subject of this order; never can the results of the approach have been more copious or more interesting; never in short can the master of a complex art have been more mastered in his turn, nor his art more penetrated, by the application of an earnest curiosity. That remark I have it at heart to make, so pre-eminently has the little volume I refer to not left the subject where it found it. It abounds in contributive light, and yet I feel on reflection that it scarce wholly dazzles another contributor away. One reason of this is that, though I enter into everything M. Faguet has said, there are things—things perhaps especially of the province of the artist, the fellow-craftsman of Flaubert—that I am conscious of his not having said; another is that inevitably there are particular possibilities of reaction in our English-speaking consciousness that hold up a light of their own. Therefore I venture to follow even on a field so laboured, only paying this toll to the latest and best work because the author has made it impossible to do less.

Flaubert's life is so almost exclusively the story of his literary application that to speak of his five or six fictions is pretty well to account for it all. He died in 1880 after a career of fifty-nine years singularly little marked by changes of scene, of fortune, of attitude, of occupation, of character, and above all, as may be said, of mind. He would be interesting to the race of novelists if only because, quite apart from the value of his work, he so personally gives us the example and the image, so presents the intellectual case. He was born a novelist, grew up, lived, died a novelist, breathing, feeling, thinking, speaking, performing every operation of life, only as that votary; and this though his production was to be small in amount and though it constituted all his diligence. It was not indeed perhaps primarily so much that he was born and lived a novelist as that he was born and lived literary, and that to be literary represented for him an almost overwhelming situation. No life was long enough, no courage great enough, no fortune kind enough to support a man under the burden of this character when once such a doom had been laid on him. His case was a doom because he felt of his vocation almost nothing but the difficulty. He had many strange sides, but this was the strangest, that if we argued from his difficulty to his work, the difficulty being registered for us in his letters and elsewhere, we should expect from the result but the smallest things. We should be prepared to find in it well-nigh a complete absence of the signs of a gift. We should regret that the unhappy man had not addressed himself to something he might have found at least comparatively easy. We should singularly miss the consecration supposedly given to a work of art by its having been conceived in joy. That is Flaubert's remarkable, his so far as I know unmatched distinction, that he has left works of an extraordinary art even the conception of which failed to help him to think in serenity. The chapter of execution, from the moment execution gets really into the shafts, is of course always and everywhere a troubled one—about which moreover too much has of late been written; but we frequently find Flaubert cursing his subjects themselves, wishing he had not chosen them, holding himself up to derision for having done so, and hating them in the very act of sitting down to them. He cared immensely for the medium, the task and the triumph involved, but was himself the last to be able to say why. He is sustained only by the rage and the habit of effort; the mere *love* of letters, let alone the love of life, appears at an early age to have deserted him. Certain passages in his correspondence make us even wonder if it be not hate that sustains him most. So, successively, his several supremely finished and crowned compositions came into the world, and we may feel sure that none others of the kind, none that were to have an equal fortune, had sprung from such adversity.

I insist upon this because his at once excited and baffled passion gives the key of his life and determines its outline. I must speak of him at least as I feel him and as in his very latest years I had the fortune occasionally to see him. I said just now, practically, that he is for many of our tribe at large *the* novelist, intent and typical, and so, gathered together and foreshortened, simplified and fixed, the lapse of time seems to show him. It has made him in his prolonged posture extraordinarily objective, made him even resemble one of his own productions, constituted him as a subject, determined him as a figure; the limit of his range, and above all of his reach, is after this fashion, no doubt, sufficiently indicated, and yet perhaps in the event without injury to his name. If our consideration of him cultivates a certain tenderness on the double ground that he suffered supremely in the cause and that there is endlessly much to be learned from him, we remember at the same time that, indirectly, the world at large possesses him not less than the *confrère*. He has fed and fertilized, has filtered through others, and so arrived at contact with that public from whom it was his theory that he was separated by a deep and impassable trench, the labour of his own spade. He is none the less more interesting, I repeat, as a failure however qualified than as a success however explained, and it is as so viewed that the unity of his career attaches and admonishes. Save in some degree by a condition of health (a liability to epileptic fits at times frequent, but never so frequent as to have been generally suspected) he was not outwardly hampered as the tribe of men of letters goes—an anxious brotherhood at the best; yet the fewest possible things appear to have ever succeeded in happening to him. The only son of an eminent provincial physician, he inherited a modest ease and no other incumbrance than, as was the case for Balzac, an over-attentive and importunate mother; but freedom spoke to him from behind a veil, and when we have mentioned the few apparent facts of experience that make up his landmarks over and beyond his interspaced publications we shall have completed his biography. Tall, strong, striking, he caused his friends to admire in him the elder, the florid Norman type, and he seems himself, as a man of imagination, to have found some transmission of race in his stature and presence, his light-coloured salient eyes and long tawny moustache.

The central event of his life was his journey to the East in 1849 with M. Maxime Du Camp, of which the latter has left in his *Impressions littéraires* a singularly interesting and, as we may perhaps say, slightly treacherous report, and which prepared for Flaubert a state of nostalgia that was not only never to leave him, but that was to work in him as a motive. He had during that year, and just in sufficient quantity, his revelation, the particular appropriate disclosure to which the gods at some moment treat the artist unless they happen too perversely to conspire against him: he tasted of the knowledge by which he was subsequently to measure everything, appeal from everything, find everything flat. Never probably was an impression so assimilated, so positively transmuted to a function; he lived on it to the end and we may say that in *Salammbô* and *La Tentation de Saint-Antoine* he almost died of it. He made afterwards no other journey of the least importance save a disgusted excursion to the Rigi-Kaltbad shortly before his death. The Franco-German War was of course to him for the time as the valley of the shadow itself; but this was an ordeal, unlike most of his other ordeals, shared after all with millions. He never married—he declared, toward the end, to the most comprehending of his confidants, that he had been from the first "afraid of life"; and the friendliest element of his later time was, we judge, that admirable comfortable commerce, in her fullest maturity, with Mme George Sand, the confidant I just referred to; which has been preserved for us in the published correspondence of each. He had in Ivan Turgénieff a friend almost as valued; he spent each year a few months in Paris, where (to mention everything) he had his natural place, so far as he cared to take it, at the small literary court of the Princess Mathilde; and, lastly, he lost toward the close of his life, by no fault of his own, a considerable part of his modest fortune. It is, however, in the long security, the almost unbroken solitude of Croisset, near Rouen, that he mainly figures for us, gouging out his successive books in the wide old room, of many windows, that, with an intervening terrace, overlooked the broad Seine and the passing boats. This was virtually a monastic cell, closed to echoes and accidents; with its stillness for long periods scarce broken save by the creak of the towing-chain of the tugs across the water. When I have added that his published letters offer a view, not very refreshing, of his youthful entanglement with Mme Louise Colet— whom we name because, apparently not a shrinking person, she long ago practically named herself—I shall have catalogued his personal vicissitudes. And I may add further that the connection with Mme Colet, such as it was, rears its head for us in something like a desert of immunity from such complications.

His complications were of the spirit, of the literary vision, and though he was thoroughly profane he was yet essentially anchoretic. I perhaps miss a point, however, in not finally subjoining that he was liberally accessible to his friends during the months he regularly spent in Paris. Sensitive, passionate, perverse, not less than *immediately* sociable—for if he detested his collective contemporaries this dropped, thanks to his humanizing shyness, before the individual encounter— he was in particular and super-excellently not *banal*, and he attached men perhaps more than women, inspiring a marked, a by no means colourless shade of respect; a respect not founded, as the air of it is apt to be, on the vague presumption, but addressed almost in especial to his disparities and oddities and thereby, no doubt, none too different from affection. His friends at all events were a rich and eager *cénacle*, among whom he was on occasion, by his picturesque personality, a natural and overtopping centre; partly perhaps because he was so much and so familiarly at home. He wore, up to any hour of the afternoon, that long colloquial dressing-gown, with trousers to match, which one has always associated with literature in France—the uniform really of freedom of talk. Freedom of talk abounded by his winter fire, for the *cénacle* was made up almost wholly of the more finely distinguished among his contemporaries; of philosophers, men of letters and men of affairs belonging to his own generation and the next. He had at the time I have in mind a small perch, far aloft, at the distant, the then almost suburban, end of the Faubourg Saint-Honoré, where on Sunday afternoons, at the very top of an endless flight of stairs, were to be encountered in a cloud of conversation and smoke most of the novelists of the general Balzac tradition. Others of a different birth and complexion were markedly not of the number, were not even conceivable as present; none of those, unless I misremember, whose fictions were at that time "serialized" in the *Revue des Deux Mondes*. In spite of Renan and Taine and two or three more, the contributor to the *Revue* would indeed at no time have found in the circle in question his foot on his native heath. One could recall if one would two or three vivid allusions to him, not of the most quotable, on the lips of the most famous of "naturalists"—allusions to him as represented for instance by M. Victor Cherbuliez and M. Octave Feuillet. The author of these pages recalls a concise qualification of this last of his fellows on the lips of Emile Zola, which that absorbed auditor had too directly, too rashly asked for; but which is alas not reproducible here. There was little else but the talk, which had extreme intensity and variety; almost nothing, as I remember, but a painted and gilded idol, of considerable size, a relic and a memento, on the chimney-piece. Flaubert was huge and diffident, but florid too and resonant, and my main remembrance is of a conception of courtesy in him, an accessibility to the human relation, that only wanted to be sure of the way taken or to take. The uncertainties of the French for the determination of intercourse have often struck me as quite matching the sharpness of their certainties, as we for the most part feel these latter, which sometimes in fact throw the indeterminate into almost touching relief. I have thought of them at such times as the people in the world one may have to go more of the way to meet than to meet any other, and this, as it were, through their being seated and embedded, provided for at home, in a manner

that is all their own and that has bred them to the positive preaccept-
ance of interest on their behalf. We at least of the Anglo-American
race, more abroad in the world, perching everywhere, so far as grounds
of intercourse are concerned, more vaguely and superficially, as well
as less intelligently, are the more ready by that fact with inexpensive
accommodations, rather conscious that these themselves forbear from
the claim to fascinate, and advancing with the good nature that is the
mantle of our obtuseness to any point whatever where entertainment
may be offered us. My recollection is at any rate simplified by the fact
of the presence almost always, in the little high room of the Faubourg's
end, of other persons and other voices. Flaubert's own voice is clearest
to me from the uneffaced sense of a winter week-day afternoon when
I found him by exception alone and when something led to his reading
me aloud, in support of some judgment he had thrown off, a poem of
Théophile Gautier's. He cited it as an example of verse intensely and
distinctively French, and French in its melancholy, which neither
Goethe nor Heine nor Leopardi, neither Pushkin nor Tennyson nor, as he
said, Byron, could at all have matched in *kind*. He converted me at the
moment to this perception, alike by the sense of the thing and by his
large utterance of it; after which it is dreadful to have to confess not
only that the poem was then new to me, but that, hunt as I will in every
volume of its author, I am never able to recover it. This is perhaps
after all happy, causing Flaubert's own full tone, which was the note
of the occasion, to linger the more unquenched. But for the rhyme in
fact I could have believed him to be spouting to me something strange
and sonorous of his own. The thing really rare would have been to
hear him do that—hear him *gueuler*, as he liked to call it. Verse, I felt,
we had always with us, and almost any idiot of goodwill could give it a
value. The value of so many a passage of *Salammbô* and of *L'Education*
was on the other hand exactly such as gained when he allowed himself,
as had by the legend ever been frequent *dans l'intimité*, to "bellow" it
to its fullest effect.
    One of the things that make him most exhibitional and most de-
scribable, so that if we had invented him as an illustration or a character
we would exactly so have arranged him, is that he was formed intellectually of two quite distinct compartments, a sense of the real and
a sense of the romantic, and that his production, for our present
cognizance, thus neatly and vividly divides itself. The divisions are
as marked as the sections on the back of a scarab, though their distinctness is undoubtedly but the final expression of much inward strife.

M. Faguet indeed, who is admirable on this question of our author's duality, gives an account of the romanticism that found its way for him into the real and of the reality that found its way into the romantic; but he none the less strikes us as a curious splendid insect sustained on wings of a different coloration, the right, a vivid red, say, and the left as frank a yellow. This duality has in its sharp operation placed *Madame Bovary* and *L'Education* on one side together and placed together on the other *Salammbô* and *La Tentation*. *Bouvard et Pécuchet* it can scarce be spoken of, I think, as having placed anywhere or anyhow. If it was Flaubert's way to find his subject impossible there was none he saw so much in that light as this last-named, but also none that he appears to have held so important for that very reason to pursue to the bitter end. Posterity agrees with him about the impossibility, but rather takes upon itself to break with the rest of the logic. We may perhaps, however, for symmetry, let *Bouvard et Pécuchet* figure as the tail—if scarabs ever have tails—of our analogous insect. Only in that case we should also append as the very tip the small volume of the *Trois Contes*, preponderantly of the deepest imaginative hue.

His imagination was great and splendid; in spite of which, strangely enough, his masterpiece is not his most imaginative work. *Madame Bovary*, beyond question, holds that first place, and *Madame Bovary* is concerned with the career of a country doctor's wife in a petty Norman town. The elements of the picture are of the fewest, the situation of the heroine almost of the meanest, the material for interest, considering the interest yielded, of the most unpromising; but these facts only throw into relief one of those incalculable incidents that attend the proceedings of genius. *Madame Bovary* was doomed by circumstances and causes—the freshness of comparative youth and good faith on the author's part being perhaps the chief—definitely to take its position, even though its subject was fundamentally a negation of the remote, the splendid and the strange, the stuff of his fondest and most cultivated dreams. It would have seemed very nearly to exclude the free play of the imagination, and the way this faculty on the author's part nevertheless presides is one of those accidents, manœuvres, inspirations, we hardly know what to call them, by which masterpieces grow. He of course knew more or less what he was doing for his book in making Emma Bovary a victim of the imaginative habit, but he must have been far from designing or measuring the total effect which renders the work so general, so complete an expression of himself. His separate idiosyncrasies, his irritated sensibility to the life about him, with the power to catch it in the fact and hold it hard, and his hunger for style and history and poetry, for the rich and the rare, great reverberations, great adumbrations, are here represented together as they are not in his later writings. There is nothing of the near, of the directly observed, though there may be much of the directly perceived and the minutely detailed, either in *Salammbô* or in *Saint Antoine*, and little enough of the extravagance of illusion in that indefinable last word of restrained evocation and cold execution *L'Education sentimentale*. M. Faguet has of course excellently noted this—that the fortune and felicity of the book were assured by the stroke that made the central figure an embodiment of helpless romanticism. Flaubert himself but narrowly escaped being such an embodiment after all, and he is thus able to express the romantic mind with extraordinary truth. As to the rest of the matter he had the luck of having been in possession from the first, having begun so early to nurse and work up his plan that, familiarity and the native air, the native soil, aiding, he had finally made out to the last lurking shade the small sordid sunny dusty village picture, its emptiness constituted and peopled. It is in the background and the accessories that the real, the real of his theme, abides; and the romantic, the romantic of his theme, accordingly occupies the front. Emma Bovary's poor adventures are a tragedy for the very reason that in a world unsuspecting, unassisting, unconsoling, she has herself to distil the rich and rare. Ignorant, unguided, undiverted, ridden by the very nature and mixture of her consciousness, she makes of the business an inordinate failure, a failure which in its turn makes for Flaubert the most pointed, the most *told* of anecdotes.

There are many things to say about *Madame Bovary*, but an old admirer of the book would be but half-hearted—so far as they represent reserves or puzzlements—were he not to note first of all the circumstances by which it is most endeared to him. To remember it from far back is to have been present all along at a process of singular interest to a literary mind, a case indeed full of comfort and cheer. The finest of Flaubert's novels is to-day, on the French shelf of fiction, one of the first of the classics; it has attained that position, slowly, but steadily, before our eyes; and we seem so to follow the evolution of the fate of a classic. We see how the thing takes place; which we rarely can, for we mostly miss either the beginning or the end, especially in the case of a consecration as complete as this. The consecrations of the past are too far behind and those of the future too far in front. That the production before us *should* have come in for the heavenly crown may be a fact to offer English and American readers a mystifying side; but it is exactly our ground and a part moreover of the total interest. The author of these remarks remembers, as with a sense of the way such things happen, that when a very young person in Paris he took up from the parental table the latest number of the periodical in which Flaubert's then duly unrecognized masterpiece was in course of publication. The moment is not historic, but it was to become in the light of history, as may be said, so unforgettable that every small feature of it yet again lives for him: it rests there like the backward end of the span. The cover of the old *Revue de Paris* was yellow, if I mistake not, like that of the new, and *Madame Bovary: Mœurs de Province*, on the inside of it, was already, on the spot, as a title, mysteriously arresting, inscrutably charged. I was ignorant of what had preceded and was not to know till much later what followed; but present to me still is the act of standing there before the fire, my back against the low beplushed and begarnished French chimney-piece and taking in what I might of that instalment, taking it in with so surprised an interest, and perhaps as well such a stir of faint foreknowledge, that the sunny little salon, the autumn day, the window ajar and the cheerful outside clatter of the Rue Montaigne are all now for me more or less in the story and the story more or less in them. The story, however, was at that moment having a difficult life; its fortune was all to make; its merit was so far from suspected that, as Maxime Du Camp—though verily with no excess of contrition—relates, its cloth of gold barely escaped the editorial shears. This with much more, contributes for us to the course of things to come. The book, on its appearance as a volume, proved a shock to the high propriety of the guardians of public morals under the second Empire, and Flaubert was prosecuted as author of a work indecent to scandal. The prosecution in the event fell to the ground, but I should perhaps have mentioned this agitation as one of the very few, of any public order, in his short list. *Le Candidat* fell at the Vaudeville Theatre, several years later, with a violence indicated by its withdrawal after a performance of but two nights, the first of these marked by a deafening uproar; only if the comedy was not to recover from this accident the misprized lustre of the novel was entirely to reassert itself. It is strange enough at present—so far have we travelled since then—that *Madame Bovary* should in so comparatively recent a past have been to that extent a cause of reprobation; and suggestive above all, in such connections, as to the large unconsciousness of superior minds. The desire of the superior mind of the day—that is the governmental, official, legal—to distinguish a book with such a destiny before it is a case conceivable, but conception breaks down before its design of making the distinction purely invidious. We can imagine its knowing so little, however face to face with the object, what it had got hold of; but for it to have been so urged on by a blind inward spring to publish to posterity the extent of its ignorance, that would have been beyond imagination, beyond everything but pity.

And yet it is not after all that the place the book has taken is so overwhelmingly explained by its inherent dignity; for here comes in the curiosity of the matter. Here comes in especially its fund of admonition for alien readers. The dignity of its substance is the dignity of Mme Bovary herself as a vessel of experience—a question as to which unmistakably, I judge, we can only depart from the consensus of French critical opinion. M. Faguet for example commends the character of the heroine as one of the most living and discriminated figures of women in all literature, praises it as a field for the display of the romantic spirit that leaves nothing to be desired. Subject to an observation I shall presently make and that bears heavily in general, I think, on Flaubert as a painter of life, subject to this restriction he is right; which is a proof that a work of art may be markedly open to objection and at the same time be rare in its kind, and that when it is perfect to this point nothing else particularly matters. *Madame Bovary* has a perfection that not only stamps it, but that makes it stand almost alone; it holds itself with such a supreme unapproachable assurance as both excites and defies judgment. For it deals not in the least, as to unapproachability, with things exalted or refined; it only confers on its sufficiently vulgar elements of exhibition a final unsurpassable form. The form is in *itself* as interesting, as active, as much of the essence of the subject as the idea, and yet so close is its fit and so inseparable its life that we catch it at no moment on any errand of its own. That verily is to *be* interesting—all round; that is to be genuine and whole. The work is a classic because the thing, such as it is, is ideally *done*, and because it shows that in such doing eternal beauty may dwell. A pretty young woman who lives, socially and morally speaking, in a hole, and who is ignorant, foolish, flimsy, unhappy, takes a pair of lovers by whom she is successively deserted; in the midst of the bewilderment of which, giving up her husband and her child, letting everything go, she sinks deeper into duplicity, debt, despair, and arrives on the spot, on the small scene itself of her poor depravities, at a pitiful tragic end. In especial she does these things while remaining absorbed in romantic intention and vision, and she remains absorbed in romantic intention and vision while fairly rolling in the dust. That is the triumph of the book as the triumph stands, that Emma interests us by the nature of her consciousness and the play of her mind, thanks to the reality and beauty with which those sources are invested. It is not only that they represent *her* state; they are so true, so observed and felt, and especially so shown, that they represent the state, actual or potential, of all persons like her, persons romantically determined. Then her setting, the medium in which she struggles, becomes in its way as important, becomes eminent with the eminence of art; the tiny world in which she revolves, the contracted cage in which she flutters, is hung out in space for her, and her companions in captivity there are as true as herself.

I have said enough to show what I mean by Flaubert's having in this picture expressed something of his intimate self, given his heroine something of his own imagination: a point precisely that brings me back to the restriction at which I just now hinted, in which M. Faguet fails to indulge and yet which is immediate for the alien reader. Our complaint is that Emma Bovary, in spite of the nature of her consciousness and in spite of her reflecting so much that of her creator, is really too small an affair. This critically speaking, is in view both of the value and the fortune of her history, a wonderful circumstance. She associates herself with Frédéric Moreau in *L'Education* to suggest for us a question that can be answered, I hold, only to Flaubert's detriment. Emma taken alone would possibly not so directly press it, but in her company the hero of our author's second study of the "real" drives it home. Why did Flaubert choose, as special conduits of the life he proposed to depict, such inferior and in the case of Frédéric such abject human specimens? I insist only in respect to the latter, the perfection of Madame Bovary scarce leaving one much warrant for wishing anything other. Even here, however, the general scale and size of Emma, who is small even of her sort, should be a warning to hyperbole. If I say that in the matter of Frédéric at all events the answer is inevitably detrimental I mean that it weighs heavily on our author's general credit. He wished in each case to make a picture of experience —middling experience, it is true—and of the world close to him; but if he imagined nothing better for his purpose than such a heroine and such a hero, both such limited reflectors and registers, we are forced to believe it to have been by a defect of his mind. And that sign of weakness remains even if it be objected that the images in question were addressed to his purpose better than others would have been: the purpose itself then shows as inferior. *L'Education sentimentale* is a strange, an indescribable work, about which there would be many more things to say than I have space for, and all of them of the deepest interest. It is moreover, to simplify my statement, very much less satisfying a thing, less pleasing whether in its unity or its variety, than its specific predecessor. But take it as we will, for a success or a failure—M. Faguet indeed ranks it, by the measure of its quantity of intention, a failure, and I on the whole agree with him—the personage offered us as bearing the weight of the drama, and in whom we are invited to that extent to interest ourselves, leaves us mainly wondering what our entertainer could have been thinking of. He takes Frédéric Moreau on the threshold of life and conducts him to the extreme of maturity without apparently suspecting for a moment either our wonder or our protest—"Why, why *him?*" Frédéric is positively too poor for his part, too scant for his charge; and we feel with a kind of embarrassment, certainly with a kind of compassion, that it is somehow the business of a protagonist to prevent in his designer an excessive waste of faith. When I speak of the faith in Emma Bovary as proportionately wasted I reflect on M. Faguet's judgment that she is from the point of view of deep interest richly or at least roundedly representative. Represent-ative of what? he makes us ask even while granting all the grounds of misery and tragedy involved. The plea for her is the plea made for all the figures that live without evaporation under the painter's hand—that they are not only particular persons but types of their kind, and as valid in one light as in the other. It is Emma's "kind" that I question for this responsibility, even if it be inquired of me why I then fail to question that of Charles Bovary, in its perfection, or that of the in-imitable, the immortal Homais. If we express Emma's deficiency as the poverty of her consciousness for the typical function, it is certainly not, one must admit, that she is surpassed in this respect either by her platitudinous husband or by his friend the pretentious apothecary. The difference is none the less somehow in the fact that they are respectively studies but of their character and office, which function in each ex-presses adequately *all* they are. It may be, I concede, because Emma is the only woman in the book that she is taken by M. Faguet as *femininely* typical, typical in the larger illustrative way, whereas the others pass with him for images specifically conditioned. Emma is this same for myself, I plead; she is conditioned to such an excess of the specific, and the specific in her case leaves out so many even of the commoner elements of conceivable life in a woman when we are invited to see that life as pathetic, as dramatic agitation, that we challenge both the author's and the critic's scale of importances. The book is a picture of the middling as much as they like, but does Emma attain even to *that*? Hers is a narrow middling even for a little imaginative person whose "social" significance is small. It is greater on the whole than her capacity of consciousness, taking this all round; and so, in a word, we feel her less illustrational than she might have been not only if the world had offered her more points of contact, but if she had had more of these to give it.

We meet Frédéric first, we remain with him long, as a *moyen*, a provincial bourgeois of the mid-century, educated and not without fortune, thereby with freedom, in whom the life of his day reflects itself. Yet the life of his day, on Flaubert's showing, hangs together with the poverty of Frédéric's own inward or for that matter outward life; so that, the whole thing being, for scale, intention and extension, a sort of epic of the usual (with the Revolution of 1848 introduced indeed as an episode), it affects us as an epic without air, without wings to lift it; reminds us in fact more than anything else of a huge balloon, all of silk pieces strongly sewn together and patiently blown up, but that absolutely refuses to leave the ground. The discrimination I here make as against our author is, however, the only one inevitable in a series of remarks so brief. What it really represents—and nothing could be more curious—is that Frédéric enjoys his position not only without the aid of a single "sympathetic" character of consequence, but even without the aid of one with whom we can directly communicate. Can we communicate with the central personage? or would we really if we could? A hundred times no, and if he himself can communicate with the people shown us as surrounding him this only proves him of their kind. Flaubert on his "real" side was in truth an ironic painter, and ironic to a tune that makes his final accepted state, his present literary dignity and "classic" peace, superficially anomalous. There is an explanation to which I shall immediately come; but I find myself feeling for a moment longer in presence of L'*Education* how much more interesting a writer may be on occasion by the given failure than by the given success. Successes pure and simple disconnect and dismiss him; failures—though I admit they must be a bit qualified— keep him in touch and in relation. Thus it is that as the work of a "grand écrivain" L'*Education*, large, laboured, immensely "written", with beautiful passages and a general emptiness, with a kind of leak in its stored sadness, moreover, by which its moral dignity escapes—thus it is that Flaubert's ill-starred novel is a curiosity for a literary museum. Thus it is also that it suggests a hundred reflections, and suggests perhaps most of them directly to the intending labourer in the same field. If in short, as I have said, Flaubert is the novelist's novelist, this performance does more than any other toward making him so.

I have to add in the same connection that I had not lost sight of Mme Arnoux, the main ornament of *L'Education*, in pronouncing just above on its deficiency in the sympathetic. Mme Arnoux is exactly the author's one marked attempt, here or elsewhere, to represent beauty otherwise than for the senses, beauty of character and life; and what becomes of the attempt is a matter highly significant. M. Faguet praises with justice his conception of the figure and of the relation, the relation that never bears fruit, that keeps Frédéric adoring her, through hindrance and change, from the beginning of life to the end; that keeps her, by the same constraint, forever immaculately "good", from youth to age, though deeply moved and cruelly tempted and sorely tried. Her contacts with her adorer are not even frequent, in proportion to the field of time; her conditions of fortune, of association and occupation are almost sordid, and we see them with the march of the drama, such as it is, become more and more so; besides which—I again remember that M. Faguet excellently notes it—nothing in the nature of "parts" is attributed to her; not only is she not presented as clever, she is scarce invested with a character at all. Almost nothing that she says is repeated, almost nothing that she does is shown. She is an image none the less beautiful and vague, an image of passion cherished and abjured, renouncing all sustenance and yet persisting in life. Only she has for real distinction the extreme drawback that she is offered us quite preponderantly through Frédéric's vision of her, that we see her practically in no other light. Now Flaubert unfortunately has not been able not so to discredit Frédéric's vision, in general, his vision of everyone and everything, and in particular of his own life, that it makes a medium good enough to convey adequately a noble impression. Mme Arnoux is of course ever so much the best thing in his life—which is saying little; but his life is made up of such queer material that we find ourselves displeased at her being "in" it on whatever terms; all the more that she seems scarcely to affect, improve or determine it. Her creator in short never had a more awkward idea than this attempt to give us the benefit of such a conception in such a way; and even though I have still something else to say about that I may as well speak of it at once as a mistake that gravely counts against him. It is but one of three, no doubt in all his work; but I shall not, I trust, pass for extravagant if I call it the most indicative. What makes it so is its being the least superficial; the two others are, so to speak, intellectual, while this is somehow moral. It was a mistake, as I have already hinted, to propose to register in so mean a consciousness as that of such a hero so large and so mixed a quantity of life as *L'Education* clearly intends; and it was a mistake of the tragic sort that is a theme mainly for silence to have embarked on *Bouvard et Pécuchet* at all, not to have given it up sooner than be given up by it. But these were at the worst not wholly compromising blunders. What *was* compromising—and the great point is that it remained so, that nothing has an equal weight against it—is the unconsciousness of error in respect to the opportunity that would have counted as his finest. We feel not so much that Flaubert misses it, for that we could bear; but that he doesn't *know* he misses it is what stamps the blunder. We do not pretend to say how he might have shown us Mme Arnoux better—that was his own affair. What is ours is that he really thought he was showing her as well as he could, or as she might be shown; at which we veil our face. For once that he had a conception quite apart, apart I mean from the array of his other conceptions and more delicate than any, he "went", as we say, and spoiled it. Let me add in all tenderness, and to make up for possibly too much insistence, that it is the only stain on his shield; let me even confess that I should not wonder if, when all is said, it is a blemish no one has ever noticed.

Perhaps no one has ever noticed either what was present to me just above as the partial makeweight there glanced at, the fact that in the midst of this general awkwardness, as I have called it, there is at the same time a danger so escaped as to entitle our author to full credit. I scarce know how to put it with little enough of the ungracious, but I think that even the true Flaubertist finds himself wondering a little that some flaw of taste, some small but unfortunate lapse by the way, *should* as a matter of fact not somehow or somewhere have waited on the demonstration of the platonic purity prevailing between this heroine and her hero—so far as we do find that image projected. It is alike difficult to indicate without offence or to ignore without unkindness a fond reader's apprehension here of a possibility of the wrong touch, the just perceptibly false note. I would not have staked my life on Flaubert's security of instinct in such a connection—as an absolutely fine and predetermined security; and yet in the event that felicity has settled, there is not so much as the lightest wrong breath (speaking of the matter in this light of tact and taste) or the shade of a crooked stroke. One exclaims at the end of the question "Dear old Flaubert after all——!" and perhaps so risks seeming to patronize for fear of not making a point. The point made for what it is worth, at any rate, I am the more free to recover the benefit of what I mean by critical "tenderness" in our general connection—expressing in it as I do our general respect, and my own particular, for our author's method and process and history, and my sense of the luxury of such a sentiment at such a vulgar literary time. It is a respect positive and settled and the thing that has most to do with consecrating for us that loyalty to him as the novelist of the novelist—unlike as it is even the best feeling inspired by any other member of the craft. He may stand for our operative conscience or our vicarious sacrifice; animated by a sense of literary honour, attached to an ideal of perfection, incapable of lapsing in fine from a self-respect, that enable us to sit at ease, to surrender to the age, to indulge in whatever comparative meannesses (and no meanness in art is so mean as the sneaking economic) we may find most comfortable or profitable. May it not in truth be said that we practise our industry, so many of us, at relatively little cost just *because* poor Flaubert, producing the most expensive fictions ever written, so handsomely paid for it? It is as if this put it in our power to produce cheap and thereby sell dear; as if, so expressing it, literary honour being by his example effectively secure for the firm at large and the general concern, on its whole æsthetic side, floated once for all, we find our individual attention free for literary and æsthetic indifference. All the while we thus lavish our indifference the spirit of the author of *Madame Bovary*, in the crosslight of the old room above the Seine, is trying to the last admiration for the thing itself. That production puts the matter into a nutshell: *Madame Bovary*, subject to whatever qualification, is absolutely the most literary of novels, so literary that it covers us with its mantle. It shows us once for all that there is no *intrinsic* call for a debasement of the type. The mantle I speak of is wrought with surpassing fineness, and we may always, under stress of whatever charge of illiteracy, frivolity, vulgarity, flaunt it as the flag of the guild. Let us therefore frankly concede that to surround Flaubert with our consideration is the least return we can make for such a privilege. The consideration moreover is idle unless it be real, unless it be intelligent enough to measure his effort and his success. Of the effort as mere effort I have already spoken, of the desperate difficulty involved for him in making his form square with his conception; and I by no means attach general importance to these secrets of the work-shop, which are but as the contortions of the fastidious muse who is the servant of the oracle. They are really rather secrets of the kitchen and contortions of the priestess of *that* tripod—they are not an upstairs matter. It is of their specially distinctive importance I am now speaking, of the light shed on them by the results before us.

They all represent the pursuit of a style, of the ideally right one for its relations, and would still be interesting if the style had not been achieved. *Madame Bovary, Salammbô, Saint Antoine, L'Education* are so written and so composed (though the last-named in a minor degree) that the more we look at them the more we find in them, under this head, a beauty of intention and of effect; the more they figure in the too often dreary desert of fictional prose a class by themselves and a little living oasis. So far as that desert is of the complexion of our own English speech it supplies with remarkable rarity this particular source of refreshment. So strikingly is that the case, so scant for the most part any dream of a scheme of beauty in these connections, that a critic betrayed at artless moments into a plea for composition may find himself as blankly met as if his plea were for trigonometry. He makes inevitably his reflections, which are numerous enough; one of them being that if we turn our back so squarely, so universally to this order of considerations it is because the novel is so preponderantly cultivated among us by women, in other words by a sex ever gracefully, comfortably, enviably unconscious (it would be too much to call them even suspicious) of the requirements of form. The case is at any rate sharply enough made for us, or against us, by the circumstance that women are held to have achieved on all our ground, in spite of this weakness and others, as great results as any. The judgment is undoubtedly founded: Jane Austen was instinctive and charming, and the other recognitions— even over the heads of the ladies, some of them, from Fielding to Pater —are obvious; without, however in the least touching my contention. For signal examples of what composition, distribution, arrangement can do, of how they intensify the life of a work of art, we have to go elsewhere; and the value of Flaubert for us is that he admirably points the moral. This is the explanation of the "classic" fortune of *Madame Bovary* in especial, though I may add that also of Hérodias and Saint-Julien l'Hospitalier in the *Trois Contes*, as well as an aspect of these works endlessly suggestive. I spoke just now of the small field of the picture in the longest of them, the small capacity, as I called it, of the vessel; yet the way the thing is done not only triumphs over the question of value but in respect to it fairly misleads and confounds us. Where else shall we find in anything proportionately so small such an air of dignity of size? Flaubert *made* things big—it was his way, his ambition and his necessity; and I say this while remembering that in *L'Education* (in proportion I mean again) the effect has not been produced. The subject of *L'Education* is in spite of Frédéric large, but an indefinable shrinkage has overtaken it in the execution. The exception so marked, however, is single; *Salammbô* and *Saint Antoine* are both at once very "heavy" conceptions and very consistently and splendidly high applications of a manner.

It is in this assured manner that the lesson sits aloft, that the spell for the critical reader resides; and if the conviction under which Flaubert labours is more and more grossly discredited among us his compact mass is but the greater. He regarded the work of art as *existing* but by its expression, and defied us to name any other measure of its life that is not a stultification. He held style to be accordingly an indefeasible part of it, and found beauty, interest and distinction as dependent on it for emergence as a letter committed to the post office is dependent on an addressed envelope. Strange enough it may well appear to us to have to apologize for such notions as eccentric. There are persons who consider that style comes of itself—we see and hear at present, I think, enough of them; and to whom he would doubtless have remarked that it goes, of itself, still faster. The thing naturally differs in fact with the nature of the imagination; the question is one of the proprieties and affinities, sympathy and proportion. The sympathy of the author of *Salammbô* was all with the magnificent, his imagination for the phrase as variously noble or ignoble in itself, contributive or destructive, adapted and harmonious or casual and common. The worse among such possibilities have been multiplied by the infection of bad writing, and he denied that the better ever do anything so obliging as to come of themselves. They scarcely indeed for Flaubert "came" at all; their arrival was determined only by fasting and prayer or by patience of pursuit, the arts of the chase, long waits and watches, figuratively speaking, among the peaks or by the waters. The production of a book was of course made inordinately slow by the fatigue of these measures; in illustration of which his letters often record that it has taken him three days[1] to arrive at one right sentence, tested by the

___

[1] It was true, delightfully true, that, extravagance in this province of his life though apparently in no other, being Flaubert's necessity and law, he deliberated and hung fire, wrestled, retreated and returned, indulged generally in a tragi-

pitch of his ideal of the right for the suggestion aimed at. His difficulties drew from the author, as I have mentioned, much resounding complaint; but those voices have ceased to trouble us and the final voice remains. No feature of the whole business is more edifying than the fact that he in the first place never misses style and in the second never appears to have beaten about for it. That betrayal is of course the worst betrayal of all, and I think the way he has escaped it the happiest form of the peace that has finally visited him. It was truly a wonderful success to be so the devotee of the phrase and yet never its victim. Fine as he inveterately desired it should be he still never lost sight of the question Fine for what? It is always so related and associated, so properly part of something else that is in turn part of something other, part of a reference, a tone, a passage, a page, that the simple may enjoy it for its least bearing and the initiated for its greatest. That surely is to be a writer of the first order, to resemble when in the hand and however closely viewed a shapely crystal box, and yet to be seen when placed on the table and opened to contain innumerable compartments, springs and tricks. One is ornamental either way, but one is in the second way precious too.

The crystal box then figures the style of *Salammbô* and *Saint Antoine* in a greater degree than that of *Bovary* because, as the two former express the writer's romantic side, he had in them, while equally covering his tracks, still further to fare and still more to hunt. Beyond this allusion to their completing his duality I shall not attempt closely to characterize them; though I admit that in not insisting on them I press most lightly on the scale in to which he had in his own view cast his greatest pressure. He lamented the doom that drove him so oddly, so ruefully, to choose his subjects, but he lamented it least when these subjects were most pompous and most exotic, feeling as he did that they had then after all most affinity with his special eloquence. In dealing with the near, the directly perceived, he had to keep down his tone, to make the eloquence small; though with the consequence, as we have seen, that in spite of such precautions the whole thing mostly, insists on being ample. The familiar, that is, under his touch, took on character, importance, extension, one scarce knows what to call it,

---

comedy of waste; which I recall a charming expression of on the lips of Edmond de Goncourt, who quite recognized the heroic legend, but prettily qualified it: "Il faut vous dire qu'il y avait là-dedans beaucoup de coucheries et d'école buissonnière." And he related how on the occasion of a stay with his friend under the roof of the Princess Mathilde, the friend, missed during the middle hours of a fine afternoon, was found to have undressed himself and gone to bed to think!

in order to carry the style or perhaps rather, as we may say, sit with proper ease in the vehicle, and there was accordingly a limit to its smallness; whereas in the romantic books, the preferred world of Flaubert's imagination, there was practically no need of compromise. The compromise gave him throughout endless trouble, and nothing would be more to the point than to show, had I space, why in particular it distressed him. It was obviously his strange predicament that the only spectacle open to him by experience and direct knowledge was the bourgeois, which on that ground imposed on him successively his three themes, which he hated, because his experience left him no alternative; his only alternative was given by history, geography, philosophy, fancy, the world of erudition and of imagination, the world especially of this last. In the bourgeois sphere his ideal of ex- pression laboured under protest, for matter, and his pursuit of them, sat no less heavily. But as his style all the while required a certain ex- ercise of pride he was on the whole more at home in the exotic than in the familiar; he escaped above all in the former connection the associations, the disparities he detested. He could be frankly noble in *Salammbô* and *Saint-Antoine*, whereas in *Bovary* and *L'Education* he could be but circuitously and insidiously so. He could in the one case cut his coat according to his cloth—if we mean by his cloth his pre- determined tone, while in the other he had to take it already cut. Singular enough in his life the situation so constituted: the comparatively meagre human consciousness—for we must come back to that in him— struggling with the absolutely large artistic; and the large artistic half wreaking itself on the meagre human and half-seeking a refuge from it, as well as a revenge against it, in something quite different.

Flaubert had in fact command of two refuges which he worked in turn. The first of these was the attitude of irony, so constant in him that *L'Education* bristles and hardens with it and *Bouvard et Pécuchet*— strangest of "poetic" justices—is made as dry as sand and as heavy as lead; the second only was, by processes, by journeys the most expensive, to get away altogether. And we inevitably ask ourselves whether, eschewing the policy of flight, he might not after all have fought out his case a little more on the spot. Might he not have addressed himself to the human still otherwise than in *L'Education* and in *Bouvard*? When one thinks of the view of the life of his country, of the vast French community and its constituent creatures, offered in these productions, one declines to believe it could make up the *whole* vision of a man of his quality. Or when all was said and done was he absolutely and exclusively condemned to irony? The second refuge I speak of, the getting away from the human, the congruously and measurably human, altogether, perhaps becomes in the light of this possibility but an irony the more. Carthage and the Thebaid, Salammbô, Spendius, Matho, Hannon, Saint Anthony, Hilarion, the Paternians, the Marcosians and the Carpocratians, what are all these, inviting because queer, but a confession of supreme impatience with the actual and the near, often queer enough too, no doubt, but not consolingly, not transcendently? Last remains the question whether, even if our author's immediate as distinguished from his remote view had had more reach, the particular gift we claim for him, the perfection of arrangement and form, would have had in certain directions the acquired flexibility. States of mind, states of soul, of the simpler kind, the kinds supposable in the Emma Bovarys, the Frédérics, the Bouvards and the Pécuchets, to say nothing of the Carthaginians and the Eremites—for Flaubert's eremites are eminently artless—these conditions represent, I think, his proved psychological range. And that throws us back remarkably, almost confoundingly, upon another face of the general anomaly. The "gift" was of the greatest, a force in itself, in virtue of which he is a consummate writer; and yet there are whole sides of life to which it was never addressed and which it apparently quite failed to suspect as a field of exercise. If he never approached the complicated character in man or woman—Emma Bovary is not the least little bit complicated—or the really furnished, the finely civilized, was this because, surprisingly, he could not? L'âme française at all events shows in him but ill.

This undoubtedly marks a limit, but limits are for the critic familiar country, and he may mostly well feel the prospect wide enough when he finds something positively well enough done. By disposition or by obligation Flaubert selected, and though his selection was in some respects narrow he stops not too short to have left us three really "cast" works and a fourth of several parts, to say nothing of the element of perfection, of the superlative for the size, in his three nouvelles. What he attempted he attempted in a spirit that gives an extension to the idea of the achievable and the achieved in a literary thing, and it is by this that we contentedly gauge the matter. As success goes in this world of the approximate it may pass for the success of the greatest. If I am unable to pursue the proof of my remark in Salammbô and Saint-Antoine it is because I have also had to select and have found the questions connected with their two companions more interesting. There are numerous judges, I hasten to mention, who, showing the

opposite preference, lose themselves with rapture in the strange bristling archæological picture—yet all amazingly vivified and co-ordinated
—of the Carthaginian mercenaries in revolt and the sacred veil of the
great goddess profaned and stolen; as well in the still more peopled
panorama of the ancient sects, superstitions and mythologies that swim
in the desert before the fevered eyes of the Saint. One may be able,
however, at once to breathe more freely in *Bovary* than in *Salammbô*
and yet to hope that there is no intention of the latter that one has missed.
The great intention certainly, and little as we may be sweetly beguiled,
holds us fast; which is simply the author's indomitable purpose of fully
pervading his field. There are countries beyond the sea in which tracts
are allowed to settlers on condition that they will really, not nominally,
cultivate them. Flaubert is on his romantic ground like one of these
settlers; he makes good with all his might his title to his tract, and in a
way that shows how it is not only for him a question of safety but a
question of honour. Honour demands that he shall set up his home
and his faith there in such a way that every inch of the surface be
planted or paved. He would have been ashamed merely to encamp and,
after the fashion of most other adventurers, knock up a log hut among
charred stumps. This was not what would have been for him taking
artistic possession, it was not what would have been for him even
personal honour, let alone literary; and yet the general lapse from in-
tegrity was a thing that, wherever he looked, he saw not only condoned
but acclaimed and rewarded. He lived, as he felt, in an age of mean
production and cheap criticism, the practical upshot of which took
on for him a name that was often on his lips. He called it the hatred
of literature, a hatred in the midst of which, the most literary of men,
he found himself appointed to suffer. I may not, however, follow him
in that direction—which would take us far; and the less that he was
for himself after all, in spite of groans and imprecations, a man of
resources and remedies, and that there was always his possibility of
building himself in.

This he did equally in all his books—built himself into literature by
means of a material put together with extraordinary art; but it leads
me again to the question of what such a stiff ideal imposed on him for
the element of exactitude. This element, in the romantic, was his
merciless law. It was perhaps even in the romantic that—if there could
indeed be degrees for him in such matters—he most despised the loose
and the more-or-less. To be intensely definite and perfectly positive,
to know so well what he meant that he could at every point strikingly

and conclusively verify it, was the first of his needs; and if in addition to being thus synthetically final he could be strange and sad and terrible, and leave the cause of these effects inscrutable, success then had for him its highest savour. We feel the inscrutability in those memorable few words that put before us Frédéric Moreau's start upon his vain course of travel, "Il connût alors la mélancolie des paquebots"; an image to the last degree comprehensive and embracing, but which haunts us, in its droll pathos, without our quite knowing why. But he was really never so pleased as when he could be both rare and precise about the dreadful. His own sense of all this, as I have already indicated, was that beauty comes with expression, that expression is creation, that it *makes* the reality, and only in the degree in which it *is*, exquisitely, expression; and that we move in literature through a world of different values and relations, a blest world in which we know nothing except by style, but in which also everything is saved by it, and in which the image is thus always superior to the thing itself. This quest and multiplication of the image, the image tested and warranted and consecrated for the occasion, was accordingly his high elegance, to which he too much sacrificed and to which *Salammbô* and partly *Saint-Antoine* are monstrous monuments. Old cruelties and perversities, old wonders and errors and terrors, endlessly appealed to him; they constitute the unhuman side of his work, and if we have not the bribe of curiosity, of a lively interest in method, or rather in evocation just *as* evocation, we tread our way among them, especially in *Salammbô*, with a reserve too dry for our pleasure. To my own view the curiosity and the literary interest are equal in dealing with the non-romantic books, and the world presented, the aspects and agents, are less deterrent and more amenable both to our own social and expressional terms. Style itself moreover, with all respect to Flaubert, never *totally* beguiles; since even when we are so queerly constituted as to be ninety-nine parts literary we are still a hundredth part something else. This hundredth part may, once we possess the book—or the book possesses us— make us imperfect as readers, and yet without it should we want or get the book at all? The curiosity at any rate, to repeat, is even greatest for me in *Madame Bovary*, say, for here I can measure, can more directly appreciate, the terms. The aspects and impressions being of an experience conceivable to me I am more touched by the beauty; my interest gets more of the benefit of the beauty even though this be not intrinsically greater. Which brings back our appreciation inevitable at last to the question of our author's lucidity.

I have sufficiently remarked that I speak from the point of view of his interest to a reader of his own craft, the point of view of his extraordinary technical wealth—though indeed when I think of the general power of *Madame Bovary* I find myself desiring not to narrow the ground of the lesson, not to connect the lesson, to its prejudice, with that idea of the "technical", that question of the way a thing is done, so abhorrent, as a call upon attention, in whatever art, to the wondrous Anglo-Saxon mind. Without proposing Flaubert as the type of the newspaper novelist, or as an easy alternative to golf or the bicycle, we should do him less than justice in failing to insist that a masterpiece like *Madame Bovary* may benefit even with the simple-minded by the way it has been done. It derives from its firm roundness that sign of all rare works that there is something in it for every one. It may be read ever so attentively, ever so freely, without a suspicion of how it is written, to say nothing of put together; it may equally be read under the excitement of these perceptions alone, one of the greatest known to the reader who is fully open to them. Both readers will have been transported, which is all any can ask. Leaving the first of them, however that may be, to state the case for himself, I state it yet again for the second, if only on this final ground. The book and its companions represent for us a practical solution, Flaubert's own troubled but settled one, of the eternal dilemma of the painter of life. From the moment this rash adventurer deals with his mysterious matter at all directly his desire is not to deal with it stintedly. It at the same time remains true that from the moment he desires to produce forms in which it shall be preserved, he desires that these forms, things of *his* creation, shall not be, as testifying to his way with them, weak or ignoble. He must make them complete and beautiful, of satisfactory production, intrinsically interesting, under peril of disgrace with those who know. Those who don't know of course don't count for him, and it neither helps nor hinders him to say that every one knows about life. Every one does not—it is distinctly the case of the few; and if it were in fact the case of the many the knowledge still might exist, on the evidence around us, even in an age of unprecedented printing, without attesting itself by a multiplication of masterpieces. The question for the artist can only be of doing the artistic utmost, and thereby of *seeing* the general task. When it is seen with the intensity with which it presented itself to Flaubert a lifetime is none too much for fairly tackling it. It must either be left alone or be dealt with, and to leave it alone is a comparatively simple matter.

To deal with it is on the other hand to produce a certain number of finished works, there being no other known method; and the quantity of life depicted will depend on this array. What will this array, however, depend on, and what will condition the number of pieces of which it is composed? The "finish", evidently, that the formula so glibly postulates and for which the novelist is thus so handsomely responsible. He has on the one side to feel his subject and on the other side to render it, and there are undoubtedly two ways in which his situation may be expressed, especially perhaps by himself. The more he feels his subject the more he *can* render it—that is the first way. The more he renders it the more he *can* feel it—that is the second way. This second way was unmistakably Flaubert's, and if the result of it for him was a bar to abundant production he could only accept such an incident as part of the game. He probably for that matter would have challenged any easy definition of "abundance", contested the application of it to the repetition, however frequent, of the thing not "done". What but the "doing" makes the thing, he would have asked, and how can a positive result from a mere iteration of negatives, or wealth proceed from the simple addition of so many instances of penury? We should here, in closer communion with him, have got into his highly characteristic and suggestive view of the fertilization of subject by form, penetration of the sense, ever, by the expression—the latter reacting creatively on the former; a conviction in the light of which he appears to have wrought with real consistency and which borrows from him thus its high measure of credit. It would undoubtedly have suffered if his books had been things of a loose logic, whereas we refer to it not only without shame but with an encouraged confidence by their showing of a logic so close. Let the phrase, the form that the whole is at the given moment staked on, be beautiful and related, and the rest will take care of itself—such is a rough indication of Flaubert's faith; which has the importance that it was a faith sincere, active and inspiring. I hasten to add indeed that we must most of all remember how in these matters everything hangs on definitions. The "beautiful", with our author, covered for the phrase a great deal of ground, and when every sort of propriety had been gathered in under it and every relation, in a complexity of such, protected, the idea itself, the presiding thought, ended surely by being pretty well provided for.

These, however, are subordinate notes, and the plain question, in the connection I have touched upon, is of whether we would really wish him to have written more books, say either of the type of *Bovary*

or of the type of *Salammbô*, and not have written them so well. When
the production of a great artist who has lived a length of years has been
small there is always the regret; but there is seldom, any more than here,
the conceivable remedy. For the case is doubtless predetermined by
the particular kind of great artist a writer happens to be, and this even
if when we come to the conflict, to the historic case, deliberation and
delay may not all have been imposed by temperament. The admirable
George Sand, Flaubert's beneficent friend and correspondent, is exactly the happiest example we could find of the genius constitutionally
incapable of worry, the genius for whom style "came", for whom the
sought effect was ever quickly and easily struck off, the book freely and
swiftly written, and who consequently is represented for us by up-
wards of ninety volumes. If the comparison were with this lady's
great contemporary the elder Dumas the disparity would be quadrupled, but that ambiguous genius, somehow never really caught by
us in the *fact* of composition, is out of our concern here: the issue is of
those developments of expression which involve a style, and as Dumas
never so much as once grazed one in all his long career, there was not
even enough of that grace in him for a fillip of the finger-nail. Flaubert
is at any rate represented by six books, so that he may on that estimate
figure as poor, while Mme Sand, falling so little short of a hundred,
figures as rich; and yet the fact remains that I can refer the congenial
mind to him with confidence and can do nothing of the sort for it in
respect to Mme Sand. She is loose and liquid and iridescent, as iridescent
as we may undertake to find her; but I can imagine compositions quite
without virtue—the virtue I mean, of sticking together—begotten
by the impulse to emulate her. She had undoubtedly herself the benefit
of her facility, but are we not left wondering to what extent *we* have
it? There is too little in her, by the literary connection, for the critical
mind, weary of much wandering, to rest upon. Flaubert himself
wandered, wandered far, went much roundabout and sometimes lost
himself by the way, but how handsomely he provided for our present
repose! He found the French language inconceivably difficult to write
with elegance and was confronted with the equal truths that elegance
is the last thing that languages, even as they most mature, seem to
concern themselves with, and that at the same time taste, asserting
rights, insists on it, to the effect of showing us in a boundless circum-
jacent waste of effort what the absence of it may mean. He saw the
lesson of this desert of death come back to that—that everything at all
saved from it for us since the beginning had been saved by a soul of

elegance within, or in other words by the last refinement of selection, by the indifference on the part of the very idiom, huge quite other than 'composing' agent, to the individual pretension. Recognizing thus that to carry through the individual pretension is at the best a battle, he adored a hard surface and detested a soft one—much more a muddled; regarded a style without rhythm and harmony as in a work of pretended beauty no style at all. He considered that the failure of complete expression so registered made of the work of pretended beauty a work of achieved barbarity. It would take us far to glance even at his fewest discriminations; but rhythm and harmony were for example most menaced in his scheme by repetition—when repetition had not a positive grace; and were above all most at the mercy of the bristling particles of which our modern tongues are mainly composed and which make of the desired surface a texture pricked through, from beneath, even to destruction, as by innumerable thorns.

On these lines production was of course slow work for him— especially as he met the difficulty, met it with an inveteracy which shows how it *can* be met; and full of interest for readers of English speech is the reflection he causes us to make as to the possibility of success at all comparable among ourselves. I have spoken of his groans and imprecations, his interminable waits and deep despairs; but what would these things have been, what would have become of him and what of his wrought residuum, had he been condemned to deal with a form of speech consisting, like ours, as to one part, of "that" and "which"; as to a second part, of the blest "it", which an English sentence may repeat in three or four opposed references without in the least losing caste; as to a third face of all the "tos" of the infinitive and the preposition; as to a fourth of our precious auxiliaries "be" and "do"; and as to a fifth, of whatever survives in the language for the precious art of pleasing? Whether or no the fact that the painter of "life" among us has to contend with a medium intrinsically indocile, on certain sides, like our own, whether this drawback accounts for his having failed, in our time, to treat us, arrested and charmed, to a single case of crowned classicism, there is at any rate no doubt that we in some degree owe Flaubert's counterweight for that deficiency to *his* having, on his own ground, more happily triumphed. By which I do not mean that *Madame Bovary* is a classic because the "thats", the "its" and the "tos" are made to march as Orpheus and his lute made the beasts, but because the element of order and harmony works as a symbol of everything else that is preserved for us by the history of the book. The history of the book remains the lesson and the important, the delightful thing, remains above all the drama that moves slowly to its climax. It is what we come back to for the sake of what it shows us. We see—from the present to the past indeed, never alas from the present to the future—how a classic almost inveterately grows. Unimportant, unnoticed, or, so far as noticed, contested, unrelated, alien, it has a cradle round which the fairies but scantly flock and is waited on in general by scarce a hint of significance. The significance comes by a process slow and small, the fact only that one perceptive private reader after another discovers at his convenience that the book is rare. The addition of the perceptive private readers is no quick affair, and would doubtless be a vain one did they not—while plenty of other much more remarkable books come and go—accumulate and count. They count by their quality and continuity of attention; so they have gathered for *Madame Bovary*, and so they are held. That is really once more the great circumstance. It is always in order for us to feel yet again what it is we are held by. Such is my reason, definitely, for speaking of Flaubert as the novelist's novelist. Are we not moreover —and let it pass this time as a happy hope!—pretty well all novelists now?

20

EMILE ZOLA

1903

IF it be true that the critical spirit to-day, in presence of the rising tide of prose fiction, a watery waste out of which old standards and landmarks are seen barely to emerge, like chimneys and the tops of trees in a country under flood—if it be true that the anxious observer, with the water up to his chin, finds himself asking for the *reason* of the strange phenomenon, for its warrant and title, so we likewise make out that these credentials rather fail to float on the surface. We live in a world of wanton and importunate fable, we breathe its air and consume its fruits; yet who shall say that we are able, when invited, to account for our preferring it so largely to the world of fact? To do so would be to make some adequate statement of the good the product in question does us. What does it do for our life, our mind, our manners, our morals—what does it do that history, poetry, philosophy may not do, as well or better, to warn, to comfort and command the countless thousands for whom and by whom it comes into being? We seem too often left with our riddle on our hands. The lame conclusion on which we retreat is that "stories" are multiplied, circulated, paid for, on the scale of the present hour, simply because people "like" them. As to why people *should* like anything so loose and mean as the preponderant mass of the "output", so little indebted for the magic of its action to any mystery in the making, is more than the actual state of our perceptions enables us to say.

This bewilderment might be our last word if it were not for the occasional occurrence of accidents especially appointed to straighten out a little our tangle. We are reminded that if the unnatural prosperity of the wanton fable cannot be adequately explained, it can at least be illustrated with a sharpness that is practically an argument. An abstract solution failing we encounter it in the concrete. We catch in short a new impression or, to speak more truly, recover an old one. It was always there to be had, but we ourselves throw off an oblivion, an indifference for which there are plenty of excuses. We become conscious, for our profit, of a *case*, and we see that our mystification came from the way cases had appeared for so long to fail us. None of the shapeless forms about us for the time had attained to the dignity of one. The one I am now conceiving as suddenly effective—for which I fear I must have been regarding it as somewhat in eclipse—is that of Emile Zola, whom, as a manifestation of the sort we are considering, three or four striking facts have lately combined to render more objective and, so to speak, more massive. His close connection with the most resounding of recent public quarrels; his premature and disastrous death; above all, at the moment I write, the appearance of his last-finished novel, bequeathed to his huge public from beyond the grave—these rapid events have thrust him forward and made him loom abruptly larger; much as if our pedestrian critic, treading the dusty highway, had turned a sharp corner.

It is not assuredly that Zola has ever been veiled or unapparent; he had, on the contrary been digging his field these thirty years, and for all passers to see, with an industry that kept him, after the fashion of one of the grand grim sowers or reapers of his brother of the brush, or at least of the canvas, Jean-François Millet, duskily outlined against the sky. He was there in the landscape of labour—he had always been; but he was there as a big natural or pictorial feature, a spreading tree, a battered tower, a lumpish round-shouldered useful hayrick, confounded with the air and the weather, the rain and the shine, the day and the dusk, merged more or less, as it were, in the play of the elements themselves. We had got used to him, and, thanks in a measure just to this stoutness of his presence, to the long regularity of his performance, had come to notice him hardly more than the dwellers in the market-place notice the quarters struck by the town-clock. On top of all accordingly, for our skeptical mood, the sense of his work—a sense determined afresh by the strange climax of his personal history—rings out almost with violence as a reply to our wonder. It is as if an earthquake or some other rude interference had shaken from the town-clock a note of such unusual depth as to compel attention. We therefore once more give heed, and the result of this is that we feel ourselves after a little probably as much enlightened as we can hope ever to be. We have worked round to the so marked and impressive anomaly of the adoption of the futile art by one of the stoutest minds and stoutest characters of our time. This extraordinarily robust worker has found it good enough for him, and if the fact is, as I say, anomalous, we are doubtless helped to conclude that by its anomalies, in future, the bankrupt business, as we are so often moved to pronounce it, will most recover credit.

What is at all events striking for us, critically speaking, is that, in the midst of the dishonour it has gradually harvested by triumphant vulgarity of practice, its pliancy and applicability can still plead for themselves. The curious contradiction stands forth for our relief— the circumstance that thirty years ago a young man of extraordinary brain and indomitable purpose, wishing to give the measure of these endowments in a piece of work supremely solid, conceived and sat down to *Les Rougon-Macquart* rather than to an equal task in physics, mathematics, politics or economics. He saw his undertaking, thanks to his patience and courage, practically to a close; so that it is exactly neither of the so-called constructive sciences that happens to have had the benefit, intellectually speaking, of one of the few most constructive achievements of our time. There then, provisionally at least, we touch bottom; we get a glimpse of the pliancy and variety, the ideal of vividness, on behalf of which our equivocal form may appeal to a strong head. In the name of what ideal on its own side, however, does the strong head yield to the appeal? What is the logic of its so deeply committing itself? Zola's case seems to tell us, as it tells us other things. The logic is in its huge freedom of adjustment to the temperament of the worker, which it carries, so to say, as no other vehicle can do. It expresses fully and directly the whole man, and big as he may be it can still be big enough for him without becoming false to its type. We see this truth made strong, from beginning to end, in Zola's work; we see the temperament, we see the whole man, with his size and all his marks, stored and packed away in the huge hold of *Les Rougon-Macquart* as a cargo is packed away on a ship. His personality is the thing that finally pervades and prevails, just as so often on a vessel the presence of the cargo makes itself felt for the assaulted senses. What has most come home to me in reading him over is that a scheme of fiction so conducted is in fact a capacious vessel. It can carry anything —with art and force in the stowage; nothing in this case will sink it. And it is the only form for which such a claim can be made. All others have to confess to a smaller scope—to selection, to exclusion, to the danger of distortion, explosion, combustion. The novel has nothing to fear but sailing too light. It will take aboard all we bring in good faith to the dock.

And intense vision of this truth must have been Zola's comfort from the earliest time—the years, immediately following the crash of the Empire, during which he settled himself to the tremendous task he had mapped out. No finer act of courage and confidence, I think, is recorded in the history of letters. The critic in sympathy with him returns again and again to the great wonder of it, in which something so strange is mixed with something so august. Entertained and carried out almost from the threshold of manhood, the high project, the work of a lifetime, announces beforehand its inevitable weakness and yet speaks in the same voice for its admirable, its almost unimaginable strength. The strength was in the young man's very person—in his character, his will, his passion, his fighting temper, his aggressive lips, his squared shoulders (when he "sat up") and overweening confidence; his weakness was in that inexperience of life from which he proposed not to suffer, from which he in fact suffered on the surface remarkably little, and from which he was never to suspect, I judge, that he had suffered at all. I may mention for the interest of it that, meeting him during his first short visit to London—made several years before his stay in England during the Dreyfus trial—I received a direct impression of him that was more informing than any previous study. I had seen him a little, in Paris, years before that, when this impression was a perceptible promise, and I was now to perceive how time had made it good. It consisted, simply stated, in his fairly bristling with the betrayal that nothing whatever had happened to him in life but to write Les Rougon-Macquart. It was even for that matter almost more as if Les Rougon-Macquart had written him, written him as he stood and sat, as he looked and spoke, as the long, concentrated, merciless effort had made and stamped and left him. Something very fundamental was to happen to him in due course, it is true, shaking him to his base; fate was not wholly to cheat him of an independent evolution. Recalling him from this London hour one strongly felt during the famous "Affair" that his outbreak in connection with it was the act of a man with arrears of personal history to make up, the act of a spirit for which life, or for which at any rate freedom, had been too much postponed, treating itself at last to a luxury of experience.

I welcomed the general impression at all events—I intimately entertained it; it represented so many things, it suggested, just as it was, such a lesson. You could neither have everything nor be everything— you had to choose; you could not at once sit firm at your job and wander through space inviting initiations. The author of Les Rougon-Macquart had had all those, certainly, that this wonderful company could bring him; but I can scarce express how it was implied in him that his time had been fruitfully passed with them alone. His artistic evolution struck one thus as, in spite of its magnitude, singularly simple, and evidence of the simplicity seems further offered by his

last production, of which we have just come into possession. *Vérité*
truly does give the measure, makes the author's high maturity join
hands with his youth, marks the rigid straightness of his course from
point to point. He had seen his horizon and his fixed goal from the
first, and no cross-scent, no new distance, no blue gap in the hills to
right or to left ever tempted him to stray. *Vérité*, of which I shall have
more to say, is in fact, as a moral finality and the crown of an edifice,
one of the strangest possible performances. Machine-minted and made
good by an immense expertness, it yet makes us ask how, for disinterested observation and perception, the writer had used so much time
and so much acquisition, and how he can all along have handled so
much material without some larger subjective consequence. We really
rub our eyes in other words to see so great an intellectual adventure
as *Les Rougon-Macquart* come to its end in deep desert sand. Difficult
truly to read, because showing him at last almost completely a prey
to the danger that had for a long time more and more dogged his steps,
the danger of the mechanical all confident and triumphant, the book is
nevertheless full of interest for a reader desirous to penetrate. It speaks
with more distinctness of the author's temperament, tone and manner
than if, like several of his volumes, it achieved or enjoyed a successful
life of its own. Its heavy completeness, with all this, as of some prodigiously neat, strong and complicated scaffolding constructed by a
firm of builders for the erection of a house whose foundations refuse
to bear it and that is unable therefore to rise—its very betrayal of a
method and a habit more than adequate, on past occasions, to similar
ends, carries us back to the original rare exhibition, the grand assurance
and grand patience with which the system was launched.

If it topples over, the system, by its own weight in these last applications of it, that only makes the history of its prolonged success the
more curious and, speaking for myself, the spectacle of its origin more
attaching. Readers of my generation, will remember well the publication of *La Conquête de Plassans* and the portent, indefinable but irresistible, after perusal of the volume, conveyed in the general rubric under
which it was a first instalment, "Natural and Social History of a Family
under the Second Empire". It squared itself there at its ease, the announcement, from the first, and we were to learn promptly enough
what a fund of life it masked. It was like the mouth of a cave with a
signboard hung above, or better still perhaps like the big booth at a
fair with the name of the show across the flapping canvas. One strange
animal after another stepped forth into the light, each in its way a

monster bristling and spotted, each a curiosity of that "natural history" in the name of which we were addressed, though it was doubtless not till the issue of *L'Assommoir* that the true type of the monstrous seemed to be reached. The enterprise, for those who had attention, was even at a distance impressive, and the nearer the critic gets to it retrospectively the more so it becomes. The pyramid had been planned and the site staked out, but the young builder stood there, in his sturdy strength, with no equipment save his two hands and, as we may say, his wheel-barrow and his trowel. His pile of material—of stone, brick and rubble or whatever—was of the smallest, but this he apparently felt as the least of his difficulties. Poor, uninstructed, unacquainted, unintroduced, he set up his subject wholly from the outside, proposing to himself wonderfully to get into it, into its depths, as he went.

If we imagine him asking himself what he knew of the "social" life of the second Empire to start with, we imagine him also answering in all honesty: "I have my eyes and my ears—I have all my senses: I have what I've seen and heard, what I've smelled and tasted and touched. And then I've my curiosity and my pertinacity; I've libraries, books, newspapers, witnesses, the material, from step to step, of an *enquête*. And then I've my genius—that is, my imagination, my passion, my sensibility to life. Lastly I've my method, and that will be half the battle. Best of all perhaps even, I've plentiful lack of doubt." Of the absence in him of a doubt, indeed of his inability, once his direction taken, to entertain so much as the shadow of one, *Vérité* is a positive monument—which again represents in this way the unity of his tone and the meeting of his extremes. If we remember that his design was nothing if not architectural, that a "majestic whole", a great balanced façade, with all its orders and parts, that a singleness of mass and a unity of effect, in fine, were before him from the first, his notion of picking up his bricks as he proceeded becomes, in operation, heroic. It is not in the least as a record of failure for him that I note this particular fact of the growth of the long series as on the whole the liveliest interest it has to offer. "I don't know my subject, but I must live into it; I don't know life, but I must learn it as I work"—that attitude and programme represent, to my sense, a drama more intense on the worker's own part than any of the dramas he was to invent and put before us.

It was the fortune, it was in a manner the doom, of *Les Rougon-Macquart* to deal with things almost always in gregarious form, to be a picture of *numbers*, of classes, crowds, confusions, movements, industries

—and this for a reason of which it will be interesting to attempt
some account. The individual life is, if not wholly absent, reflected in
coarse and common, in generalized terms; whereby we arrive precisely
at the oddity just named, the circumstance that, looking out somewhere
and often woefully athirst, for the taste of fineness, we find it not in the
fruits of our author's fancy, but in a different matter altogether. We
get it in the very history of his effort, the image itself of his lifelong
process, comparatively so personal, so spiritual even, and, through all
its patience and pain, of a quality so much more distinguished than
the qualities he succeeds in attributing to his figures even when he
most aims at distinction. There can be no question in these narrow
limits of my taking the successive volumes one by one—all the more
that our sense of the exhibition is as little as possible an impression of
parts and books, of particular "plots" and persons. It produces the
effect of a mass of imagery in which shades are sacrificed, the effect of
character and passion in the lump or by the ton. The fullest, the most
characteristic episodes affect us like a sounding chorus or procession, as
with a hubbub of voices and a multitudinous tread of feet. The setter
of the mass into motion, he himself, in the crowd, figures best, with
whatever queer idiosyncrasies, excrescences and gaps, a being of a substance akin to our own. Taking him as we must, I repeat, for quite
heroic, the interest of detail in him is the interest of his struggle at every
point with his problem.

The sense for crowds and processions, for the gross and the general
was largely the *result* of this predicament, of the disproportion between
his scheme and his material—though it was certainly also in part an
effect of his particular turn of mind. What the reader easily discerns
in him is the sturdy resolution with which breadth and energy supply
the place of penetration. He rests to his utmost on his documents,
devours and assimilates them, makes them yield him extraordinary
appearances of life; but in this way he too improvises in the grand
manner, the manner of Walter Scott and of Dumas the elder. We feel
that he *has* to improvise for his moral and social world, the world as
to which vision and opportunity must come, if they are to come at all,
unhurried and unhustled—must take their own time, helped undoubtedly
more or less by blue-books, reports and interviews, by inquiries "on
the spot", but never wholly replaced by such substitutes without a
general disfigurement. Vision and opportunity reside in a personal
sense and a personal history, and no short cut to them in the interest
of plausible fiction has ever been discovered. The short cut, it is not

too much to say, was with Zola the subject of constant ingenious experiment, and it is largely to this source, I surmise, that we owe the
celebrated element of his grossness. He was *obliged* to be gross, on his
system, or neglect to his cost an invaluable aid to representation, as
well as one that apparently struck him as lying close at hand; and I
cannot withhold my frank admiration from the courage and consistency with which he faced his need.

His general subject in the last analysis was the nature of man; in
dealing with which he took up, obviously, the harp of most numerous
strings. His business was to make these strings sound true, and there
were none that he did not, so far as his general economy permitted,
persistently try. What happened then was that many—say about half,
and these, as I have noted, the most silvered, the most golden—refused
to give out their music. They would only sound false, since (as with
all earnestness he must have felt) he could command them, through
want of skill, of practice, of ear, to none of the right harmony. What
therefore was more natural than that, still splendidly bent on producing his illusion, he should throw himself on the strings he might
thump with effect, and should work them, as our phrase is, for all they
were worth? The nature of man, he had plentiful warrant for holding,
is an extraordinary mixture, but the great thing was to represent a
sufficient part of it to show that it was solidly, palpably, commonly
the nature. With this preoccupation he doubtless fell into extravagance
—there was clearly so much to lead him on. The coarser side of his
subject, based on the community of all the instincts, was for instance
the more practicable side, a sphere the vision of which required but
the general human, scarcely more than the plain physical, initiation, and
dispensed thereby conveniently enough with special introductions or
revelations. A free entry into this sphere was undoubtedly compatible
with a youthful career as hampered right and left even as Zola's own.

He was in prompt possession thus of the range of sympathy that he
could cultivate, though it must be added that the complete exercise of
that sympathy might have encountered an obstacle that would somewhat undermine his advantage. Our friend might have found himself
able, in other words, to pay to the instinctive, as I have called it, only
such tribute as protesting taste (his own dose of it) permitted. Yet
there it was again that fortune and his temperament served him.
Taste as he knew it, taste as his own constitution supplied it, proved
to have nothing to say to the matter. His own dose of the precious
elixir had no perceptible regulating power. Paradoxical as the remark

may sound, this accident was positively to operate as one of his greatest felicities. There are parts of his work, those dealing with romantic or poetic elements, in which the inactivity of the principle in question is sufficiently hurtful; but it surely should not be described as hurtful to such pictures as *Le Ventre de Paris*, as *L'Assommoir*, as *Germinal*. The conception on which each of these productions rests is that of a world with which taste has nothing to do, and though the act of representation may be justly held, as an artistic act, to involve its presence, the discrimination would probably have been in fact, given the particular illusion sought, more detrimental than the deficiency. There was a great outcry, as we all remember, over the rank materialism of *L'Assommoir*, but who cannot see to-day how much a milder infusion of it would have told against the close embrace of the subject aimed at? *L'Assommoir* is the nature of man—but not his finer, nobler, cleaner or more cultivated nature; it is the image of his free instincts, the better and the worse, the better struggling as they can, gasping for light and air, the worst making themselves at home in darkness, ignorance and poverty. The whole handling makes for emphasis and scale, and it is not to be measured how, as a picture of conditions, the thing would have suffered from timidity. The qualification of the painter was precisely his stoutness of stomach, and we scarce exceed in saying that to have taken in and given out again less of the infected air would, with such a resource, have meant the waste of a faculty.

I may add in this connection moreover that refinement of intention did on occasion and after a fashion of its own unmistakably preside at these experiments; making the remark in order to have done once for all with a feature of Zola's literary physiognomy that appears to have attached the gaze of many persons to the exclusion of every other. There are judges in these matters so perversely preoccupied that for them to see anywhere the "improper" is for them straightway to cease to see anything else. The said improper, looming supremely large and casting all the varieties of the proper quite into the shade, suffers thus in their consciousness a much greater extension than it ever claimed, and this consciousness becomes, for the edification of many and the information of a few, a colossal reflector and record of it. Much may be said, in relation to some of the possibilities of the nature of man, of the nature in especial of the "people", on the defect of our author's sense of proportion. But the sense of proportion of many of those he has scandalized would take us further yet. I recall at all events as relevant—for it comes under a very attaching general head—two occasions of long ago, two Sunday afternoons in Paris, on which I found the question of intention very curiously lighted. Several men of letters of a group in which almost every member either had arrived at renown or was well on his way to it, were assembled under the roof of the most distinguished of their number, where they exchanged free confidences on current work, on plans and ambitions, in a manner full of interest for one never previously privileged to see artistic conviction, artistic passion (at least on the literary ground) so systematic and so articulate. "Well, I on my side," I remember Zola's saying, "am engaged on a book, a study of the *mœurs* of the people, for which I am making a collection of all the 'bad words', the *gros mots*, of the language, those with which the vocabulary of the people, those with which their familiar talk, bristles." I was struck with the tone in which he made the announcement—without bravado and without apology, as an interesting idea that had come to him and that he was working, really to arrive at character and particular truth, with all his conscience; just as I was struck with the unqualified interest that his plan excited. It was *on* a plan that he was working—formidably, almost grimly, as his fatigued face showed; and the whole consideration of this interesting element partook of the general seriousness.

But there comes back to me also as a companion-piece to this another day, after some interval, on which the interest was excited by the fact that the work for love of which the brave license had been taken was actually under the ban of the daily newspaper that had engaged to "serialize" it. Publication had definitively ceased. The thing had run a part of its course, but it had outrun the courage of editors and the curiosity of subscribers—that stout curiosity to which it had evidently in such good faith been addressed. The chorus of contempt for the ways of such people, their pusillanimity, their superficiality, vulgarity, intellectual platitude, was the striking note on this occasion; for the journal impugned had declined to proceed and the serial, broken off, been obliged, if I am not mistaken, to seek the hospitality of other columns, secured indeed with no great difficulty. The composition so qualified for future fame was none other, as I was later to learn, than *L'Assommoir*; and my reminiscence has perhaps no greater point than in connecting itself with a matter always dear to the critical spirit, especially when the latter has not too completely elbowed out the romantic—the matter of the "origins", the early consciousness, early steps, early tribulations, early obscurity, as so often happens, of productions finally crowned by time.

Their greatness is for the most part a thing that has originally begun so small; and this impression is particularly strong when we have been in any degree present, so to speak, at the birth. The course of the matter is apt to tend preponderantly in that case to enrich our stores of irony. In the eventual conquest of consideration by an abused book we recognize, in other terms, a drama of romantic interest, a drama often with large comic no less than with fine pathetic interweavings. It may of course be said in this particular connection that *L'Assommoir* had not been one of the literary things that creep humbly into the world. Its "success" may be cited as almost insolently prompt, and the fact remains true if the idea of success be restricted, after the inveterate fashion, to the idea of circulation. What remains truer still, however, is that for the critical spirit circulation mostly matters not the least little bit, and it is of the success with which the history of Gervaise and Coupeau nestles in *that* capacious bosom, even as the just man sleeps in Abraham's, that I here speak. But it is a point I may better refer to a moment hence.

Though a summary study of Zola need not too anxiously concern itself with book after book—always with a partial exception from this remark for *L'Assommoir*—groups and varieties none the less exist in the huge series, aids to discrimination without which no measure of the presiding genius is possible. These divisions range themselves to my sight, roughly speaking, however, as scarce more than three in number—I mean if the ten volumes of the *Œuvres critiques* and the *Théâtre* be left out of account. The critical volumes in especial abound in the characteristic, as they were also a wondrous addition to his sum of achievement during his most strenuous years. But I am forced not to consider them. The two groups constituted after the close of *Les Rougon-Macquart*—*Les Trois Villes* and the incomplete *Quatre Evangiles* —distribute themselves easily among the three types, or, to speak more exactly, stand together under one of the three. This one, so comprehensive as to be the author's main exhibition, includes to my sense all his best volumes—to the point in fact of producing an effect of distinct inferiority for those outside of it, which are, luckily for his general credit, the less numerous. It is so inveterately pointed out in allusion to him that one shrinks, in repeating it, from sounding flat; but as he was admirably equipped from the start for the evocation of number and quantity, so those of his social pictures that most easily surpass the others are those in which appearances, the appearances familiar to him, are at once most magnified and most multiplied.

To make his characters swarm, and to make the great central thing they swarm about "as large as life", portentously, heroically big, that was the task he set himself very nearly from the first, that was the secret he triumphantly mastered. Add that the big central thing was always some highly representative institution or industry of the France of his time, some seated Moloch of custom, of commerce, of faith, lending itself to portrayal through its abuses and excesses, its idol-face and great devouring mouth and we embrace the main lines of his attack. In *Le Ventre de Paris* he had dealt with the life of the huge Halles, the general markets and their supply, the personal forces, personal situations, passions, involved in (strangest of all subjects) the alimentation of the monstrous city, the city whose victualling occupies so inordinately much of its consciousness. Paris richly gorged, Paris sublime and indifferent in her assurance (so all unlike poor Oliver's) of "more", figures here the theme itself, lies across the scene like some vast ruminant creature breathing in a cloud of parasites. The book was the first of the long series to show the full freedom of the author's hand, though *La Curée* had already been symptomatic. This freedom, after an interval, broke out on a much bigger scale in *L'Assommoir* in *Au bonheur des dames*, in *Germinal*, in *La Bête humaine*, in *L'Argent*, in *La Débâcle*, and then again, though more mechanically and with much of the glory gone, in the more or less wasted energy of *Lourdes*, *Rome*, *Paris*, of *Fécondité*, *Travail* and *Vérité*.

Au bonheur des dames* handles the colossal modern shop, traces the growth of such an organization as the Bon Marché or the Magasin-du-Louvre, sounds the abysses of its inner life, marshals its population, its hierarchy of clerks, counters, departments, divisions and sub-divisions, plunges into the labyrinth of the mutual relations of its staff, and above all traces its ravage amid the smaller fry of the trade, of all the trades, pictures these latter gasping for breath in an air pumped clean by its mighty lungs. *Germinal* revolves about the coal mines of Flemish France, with the subterranean world of the pits for its central presence, just as *La Bête humaine* has for its protagonist a great railway and *L'Argent* presents in terms of human passion—mainly of human baseness—the fury of the Bourse and the monster of Credit. *La Débâcle* takes up with extraordinary breadth the first act of the Franco-Prussian war, the collapse at Sedan, and the titles of the six volumes of *The Three Cities* and the *Four Gospels* sufficiently explain them. I may mention, however, for the last lucidity, that among these *Fécondité* manipulates, with an amazing misapprehension of means to ends, of remedies to ills, no less thickly peopled a theme than that of the decline in the French birth-rate, and that *Vérité* presents a fictive equivalent of the Dreyfus case, with a vast and elaborate picture of the battle in France between lay and clerical instruction. I may even further mention to clear the ground, that with the close of *Les Rougon-Macquart* the diminution of freshness in the author's energy, the diminution of intensity and, in short, of quality, becomes such as to render sadly difficult a happy life with some of the later volumes. Happiness of the purest strain never indeed, in old absorptions of Zola, quite sat at the feast; but there was mostly a measure of coercion, a spell without a charm. From these last-named productions of the climax everything strikes me as absent but quantity (*Vérité*, for instance, is, with the possible exception of *Nana*, the longest of the list); though indeed there is something impressive in the way his quantity represents his patience.

There are efforts here at stout perusal that, frankly, I have been unable to carry through, and I should verily like, in connection with the vanity of these, to dispose on the spot of the sufficiently strange phenomenon constituted by what I have called the climax. It embodies in fact an immense anomaly; it casts back over Zola's prime and his middle years the queerest grey light of eclipse. Nothing moreover—nothing "literary"—was ever so odd as in this matter the whole turn of the case, the consummation so logical yet so unexpected. Writers have grown old and withered and failed; they have grown weak and sad; they have lost heart, lost ability, yielded in one way or another—the possible ways being so numerous—to the cruelty of time. But the singular doom of this genius, and which began to multiply its symptoms ten years before his death, was to find, with life, at fifty, still rich in him, strength only to undermine all the "authority" he had gathered. He had not grown old and he had not grown feeble; he had only grown all too wrongly insistent, setting himself to wreck, poetically, his so massive identity—to wreck it in the very waters in which he had formally arrayed his victorious fleet. (I say "poetically" on purpose to give him the just benefit of all the beauty of his power.) The process of the disaster, so full of the effect, though so without the intention, of perversity, is difficult to trace in a few words; it may best be indicated by an example or two of its action.

The example that perhaps most comes home to me is again connected with a personal reminiscence. In the course of some talk that I had with him during his first visit to England I happened to ask him what opportunity to travel (if any) his immense application had ever left him, and whether in particular he had been able to see Italy, a country from which I had either just returned or which I was luckily— not having the "Natural History of a Family" on my hands—about to revisit. "All I've done, alas", he replied, "was, the other year, in the course of a little journey to the south, to my own *pays*—all that has been possible was then to make a little dash as far as Genoa, a matter of only a few days." *Le Docteur Pascal*, the conclusion of *Les Rougon-Macquart*, had appeared shortly before, and it further befell that I asked him what plans he had for the future, now that, still *dans la force de l'âge*, he had so cleared the ground. I shall never forget the fine promptitude of his answer—"Oh, I shall begin at once *Les Trois Villes*." "And which cities are they to be?" The reply was finer still —"Lourdes, Paris, Rome".

It was splendid for confidence and cheer, but it left me, I fear, more or less gaping, and it was to give me afterwards the key, critically speaking, to many a mystery. It struck me as breathing to an almost tragic degree the fatuity of those in whom the gods stimulate that vice to their ruin. He was an honest man—he had always bristled with it at every pore; but no artistic reverse was inconceivable for an adven-turer who, stating in one breath that his knowledge of Italy consisted of a few days spent at Genoa, was ready to declare in the next that he had planned, on a scale, a picture of Rome. It flooded his career, to my sense, with light; it showed how he had marched from subject to subject and had "got up" each in turn—showing also how consum-mately he had reduced such getting-up to an artifice. He had success and a rare impunity behind him, but nothing would now be so in-teresting as to see if he could again play the trick. One would leave him, and welcome, Lourdes and Paris—he had already dealt, on a scale, with his own country and people. But was the adored Rome also to be his on such terms, the Rome he was already giving away before possessing an inch of it? One thought of one's own frequentations, saturations—a history of long years, and of how the effect of them had somehow been but to make the subject too august. Was *he* to find it easy through a visit of a month or two with "introductions" and a Bædeker?

It was not indeed that the Bædeker and the introductions didn't show, to my sense, at that hour, as extremely suggestive; they were positively a part of the light struck out by his announcement. They defined the system on which he had brought *Les Rougon-Macquart*

safely into port. He had had his Bædeker and his introductions for
Germinal, for *L'Assommoir*, for *L'Argent*, for *La Débâcle*, for *Au bonheur
des dames*; which advantages, which researches, had clearly been all
the more in character for being documentary, extractive, a matter of
renseignements, published or private, even when most mixed with personal impressions snatched, with *enquêtes sur les lieux*, with facts ob-
tained from the best authorities, proud and happy to co-operate in
so famous a connection. That was, as we say, all right, all the more
that the process, to my imagination, became vivid and was wonderfully reflected back from its fruits. There *were* the fruits—so it hadn't
been presumptuous. Presumption, however, was now to begin, and
what omen mightn't there be in its beginning with such complacency?
Well time would show—as time in due course effectually did. *Rome*, as
the second volume of *The Three Cities*, appeared with high punctuality
a year or two later; and the interesting question, an occasion really
for the moralist, was by that time not to recognize in it the mere
triumph of a mechanical art, a "receipt" applied with the skill of long
practice, but to do much more than this—that is really to give a name
to the particular shade of blindness that could constitute a trap for so
great an artistic intelligence. The presumptuous volume, without
sweetness, without antecedents, superficial and violent, has the minimum instead of the maximum of *value;* so that it betrayed or "gave
away" just in this degree the state of mind on the author's part responsible for its inflated hollowness. To put one's finger on the state
of mind was to find out accordingly what was, as we say, the matter
with him.

It seemed to me, I remember, that I found out as never before when,
in its turn, *Fécondité* began the work of crowning the edifice. *Fécondité*
is physiological, whereas *Rome* is not, whereas *Vérité* likewise is not;
yet these three productions joined hands at a given moment to fit into
the lock of the mystery the key of my meditation. They came to the
same thing, to the extent of permitting me to read into them together
the same precious lesson. This lesson may not, barely stated, sound
remarkable; yet without being in possession of it I should have ventured
on none of these remarks. "The matter with" Zola then, so far as it
goes, was that, as the imagination of the artist is in the best cases not
only clarified but intensified by his equal possession of Taste (deserving
here if ever the old-fashioned honour of a capital), so when he has
lucklessly never inherited that auxiliary blessing the imagination itself
inevitably breaks down as a consequence. There is simply no limit, in

fine, to the misfortune of being tasteless; it does not merely disfigure
the surface and the fringe of your performance—it eats back into the
very heart and enfeebles the sources of life. When you have no taste
you have no discretion, which is the conscience of taste, and when
you have no discretion you perpetrate books like *Rome*, which are
without intellectual modesty, books like *Fécondité*, which are without
a sense of the ridiculous, books like *Vérité*, which are without the finer
vision of human experience.

It is marked that in each of these examples the deficiency has been
directly fatal. No stranger doom was ever appointed for a man so
plainly desiring only to be just than the absurdity of not resting till he
had buried the felicity of his past, such as it was, under a great flat
leaden slab. *Vérité* is a plea for science, as science, to Zola, is *all* truth,
the mention of any other kind being mere imbecility; and the simplification of the human picture to which his negations and exasperations
have here conducted him was not, even when all had been said,
credible in advance. The result is amazing when we consider that the
finer observation is the supposed basis of all such work. It is not that
even here the author has not a queer idealism of his own; this idealism
is on the contrary so present as to show positively for the falsest of his
simplifications. In *Fécondité* it becomes grotesque, makes of the book
the most muscular mistake of *sense* probably ever committed. Where
was the judgment of which experience is supposed to be the guarantee
when the perpetrator could persuade himself that the lesson he wished
in these pages to convey could be made immediate and direct, chalked,
with loud taps and a still louder commentary, the sexes and generations
all convoked, on the blackboard of the "family sentiment"?

I have mentioned, however, all this time but one of his categories.
The second consists of such things as *La Fortune des Rougon* and *La
Curée*, as *Eugène Rougon* and even *Nana*, as *Pot-Bouille*, as *L'Œuvre* and
La Joie de vivre. These volumes may rank as social pictures in the
narrowest sense, studies, comprehensively speaking, of the manners,
the morals, the miseries—for it mainly comes to that—of a bourgeoisie
grossly materialized. They deal with the life of individuals in the
liberal professions and with that of political and social adventures, and
offer the personal character and career, more or less detached, as the
centre of interest. *La Curée* is an evocation, violent and "romantic",
of the extravagant appetites, the fever of the senses, supposedly
fostered, for its ruin, by the hapless second Empire, upon which general
ills and turpitudes at large were at one time so freely and conveniently

fathered. *Eugène Rougon* carries out this view in the high colour of a political portrait, not other than scandalous, for which one of the ministerial *âmes damnées* of Napoleon III, M. Rouher, is reputed, I know not how justly, to have sat. *Nana*, attaching itself by a hundred strings to a prearranged table of kinships, heredities, transmissions, is the vast crowded epos of the daughter of the people filled with poisoned blood and sacrificed as well as sacrificing on the altar of luxury and lust; the panorama of such a "progress" as Hogarth would more definitely have named—the progress across the high plateau of "pleasure" and down the facile descent on the other side. *Nana* is truly a monument to Zola's patience; the subject being so ungrateful, so formidably special, that the multiplication of illustrative detail, the plunge into pestilent depths, represents a kind of technical intrepidity.

There are other plunges, into different sorts of darkness; of which the æsthetic, even the scientific, even the ironic motive fairly escapes us—explorations of stagnant pools like that of *La Joie de vivre*, as to which granting the nature of the curiosity and the substance laboured in, the patience is again prodigious, but which make us wonder what pearl of philosophy, of suggestion or just of homely recognition, the general picture, as of rats dying in a hole, has to offer. Our various senses, sight, smell, sound, touch, are, as with Zola always, more or less convinced; but when the particular effect upon each of these is added to the effect upon the others the mind still remains bewilderedly unconscious of any use for the total. I am not sure indeed that the case is in this respect better with the productions of the third order—*La Faute de l'Abbé Mouret*, *Une Page d'amour*, *Le Rêve*, *Le Docteur Pascal*—in which the appeal is more directly, is in fact quite earnestly, to the moral vision; so much, on such ground, was to depend precisely on those discriminations in which the writer is least at home. The volumes whose names I have just quoted are his express tribute to the "ideal", to the select and the charming—fair fruits of invention intended to remove from the mouth so far as possible the bitterness of the ugly things in which so much of the rest of his work had been condemned to consist. The subjects in question then are "idyllic" and the treatment poetic, concerned essentially to please on the largest lines and involving at every turn that salutary need. They are matters of conscious delicacy, and nothing might interest us more than to see what, in the shock of the potent forces enlisted, becomes of this shy element. Nothing might interest us more, literally, and might positively affect us more, even very nearly to tears, though indeed sometimes also to smiles, than to see the constructor of *Les Rougon-Macquart* trying, "for all he is worth", to be fine with fineness, finely tender, finely true —trying to be, as it is called, distinguished—in face of constitutional hindrance.

The effort is admirably honest, the tug at his subject splendidly strong; but the consequences remain of the strangest, and we get the impression that—as representing discriminations unattainable—they are somehow the price he paid. *Le Docteur Pascal*, for instance, which winds up the long chronicle on the romantic note, on the note of in-voked beauty, in order to sweeten, as it were, the total draught—*Le Docteur Pascal*, treating of the erotic ardour entertained for each other by an uncle and his niece, leaves us amazed at such a conception of beauty, such an application of romance, such an estimate of sweetness, a sacrifice to poetry and passion so little in order. Of course, we definitely remind ourselves, the whole long chronicle is explicitly a scheme, solidly set up and intricately worked out, lighted, according to the author's pretension, by "science", high, dry and clear, and with each part involved and necessitated in all the other parts, each block of the edifice, each "morceau de vie", *physiologically* determined by previous combinations. "How can I help it", we hear the builder of the pyramid ask, "if experience (by which alone I proceed) shows me certain plain results—if, holding up the torch of my famous 'experi-mental method', I find it stare me in the face that the union of certain types, the conflux of certain strains of blood, the intermarriage, in a word, of certain families, produces nervous conditions, conditions temperamental, psychical and pathological, in which nieces *have* to fall in love with uncles and uncles with nieces? Observation and imagination, for any picture of life," he as audibly adds, "know no light but science, and are false to all intellectual decency, false to their own honour, when they fear it, dodge it, darken it. To pretend to any other guide or law is mere base humbug."

That is very well, and the value, in a hundred ways, of a mass of production conceived in such a spirit can never (when robust execution has followed) be small. But the formula really sees us no further. It offers a definition which is no definition. "Science" is soon said—the whole thing depends on the ground so covered. Science accepts surely *all* our consciousness of life; even, rather, the latter closes maternally round it—so that, becoming thus a force within us, not a force outside, it exists, it illuminates only as we apply it. We do emphatically apply it in art. But Zola would apparently hold that it much more applies *us*. On the showing of many of his volumes then it makes but a dim use of us, and this we should still consider the case even were we sure that the article offered us in the majestic name is absolutely at one with its own pretension. This confidence we can on too many grounds never have. The matter is one of appreciation, and when an artist answers for science who answers for the artist—who at the least answers for art? Thus it is with the mistakes that affect us, I say, as Zola's penalties. We are reminded by them that the game of art has, as the phrase is, to be played. It may not with any sure felicity for the result be both taken and left. If you insist on the common you must submit to the common; if you discriminate, on the contrary, you must, however invidious your discriminations may be called, trust to them to see you through.

To the common then Zola, often with splendid results, inordinately sacrifices, and this fact of its overwhelming him is what I have called his paying for it. In *L'Assommoir*, in *Germinal*, in *La Débâcle*, productions in which he must most survive, the sacrifice is ordered and fruitful, for the subject and the treatment harmonize and work together. He describes what he best feels, and feels it more and more as it naturally comes to him—quite, if I may allow myself the image, as we zoologically see some mighty animal, a beast of a corrugated hide and a portentous snout, soaking with joy in the warm ooze of an African riverside. In these cases everything matches, and "science", we may be permitted to believe, has had little hand in the business. The author's perceptions go straight, and the subject, grateful and responsive, gives itself wholly up. It is no longer a case of an uncertain smoky torch, but of a personal vision, the vision of genius, springing from an inward source. Of this genius *L'Assommoir* is the most extraordinary record. It contains, with the two companions I have given it, all the best of Zola, and the three books together are solid ground —or would be could I now so take them—for a study of the particulars of his power. His strongest marks and features abound in them; *L'Assommoir* above all is (not least in respect to its bold free linguistic reach, already glanced at) completely genial, while his misadventures, his unequipped and delusive pursuit of the life of the spirit and the tone of culture, are almost completely absent.

It is a singular sight enough this of a producer of illusions whose interest for us is so independent of our pleasure or at least of our complacency—who touches us deeply even while he most "puts us off", who makes us care for his ugliness and yet himself at the same time pitilessly (pitilessly, that is, for *us*) makes a mock of it, who fills us with a sense of the rich which is none the less never the rare. Gervaise, the most immediately "felt", I cannot but think, of all his characters, is a lame washerwoman, loose and gluttonous, without will, without any principle of cohesion, the sport of every wind that assaults her exposed life, and who, rolling from one gross mistake to another, finds her end in misery, drink and despair. But her career, as presented, has fairly the largeness that, throughout the chronicle, we feel as epic, and the intensity of her creator's vision of it and of the dense sordid life hanging about it is one of the great things the modern novel has been able to do. It has done nothing more completely constitutive and of a tone so rich and full and sustained. The tone of *L'Assommoir* is, for mere "keeping up", unsurpassable, a vast deep steady tide on which every object represented is triumphantly borne. It never shrinks nor flows thin, and nothing for an instant drops, dips or catches; the high-water mark of sincerity, of the genial, as I have called it, is unfailingly kept.

For the artist in the same general "line" such a production has an interest almost inexpressible, a mystery as to origin and growth over which he fondly but rather vainly bends. How after all does it so get itself *done*?—the "done" being admirably the sign and crown of it. The light of the richer mind has been elsewhere, as I have sufficiently hinted, frequent enough, but nothing truly in all fiction was ever built so strong or made so dense as here. Needless to say there are a thousand things with more charm in their truth, with more beguilement of every sort, more prettiness of pathos, more innocence of drollery, for the spectator's sense of truth. But I doubt if there has ever been a more totally *represented* world, anything more founded and established, more provided for all round, more organized and carried on. It is a world practically workable, with every part as functional as every other, and with the parts all chosen for direct mutual aid. Let it not be said either that the equal constitution of parts makes for repletion or excess; the air circulates and the subject blooms; deadness comes in these matters only when the right parts are absent and there is vain beating of the air in their place—the refuge of the fumbler incapable of the thing "done" at all.

The mystery I speak of, for the reader who reflects as he goes, is the wonder of the scale and energy of Zola's assimilations. This wonder besets us above all throughout the three books I have placed first. How, all sedentary and "scientific", did he get so *near*? By what art,

inscrutable, immeasurable, indefatigable, did he arrange to make of
his documents in these connections, a use so vivified? Say he was
"near" the subject of *L'Assommoir* in imagination, in more or less
familiar impression, in temperament and humour, he could not after
all have been near it in personal experience, and the copious person-
alism of the picture, not to say its frank animalism, yet remains its
note and its strength. When the note had been struck in a thousand
forms we had, by multiplication, as a kind of cumulative consequence,
the finished and rounded book; just as we had the same result by the
same process in *Germinal*. It is not of course that multiplication and
accumulation, the extraordinary pair of legs on which he walks, are
easily or directly consistent with his projecting himself morally; this
immense diffusion, with its appropriation of everything it meets,
affects us on the contrary as perpetually delaying access to what we
may call the private world, the world of the individual. Yet since the
individual—for it so happens—is simple and shallow our author's
dealings with him, as met and measured, maintain their resemblance
to those of the lusty bee who succeeds in plumping for an instant, of
a summer morning, into every flower-cup of the garden.

Grant—and the generalization may be emphatic—that the shallow
and the simple are *all* the population of his richest and most crowded
pictures, and that his "psychology", in a psychologic age, remains
thereby comparatively coarse, grant this and we but get another view
of the miracle. We see enough of the superficial among novelists
at large, assuredly, without deriving from it, as we derive from Zola
at his best, the concomitant impression of the solid. It is in general—
I mean among the novelists at large—the impression of the *cheap*,
which the author of *Les Rougon-Macquart*, honest man, never faithless
for a moment to his own stiff standard, manages to spare us even in
the prolonged sand-storm of *Vérité*. The Common is another matter;
it is one of the forms of the superficial—pervading and consecrating
all things in such a book as *Germinal*—and it only adds to the number
of our critical questions. How in the world is it made, this deplorable
democratic malodorous Common, so strange and so interesting?
How is it taught to receive into its loins the stuff of the epic and still,
in spite of that association with poetry, never depart from its nature?
It is in the great lusty game he plays with the shallow and the simple
that Zola's mastery resides, and we see of course that when values are
small it takes innumerable items and combinations to make up the
sum. In *L'Assommoir* and in *Germinal*, to some extent even in *La*

Débâcle, the values are all, morally, personally, of the lowest—the highest is poor Gervaise herself, richly human in her generosities and follies—yet each is as distinct as a brass-headed nail.

What we come to accordingly is the unprecedented case of such a combination of parts. Painters, of great schools, often of great talent, have responded liberally on canvas to the appeal of ugly things, of Spanish beggars, squalid and dusty-footed, of martyred saints or other convulsed sufferers, tortured and bleeding, of boors and louts soaking a Dutch proboscis in perpetual beer; but we had never before had to reckon with so literary a treatment of the mean and vulgar. When we others of the Anglo-Saxon race are vulgar we are, handsomely and with the best conscience in the world, vulgar all through, too vulgar to be in any degree literary, and too much so therefore to be critically reckoned with at all. The French are different—they separate their sympathies, multiply their possibilities, observe their shades, remain more or less outside of their worst disasters. They mostly contrive to get the *idea*, in however dead a faint, down into the lifeboat. They may lose sight of the stars, but they save in some such fashion as that their intellectual souls. Zola's own reply to all puzzlements would have been, at any rate, I take it, a straight summary of his inveterate professional habits. "It is all very simple—I produce, roughly speaking, a volume a year, and of this time some five months go to preparation, to special study. In the other months, with all my *cadres* established, I write the book. And I can hardly say which part of the job is stiffest."

The story was not more wonderful for him than that, nor the job more complex; which is why we must say of his whole process and its results that they constitute together perhaps the most extraordinary *imitation* of observation that we possess. Balzac appealed to "science" and proceeded by her aid; Balzac had *cadres* enough and a tabulated world, rubrics, relationships and genealogies; but Balzac affects us in spite of everything as personally overtaken by life, as fairly hunted and run to earth by it. He strikes us as struggling and all but submerged, as beating over the scene such a pair of wings as were not soon again to be wielded by any visitor of his general air and as had not at all events attached themselves to Zola's rounded shoulders. His bequest is in consequence immeasurably more interesting, yet who shall declare that his adventure was in its greatness more successful? Zola "pulled it off", as we say, supremely, in that he never but once found himself obliged to quit, to our vision, his magnificent treadmill of the pigeon-holed and documented—the region we may qualify as that of experience by imitation. His splendid economy saw him through, he laboured to the end within sight of his notes and his charts.

The extraordinary thing, however, is that on the single occasion when publicly—as his whole manifestation was public—life did swoop down on him, the effect of the visitation was quite perversely other than might have been looked for. His courage in the Dreyfus connection testified admirably to his ability to live for himself and out of the order of his volumes—little indeed as living at all might have seemed a question for one exposed, when his crisis was at its height and he was found guilty of "insulting" the powers that were, to be literally torn to pieces in the precincts of the Palace of Justice. Our point is that nothing was ever so odd as that these great moments should appear to have been wasted, when all was said, for his creative intelligence. *Vérité*, as I have intimated, the production in which they might most have been reflected, is a production unrenewed and un-refreshed by them, spreads before us as somehow flatter and greyer, not richer and more relieved, by reason of them. They really arrived, I surmise, too late in the day; the imagination they might have vivified was already fatigued and spent.

I must not moreover appear to say that the power to evoke and present has not even on the dead level of *Vérité* its occasional minor revenges. There are passages, whole pages, of the old full-bodied sort, pictures that elsewhere in the series would in all likelihood have seemed abundantly convincing. Their misfortune is to have been discounted by our intensified, our finally fatal sense of the *procédé*. Quarrelling with all conventions, defiant of them in general, Zola was yet inevitably to set up his own group of them—as, for that matter, without a sufficient collection, without their aid in simplifying and making possible, how could he ever have seen his big ship into port? Art welcomes them, feeds upon them always; no sort of form is practicable without them. It is only a question of what particular ones we use—to wage war on certain others and to arrive at particular forms. The convention of the blameless being, the thoroughly "scientific" creature possessed impeccably of all truth and serving as the mouthpiece of it and of the author's highest complacencies, this character is for instance a con-vention inveterate and indispensable, without whom the "sympathetic" side of the work could never have been achieved. Marc in *Vérité*, Pierre Froment in *Lourdes* and in *Rome*, the wondrous representatives of the principle of reproduction in *Fécondité*, the exemplary painter of

L'Œuvre, sublime in his modernity and paternity, the patient Jean Macquart of *La Débâcle*, whose patience is as guaranteed as the exactitude of a well-made watch, the supremely enlightened Docteur Pascal even, as I recall him, all amorous nepotism but all virtue too and all beauty of life—such figures show us the reasonable and the good not merely in the white light of the old George Sand novel and its improved moralities, but almost in that of our childhood's nursery and schoolroom, that of the moral tale of Miss Edgeworth and Mr. Thomas Day.

Yet let not these restrictions be my last word. I had intended, under the effect of a reperusal of *La Débâcle*, *Germinal* and *L'Assommoir*, to make no discriminations that should not be in our hero's favour. The long-drawn incident of the marriage of Gervaise and Cadet-Cassis and that of the Homeric birthday feast later on in the laundress's workshop, each treated from beginning to end and in every item of their coarse comedy and humanity, still show the unprecedented breadth by which they originally made us stare, still abound in the particular kind and degree of vividness that helped them, when they appeared, to mark a date in the portayal of manners. Nothing had then been sustained and at every moment of its grotesque and pitiful existence lived into as the nuptial day of the Coupeau pair in especial, their fantastic processional pilgrimage through the streets of Paris in the rain, their bedraggled exploration of the halls of the Louvre museum, lost as in the labyrinth of Crete, and their arrival at last, ravenous and exasperated, at the *guinguette* where they sup at so much a head, each paying, and where we sit down with them in the grease and the perspiration and succumb, half in sympathy, half in shame, to their monstrous pleasantries, acerbities and miseries. I have said enough of the mechanical in Zola; here in truth is, given the elements, almost insupportably the sense of life. That effect is equally in the historic chapter of the strike of the miners in *Germinal*, another of those illustrative episodes, viewed as great passages to be "rendered", for which our author established altogether a new measure and standard of handling, a new energy and veracity, something since which the old trivialities and poverties of treatment of such aspects have become incompatible, for the novelist, with either rudimentary intelligence or rudimentary self-respect.

As for *La Débâcle*, finally, it takes its place with Tolstoi's very much more universal but very much less composed and condensed epic as an incomparably human picture of war. I have been re-reading it, I confess, with a certain timidity, the dread of perhaps impairing the deep impression received at the time of its appearance. I recall the effect it then produced on me as a really luxurious act of submission. It was early in the summer; I was in an old Italian town; the heat was oppressive, and one could but recline, in the lightest garments, in a great dim room and give one's self up. I like to think of the conditions and the emotion, which melt for me together into the memory I fear to imperil. I remember that in the glow of my admiration there was not a reserve I had ever made that I was not ready to take back. As an application of the author's system and his supreme faculty, as a triumph of what these things could do for him, how could such a performance be surpassed? The long, complex, horrific, pathetic battle, embraced, mastered, with every crash of its squadrons, every pulse of its thunder and blood resolved for us, by reflection, by communication from two of the humblest and obscurest of the military units, into immediate vision and contact, into deep human thrills of terror and pity—this bristling centre of the book was such a piece of "doing" (to come back to our word) as could only shut our mouths. That doubtless is why a generous critic, nursing the sensation, may desire to drop for a farewell no term into the other scale. That our author was clearly great at congruous subjects—this may well be our conclusion. If the others, subjects of the private and intimate order, gave him more or less inevitably "away", they yet left him the great distinction that the more he could be promiscuous and collective, the more even he could (to repeat my imputation) illustrate our large natural allowance of health, heartiness and grossness, the more he could strike us as penetrating and true. It was a distinction not easy to win and that his name is not likely soon to lose.

21

GABRIELE D'ANNUNZIO

1904

THE great feast-days of all, for the restless critic, are those much inter-spaced occasions of his really meeting a "case", as he soon enough learns to call, for his convenience and assistance, any supremely contributive or determinant party to the critical question. These are recognitions that make up for many dull hours and dry contacts, many a thankless, a disconcerted gaze into faces that have proved expressionless. Always looking, always hoping for his happiest chance, the inquirer into the reasons of things—by which I mean especially into the reasons of books—so often misses it, so often wastes his steps and withdraws his confidence, that he inevitably works out for himself, sooner or later, some handy principle of recognition. It may be a rough thing, a mere home-made tool of his trade, but it serves his purpose if it keeps him from beginning with mistakes. He becomes able to note in its light the signs and marks of the possible precious identity, able to weigh with some exactitude the appearances that make for its reality. He ends, through much expenditure of patience, by seeing when, how, why, the "case" announces and presents itself, and he perhaps even feels that failure and felicity have worked together to produce in him a sense for it that may at last be trusted as an instinct. He thus arrives at a view of all the candidates, frequently interesting enough, who fall short of the effective title, because he has at need, perhaps even from afar, scented along the wind the strongest member of the herd. He may perhaps not always be able to give us the grounds of his certainty, but he is at least never without knowing it in presence of one of the full-blown products that are the joy of the analyst. He recognizes as well how the state of being full-blown comes above all from the achievement of consistency, of that last consistency which springs from the unrestricted enjoyment of freedom.

Many of us will doubtless not have forgotten how we were witnesses a certain number of years since to a season and a society that had found themselves of a sudden roused, as from some deep drugged sleep, to the conception of the "æsthetic" law of life; in consequence of which this happy thought had begun to receive the honours of a lively appetite and an eager curiosity, but was at the same time surrounded and manipulated by as many different kinds of inexpertness as probably ever huddled together on a single pretext. The spectacle was strange and finally was wearisome, for the simple reason that the principle in question, once it was proclaimed—a principle not easily formulated, but which we may conveniently speak of as that of beauty at any price, beauty appealing alike to the senses and to the mind—was never felt to fall into its place as really adopted and efficient. It remained for us a queer high-flavoured fruit from overseas, grown under another sun than ours, passed round and solemnly partaken of at banquets organized to try it, but not found on the whole really to agree with us, not proving thoroughly digestible. It brought with it no repose, brought with it only agitation. We were not really, not fully convinced, for the state of conviction is quiet. This was to have been the state itself —that is the state of mind achieved and established—in which we were to know ugliness no more, to make the æsthetic consciousness feel at home with us, or learn ourselves at any rate to feel at home with it. That would have been the reign of peace, the supreme beatitude; but stability continued to elude us. We had mustered a hundred good reasons for it, yet the reasons but lighted up our desert. They failed to flower into a single concrete æsthetic "type". One authentic, one masterful specimen would have done wonders for us, would at least have assuaged our curiosity. But we were to be left till lately with our curiosity on our hands.

This is a yearning, however, that Signor D'Annunzio may at last strike us as supremely formed to gratify; so promptly we find in him as a literary figure the highest expression of the reality that our own conditions were to fail of making possible. He has immediately the value of giving us by his mere logical unfolding the measure of our shortcomings in the same direction, that of our timidities and penuries and failures. He throws a straighter and more inevitable light on the æsthetic consciousness than has, to my sense, in our time, reached it from any other quarter; and there is many a mystery that properly interrogated he may help to clear up for us, many an explanation of our misadventure that—as I have glanced at it—he may give. He starts with the immense advantage of enjoying an invoked boon by grace and not by effort, of claiming it under another title than the sweat of his brow and the aspiration of his culture. He testifies to the influence of things that have had time to get themselves taken for granted. Beauty at any price is an old story to him; art and form and style as the aim of the superior life are a matter of course; and it may be said of him, I think, that, thanks to these transmitted and implanted instincts and aptitudes, his individual development begins where the struggle of the mere earnest questioner ends. Signor D'Annunzio is earnest in his way, quite extraordinarily—which is a feature of his physiognomy that we shall presently come to and about which there will be something to say; but we feel him all the while in such secure possession of his heritage of favouring circumstance that his sense of intellectual responsibility is almost out of proportion. This is one of his interesting special marks, the manner in which the play of the æsthetic instinct in him takes on, for positive extravagance and as a last refinement of freedom, the crown of solicitude and anxiety. Such things but make with him for ornament and parade; they are his tribute to civility; the essence of the matter is meanwhile in his blood and his bones. No mistake was possible from the first as to his being of the inner literary camp—a new form altogether of perceptive and expressive energy; the question was settled by the intensity and variety, to say nothing of the precocity, of his early poetic production.

Born at Pescara, in the Regno, the old kingdom of Naples, "towards" 1863, as I find noted by a cautious biographer, he had while scarce out of his teens allowed his lyric genius full opportunity of scandalizing even the moderately austere. He defined himself betimes very much as he was to remain, a rare imagination, a poetic, an artistic intelligence of extraordinary range and fineness concentrated almost wholly on the life of the senses. For the critic who simplifies a little to state clearly, the only ideas he urges upon us are the erotic and the plastic, which have for him about an equal intensity, or of which it would be doubtless more correct to say that he makes them interchangeable faces of the same figure. He began his career by playing with them together in verse, to innumerable light tunes and with an extraordinary general effect of curiosity and brilliancy. He has continued still more strikingly to play with them in prose; they have remained the substance of his intellectual furniture. It is of his prose only, however, that, leaving aside the *Intermezzo*, *L'Isottèo*, *La Chimera*, *Odi Navali* and other such matters, I propose to speak, the subject being of itself ample for one occasion. His five novels and his four plays have extended his fame; they suggest by themselves as many observations as we shall have space for. The group of productions, as the literary industry proceeds among us to-day, is not large, but we may doubt if a talent and temperament, if indeed a whole "view of life",

ever built themselves up as vividly for the reader out of so few blocks.
The writer is even yet enviably young; but this solidity of his literary
image, as of something already seated on time and accumulation, makes
him a rare example. Precocity is somehow an inadequate name for it,
as precocity seldom gets away from the element of promise, and it is
not exactly promise that blooms in the hard maturity of such a performance as *The Triumph of Death*. There are certain expressions of
experience, of the experience of the whole man, that are like final
milestones, milestones for his possible fertility if not for his possible
dexterity; a truth that has not indeed prevented *Il Fuoco*, with its
doubtless still ampler finality, from following the work just mentioned.
And we have had particularly before us, in verse, I must add, *Francesca
da Rimini*, with the great impression a great actress has enabled this
drama to make.

Only I must immediately in this connection also add that Signor
D'Annunzio's plays are, beside his novels, of decidedly minor weight;
testifying abundantly to his style, his romantic sense and his command
of images, but standing in spite of their eloquence only for half of his
talent, largely as he yet appears in *Il Fuoco* to announce himself by
implication as an intending, indeed as a pre-eminent dramatist. The
example is interesting when we catch in the fact the opportunity for
comparing with the last closeness the capacity of the two rival canvases, as they become for the occasion, on which the picture of life
may be painted. The closeness is never so great, the comparison never
so pertinent, as when the separate efforts are but different phases of
the same talent. It is not at any rate under this juxtaposition that the
infinitely greater amplitude of portrayal resident in the novel strikes
us least. It in fact strikes us the more, in this quarter, for Signor
D'Annunzio, that his plays have been with one exception successes.
We must none the less take *Francesca* but for a success of curiosity; on
the part of the author I mean even more than on the part of the public.
It is primarily a pictorial and ingenious thing and, as a picture of
passion, takes, in the total collection, despite its felicities of surface and
arrangement, distinctly a "back seat". Scarcely less than its companions
it overflows with the writer's plenitude of verbal expression, thanks
to which, largely, the series will always prompt a curiosity and even a
tenderness in any reader interested precisely in this momentous
question of "style in a play"—interested in particular to learn by what
æsthetic chemistry a play would as a work of art propose to eschew it.
It is in any such connection so inexpugnable that we have only to be

cheated of it in one place to feel the subject cry aloud for it, like a sick man forsaken, in another.

I may mention at all events the slightly perverse fact that, thanks, on this side, to the highest watermark of translation, Signor D'Annunzio makes his best appeal to the English public as a dramatist. Of each of the three English versions of other examples of his work whose titles are inscribed at the beginning of these remarks it may be said that they are adequate and respectable considering the great difficulty encountered. The author's highest good fortune has nevertheless been at the hands of his French interpreter, who has managed to keep constantly close to him—allowing for an occasional inconsequent failure of courage when the directness of the original *brave l'honnêteté* —and yet to achieve a tone not less idiomatic, and above all not less marked by "authority", than his own. Mr. Arthur Symons, among ourselves, however, has rendered the somewhat insistent eloquence of *La Gioconda* and the intricate and difficult verse of *Francesca* with all due sympathy, and in the latter case especially—a highly arduous task— with remarkably patient skill. It is not his fault, doubtless, if the feet of his English text strike us as moving with less freedom than those of his original; such being the hard price paid always by the translator who tries for correspondence from step to step, tries for an identical order. Even less is he responsible for its coming still more home to us in a translation that the meagre anecdote here furnishing the subject, and on which the large superstructure rests, does not really lend itself to those developments that make a full or an interesting tragic com- plexity. Behind the glamour of its immense literary association the subject of *Francesca* is for purposes of essential, of enlarged exhibition delusive and "short".

These, however, are for the moment side-issues; what is more relevant is the stride taken by our author's early progress in his first novel and his second, *Il Piacere* and *L'Innocente*; a pair from the freshness, the direct young energy of which he was for some of his admirers, too promptly and too markedly to decline. We may take it as characteristic of the intensity of the literary life in him that his brief career falls already thus into periods and supplies a quantity of history sufficient for those differences among students by which the dignity of history appears mainly to be preserved. The nature of his prime inspiration I have already glanced at; and we are helped to a characterization if I say that the famous enthroned "beauty" which operates here, so straight, as the great obsession, is not in any perceptible degree moral beauty. It would be difficult perhaps to find elsewhere in the same compass so much expression of the personal life resting so little on any picture of the personal character and the personal will. It is not that Signor D'Annunzio has not more than once pushed his furrow in this latter direction; but nothing is exactly more interesting, as we shall see, than the seemingly inevitable way in which the attempt falls short.

Il Piacere, the first in date of the five tales, has, though with imperfections, the merit of giving us strongly at the outset the author's scale and range of view, and of so constituting a sort of prophetic summary of his elements. All that is done in the later things is more or less done here, and nothing is absent here that we are not afterwards also to miss. I propose, however, that it shall not be prematurely a question with us of what we miss; no intelligible statement of which, for that matter, in such considerations as these, is ever possible till there has been some adequate statement of what we find. Count Andrea Sperelli is a young man who pays, pays heavily, as we take it that we are to understand, for an unbridled surrender to the life of the senses; whereby it is primarily a picture of that life that the story gives us. He is represented as inordinately, as quite monstrously, endowed for the career that from the first absorbs and that finally is to be held, we suppose, to engulf him; and it is a tribute to the truth with which his endowment is presented that we should scarce know where' else to look for so complete and convincing an account of such adventures. Casanova de Seingalt is of course infinitely more copious, but his autobiography is cheap loose journalism compared with the directed, finely-condensed iridescent epic of Count Andrea.

This young man's years have run but half their course from twenty to thirty when he meets and becomes entangled with a woman more infernally expert even than himself in the matters in which he is most expert—and he is given us as a miracle of social and intellectual accomplishment—the effect of whom is fatally to pervert and poison his imagination. As his imagination is applied exclusively to the employments of "love", this means, for him, a frustration of all happiness, all comfortable consistency, in subsequent relations of the same order. The author's view—this is fundamental—is all of a world in which relations of any other order whatever mainly fail to offer themselves in any attractive form. Andrea Sperelli, loving, accordingly—in the manner in which D'Annunzio's young men love and to which we must specifically return—a woman of good faith, a woman as different as possible from the creature of evil communications, finds the vessel of his spirit itself so infected and disqualified that it falsifies and dries up everything that passes through it. The idea that has virtually determined the situation appears in fact to be that the hero *would* have loved in another manner, or would at least have wished to, but that he had too promptly put any such fortune, so far as his capacity is concerned, out of court. We have our reasons, presently manifest, for doubting the possibility itself; but the theory has nevertheless given its direction to the fable.

For the rest the author's three sharpest signs are already unmistakable: first his rare notation of states of excited sensibility; second his splendid visual sense, the quick generosity of his response to the message, as we nowadays say, of aspects and appearances, to the beauty of places and things; third his ample and exquisite style, his curious, various, inquisitive, always active employment of language as a means of communication and representation. So close is the marriage between his power of "rendering", in the light of the imagination, and whatever he sees and feels, that we should much mislead in speaking of his manner as a thing distinct from the matter submitted to it. The fusion is complete and admirable, so that, though his work is nothing if not "literary", we see at no point of it where literature or where life begins or ends: we swallow our successive morsels with as little question as we swallow food that has by proper preparation been reduced to singleness of savour. It is brought home to us afresh that there is no complete creation without style any more than there is complete music without sound; also that when language becomes as closely applied and impressed a thing as for the most part in the volumes before us the fact of artistic creation is registered at a stroke. It is never more present than in the thick-sown illustrative images and figures that fairly bloom under D'Annunzio's hand. I find examples in *Il Piacere*, as elsewhere, by simply turning the pages. "His will"—of the hero's weakness—"useless as a sword of base temper hung at the side of a drunkard or a dullard." Or of his own southern land in September: "I scarce know why, looking at the country in this season, I always think of some beautiful woman after childbirth, who lies back in her white bed, smiling with a pale, astonished, inextinguishable smile." Or the incision of this: "Where for him now were those unclean short-lived loves that left in the mouth the strange acidity of fruit cut with a steel knife?" Or the felicity of the following, of a southern night seen and felt from the terrace of a villa. "Clear meteors at intervals, streaked the motionless air, running over it as lightly and silently as drops of water on a crystal pane." "The sails on the sea," he says of the same look-out by day, "were as pious and numberless as the wings of cherubim on the gold grounds of old Giottesque panels."

But it is above all here for two things that his faculty is admirable; one of them his making us feel through the windows of his situation, or the gaps, as it were, of his flowering wood, the golden presence of Rome, the charm that appeals to him as if he were one of the pilgrims from afar, save that he reproduces it with an authority in which, as we have seen, the pilgrims from afar have mainly been deficient. The other is the whole category of the phenomena of "passion", as passion prevails between his men and his women—and scarcely anything else prevails; the states of feeling, of ecstasy and suffering engendered, the play of sensibility from end to end of the scale. In this direction he has left no dropped stitches for any worker of like tapestries to pick up. We shall here have made out that many of his "values" are much to be contested, but that where they are true they are as fresh as discoveries; witness the passage where Sperelli, driving back to Rome after a steeple-chase in which he has been at the supreme moment worsted, meets nothing that does not play with significance into his vision and act with force on his nerves. He has before the race had "words", almost blows, on the subject of one of the ladies present, with one of the other riders, of which the result is that they are to send each other their seconds; but the omens are not for his adversary, in spite of the latter's success on the course.

> From the mail-coach, on the return, he overtook the flight towards Rome of Giannetto Rutolo, seated in a small two-wheeled trap, behind the quick trot of a great roan, over whom he bent with tight reins, holding his head down and his cigar in his teeth, heedless of the attempts of policemen to keep him in line. Rome, in the distance, stood up dark against a zone of light as yellow as sulphur; and the statues crowning St. John Lateran looked huge, above the zone, in their violet sky. *Then it was that Andrea fully knew the pain he was making another soul suffer.*

Nothing could be more characteristic of the writer than the way what has preceded flowers into that last reality; and equally in his best manner, doubtless, is such a passage as the following from the same volume, which treats of the hero's first visit to the sinister great lady whose influence on his soul and his senses is to become as the trail of a serpent. She receives him, after their first accidental meeting, with extraordinary promptitude and the last intimacy, receives him in the depths of a great Roman palace which the author, with a failure of taste that is, unfortunately for him, on ground of this sort, systematic, makes a point of naming. "Then they ceased to speak. Each felt the presence of the other flow and mingle with his own, with her own, very blood; till it was *her* blood at last that seemed to have become his life, and his that seemed to have become hers. The room grew larger in the deep silence; the crucifix of Guido Reni made the shade of the canopy and curtains religious; the rumour of the city came to them like the murmur of some far-away flood." Or take for an instance of the writer's way of showing the consciousness as a full, mixed cup, of touching us ourselves with the mystery at work in his characters, the description of the young man's leaving the princely apartments in question after the initiation vouchsafed to him. He had found the great lady ill in bed, with remedies and medicine-bottles at her side, but not too ill, as we have seen, to make him welcome. "Farewell," she has said. "Love me! Remember!"

> It seemed to him, crossing the threshold again, that he heard behind him a burst of sobs. But he went on, a little uncertain, wavering like a man who sees imperfectly. The odour of the chloroform clung to his sense like some fume of intoxication; but at each step something intimate passed away from him, wasting itself in the air, so that, impulsively, instinctively, he would have kept himself as he was, have closed himself in, have wrapped himself up to prevent the dispersion. The rooms in front of him were deserted and dumb. At one of the doors "Mademoiselle" appeared, with no sound of steps, with no rustle of skirts, standing there like a ghost. "This way, signor conte. You won't find it." She had an ambiguous, irritating smile, and her curiosity made her grey eyes more piercing. Andrea said nothing. The woman's presence again disconcerted and troubled him, affected him with a vague repugnance, stirred indeed his wrath.

Even the best things suffer by detachment from their context; but so it is that we are in *possession* of the young man's exit, so it is that the act interests us. Fully announced from the first, among these things, was D'Annunzio's signal gift of never approaching the thing particularly to be done, the thing that so presents itself to the painter, without consummately doing it. Each of his volumes offers thus its little gallery of episodes that stand out like the larger pearls occurring at intervals on a string of beads. The steeplechase in *Il Piacere*, the auction sale of precious trinkets in Via Sistina on the wet afternoon, the morning in the garden at Schifanoia, by the southern sea, when Donna Maria, the new revelation, first comes down to Andrea, who awaits her there in the languor of convalescence from the almost fatal wound received in the duel of which the altercation on the race-course has been the issue: the manner of such things as these has an extraordinary completeness of beauty. But they are, like similar pages in *Il Trionfo* and *Il Fuoco*, not things for adequate citation, not things that lend themselves as some of the briefer felicities. Donna Maria, on the September night at Schifanoia, has been playing for Andrea and their hostess certain old quaint gavottes and toccatas.

> It lived again wondrously beneath her fingers, the eighteenth-century music, so melancholy in its dance-tunes—tunes that might have been composed to be danced, on languid afternoons of some St. Martin's summer, in a deserted park, among hushed fountains and pedestals without their statues, over carpets of dead roses, by pairs of lovers soon to love no more.

Autobiographic in form, *L'Innocente* sticks closely to its theme, and though the form is on the whole a disadvantage to it the texture is admirably close. The question is of nothing less than a young husband's relation to the illegitimate child of his wife, born confessedly as such, and so born, marvellous to say, in spite of the circumstance that the wife adores him, and of the fact that, though long grossly, brutally false to her, he also adores his wife. To state these data is sufficiently to express the demand truly made by them for superiority of treatment; they require certainly two or three almost impossible postulates. But we of course never play the fair critical game with an author, never get into relation with him at all, unless we grant him his postulates. His subject is what is given him—given him by influences, by a process, with which we have nothing to do; since what art, what revelation, can ever really make such a mystery, such a passage in the private life of the intellect, adequately traceable for us? His treatment of it, on the other hand, is what he actively gives; and it is with what he gives that we are critically concerned. If there is nothing in him that effectually induces us to make the postulate, he is then empty for us altogether, and the sooner we have done with him the better; little as the truly curious critic enjoys, as a general thing, having publicly to throw up the sponge.

Tullio Hermil, who finally compasses the death of the little "innocent", the small intruder whose presence in the family life has become too intolerable, retraces with a master's hand each step of the process by which he has arrived at this sole issue. Save that his wife dumbly divines and accepts it, his perpetration of the deed is not suspected, and we take the secret confession of which the book consists as made for the relief and justification of his conscience. The action all goes forward in that sphere of exasperated sensibility which Signor D'Annunzio has made his own so triumphantly that other story-tellers strikes us in comparison as remaining at the door of the inner precinct, as listening there but to catch an occasional faint sound, while he alone is well within and moving through the place as its master. The sensibility has again in itself to be qualified; the exasperation of feeling is ever the essence of the intercourse of some man with some woman who has reduced him, as in *L'Innocente* and in *Il Trionfo*, to homicidal madness, or of some woman with some man who, as in *Il Fuoco*, and also again by a strange duplication of its office in *L'Innocente*, causes her atrociously to suffer. The plane of the situation is thus visibly a singularly special plane; that, always, of the more or less insanely demoralized pair of lovers, for neither of whom is any other personal relation indicated either as actual or as conceivably possible. Here, it may be said on such a showing is material rather alarmingly cut down as to range, as to interest and, not least, as to charm; but here precisely it is that, by a wonderful chance, the author's magic comes effectively into play.

Little in fact as the relation of the erotically exasperated *with* the erotically exasperated, when pushed on either side to frenzy, would appear to lend itself to luminous developments, the difficulty is surmounted each time in a fashion that, for consistency no less than for brilliancy, is all the author's own. Though surmounted triumphantly as to interest, that is, the trick is played without the least falsification of the luckless subjects of his study. They remain the abject victims of sensibility that his plan has originally made them; they remain exasperated, erotic, hysterical, either homicidally or suicidally determined, cut off from any personal source of life that does not poison them; notwithstanding all of which they neither starve dramatically nor suffer us to starve with them. How then is this seemingly inevitable catastrophe prevented? We ask it but to find on reflection that the answer opens the door to their historian's whole secret. The unfortunates are deprived of any enlarging or saving personal relation, that is of any beneficent reciprocity; but they make up for it by their relation both to the *idea* in general and to the whole world of the senses, which is the completest that the author can conceive for them. He may be described as thus executing on their behalf an artistic *volte-face* of the most effective kind, with results wonderful to note. The world of the senses, with which he surrounds them—a world too of the idea, that is of a few ideas admirably expressed—yields them such a crop of impressions that the need of other occasions to vibrate and respond, to act or to aspire, is superseded by their immense factitious agitation. This agitation runs its course in strangely brief periods—a singular note, the brevity, of every situation; but the period is while it lasts, for all its human and social poverty, quite inordinately peopled and furnished. The innumerable different ways in which his concentrated couples are able to feel about each other and about their enclosing cage of golden wire, the nature and the art of Italy—these things crowd into the picture and pervade it, lighting it scarcely less, strange to say, because they are things of bitterness and woe.

It is one of the miracles of the imagination; the great shining element in which the characters flounder and suffer becomes rich and beautiful for them, as well as in so many ways for us, by the action of the writer's mind. They not only live in his imagination, but they borrow it from him in quantities; indeed without this charitable advance they would be poor creatures enough, for they have in each case almost nothing of their own. On the aid thus received they start, they get into motion; it makes their common basis of "passion", desire, enchantment, aversion. The essence of the situation is the same in *Il Trionfo* and *Il Fuoco* as in *L'Innocente*: the temporarily-united pair devour each other, tear and rend each other, wear each other out through a series of erotic convulsions and nervous reactions that are made interesting—interesting to *us*—almost exclusively by the special wealth of their consciousness. The medium in which they move is admirably reflected in it; the autumn light of Venice, the afterglow of her past, in the drama of the elderly actress and the young rhetorician of *Il Fuoco*; the splendour of the summer by the edge of the lower Adriatic in that of the two isolated erotomaniacs of *Il Trionfo*, indissolubly linked at last in the fury of physical destruction into which the man drags the woman by way of retribution for the fury of physical surrender into which she has beguiled him.

As for *L'Innocente* again, briefly, there is perhaps nothing in it to match the Roman passages of *Il Piacere*; but the harmony of the general, the outer conditions pervades the picture; the sweetness of the *villeggiatura* life, the happiness of place and air, the lovability of the enclosing scene, all at variance with the sharpness of the inner tragedy. The inner tragedy of *L'Innocente* has a concentration that is like the carrying, through turns and twists, upstairs and down, of some cup filled to the brim, of which no drop is yet spilled; such cumulative truth rules the scene after we have once accepted the postulate. It is true that the situation as exhibited involves for Giuliana, the young wife, the vulgarest of adventures; yet she becomes, as it unfolds, the figure of the whole gallery in whom the pathetic has at once most of immediate truth and of investing poetry. I much prefer her for beauty and interest to Donna Maria in *Il Piacere* the principal other image of faith and patience sacrificed. We see these virtues as still supreme in her even while she faces, in advance, her ordeal, in respect of which it has been her hope, in fact her calculation, that her husband will have been deceived about the paternity of her child; and she is so truthfully touching when this possibility breaks down that even though we rub our eyes at the kind of dignity claimed for her we participate without reserve in her predicament. The origin of the infant is frankly ignoble, whereas it is on the nobleness of Giuliana that the story essentially hinges; but the contradiction is wonderfully kept from disconcerting us altogether. What the author has needed for his strangest truth is that the mother shall feel exactly as the husband does, and that the husband shall after the first shock of his horror feel intimately and explicitly with the mother. They take in this way the same view of their woeful excrescence; and the drama of the child's advent and of the first months of his existence, his insistent and hated survival, becomes for them in respect to the rest of the world a drama of silence and dissimulation, in every step of which we feel a terror.

The effect, I may add, gains more than one kind of intensity from that almost complete absence of *other* contacts to which D'Annunzio systematically condemns his creatures; introducing here, however, just the two or three that more completely mark the isolation. It may doubtless be conceded that our English-speaking failure of insistence, of inquiry and penetration, in certain directions, springs partly from our deep-rooted habit of dealing with man, dramatically, on his social and gregarious side, as a being the variety of whose intercourse with his fellows, whatever forms his fellows may take, is positively half his interesting motion. We fear to isolate him, for we remember that as we see and know him he scarce understands himself save in action, action which inevitably mixes him with his kind. To see and know him, like Signor D'Annunzio, almost only in passion is another matter, for passion spends itself quickly in the open and burns hot mainly in nooks and corners. Nothing, too, in the picture is more striking than the manner in which the merely sentimental abyss—that of the couple

brought together by the thing that might utterly have severed them—
is consistently and successfully avoided. We should have been certain
to feel it in many other hands yawning but a few steps off. We see the
dreadful facts in themselves, are brought close to them with no interposing vaguenesses or other beggings of the question, and are forcibly
reminded how much more this "crudity" makes for the communication of tenderness—what is aimed at—than an attitude conventionally
more reticent. We feel what the tenderness can be when it rests on *all*
the items of a constituted misery, not one of which is illogically blinked.

For the pangs and pities of the flesh in especial D'Annunzio has in
all his work the finest hand—those of the spirit exist with him indeed
only as proceeding from these; so that Giuliana for instance affects us,
beyond any figure in fiction we are likely to remember, as living and
breathing under our touch and before our eyes, as a creature of organs,
functions and processes, palpable, audible, pitiful physical conditions.
These are facts, many of them, of an order in pursuit of which many
a spectator of the "picture of life" will instinctively desire to stop short,
however great in general his professed desire to enjoy the borrowed
consciousness that the picture of life gives us; and nothing, it may well
be said, is more certain than that we have a right in such matters to
our preference, a right to choose the kind of adventure of the imagination we like best. No obligation whatever rests on us in respect to a
given kind—much light as our choice may often throw for the critic
on the nature of our own intelligence. *There*, at any rate, we are
disposed to say of such a piece of penetration as *L'Innocente*, there is a
particular dreadful adventure, as large as life, for those who can bear
it. The conditions are all present; it is only the reader himself who
may break down. When in general, it may be added, we see readers
do so, this is truly more often because they are shocked at really
finding the last consistency than because they are shocked at missing
it.

Il Trionfo della Morte and *Il Fuoco* stand together as the amplest and
richest of our author's histories, and the earlier, the more rounded and
faultless thing of the two, is not unlikely to serve, I should judge, as an
unsurpassable example of his talent. His accomplishment here reaches its
maximum; all his powers fight for him; the wealth of his expression
drapes the situation represented in a mantle of voluminous folds, stiff
with elaborate embroidery. The "story" may be told in three words:
how Giorgio Aurispa meets in Rome the young and extremely pretty
wife of a vulgar man of business, her unhappiness with whom is

complete, and, falling in love with her on the spot, eventually persuades her—after many troubled passages—to come and pass a series of weeks with him in a "hermitage" by the summer sea, where, in a delirium of free possession, he grows so to hate her, and to hate himself for his subjection to her, and for the prostration of all honour and decency proceeding from it, that his desire to destroy her even at the cost of perishing with her at last takes uncontrollable form and he drags her, under a pretext, to the edge of a sea-cliff and hurls her, interlocked with him in appalled resistance, into space. We get at an early stage the note of that aridity of agitation in which the narrator has expended treasures of art in trying to interest us. "Fits of indescribable fury made them try which could torture each other best, which most lacerate the other's heart and keep it in martyrdom." But they understand, at least the hero does; and he formulates for his companion the essence of their *impasse*. It is not her fault when she tears and rends.

Each human soul carries in it for love but a determinate quantity of sensitive force. It is inevitable that this quantity should use itself up with time, as everything else does; so that when it is used up no effort has power to prevent love from ceasing. Now it's a long time that you have been loving me; nearly two years!

The young man's intelligence is of the clearest; the woman's here is inferior, though in *Il Fuoco* the two opposed faculties are almost equal; but the pair are alike far from living in their intelligence, which only serves to bestrew with lurid gleams the black darkness of their sensual life. So far as the intelligence is one with the will our author fundamentally treats it as cut off from all communication with any other quarter—that is with the senses arrayed and encamped. The most his unfortunates arrive at is to carry their extremely embellished minds with them through these dusky passages as a kind of gilded glimmering lantern, the effect of which is merely fantastic and ironic —a thing to make the play of their shadows over the walls of the catacomb more monstrous and sinister. Again in the first pages of *Il Trionfo* the glimmer is given.

He recognized the injustice of any resentment against her, because he recognized the fatal necessities that controlled them alike. No, his misery came from no other human creature; it came from the very essence of life. The lover had not the lover to complain of, but simply love itself. Love, towards which his whole being reached out, from within, with a rush not to be checked, love was of all the sad things of this earth the most lamentably sad. And to this supreme sadness he was perhaps condemned till death.

That, in a nutshell, is D'Annunzio's subject-matter; not simply that his characters sees in advance what love is worth for them, but that they nevertheless need to make it the totality of their consciousness. In *Il Trionfo* and *Il Fuoco* the law just expressed is put into play at the expense of the woman, with the difference, however, that in the latter tale the woman perceives and judges, suffers in mind, so to speak, as well as in nerves and in temper. But it would be hard to say in which of these two productions the inexhaustible magic of Italy most helps the effect, most hangs over the story in such a way as to be one with it and to make the ugliness and the beauty melt together. The ugliness, it is to be noted, is continually *presumed* absent; the pursuit and cultivation of beauty—that fruitful preoccupation which above all, I have said, gives the author his value as our "case"—being the very ground on which the whole thing rests. The ugliness is an accident, a treachery of fate, the intrusion of a foreign substance—having for the most part in the scheme itself no admitted inevitability. Against it every provision is made that the most developed taste in the world can suggest; for, ostensibly, transcendently, Signor D'Annunzio's *is* the most developed taste in the world—his and that of the ferocious yet so contracted *conoscenti* his heroes, whose virtual identity with himself, affirmed with a strangely misplaced complacency by some of his critics, one would surely hesitate to take for granted. It is the wondrous physical and other endowments of the two heroines of *Il Piacere*, it is the joy and splendour of the hero's intercourse with them, to say nothing of the lustre of his own person, descent, talents, possessions, and of the great general setting in which everything is offered—it is all this that makes up the picture, with the constant suggestion that nothing of a baser quality for the æsthetic sense, or at the worst for a pampered curiosity, might hope so much as to live in it. The case is the same in *L'Innocente*, a scene all primarily smothered in flowers and fruits and fragrances and soft Italian airs, in every implication of flattered embowered constantly-renewed desire, which happens to be a blighted felicity only for the very reason that the cultivation of delight—in the form of the wife's luckless experiment—has so awkwardly overleaped itself. Whatever furthermore we may reflectively think either of the Ippolita of *Il Trionfo* or of her companion's scheme of existence with her, it is enchanting grace, strange, original, irresistible in kind and degree, that she is given us as representing; just as her material situation with her young man during the greater part of the tale is a constant communion, for both of them, with the poetry and the nobleness of classic landscape, of nature consecrated by association.

The mixture reaches its maximum, however, in *Il Fuoco*, if not perhaps in *The Virgins of the Rocks*; the mixture I mean of every exhibited element of personal charm, distinction and interest, with every insidious local influence, every glamour of place, season and surrounding object. The heroine of the first-named is a great tragic actress, exquisite of aspect, intelligence and magnanimity, exquisite for everything but for being unfortunately middle-aged, battered, marked, as we are constantly reminded, by all the aftersense of a career of promiscuous carnal connections. The hero is a man of letters, a poet, a dramatist of infinite reputation and resource, and their union is steeped to the eyes in the gorgeous medium of Venice, the moods of whose melancholy and the voices of whose past are an active part of the perpetual concert. But we see *all* the persons introduced to us yearn and strain to exercise their perceptions and taste their impressions as deeply as possible, conspiring together to interweave them with the pleasures of passion. They "go in", as the phrase is, for beauty at any cost—for each other's own to begin with; their creator, in the inspiring quest, presses them hard, and the whole effect becomes for us that of an organized general sacrifice to it and an organized general repudiation of everything else. It is not idle to repeat that the value of the Italian background has to this end been inestimable, and that every spark of poetry it had to contribute has been struck from it—with what supreme felicity we perhaps most admiringly learn in *The Virgins of the Rocks*. To measure the assistance thus rendered, and especially the immense literary lift given, we have only to ask ourselves what appearance any one of the situations presented would have made in almost any Cisalpine or "northern" frame of circumstance whatever. Supported but by such associations of local or of literary elegance as *our* comparatively thin resources are able to furnish, the latent weakness in them all, the rock, as to final effect, on which they split and of which I shall presently speak, would be immeasurably less dissimulated. All this is the lesson of style, by which we here catch a writer in the very act of profiting after a curious double fashion. D'Annunzio arrives at it both by expression and by material—that is, by a whole side of the latter; so that with such energy at once and such a good fortune it would be odd indeed if he had not come far. It is verily in the very name and interest of beauty, of the lovely impression, that Giorgio Aurispa becomes homicidal in thought and finally in act.

She would in death become for me matter of thought, pure ideality. From a precarious and imperfect existence she would enter into an existence complete and definitive, forsaking for ever the infirmity of her weak luxurious flesh. Destroy to possess— there is no other way for him who seeks the absolute in love.

To these reflections he has been brought by the long, dangerous past which, as the author says, his connection with his mistress has behind it—a past of recriminations of which the ghosts still walk. "It dragged behind it, through time, an immense dark net, all full of dead things." To quote here at all is always to desire to continue, and *Il Trionfo* abounds in the illustrative episodes that are ever made so masterfully concrete. Offering in strictness, incidentally, the only exhibition in all the five volumes of a human relation other than the acutely sexual, it deals admirably enough with this opportunity when the hero pays his visit to his provincial parents before settling with his mistress at their hermitage. His people are of ancient race and have been much at their ease; but the home in the old Apulian town, over-darkened by the misdeed of a demoralized father, is on the verge of ruin, and the dull mean despair of it all, lighted by outbreaks of helpless rage on the part of the injured mother, is more than the visitor can bear, absorbed as he is in impatiences and concupiscences which make everything else cease to exist for him. His terror of the place and its troubles but exposes of course the abjections of his weakness, and the sordid squabbles, the general misery and mediocrity of life that he has to face, constitute precisely, for his personal design, the abhorred challenge of ugliness, the interference of a call other than erotic. He flees before it, leaving it to make shift as it can; but nothing could be more "rendered" in detail than his overwhelmed vision of it.

So with the other finest passages of the story, notably the summer day spent by the lovers in a long dusty dreadful pilgrimage to a famous local miracle-working shrine, where they mingle with the multitude of the stricken, the deformed, the hideous, the barely human, and from which they return, disgusted and appalled, to plunge deeper into consoling but too temporary transports; notably also the incident, masterly in every touch, of the little drowned *contadino*, the whole scene of the small starved dead child on the beach, in all the beauty of light and air and view, with the effusions and vociferations and grimnesses round him, the sights and sounds of the quasi-barbaric life that have the relief of antique rites portrayed on old tombs and urns, that quality and dignity of looming larger which a great feeling on the painter's part ever gives to small things. With this ampler truth the last page of the book is above all invested, the description of the supreme moment— for some time previous creeping nearer and nearer—at which the delirious protagonist beguiles his vaguely but not fully suspicious companion into coming out with him towards the edge of a dizzy place over the sea, where he suddenly grasps her for her doom and the sense of his awful intention, flashing a light back as into their monstrous past, makes her shriek for her life. She dodges him at the first betrayal, panting and trembling.

"Are you crazy?" she cried with wrath in her throat. "Are you crazy?" But as she saw him make for her afresh in silence, as she felt herself seized with still harsher violence and dragged afresh towards her danger, she understood it all in a great sinister flash which blasted her soul with terror. "No no, Giorgio! Let me go! Let me go! Another minute—listen, listen! Just a minute! I want to say——!" She supplicated, mad with terror, getting herself free and hoping to make him wait, to put him off with pity. "A minute! Listen! I love you! Forgive me! Forgive me!" She stammered incoherent words, desperate, feeling herself overcome, losing her ground, seeing death close. "Murder!" she then yelled in her fury. And she defended herself with her nails, with her teeth, biting like a wild beast. "Murder!" she yelled, feeling herself seized by the hair, felled to the ground on the edge of the precipice, lost. The dog meanwhile barked out at the scuffle. The struggle was short and ferocious, as between implacable enemies who had been nursing to this hour in the depth of their souls an intensity of hate. And they plunged into death locked together.

The wonder-working shrine of the Abruzzi, to which they have previously made their way, is a local Lourdes, the resort from far and wide of the physically afflicted, the evocation of whose multitudinous presence, the description of whose unimaginable miseries and ecstasies, grovelling struggles and supplications, has the mark of a pictorial energy for such matters not inferior to that of Emile Zola—to the degree even that the originality of the pages in question was, if I remember rightly, rather sharply impugned in Paris. D'Annunzio's defence, however, was easy, residing as it does in the fact that to handle any subject successfully handled by Zola (his failures are another matter) is quite inevitably to walk more or less in his footsteps, in prints so wide and deep as to leave little margin for passing round them. To which I may add that, though the judgment may appear odd, the truth and force of the young man's few abject days at Guardiagrele, his *casa paterna*, are such as to make us wish that other such corners of life were more frequent in the author's pages. He has the supremely interesting quality in the novelist that he *fixes*, as it were, the tone of every cluster of objects he approaches, fixes it by the consistency and intensity of his reproduction. In *The Virgins of the Rocks* we have also a *casa paterna*, and a thing, as I have indicated, of exquisite and wonderful tone; but the tone here is of poetry, the truth and the force are less measurable and less familiar, and the whole question, after all, in its refined and attenuated form, is still that of sexual pursuit, which keeps it within the writer's too frequent limits. Giorgio Aurispa, in *Il Trionfo*, lives in communion with the spirit of an amiable and melancholy uncle who had committed suicide and made him heir of his fortune, and one of the nephew's most frequent and faithful loyalties is to hark back, in thought, to the horror of his first knowledge of the dead man's act, put before us always with its accompaniment of loud southern resonance and confusion. He is in the place again, he is in the room, at Guardiagrele, of the original appalled vision.

> He heard, in the stillness of the air and of his arrested soul, the small shrill of an insect in the wainscot. And the little fact sufficed to dissipate for the moment the extreme violence of his nervous tension, as the puncture of a needle suffices to empty a swollen bladder. Every particular of the terrible day came back to his memory: the news abruptly brought to Torretta di Sarsa, towards three in the afternoon, by a panting messenger who stammered and whimpered; the ride on horseback, at lightning speed, under the canicular sky and up the torrid slopes, and, during the rush, the sudden faintnesses that turned him dizzy in his saddle; then the house at home, filled with sobs, filled with a noise of doors slamming in the general scare, filled with the strumming of his own arteries; and at last his irruption into the room, the sight of the corpse, the curtains inflated and rustling, the tinkle on the wall of the little font for holy water.

This young man's great mistake, we are told, had been his insistence on regarding love as a form of enjoyment. He would have been in a possible relation to it only if he had learned to deal with it as a form of suffering. This is the lesson brought home to the heroine of *Il Fuoco*, who suffers indeed, as it seems to us, so much more than is involved in the occasion. We ask ourselves continually why; that is we do so at first; we do so before the special force of the book takes us captive and reduces us to mere charmed absorption of its successive parts and indifference to its moral sense. Its defect is verily that it has no moral sense proportionate to the truth, the constant high style of the general picture; and this fact makes the whole thing appear given us simply because it has happened, because it was material that the author had become possessed of, and not because, in its almost journalistic "actuality", it has any large meaning. We get the impression of a direct transfer, a "lift", bodily, of something seen and known, something not really produced by the chemical process of art, the crucible or retort from which things emerge for a new function. Their meaning here at any rate, extracted with difficulty, would seem to be that there is an inevitable leak of ease and peace when a mistress happens to be considerably older than her lover; but even this interesting yet not unfamilar truth loses itself in the great poetic, pathetic, psychologic ceremonial.

That matters little indeed, as I say, while we read; the two sensibilities concerned bloom, in all the Venetian glow, like wondrous water-plants, throwing out branches and flowers of which we admire the fantastic growth even while we remain, botanically speaking, bewildered. They are other sensibilities than those with which we ourselves have community—one of the main reasons of their appearing so I shall presently explain; and, besides, they are isolated, sequestrated, according to D'Annunzio's constant view of such cases, for an exclusive, an intensified and arid development. The mistress has, abnormally, none of the protection, the alternative life, the saving sanity of other interests, ties, employments; while the hero, a young poet and dramatist with an immense consciousness of genius and fame, has for the time at least only those poor contacts with existence that the last intimacies of his contact with his friend's person, her poor *corpo non piu giovane*, as he so frequently repeats, represent for him. It is not for us, however, to contest the relation; it is in the penetrating way again in which the relation is rendered that the writer has his triumph; the way above all in which the world-weary interesting sensitive woman, with her infinite intelligence, yet with her longing for some happiness still among all her experiments untasted, and her genius at the same time for familiar misery, is marked, featured, individualized for us, and, with the strangest art in the world—one of those mysteries of which great talents alone have the trick—at once ennobled with beauty and desecrated by a process that we somehow feel to be that of exposure, to spring from some violation of a privilege. " 'Do with me,' " says the Foscarina on a certain occasion, " 'whatever you will'; and she smiled in her offered abjection. She belonged to him like the thing one holds in one's fist, like the ring on one's finger, like a glove, like a garment, like a word that may be spoken or not, like a draught that may be drunk or poured on the ground." There are some lines describing an hour in which she has made him feel as never before "the incalculable capacity of the heart of man. And it seemed to him as he heard the beating of his own heart and divined the violence of the other beside him that he had in his ears the loud repercussion of the hammer on the hard anvil where human destiny is forged." More than ever here the pitch of the personal drama is taken up by everything else in the scene—everything else being in fact but the immediate presence of Venice, her old faded colour and old vague harmonies, played with constantly as we might play with some rosy fretted faintly-sounding sea-shell.

It would take time to say what we play with in the silver-toned *Virgins of the Rocks*, the history of a visit paid by a transcendent young man—always pretty much the same young man—to an illustrious family whose fortunes have tragically shrunken with the expulsion of the Bourbons from the kingdom of Naples, and the three last lovely daughters of whose house are beginning to wither on the stem, undiscovered, unsought, in a dilapidated old palace, an old garden of neglected pomp, a place of fountains and colonnades, marble steps and statues, all circled with hard bright sun-scorched volcanic scenery. They are tacitly candidates for the honour of the hero's hand, and the subject of the little tale, which deals with scarce more than a few summer days, is the manner of their presenting themselves for his admiration and his choice. I decidedly name this exquisite composition as my preferred of the series; for if its tone is thoroughly romantic the romance is yet of the happiest kind, the kind that consists in the imaginative development of observable things, things present, significant, related to us, and not in a weak false fumble for the remote and the disconnected.

It is indeed the romantic mind itself that makes the picture, and there could be no better case of the absolute artistic vision. The mere facts are soon said; the main fact, above all, of the feeble remnant of an exhausted race waiting in impotence to see itself cease to be. The father has nothing personal left but the ruins of his fine presence and of his old superstitions, a handful of silver dust; the mother, mad and under supervision, stalks about with the delusion of imperial greatness (there is a wonderful page on her parading through the gardens in her rococo palanquin, like a Byzantine empress, attended by sordid keepers, while the others are hushed into pity and awe); the two sons hereditarily tainted, are virtually imbecile; the three daughters, candidly considered, are what we should regard in our Anglo-Saxon world as but the stuff of rather particularly dreary and shabby, quite unutterably idle old maids. Nothing, within the picture, occurs; nothing is done or, more acutely than usual, than everywhere, suffered; it is all a mere affair of the rich impression, the complexity of images projected upon the quintessential spirit of the hero, whose own report is what we have— an affair of the quality of observation, sentiment and eloquence brought to bear. It is not too much to say even that the whole thing is in the largest sense but a theme for style, style of substance as well as of form. Within this compass it blooms and quivers and shimmers with light, becomes a wonderful little walled garden of romance. The young man has a passage of extreme but respectful tenderness with each of the sisters in turn, and the general cumulative effect is scarcely impaired by the fact that "nothing comes" of any of these relations. Too little comes of anything, I think, for any very marked human analogy, inasmuch as if it is interesting to be puzzled to a certain extent by what an action, placed before us, is designed to show or to signify, so we require for this refined amusement at least the sense that some general idea is represented. We must feel it present.

Therefore if making out nothing very distinct in *Le Vergini* but the pictorial idea, and yet cleaving to the preference I have expressed, I let the anomaly pass as a tribute extorted by literary art, I may seem to imply that a book may have a great interest without showing a perfect sense. The truth is undoubtedly that I am in some degree beguiled and bribed by the particularly intense expression given in these pages to the author's æsthetic faith. If he is so supremely a "case" it is because this production has so much to say for it, and says it with such a pride of confidence, with an assurance and an elegance that fairly make it the last conceivable word of such a profession. The observations recorded have their origin in the narrator's passionate reaction against the vulgarity of the day. All the writer's young men react; but Cantelmo, in the volume before us, reacts with the finest contempt. He is, like his brothers, a *raffiné* conservative, believing really, so far as we understand it, only in the virtue of "race" and in the grand manner. The blighted Virgins, with all that surrounds them, are an affirmation of the grand manner—that is of the shame and scandal of what in an odious age it has been reduced to. It consists indeed of a number of different things which I may not pretend to have completely fitted together, but which are, with other elements, the sense of the supremacy of beauty, the supremacy of style and, last not least, of the personal will, manifested for the most part as a cold insolence of attitude

—not manifested as anything much more edifying. What it really appears to come to is that the will is a sort of romantic ornament, the application of which, for life in the present and the future, remains awkwardly vague, though we are always to remember that it has been splendidly forged in the past. The will in short *is* beauty, is style, is elegance, is art—especially in members of great families and possessors of large fortunes. That of the hero of *Le Vergin* has been handed down to him direct, as by a series of testamentary provisions, from a splendid young ancestor for whose memory and whose portrait he has a worship, a warrior and virtuoso of the Renaissance, the model of his spirit.

> He represents for me the mysterious meaning of the power of style, not violable by any one, and least of all ever by myself in my own person.

And elsewhere—

> The sublime hands of Violante [the beauty and interest of hands play a great part, in general, in the picture], pressing out in drops the essence of the tender flowers and letting them fall bruised to the ground, performed an act which, as a symbol, corresponded perfectly to the character of my style; this being ever to extract from a thing its very last scent of life, to take from it all it could give and leave it exhausted. Was not this one of the most important offices of my art of life?

The book is a singularly rich exhibition of an inward state, the state of private poetic intercourse with things, the kind of current that in a given personal experience flows to and fro between the imagination and the world. It represents the aesthetic consciousness, proud of its conquests and discoveries, and yet trying, after all, as with the vexed sense of a want, to look through other windows and eyes. It goes all lengths, as is of course indispensable on behalf of a personage constituting a case. "I firmly believe that the greatest sum of future dominion will be precisely that which shall have its base and its apex in Rome" such being in our personage the confidence of the "Latin" spirit. Does it not really all come back to style? It was to the Latin spirit that the Renaissance was primarily vouchsafed; and was not, for a simplified statement, the last word of the Renaissance the question of taste? That is the aesthetic question; and when the Latin spirit after many misadventures again clears itself we shall see how all the while this treasure has been in its keeping. Let us as frankly as possible add that there is a whole side on which the clearance may appear to have made quite a splendid advance with Signor D'Annunzio himself.

But there is another side, which I have been too long in coming to, yet which I confess is for me much the more interesting. No account of our author is complete unless we really make out what becomes of that aesthetic consistency in him which, as I have said, our own collective and cultivated effort is so earnestly attempting and yet so pathetically, if not so grotesquely, missing. We are struck, unmistakably, early in our acquaintance with these productions, by the fact that their total beauty somehow extraordinarily fails to march with their beauty of parts, and that something is all the while at work undermining that bulwark against ugliness which it is their obvious theory of their own office to throw up. The disparity troubles and haunts us just in proportion as we admire; and our uneasy wonderment over the source of the weakness fails to spoil our pleasure only because such questions have so lively an interest for the critic. We feel ourselves somehow in presence of a singular incessant *leak* in the effect of distinction so artfully and copiously produced, and we apply our test up and down in the manner of the inquiring person who, with a tin implement and a small flame, searches our premises for an escape of gas. The bad smell has, as it were, to be accounted for; and yet where, amid the roses and lilies and pomegranates, the thousand essences and fragrances, can such a thing possibly be? Quite abruptly, I think, at last (if we have been much under the spell) our test gives us the news, not unaccompanied with the shock with which we see our escape of gas spring into flame. There is no mistaking it; the leak of distinction is produced by a positive element of the vulgar; and that the vulgar should flourish in an air so charged, intellectually speaking, with the "aristocratic" element, becomes for us straightway the greatest of oddities and at the same time, critically speaking, one of the most interesting things conceivable.

The interest then springs from its being involved for us in the "case". We recognize so many suggested consequences if the case is really to prove responsible for it. We ask ourselves if there be not a connection, we almost tremble lest there shouldn't be; since what is more obvious than that, if a high example of exclusive aestheticism—as high a one as we are likely ever to meet—is bound sooner or later to spring a leak, the general question receives much light? We recognize here the value of our author's complete consistency: he would have kept his bottom sound, so to speak, had he not remained so long at sea. If those imperfect exponents of his faith whom we have noted among ourselves fail to flower, for a climax, in any proportionate way, we make out that they are embarrassed not so much by any force they possess as by a force—a force of temperament—that they lack. The anomaly I speak of presents itself thus as the dilemma in which Signor D'Annunzio's consistency has inexorably landed him; and the disfigurement breaks out, strikingly enough, in the very forefront of his picture, at the point where he has most lavished his colour. It is where he has most trusted and depended that he is most betrayed, the traitor sharing certainly his tent and his confidence. What is it that in the interest of beauty he most elaborately builds on if not on the love-affairs of his heroes and heroines, if not on his exhibition of the free play, the sincere play, the play closely studied and frankly represented, of the sexual relation? It is round this exercise, for him, that expressible, demonstrable, communicable beauty prevailingly clusters; a view indeed as to which we all generously go with him, subject to the reserve for each of us of our own expression and demonstration. It is these things on his part that break down, it is his discrimination that falls short, and thereby the very kind of intellectual authority most implied by his pretension. There is according to him an immense amenity that can be saved—saved by style—from the general wreck and welter of what is most precious, from the bankruptcy determined more and more by our basely democratic conditions. As we watch the actual process, however, it is only to see the lifeboat itself founder. The vulgarity into which he so incongruously drops is, I will not say the space he allots to love-affairs, but the weakness of his sense of "values" in depicting them.

We begin to ask ourselves at an early stage what this queer passion may be in the representation of which the sense of beauty ostensibly finds its richest expression and which is yet attended by nothing else at all—neither duration, nor propagation, nor common kindness, nor common consistency with other relations, common congruity with the rest of life—to make its importance good. If beauty is the supreme need so let it be; nothing is more certain than that we can never get too much of it if only we get it of the right sort. It is therefore on this very ground—the ground of its own sufficiency—that Signor D'Annunzio's invocation of it collapses at our challenge. The vulgarity comes from the disorder really introduced into values, as I have called them; from the vitiation suffered—that we should have to record so mean an accident—by taste, impeccable taste, itself. The truth of this would come out fully in copious examples, now impossible; but it is not too much to say, I think, that in every principal situation presented the fundamental weakness causes the particular interest to be inordinately compromised.

I must not, I know, make too much of *Il Piacere*—one of those works of promising youth with which criticism is always easy—and I should indeed say nothing of it if it were also a work of less ability. It really, however, to my mind, quite gives us the key, all in the morning early, to our author's general misadventure. Andrea Sperelli is the key; Donna Maria is another key of a slightly different shape. They have neither of them the aesthetic importance, any more than the moral, that their narrator claims for them and in his elaborate insistence on which he has so hopelessly lost his way. If they *were* important—by which I mean if they showed in any other light than that of their particular erotic exercise—they would justify the claim made for them with such superior art. They have no general history, since their history is only, and immediately and extravagantly, that of their too cheap and too easy romance. Why should the career of the young man be offered as a sample of pathetic, of tragic, of edifying corruption?— in which case it might indeed be matter for earnest exhibition. The march of corruption, the insidious influence of propinquity, oppor- tunity, example, the ravage of false estimates and the drama of sterilizing passion—all this is a thinkable theme, thinkable especially in the light of a great talent. But for Andrea Sperelli there is not only no march, no drama, there is not even a weakness to give him the semblance of dramatic, of plastic material; he is solidly, invariably, vulgarly strong, and not a bit more corrupt at the end of his disorders than at the beginning. His erudition, his intellectual accomplishments and elevation, are too easily spoken for; no view of him is given in which we can feel or taste them. Donna Maria is scarcely less signal an instance of the apparent desire on the author's part to impute a "value" defeated by his apparently not knowing what a value is. She is apparently an immense value for the occasions on which the couple secretly meet, but how is she otherwise one? and what becomes there- fore of the beauty, the interest, the pathos, the struggle, or whatever else, of her relation—relation of character, of judgment, even of mere taste—to her own collapse? The immediate physical sensibility that surrenders in her is, as throughout, exquisitely painted; but since nothing operates for her, one way or the other, *but* that familiar faculty, we are left casting about us almost as much for what else she has to give as for what, in any case, she may wish to keep.

The author's view of the whole matter of durations and dates, in these connections, gives the scale of "distinction" by itself a marked downward tilt; it confounds all differences between the trivial and the grave. Giuliana, in *L'Innocente*, is interesting because she has had a misadventure, and she is exquisite in her delineator's view because she has repented of it. But the misadventure, it appears, was a matter but of a minute; so that we oddly see this particular romance attenuated on the ground of its brevity. Given the claims of the exquisite the attenuation should surely be sought in the very opposite quarter; since, where these remarkable affections are concerned, how otherwise than by the element of comparative duration do we obtain the element of comparative good faith, on which we depend for the element, in turn, of comparative dignity? Andrea Sperelli becomes in the course of a few weeks in Rome the lover of some twenty or thirty women of fashion—the number scarce matters; but to make this possible his connection with each has but to last a day or two; and the effect of that in its order is to reduce to nothing, by vulgarity, by frank grotesqueness of association, the romantic capacity in him on which the chronicler's whole appeal to us is based. The association rising before us more nearly than any other is that of the manners observable in the most mimetic department of any great menagerie.

The most serious relation depicted—in the sense of being in some degree the least suggestive of mere zoological sociability—is that of the lovers in *Il Fuoco*, as we also take this pair for their creator's sanest and most responsible spirits. It is a question between them of an heroic affection, and yet the affection appears to make good for itself no place worth speaking of in their lives. It holds but for a scant few weeks; the autumn already reigns when the connection begins, and the connection is played out (or if it be not the ado is about nothing) with the first flush of the early Italian spring. It suddenly, on our hands, becomes trivial, with all our own estimate of reasons and realities and congruities falsified. The Foscarina has, on professional business, to "go away", and the young poet has to do the same; but such a separation, so easily bridged over by such great people, makes a beggarly climax for an intercourse on behalf of which all the forces of poetry and tragedy have been set in motion. Where then we ask ourselves is the weakness?—as we ask it, very much in the same way, in respect to the vulgarized aspect of the tragedy of Giorgio Aurispa. The pang of pity, the pang that springs from a conceivable community in doom, is in this latter case altogether wanting. Directly we lift a little the embroidered mantle of that gift for appearances which plays, on Signor D'Annunzio's part, such tricks upon us, we find ourselves put off, as the phrase is, with an inferior article. The inferior article is the hero's poverty of life, which cuts him down for pathetic interest just as the same limitation in *Il Piacere* cuts down Donna Maria. Presented each as victims of another rapacious person who has got the better of them, there is no process, no complexity, no suspense in their story; and thereby, we submit, there is no aesthetic beauty. Why *shouldn't* Giorgio Aurispa go mad? Why shouldn't Stelio Effrena go away? We make the inquiry as disconcerted spectators, not feeling in the former case that we have had any communication with the wretched youth's sanity, and not seeing in the latter why the tie of all the passion that has been made so admirably vivid for us should not be able to weather change.

Nothing is so singular with D'Annunzio as that the very basis and subject of his work should repeatedly go aground on such shallows as these. He takes for treatment a situation that is substantially none— the most fundamental this of his values, and all the more compromising that his immense art of producing illusions still leaves it exposed. The idea in each case is superficially specious, but *where* it breaks down is what makes all the difference. *Il Piacere* would have meant what it seems to try to mean only if a provision had been made in it for some adequate "inwardness" on the part either of the nature disintegrated or of the other nature to which this poisoned contact proves fatal. *L'Innocente* of the group, comes nearest to justifying its idea; and I leave it unchallenged, though its meaning surely would have been written larger if the attitude of the wife towards her misbegotten child had been, in face of the husband's, a little less that of the dumb detached animal suffering in her simplicity. As a picture of such suffering, the pain of the mere dumb animal, the work is indeed magnificent; only its connections are poor with the higher dramatic, the higher poetic, complexity of things.

I can only repeat that to make *The Triumph of Death* a fruitful thing we should have been able to measure the triumph by its frustration of some conceivable opportunity at least for life. There is a moment at which we hope for something of this kind, the moment at which the young man pays his visit to his family, who have grievous need of him and towards whom we look to see some one side or other of his fine sensibility turn. But nothing comes of that for the simple reason that the personage is already dead—that nothing exists in him but the established *fear* of life. He turns his back on everything but a special sensation, and so completely shuts the door on the elements of contrast and curiosity. Death really triumphs, in the matter, but over the physical terror of the inordinate woman; a pang perfectly communicated to us, but too small a surface to bear the weight laid on it, which accordingly affects us as that of a pyramid turned over on its point. It is throughout one of D'Annunzio's strongest marks that he treats "love" as a matter not to be mixed with life, in the larger sense of the word, at all—as a matter all of whose other connections are dropped; a sort of secret game that can go on only if each of the parties has nothing to do, even on any *other* terms, with any one else.

I have dwelt on the fact that the sentimental intention in *Il Fuoco* quite bewilderingly fails, in spite of the splendid accumulation of material. We wait to the end to see it declare itself, and then are left, as I have already indicated, with a mere meaningless anecdote on our hands. Brilliant and free, each freighted with a talent that is given us as incomparable, the parties to the combination depicted have, for their affection, the whole world before them—and not the simple terraqueous globe, but that still vaster sphere of the imagination in which, by an exceptionally happy chance, they are able to move together on very nearly equal terms. A tragedy is a tragedy, a comedy is a comedy, when the effect, in either sense, is *determined* for us, determined by the interference of some element that starts a complication or precipitates an action. As in *Il Fuoco* nothing whatever interferes—or nothing certainly that need weigh with the high spirits represented—we ask why such precious revelations are made us for nothing. Admirably made in themselves they yet strike us as, aesthetically speaking, almost cruelly wasted.

This general remark would hold good, as well, of *Le Vergini*, if I might still linger, though its application has already been virtually made. Anatolia, in this tale, the most robust of the three sisters, declines marriage in order to devote herself to a family who have, it would certainly appear, signal need of her nursing. But this, though it sufficiently represents *her* situation, covers as little as possible the ground of the hero's own, since he, quivering intensely with the treasure of his "will", inherited in a straight line from the *cinque-cento*, only asks to affirm his sublimated energy. The temptation to affirm it erotically, at least, has been great for him in relation to each of the young women in turn; but it is for Anatolia that his admiration and affection most increase in volume, and it is accordingly for her sake that, with the wonderful moral force behind him (kept as in a Florentine casket), we

must look to see him justified. He has a fine image—and when has
the author not fine images?—to illustrate the constant readiness of this
possession. The young woman says something that inspires him,
whereupon, "as a sudden light playing over the dusky wall of a room
causes the motionless sword in a trophy to shine, so her word drew a
great flash from my suspended *volontà*. There was a virtue in her," the
narrator adds, "which could have produced portentous fruit. Her
substance might have nourished a superhuman germ." In spite of which
it never succeeds in becoming so much as a question that his affection
for her shall. *act*, that this grand imagination in him shall operate, that
he himself is, in virtue of such things, exactly the person to come to her
aid and to combine with her in devotion. The talk about the *volontà*
is amusing much in the same way as the complacency of a primitive
man, unacquainted with the uses of things, who becomes possessed
by some accident of one of the toys of civilization, a watch or a motor-
car. And yet artistically and for our author the will *has* an application,
since without it he could have done no rare vivid work.

Here at all events we put our finger, I think, on the very point at
which his aesthetic plenitude meets the misadventure that discredits it.
We see just where it "joins on" with vulgarity. That sexual passion
from which he extracts such admirable detached pictures insists on
remaining for him *only* the act of a moment, beginning and ending in
itself and disowning any representative character. From the moment
it depends on itself alone for its beauty it endangers extremely its
distinction, so precarious at the best. For what it represents, precisely,
is it poetically interesting; it finds its extension and consummation
only in the rest of life. Shut out from the rest of life, shut out from
all fruition and assimilation, it has no more dignity than—to use a
homely image—the boots and shoes that we see, in the corridors of
promiscuous hotels, standing, often in double pairs, at the doors of
rooms. Detached and unassociated these clusters of objects present,
however obtruded, no importance. What the participants do with
their agitation, in short, or even what it does with them, *that* is the
stuff of poetry, and it is never really interesting save when something
finely contributive in themselves makes it so. It is this absence of anything finely contributive in themselves, on the part of the various
couples here concerned, that is the open door to the trivial. I have said,
with all appreciation, that they present the great "relation", for intimacy, as we shall nowhere else find it presented; but to see it
related, in its own turn, to nothing in the heaven above or the earth

beneath, this undermines, we definitely learn, the charm of that achievement.

And so it is, strangely, that our aesthetic "case" enlightens us. The only question is whether it be the only case of the kind conceivable. May we not suppose another with the elements differently mixed? May we not in imagination alter the proportions within or the influences without, and look with cheerfulness for a different issue? *Need* the aesthetic adventure, in a word, organized for real discovery, give us no more comforting news of success? Are there not, so to speak, finer possible combinations? are there not safeguards against futility that in the example before us were but too presumably absent? To which the sole answer probably is that no man can say. It is Signor D'Annunzio alone who has really sailed the sea and brought back the booty. The actual case is so good that all the potential fade beside it. It has for it that it exists, and that, whether for the strength of the original outfit or for the weight of the final testimony, it could scarce thinkably be bettered.

22

THE TEMPEST[1]

1907

IF the effect of the Plays and Poems, taken in their mass, be most of all to appear often to mock our persistent ignorance of so many of the conditions of their birth, and thereby to place on the rack again our strained and aching wonder, this character has always struck me as more particularly kept up for them by *The Tempest*; the production, of the long series, in which the Questions, as the critical reader of Shakespeare must ever comprehensively and ruefully call them and more or less resignedly live with them, hover before us in their most tormenting form. It may seem no very philosophic state of mind, the merely baffled and exasperated view of one of the supreme works of all litera-ture; though I feel, for myself, that to confess to it now and then, by way of relief, is no unworthy tribute to the work. It is not, certainly, the tribute most frequently paid, for the large body of comment and criticism of which this play alone has been the theme abounds much rather in affirmed conclusions, complacencies of conviction, full apprehensions of the meaning and triumphant pointings of the moral. The Questions, in the light of all this wisdom, convert themselves, with comparatively small difficulty, into smooth and definite answers; the innumerable dim ghosts that flit, like started game at eventide, through the deep dusk of our speculation, with just form enough to quicken it and no other charity for us at all, bench themselves along the vista as solidly as Falstaff and as vividly as Hotspur. Everything has thus been attributed to the piece before us, and every attribution so made has been in turn brushed away; merely to glance at such a monument to the interest inspired is to recognize a battleground of opposed factions, not a little enveloped in sound and smoke. Of these copious elements, produced for the most part to the best intention, as we can but familiarly name it, for whatever purpose, we have to cross the scene of action at a mortal risk, making the fewest steps of it and trusting to the probable calm at the centre of the storm. There in fact, though there only, we find that serenity; find the subject itself intact and unconscious, seated as unwinking and inscrutable as a divinity in a

[1] Introduction to Volume XVI of the Renaissance Edition of *The Complete Works of William Shakespeare*, edited by Sidney Lee, 1907.

temple, save for that vague flicker of derision, the only response to our interpretative heat, which adds the last beauty to its face. The divinity never relents—never, like the image of life in *The Winter's Tale*, steps down from its pedestal; it simply leaves us to stare on through the ages, with this fact indeed of having crossed the circle of fire, and so got into the real and right relation to it, for our one comfort.

The position of privilege of *The Tempest* as the latest example, to all appearance, of the author's rarer work, with its distance from us in time thereby shortened to the extent of the precious step or two, was certain to expose it, at whatever final cost, we easily see, to any amount of interpretative zeal. With its first recorded performance that of February 1613, when it was given in honour of the marriage of the Princess Elizabeth, its finished state cannot have preceeded his death by more than three years, and we accordingly take it as the finest flower of his experience. Here indeed, as on so many of the Questions, judgments sharply differ, and this use of it as an ornament to the nuptials of the daughter of James I and the younger Elector Palatine may have been but a repetition of previous performances; though it is not in such a case supposable that these can have been numerous. They would antedate the play, at the most, by a year or two, and so not throw it essentially further back from us. *The Tempest* speaks to us, somehow, convincingly, as a *pièce de circonstance*, and the suggestion that it was addressed, in its brevity, its rich simplicity, and its free elegance, to court-production, and above all to providing, with a string of other dramas, for the "intellectual" splendour of a wedding-feast, is, when once entertained, not easily dislodged. A few things fail to fit, but more fit strikingly. I like therefore to think of the piece as of 1613. To refer it, as it is referred by other reckonings, to 1611 is but to thicken that impenetrability of silence in which Shakespeare's latest years enfold him. Written as it must have been on the earlier calculation, before the age of forty-seven, it has that rare value of the richly mature note of a genius who, by our present measure of growth and fullness, was still young enough to have had in him a world of life: we feel behind it the immense procession of its predecessors, while we yet stare wistfully at the plenitude and the majesty, the expression as of something broad-based and ultimate, that were not, in any but a strained sense, to borrow their warrant from the weight of years. Nothing so enlarges the wonder of the whole time-question in Shakespeare's career as the fact of this date, in easy middle life, of his time-climax; which, if we knew less, otherwise, than we do about him.

might affect us as an attempt, on the part of treacherous History, to pass him off as one of those monsters of precocity who, fortunately for their probable reputation, the too likely betrayal of shortwindedness, are cut off in their comparative prime. The transmuted young rustic who, after a look over London, brief at the best, was ready at the age of thirty to produce *The Merchant of Venice* and *A Midsummer Night's Dream* (and this after the half-dozen splendid prelusive things that had included, at twenty-eight, *Romeo and Juliet*), had been indeed a monster of precocity—which all geniuses of the first order are not; but the day of his paying for it had neither arrived nor, however faintly, announced itself, and the fathomless strangeness of his story, the abrupt stoppage of his pulse after *The Tempest*, is not, in charity, lighted for us by a glimmer of explanation. The explanation by some interposing accident is as absent as any symptom of "declining powers".

His powers declined, that is—but declined merely to obey the spring we should have supposed inherent in them; and their possessor's case derives from this, I think, half the secret of its so inestimably mystifying us. He died, for a nature so organized, too lamentably soon; but who knows where we should have been with him if he had not lived long enough so to affirm, with many other mysteries, the mystery of his abrupt and complete cessation: There is that in *The Tempest*, specifically, though almost all indefinably, which seems to show us the artist consciously tasting of the first and rarest of his gifts, that of imaged creative Expression, the instant sense of some copious equivalent of thought for every grain of the grossness of reality; to show him as unresistingly aware, in the depths of his genius, that nothing like it had ever been known, or probably would ever be again known, on earth, and as so given up, more than on other occasions, to the joy of sovereign *science*. There are so many sides from which any page that shows his stamp may be looked at that a handful of reflections can hope for no coherency, in the chain of association immediately formed, unless they happen to bear upon some single truth. Such a truth then, for me, is this comparative—by which one can really but mean this superlative—artistic value of the play seen in the meagre circle of the items of our knowledge about it. Let me say that our knowledge, in the whole connection, is a quantity that shifts, surprisingly, with the measure of a felt need; appearing to some of us, on some sides, adequate, various, large, and appearing to others, on whatever side, a scant beggar's portion. We are concerned, it must be remembered, here— that is for getting *generally* near our author—not only with the number

of the mustered facts, but with the kind of fact that each may strike us
as being: never unmindful that such matters, when they are few, may
go far for us if they be individually but ample and significant; and when
they are numerous, on the other hand, may easily fall short enough to
break our hearts if they be at the same time but individually small and
poor. Three or four stepping-stones across a stream will serve if they
are broad slabs, but it will take more than may be counted if they are
only pebbles. Beyond all gainsaying then, by many an estimate, is
the penury in which even the most advantageous array of the Shakespearean facts still leaves us: strung together with whatever ingenuity
they remain, for our discomfiture, as the pebbles across the stream.

To balance, for our occasion, this light scale, however, *The Tempest*
affects us, taking its complexity and its perfection together, as the
rarest of all examples of literary art. There may be other things as
exquisite, other single exhalations of beauty reaching as high a mark
and sustained there for a moment, just as there are other deep wells of
poetry from which cupfuls as crystalline may, in repeated dips, be
drawn; but nothing, surely, of equal length and variety lives so happily
and radiantly as a whole: no poetic birth ever took place under a star
appointed to blaze upon it so steadily. The felicity enjoyed is enjoyed
longer and more intensely, and the art involved, completely revealed,
as I suggest, to the master, holds the securest revel. The man himself,
in the Plays, we directly touch, to my consciousness, positively nowhere: we are dealing too perpetually with the artist, the monster and
magician of a thousand masks, not one of which we feel him drop
long enough to gratify with the breath of the interval that strained
attention in us which would be yet, so quickened, ready to become
deeper still. Here at last the artist is, comparatively speaking, so
generalized, so consummate and typical, so frankly amused with himself, that is with his art, with his power, with his theme, that it is as if
he came to meet us more than his usual half-way, and as if, thereby,
in meeting *him*, and touching him, we were nearer to meeting and
touching the man. The man everywhere, in Shakespeare's work, is
so effectually locked up and imprisoned in the artist that we but hover
at the base of thick walls for a sense of him; while, in addition, the
artist is so steeped in the abysmal objectivity of his characters and
situations that the great billows of the medium itself play with him,
to our vision, very much as, over a ship's side, in certain waters, we
catch, through transparent tides, the flash of strange sea-creatures.
What we are present at in this fashion is a series of incalculable plunges

—the series of those that have taken effect, I mean, after the great primary plunge, made once for all, of the man into the artist: the successive plunges of the artist himself into Romeo and into Juliet, into Shylock, Hamlet, Macbeth, Coriolanus, Cleopatra, Antony, Lear, Othello, Falstaff, Hotspur; immersions during which, though he always ultimately finds his feet, the very violence of the movements involved troubles and distracts our sight. In *The Tempest*, by the supreme felicity I speak of, is no violence; he sinks as deep as we like, but what he sinks into, beyond all else, is the lucid stillness of his style.

One can speak, in these matters, but from the impression determined by one's own inevitable standpoint; again and again, at any rate, such a masterpiece puts before me the very act of the momentous conjunction taking place for the poet, at a given hour, between his charged inspiration and his clarified experience: or, as I should perhaps better express it, between his human curiosity and his aesthetic passion. Then, if he happens to have been, all his career, with his equipment for it, more or less the victim and the slave of the former, he yields, by way of a change, to the impulse of allowing the latter, for a magnificent moment, the upper hand. The human curiosity, as I call it, is always there—with no more need of making provision for it than use in taking precautions against it; the surrender to the luxury of expertness may therefore go forward on its own conditions. I can offer no better description of *The Tempest* as fresh re-perusal lights it for me than as such a surrender, sublimely enjoyed; and I may frankly say that, under this impression of it, there is no refinement of the artistic consciousness that I do not see my way—or feel it, better, perhaps, since we but grope, at the best, in our darkness—to attribute to the author. It is a way that one follows to the end, because it is a road, I repeat, on which one least misses some glimpse of him face to face. If it be true that the thing was concocted to meet a particular demand, that of the master of the King's revels, with his prescription of date, form, tone and length, this, so far from interfering with the Poet's perception of a charming opportunity to taste for *himself*, for himself above all, and as he had almost never so tasted, not even in *A Midsummer Night's Dream*, of the quality of his mind and the virtue of his skill, would have exceedingly favoured the happy case. Innumerable one may always suppose these delicate debates and intimate understandings of an artist with himself. "How much *taste*, in the world, may I conceive that I have?—and what a charming idea to snatch a moment for finding out! What moment could be better than this—a bridal evening before the Court, with

extra candles and the handsomest company—if I can but put my hand
on the right 'scenario'?" We can catch, across the ages, the searching
sight and the look about; we receive the stirred breath of the ripe,
amused genius; and, stretching, as I admit I do at least, for a still closer
conception of the beautiful crisis, I find it pictured for me in some such
presentment as that of a divine musician who, alone in his room,
preludes or improvises at close of day. He sits at the harpsichord, by
the open window, in the summer dusk; his hands wander over the keys.
They stray far, for his motive, but at last he finds and holds it; then he
lets himself go, embroidering and refining: it is the thing for the hour
and his mood. The neighbours may gather in the garden, the nightin-
gale be hushed on the bough; it is none the less a private occasion, a
concert of one, both performer and auditor, who plays for his own ear
his own hand, his own innermost sense, and for the bliss and capacity
of his instrument. Such are the only hours at which the artist *may*,
by any measure of his own (too many things, at others, make heavily
against it); and their challenge to him is irresistible if he has known, all
along, too much compromise and too much sacrifice.

The face that beyond any other, however, I seem to see *The Tempest*
turn to us is the side on which it so superlatively speaks of that endowment for Expression, expression as a primary force, a consuming, an
independent passion, which was the greatest ever laid upon man. It is
for Shakespeare's power of constitutive speech quite as if he had swum
into our ken with it from another planet, gathering it up there, in its
wealth, as something antecedent to the occasion and the need, and if
possible quite in excess of them; something that was to make of our
poor world a great flat table for receiving the glitter and clink of
outpoured treasure. The idea and the motive are more often than not
so smothered in it that they scarce know themselves, and the resources
of such a style, the provision of images, emblems, energies of every
sort, laid up in advance, affects us as the storehouse of a kind before a
famine or a siege—which not only, by its scale, braves depletion or
exhaustion, but bursts, through mere excess of quantity or presence,
out of all doors and windows. It renders the poverties and obscurities
of our world, as I say, in the dazzling terms of a richer and better. It
constitutes, by a miracle, more than half the author's material; so much
more usually does it happen, for the painter or the poet, that life itself,
in its appealing, overwhelming crudity, offers itself as the paste to be
kneaded. Such a personage works in general in the very elements of
experience; whereas we see Shakespeare working predominantly in

the terms of expression, *all* in the terms of the artist's specific vision and genius; with a thicker cloud of images to attest his approach, at any point, than the comparatively meagre given case ever has to attest its own identity. He points for us as no one else the relation of style to meaning and of manner to motive; a matter on which, right and left, we hear such rank ineptitudes uttered. Unless it be true that these things, on either hand, are inseparable; unless it be true that the phrase, the cluster and order of terms, *is* the object and the sense, in as close a compression as that of body and soul, so that any consideration of them as distinct, from the moment style is an active, applied force, becomes a gross stupidity: unless we recognize this reality the author of *The Tempest* has no lesson for us. It is by his expression of it exactly as the expression stands that the particular thing is created, created as interesting, as beautiful, as strange, droll or terrible—as related, in short, to our understanding or our sensibility; in consequence of which we reduce it to naught when we begin to talk of either of its presented parts as matters by themselves.

All of which considerations indeed take us too far; what is important to note being simply our Poet's high testimony to this independent, absolute value of Style, and to its need thoroughly to project and seat itself. It had been, as so seating itself, the very home of his mind, for his all too few twenty years; it had been the supreme source to him of the joy of life. It had been in fine his material, his plastic clay; since the more subtly he applied it the more secrets it had to give him, and the more these secrets might appear to him, at every point, one with the myriad pulses of the spirit of man. Thus it was that, as he passed from one application of it to another, tone became, for all its suggestions, more and more sovereign to him, and the subtlety of its secrets an exquisite interest. If I see him, at the last, over *The Tempest*, as the composer, at the harpsichord or the violin, extemporizing in the summer twilight, it is exactly that he is feeling there for tone and, by the same token, finding it—finding it as *The Tempest*, beyond any register of ours, immortally gives it. This surrender to the highest sincerity of virtuosity, as we nowadays call it, is to my perception *all* *The Tempest*; with no possible depth or delicacy in it that such an imputed character does not cover and provide for. The subject to be treated was the simple fact (if one may call anything in the matter simple) that refinement, selection, economy, the economy not of poverty, but of wealth a little weary of congestion—the very air of the lone island and the very law of the Court celebration—were here implied and imperative things. Anything was a subject, always, that offered to sight an aperture of size enough for expression and its train to pass in and deploy themselves. If they filled up all the space, none the worse; they occupied it as nothing else could do. The subjects of the Comedies are, without exception, old wives' tales—which we are not too insufferably aware of only because the iridescent veil so perverts their proportions. The subjects of the Histories are no subjects at all; each is but a row of pegs for the hanging of the cloth of gold that is to muffle them. Such a thing as *The Merchant of Venice* declines, for very shame, to be reduced to its elements of witless "story"; such things as the two Parts of *Henry the Fourth* form no more than a straight convenient channel for the procession of evoked images that is to pour through it like a torrent. Each of these productions is none the less of incomparable splendour; by which splendour we are bewildered till we see how its comes. Then we see that every inch of it is personal tone, or in other words brooding expression raised to the highest energy. Push such energy far enough—far enough if you can!—and, being what it is, it then inevitably provides for Character. Thus we see character, in every form of which the "story" gives the thinnest hint, marching through the pieces I have named in its habit as it lives, and so filling out the scene that nothing is missed. The "story" in *The Tempest* is a thing of naught, for any story will provide a remote island, a shipwreck and a coincidence. Prospero and Miranda, awaiting their relatives, are, in the present case, *for* the relatives, the coincidence— just as the relatives are the coincidence for them. Ariel and Caliban, and the island-airs and island-scents, and all the rest of the charm and magic and the ineffable delicacy (a delicacy positively at its highest in the conception and execution of Caliban) are the style handed over to its last disciplined passion of curiosity; a curiosity which flowers, at this pitch, into the freshness of each of the characters.

There are judges for whom the piece is a tissue of symbols; symbols of the facts of State then apparent, of the lights of philosophic and political truth, of the "deeper meanings of life", above all, of a high crisis in its author's career. At this most relevant of its mystic values only we may glance; the consecrated estimate of Prospero's surrender of his magic robe and staff as a figure for Shakespeare's own self-despoilment, his considered purpose, at this date, of future silence. Dr. George Brandes works out in detail that analogy; the production becomes, on such a supposition, Shakespeare's "farewell to the stage"; his retirement to Stratford, to end his days in the care of his property

and in oblivion of the theatre, was a course for which his arrangements
had already been made. The simplest way to put it, since I have
likened him to the musician at the piano, is to say that he had decided
upon the complete closing of this instrument, and that in fact he was
to proceed to lock it with the sharp click that has reverberated through
the ages, and to spend what remained to him of life in walking about a
small, squalid country-town with his hands in his pockets and an ear
for no music now but the chink of the coin they might turn over there.
This is indeed in general the accepted, the imposed view of the position
he had gained: this freedom to "elect", as we say, to cease, intellectually,
to exist: this ability, exercised at the zenith of his spendour, to shut
down the lid, from one day to another, on the most potent aptitude
for vivid reflection ever lodged in a human frame and to conduct himself thereafter, in all ease and comfort, not only as if it were not, but as
if it had never been. I speak of our "accepting" the prodigy, but
by the established record we have no choice whatever; which is why
it is imposed, as I say, on our bewildered credulity. With the impossibility of proving that the author of *The Tempest* did after the date
of that production, ever again press the spring of his fountain, ever
again reach for the sacred key or break his heart for an hour over his
inconceivable act of sacrifice, we are reduced to behaving as if we
understood the strange case; so that any rubbing of our eyes as under
the obsession of a wild dream, has been held a gesture that, for common
decency, must mainly take place in private. If I state that my small
contribution to any renewed study of the matter can amount, accordingly, but to little more than an irresistible need to rub mine in public,
I shall have done the most that the condition of our knowledge
admits of. We can "accept", but we can accept only in stupefaction—
a stupefaction that, in presence of *The Tempest*, and of the intimate
meaning so imputed to it, must despair of ever subsiding. These things
leave us in darkness—in gross darkness about the Man; the case of
which they are the warrant is so difficult to embrace. None ever
appealed so sharply to some light of knowledge, and nothing could
render our actual knowledge more contemptible. What manner of
human being was it who *could* so, at a given moment, announce his
intention of capping his divine flame with a twopenny extinguisher,
and who then, the announcement made, could serenely succeed in
carrying it out? Were it a question of a flame spent or burning thin,
we might feel a little more possessed of matter for comprehension; the
fact being, on the contrary, one can only repeat, that the value of *The*

Tempest is, exquisitely, in its refinements of power, its renewed artistic freshness and roundness, its mark as of a distinction unequalled, on the whole (though I admit that we here must take subtle measures), in any predecessor. Prospero has simply waited, to cast his magic ring into the sea, till the jewel set in it shall have begun to burn as never before.

So it is then; and it puts into a nutshell the eternal mystery, the most insoluble that ever was, the complete rupture, for our understanding, between the Poet and the Man. There are moments, I admit, in this age of sound and fury, of connections, in every sense, too maddeningly multiplied, when we are willing to let it pass as a mystery, the most soothing, cooling, consoling too perhaps, that ever was. But there are others when, speaking for myself, its power to torment us intellectually seems scarcely to be borne; and we know these moments best when we hear it proclaimed that a comfortable clearness reigns. I have been for instance reading over Mr. Halliwell-Phillipps, and I find him apparently of the opinion that it is all our fault if everything in our author's story, and above all in this last chapter of it, be not of a primitive simplicity. The complexity arises from our suffering our imagination to meddle with the Man at all; who is quite sufficiently presented to us on the face of the record. For critics of this writer's complexion the only facts we are urgently concerned with are the facts of the Poet, which are abundantly constituted by the Plays and the Sonnets. The poet is *there*, and the Man is outside: the Man is for instance in such a perfectly definite circumstance as that he could never miss, after *The Tempest*, the key of his piano, as I have called it, since he could play so freely with the key of his cashbox. The supreme master of expression had made, before fifty, all the money he wanted; therefore what was there more to express? This view is admirable if you can get your mind to consent to it. It must ignore any impulse, in presence of Play or Sonnet (whatever vague stir behind either may momentarily act as provocation) to try for a lunge at the figured arras. In front of the tapestry sits the immitigably respectable person whom our little slateful of gathered and numbered items, heaven knows, does amply account for, since there is nothing in him to explain; while the undetermined figure, on the other hand—undetermined whether in the sense of respectability or of anything else—the figure who supremely interests us, remains as unseen of us as our Ariel, on the enchanted island, remains of the bewildered visitors. Mr. Halliwell-Phillipps's theory, as I understand it—and I refer to it but as an advertisement of a hundred others—is that we too are but bewildered visitors, and that the state of mind of the Duke of Naples and his companions is our proper critical portion.

If our knowledge of the greatest of men consists therefore but of the neat and "proved" addition of two or three dozen common particulars, the rebuke to a morbid and monstrous curiosity is no more than just. We know enough, by such an implication, when we admire enough, and as difficulties would appear to abound on our attempting to push further, this is an obvious lesson to us to stand as still as possible. Not difficulties—those of penetration, exploration, interpretation, those, in the word that says everything, of appreciation—are the approved field of criticism, but the very forefront of the obvious and the palpable, where we may go round and round, like holiday-makers on hobby-horses, at the turning of a crank. Differences of estimate, in this relation, come back, too clearly, let us accordingly say, to differences of view of the character of genius in general—if not, in truth, more exactly stated, to that strangest of all fallacies, the idea of the separateness of a great man's parts. His genius places itself, under this fallacy, on one side of the line and the rest of his identity on the other; the line being that, for instance, which, to Mr. Halliwell-Phillipps's view, divides the author of *Hamlet* and *The Tempest* from the man of exemplary business-method whom alone we may propose to approach at all intimately. The stumbling-block here is that the boundary exists only in the vision of those able to content themselves with arbitrary marks. A mark becomes arbitrary from the moment we have no authoritative sign of where to place it, no sign of higher warrant than that it smooths and simplifies the ground. But though smoothing and simplifying, on such terms, may, by restricting our freedom of attention and specula-tion, make, on behalf of our treatment of the subject, for a livelier effect of business—that business as to a zealous care for which we seem taught that our author must above all serve as our model—it will see us little further on any longer road. The fullest appreciation possible is the high tribute we must offer to greatness, and to make it worthy of its office we must surely know where we are with it. In greatness as much as in mediocrity the man is, under examination, *one*, and the elements of character melt into each other. The genius is a part of the mind, and the mind a part of the behaviour; so that, for the attitude of inquiry, without which appreciation means nothing, where does one of these provinces end and the other begin? We may take the genius first or the behaviour first, but we inevitably proceed from the one to the other; we inevitably encamp, as it were, on the high central table-land that they have in common. How are we to arrive at a relation with the object to be penetrated if we are thus for ever met by a locked door flanked with a sentinel who merely invites us to take it for edifying? We take it ourselves for attaching—which is the very essence of mysteries—and profess ourselves doomed for ever to hang yearningly about it. An obscurity endured, in fine, one inch further, or one hour longer, than our neceessity truly holds us to, strikes us but as an artificial spectre, a muffled object with waving arms, set up to keep appreciation down.

For it is never to be forgotten that we are here in presence of the human character the most magnificently endowed, in all time, with the sense of the life of man, and with the apparatus for recording it; so that of *him*, inevitably, it goes hardest of all with us to be told that we have nothing, or next to nothing, to do with the effect in him of this gift. If it does not satisfy us that the effect was to make him write *King Lear* and *Othello*, we are verily difficult to please: so it is meanwhile, that the case for the obscurity is argued. That is sovereign, we reply, so far as it goes; but it tells us nothing of the effect on him of being *able* to write *Lear* and *Othello*. No scrap of testimony of what this may have been is offered us; it is the quarter in which our blankness is most blank, and in which we are yet most officiously put off. It is true of the poet in general—in nine examples out of ten—that his life is mainly inward, that its events and revolutions are his great impressions and deep vibrations, and that his "personality" is all pictured in the publication of his verse. Shakespeare, we essentially feel, is the tenth, is the millionth example; not the sleek bachelor of music, the sensitive harp set once for all in the window to catch the air, but the spirit in hungry quest of every possible experience and adventure of the spirit, and which, betimes, with the boldest of all intellectual movements, was to leap from the window into the street. We are in the street, as it were, for admiration and wonder, when the incarnation alights, and it is of no edification to shrug shoulders at the felt impulse (when made manifest) to follow, to pursue, all breathlessly to track it on its quickly-taken way. Such a quest of imaginative experience, we can only feel, has itself constituted one of the greatest observed adventures of mankind; so that no point of the history of it, however far back seized, is premature for our fond attention. Half our connection with it is our desire to "assist" at it; so how can we fail of curiosity and sympathy? The answer to which is doubtless again that these impulses are very well, but that as the case stands they can move but in one channel. We are free to assist in the Plays themselves—to assist at whatever we like; so long, that is, as, after the fashion I have noted, we rigidly limit our inductions from them. It is put to us once more that we can make no bricks without straw, and that, rage as we may against our barrier, it none the less stubbornly exists. Granted on behalf of the vaulting spirit all that we claim for it, it still, in the street, as we say—and in spite of the effect we see it as acrobatically producing there—absolutely defies pursuit. Beyond recovery, beyond curiosity, it was to lose itself in the crowd. The crowd, for that matter, the witnesses we must take as astonished and dazzled, has, though itself surviving but in a dozen or two dim, scarce articulate ghosts, been interrogated to the last man and the last distinguishable echo. This has practically elicited nothing—nothing, that is, of a nature to gratify the indiscreetly, the morbidly inquisitive; since we find ourselves not rarely reminded that morbidity may easily become a vice. *He* was notoriously not morbid; he stuck to his business—save when he so strangely gave it up; wherefore his own common sense about things in general is a model for the tone he should properly inspire. "You speak of his career as a transcendent 'adventure', as *the* conspicuously transcendent adventure—even to the sight of his contemporaries—of the mind of man; but no glimmer of any such story, of any such figure or 'presence', to use your ambiguous word, as you desire to read into the situation, can be discerned in any quarter. So what is it you propose we should do? What evidence do you suggest that, with this absence of material, we should put together? We have what we have; we are not concerned with what we have not."

In some such terms as that, one makes out, does the best attainable "appreciation" appear to invite us to let our great personage, the mighty adventurer, slink past. He slunk past in life: that was good enough for him, the contention appears to be. Why therefore should he not slink past in immortality? One's reply can indeed only be that he evidently must; yet I profess that, even while saying so, our poor point, for which *The Tempest* once more gives occasion, strikes me as still, as always, in its desperate way, worth the making. The question, I hold, will eternally interest the student of letters and of the human understanding, and the envied privilege of our play in particular will be always to keep it before him. *How* did the faculty so radiant there contrive, in such perfection, the arrest of its divine flight? By what inscrutable process was the extinguisher applied and, when

once applied, kept in its place to the end? What became of the checked
torrent, as a latent, bewildered presence and energy, in the life across
which the dam was constructed? What other mills did it set itself
turning, or what contiguous country did it—rather indeed did it *not*,
in default of these—inevitably ravage? We referred, for an account
of the matter, to recorded circumstances which are only not supremely
vulgar because they are supremely dim and few; in which character
they but mock, and as if all consciously, as I have said, at our unrest.
The one at all large indication they give is that our hero may have
died—since he did so soon—of his unnatural effort. Their quality,
however, redeems them a little by having for its effect that they throw
us back on the work itself with a rebellious renewal of appetite and
yearning. The secret that baffles us being the secret of the Man, we
know, as I have granted, that we shall never touch the Man *directly*
in the Artist. We stake our hopes thus on indirectness, which may
contain possibilities; we take that very truth for our counsel of despair,
try to look at it as helpful for the Criticism of the future. That of the
past had been too often infantile; one has asked one's self how it *could*,
on such lines, get at him. The figured tapestry, the long arras that hides
him, is always there, with its immensity of surface and its proportionate
underside. May it not then be but a question, for the fullness of time,
of the finer weapon, the sharper point, the stronger arm, the more
extended lunge?

23

THE NEW NOVEL

1914

WE feel it not to be the paradox it may at the first blush seem that the state of the novel in England at the present time is virtually very much the state of criticism itself; and this moreover, at the risk perhaps of some added appearance of perverse remark, by the very reason that we see criticism so much in abeyance. So far as we miss it altogether how and why does its "state" matter, and why and how can it or should it, as an absent force, enjoy a relation to that constant renewal cf our supply of fiction which is a present one so far as a force at all? The relation is this, in the fewest words: that no equal outpouring of matter into the mould of literature, or what roughly passes for such, has been noted to live its life and maintain its flood, its level at least of quantity and mass, in such free and easy independence of ciitical attention. It constitutes a condition and a perversity on the part of this element to remain irresponsive before an appeal so vociferous at least and so incessant; therefore how can such a neglect of occasions, so careless a habit in spite of marked openings, be better described than as responsibility declined in the face of disorder? The disorder thus determines the relation, from the moment we feel that it might be less, that it might be different, that something in the way of an order even might be disengaged from it and replace it; from the moment in fact that the low critical pitch is logically *reflected* in the poetic or, less pedantically speaking, the improvisational at large. The effect, if not the prime office, of criticism is to make our absorption and our enjoyment of the things that feed the mind as aware of itself as possible, since that awareness quickens the mental demand, which thus in turn wanders further and further for pasture. This action on the part of the mind practically amounts to a reaching out for the reasons of its interest, as only by its so ascertaining them can the interest grow more various. This is the very education of our imaginative life; and thanks to it the general question of how to refine, and of why certain things refine more and most, on that happy consciousness, becomes for us of the last importance. Then we cease to be only instinctive and at the mercy of chance, feeling that we can ourselves take a hand in our satisfaction and provide for it, making ourselves safe against dearth, and through the door opened by that perception criticism enters, if we but give it time, as a flood, the great flood of awareness; so maintaining its high tide unless through some lapse of our sense for it, some flat reversion to instinct alone, we block up the ingress and sit in stale and shrinking waters. Stupidity may arrest any current and fatuity transcend any privilege. The comfort of those who at such a time consider the scene may be a little, with *their* curiosity still insistent, to survey its platitude and record the exhibited shrinkage; which amounts to the attempt to understand how stupidity could so have prevailed. We take it here that the answer to that inquiry can be ever the same. The flood of "production" has so inordinately exceeded the activity of control that this latter anxious agent, first alarmed but then indifferent, has been forced backward out of the gate, leaving the contents of the reservoir to boil and evaporate. It is verily on the wrong side of the gate that we just now seem to see criticism stand, for never was the reservoir so bubblingly and noisily full, at least by the superficial measure of life. We have caught the odd accident in the very fact of its occurrence; we have seen the torrent swell by extravagant cheap contribution, the huge increase of affluents turbid and unrestrained. Beyond number are the ways in which the democratic example, once gathering momentum, sets its mark on societies and seasons that stand in its course. Nowhere is that example written larger, to our perception, than in "the new novel"; though this, we hasten to add, not in the least because prose fiction now occupies itself as never before with the "condition of the people", a fact quite irrelevant to the nature it has taken on, but because that nature amounts exactly to the complacent declaration of a common literary level, a repudiation the most operative even if the least reasoned of the idea of differences, the virtual law, as we may call it, of sorts and kinds, the values of individual quality and weight in the presence of undiscriminated quantity and rough-and-tumble "output"—these attestations made, we naturally mean, in the air of composition and on the aesthetic plane, if such terms have still an attenuated reference to the case before us. With which, if we be asked, in the light of that generalization, whether we impute to the novel, or in other words the novelist, *all* the stupidity against which the spirit of appreciation spends itself in vain, we reply perforce that we stop short of that, it being too obvious that of an exhibition so sterilized, so void of all force and suggestion, there would be nothing whatever to say. Our contention is exactly that, in spite of all vain aspects, it does yet present an interest, and that here and there seem written on it likelihoods of its presenting still more—always on condition of its consenting to that more intimate education which is precisely what democratized movements look most askance at. It strikes us as not too much to say that our actual view of the practice of fiction gives as just a measure as could be desired of the general, the incurable democratic suspicion of the selective and comparative principles in almost any application, and the tendency therewith to regard, and above all to treat, one manner of book, like one manner of person, as, if not absolutely as good as another, yet good enough for any democratic use. Criticism reflects contentiously on that appearance, though it be an appearance in which comfort for the book and the manner much resides; so that the idea prompting these remarks of our own is that the comfort may be deeply fallacious.

I

Still not to let go of our imputation of interest to some part at least of what is happening in the world of production in this kind, we may say that non-selective and non-comparative practice appears bent on showing us all it can do and how far or to what appointed shores, what waiting havens and inviting inlets, the current that is mainly made a current by looseness, by want of observable direction, shall succeed in carrying it. We respond to any sign of an intelligent view or even of a lively instinct—which is why we give the appearance so noted the benefit of every presumption as to its life and health. It may be that the dim sense is livelier than the presentable reason, but even that is no graceless fact for us, especially when the keenness of young curiosity and energy is betrayed in its pace, and betrayed, for that matter, in no small abundance and variety. The new or at least the young novel is up and doing, clearly, with the best faith and the highest spirits in the world; if we but extend a little our measure of youth indeed, as we are happily more and more disposed to, we may speak of it as already chin-deep in trophies. The men who are not so young as the youngest were but the other day very little older than these: Mr. Joseph Conrad, Mr. Maurice Hewlett and Mr. Galsworthy, Mr. H. G. Wells and Mr. Arnold Bennett, have not quite perhaps the early bloom of Mr. Hugh Walpole, Mr. Gilbert Cannan, Mr. Compton Mackenzie and Mr. D. H. Lawrence, but the spring unrelaxed is still, to our perception, in their step, and we see two or three of them sufficiently related to the still newer generation in a quasi-parental way to make our whole enumeration as illustrational as we need it. Mr. Wells and Mr. Arnold Bennett have their strongest mark, the aspect by which we may most classify them, in common—even if their three named contemporaries are doubtless most interesting in one of the connections we are not now seeking to make. The author of *Tono-Bungay* and of *The New Machiavelli*, and the author of *The Old Wives' Tale* and of *Clayhanger*, have practically launched the boat in which we admire the fresh play of oar of the author of *The Duchess of Wrexe*, and the documented aspect exhibited successively by *Round the Corner*, by *Carnival* and *Sinister Street*, and even by *Sons and Lovers* (however much we may find Mr. Lawrence, we confess, hang in the dusty rear). We shall explain in a moment what we mean by this designation of the element that these best of the younger men strike us as more particularly sharing, our point being provisionally that Mr. Wells and Mr. Arnold Bennett (speaking now only of them) began some time back to show us, and to show sundry emulous and generous young spirits than in the act of more or less waking up, what the state in question might amount to. We confound the author of *Tono-Bungay* and the author of *Clayhanger* in this imputation for the simple reason that with the sharpest differences of character and range they yet come together under our so convenient measure of value by *saturation*. This is the greatest value, to our sense, in either of them, their other values, even when at the highest, not being quite in proportion to it; and as to be documented, to be able even on occasion to prove quite enviably and potently so, they are alike in the authority that creates emulation. It little signifies that Mr. Wells's documented or saturated state in respect to a particular matter in hand is but one of the faces of his *generally* informed condition, of his extraordinary mass of gathered and assimilated knowledge, a miscellaneous collection more remarkable surely than any teller of "mere" tales, with the possible exception of Balzac, has been able to draw upon, whereas Mr. Arnold Bennett's corresponding provision affects us as, though singularly copious, special, exclusive and artfully economic. This distinction avails nothing against that happy fact of the handiest possession by Mr. Wells of immeasurably more concrete material, amenable for straight and vivid reference, convertible into apt illustration, than we should know where to look for examples of. The author of *The New Machiavelli* knows, somehow, to our mystified and dazzled apprehension, because he writes and because that act constitutes for him the need, on occasion a most desperate, of absorbing knowledge at the pores; the chronicler of the *Five Towns* writing so much more discernibly, on the other hand, because he knows, and conscious of no need more desperate than that particular circle of civilization may satisfy.

. Our argument is that each is ideally immersed in his own body of reference, and that immersion in any such degree and to the effect of any such variety, intensity and plausibility is really among us a new feature of the novelist's range of resource. We have seen him, we have even seen *her*, otherwise auspiciously endowed, seen him observant, impassioned, inspired, and in virtue of these things often very charming, very interesting, very triumphant, visibly qualified for the highest distinction before the fact and visibly crowned by the same after it— we have seen him with a great imagination and a great sense of life, we have seen him even with a great sense of expression and a considerable sense of art: so that we have only to re-ascend the stream of our comparatively recent literature to meet him serene and immortal, browbound with the bay and erect on his particular pedestal. We have only to do that, but have only also, while we do it, to recognize that meantime other things still than these various apotheoses have taken place, and that, to the increase of our recreation, and even if our limited space condemns us to put the matter a trifle clumsily, a change has come over our general receptive sensibility not less than over our productive tradition. In these connections, we admit, overstatement is easy and overemphasis tempting; we confess furthermore to a frank desire to enrich the case, the historic, with all the meaning we can stuff into it. So viewed accordingly it gives us the "new", to repeat our expression, as an appetite for a closer notation, a sharper specification of the signs of life, of consciousness, of the human scene and the human subject in general, than the three or four generations before us had been at all moved to insist on. They had insisted indeed, these generations, we see as we look back to them, on almost nothing whatever; what was to come to them had come, in enormous affluence and freshness at its best, and to our continued appreciation as well as to the honour of their sweet susceptibility, because again and again the great miracle of genius took place, while they gaped, in their social and sentimental sky. For ourselves that miracle has not been markedly renewed, but it has none the less happened that by hook and by crook the case for appreciation remains interesting. The great thing that saves it, under the drawback we have named, is, no doubt, that we have simply—always for appreciation—learned a little to insist, and that we thus get back on one hand something of what we have lost on the other. We are unable of course, with whatever habit of presumption engendered, to insist upon genius; so that who shall describe the measure of success we still achieve as not virtually the search for freshness, and above all for closeness, in quite a different direction? To this nearer view of commoner things Mr. Wells, say, and Mr. Arnold Bennett, and in their degree, under the infection communicated, Mr. D. H. Lawrence and Mr. Gilbert Cannan and Mr. Compton Mackenzie and Mr. Hugh Walpole, strike us as having all gathered themselves up with a movement never yet undertaken on our literary scene, and beyond anything else, with an instinctive divination of what had most waved their predecessors off it. What had this lion in the path been, we make them out as after a fashion asking themselves, what had it been from far back and straight down through all the Victorian time, but the fond superstition that the key of the situation, of each and every situation that could turn up for the novelist, was the sentimental key, which might fit into no door or window opening on closeness or on freshness at all? Was it not for all the world as if even the brightest practitioners of the past, those we now distinguish as saved for glory in spite of themselves, had been as sentimental as they could, or, to give the trick another name, as romantic and thereby as shamelessly "dodgy"?—just in order *not* to be close and fresh, not to be authentic, as that takes trouble, takes talent, and you can be sentimental, you can be romantic, you can be dodgy, alas, not a bit less on the footing of genius than on the footing of mediocrity or even of imbecility? Was it not as if the sentimental had been more and more noted as but another name for the romantic, if not indeed the romantic as but another name for the sentimental, and as if these things, whether separate or united, had been in the same degree recognized as unamenable, or at any rate unfavourable, to any consistent fineness of notation, once the tide of the copious as a condition of the thorough had fairly set in?

So, to express it briefly, the possibility of hugging the shore of the real as it had not, among us, been hugged, and of pushing inland, as far as a keel might float, wherever the least opening seemed to smile, dawned upon a few votaries and gathered further confidence with exercise. Who could say, of course, that Jane Austen had not been close, just as who could ask if Anthony Trollope had not been copious? —just as who could *not* say that it all depended on what was meant by these terms? The demonstration of what was meant, it presently appeared, could come but little by little, quite as if each tentative adventurer had rather anxiously to learn for himself what *might* be meant—this failing at least the leap into the arena of some great demonstrative, some sudden athletic and epoch-making authority. Who could pretend that Dickens was anything but romantic, and even more romantic in his humour, if possible, than in pathos or in queer perfunctory practice of the "plot"? Who could pretend that Jane Austen didn't leave much more untold than told about the aspects and manners even of the confined circle in which her muse revolved? Why shouldn't it be argued against her that where her testimony complacently ends the pressure of appetite within us presumes exactly to begin? Who could pretend that the reality of Trollope didn't owe much of its abundance to the diluted, the quite extravagantly watered strain, no less than to the heavy hand, in which it continued to be ladled out? Who of the younger persuasion would not have been ready to cite, as one of the liveliest opportunities for the critic eager to see representation searching, such a claim for the close as Thackeray's sighing and protesting "look-in" at the acquaintance between Arthur Pendennis and Fanny Bolton, the daughter of the Temple laundress, amid the purlieus of that settlement? The sentimental habit and the spirit of romance, it was unmistakably chargeable, stood out to sea as far as possible the moment the shore appeared to offer the least difficulty to hugging, and the Victorian age bristled with perfect occasions for our catching them in the act of this showy retreat. All revolutions have been prepared in spite of their often striking us as sudden, and so it was doubtless that when scarce longer ago than the other day Mr. Arnold Bennett had the fortune to lay his hand on a general scene and a cluster of agents deficient to a peculiar degree in properties that might interfere with a desirable density of illustration—deficient, that is, in such connections as might carry the imagination off to some sport on its own account—we recognized at once a set of conditions auspicious to the newer kind of appeal. Let us confess that we were at the same time doubtless to master no better way of describing these conditions than by the remark that they were, for some reason beautifully inherent in them, susceptible at once of being entirely known and of seeming delectably thick. Reduction to exploitable knowledge is apt to mean for many a case of the human complexity reduction to comparative thinness; and nothing was thereby at the first blush to interest us more than the fact that the air and the very smell of packed actuality in the subject-matter of such things as the author's two longest works was clearly but another name for his personal competence in that matter, the fullness and firmness of his embrace of it. This was a fresh and beguiling impression—that the state of inordinate possession on the chronicler's part, the mere state as such and as an energy directly displayed, *was* the interest, neither more nor less, *was* the sense and the meaning and the picture and the drama, all so sufficiently constituting them that it scarce mattered what they were in themselves. Of what they were in themselves their being in Mr. Bennett, as Mr. Bennett to such a tune harboured them, represented their one conceivable account—not to mention, as reinforcing this, our own great comfort and relief when certain high questions and wonderments about them, or about our mystified relation to them, began one after another to come up.

Because such questions did come, we must at once declare, and we are still in presence of them, for all the world as if that case of the perfect harmony, the harmony between subject and author, were just marked with a flaw and didn't meet the whole assault of restless criticism. What we make out Mr. Bennett as doing is simply recording his possession or, to put it more completely, his saturation; and to see him as virtually shut up to that process is a note of all the more moment that we see our selected cluster of his interesting juniors, and whether by his direct action on their collective impulse or not, embroiled, as we venture to call it, in the same predicament. The act of squeezing out to the utmost the plump and more or less juicy orange of a particular acquainted state and letting this affirmation of energy, however directed or undirected, constitute for them the "treatment" of a theme—*that* is what we remark them as mainly engaged in, after remarking the example so strikingly, so originally set, even if an undue subjection to it be here and there repudiated. Nothing is further from our thought than to undervalue saturation and possession, the fact of the particular experience, the state and degree of acquaintance incurred, however such a consciousness may have been determined; for these things represent on the part of the novelist, as on the part of any painter of things seen, felt or imagined, just one half of his authority—the other half being represented of course by the application he is inspired to make of them. Therefore that fine secured half is so much gained at the start, and the fact of its brightly being there may really by itself project upon the course so much colour and form as to make us on occasion, under the genial force, almost not miss the answer to the question of application.

When the author of *Clayhanger* has put down upon the table, in dense unconfused array, every fact required, every fact in any way invocable, to make the life of the *Five Towns* press upon us, and to make our sense of it, so full-fed, content us, we may very well go on for the time in the captive condition, the beguiled and bemused condition, the acknowledgment of which is in general our highest tribute to the temporary master of our sensibility. Nothing at such moments—or rather at the end of them, when the end begins to threaten—may be of a more curious strain than the dawning unrest that suggests to us fairly our first critical comment: "Yes, yes—but is this *all*? These are the circumstances of the interest—we see, we see; but where is the interest itself, where and what is its centre, and how are we to measure it in relation to *that*?" Of course we may in the act of exhaling that plaint (which we have just expressed at its mildest) well remember how many people there are to tell us that to "measure" an interest is none of our affair; that we have but to take it on the cheapest and easiest terms and be thankful; and that if by our very confession we have been led the imaginative dance the music has done for us all it pretends to. Which words, however, have only to happen to be for us the most intelligent conceivable not in the least to arrest our wonderment as to where our bedrenched consciousness may still not awkwardly leave us for the pleasure of appreciation. That appreciation is also a mistake and a priggishness, being reflective and thereby corrosive, is another of the fond dicta which we are here concerned but to brush aside—the more closely to embrace the welcome induction that appreciation, attentive and reflective, inquisitive and conclusive, is in this connection absolutely the golden *key* to our pleasure. The more it plays up, the more we recognize and are able to number the sources of our enjoyment, the greater the provision made for security in that attitude, which corresponds, by the same stroke, with the reduced danger of waste in the undertaking to amuse us. It all comes back to our amusement, and to the noblest surely, on the whole, we know; and it is in the very nature of clinging appreciation not to sacrifice consentingly a single shade of the art that makes for that blessing. From this solicitude spring our questions, and not least the one to which we give ourselves for the moment here—this moment of our being regaled as never yet with the fruits of the movement (if the name be not of too pompous an application where the flush and the heat of accident too seem so candidly to look forth), in favour of the "expression of life" in terms as loose as may pretend to an effect of expression at all.

The relegation of terms to the limbo of delusions outlived so far as ever really cultivated becomes of necessity, it will be plain, the great mark of the faith that for the novelist to show he "knows all about" a certain congeries of aspects, the more numerous within their mixed circle the better, is thereby to set in motion, with due intensity, the pretension to interest. The state of knowing all about whatever it may be has thus only to become consistently and abundantly active to pass for his supreme function; and to its so becoming active few difficulties appear to be described—so great may on occasion be the mere excitement of activity. To the fact that the exhilaration is, as we have hinted, often infectious, to this and to the charming young good faith and general acclamation under which each case appears to proceed—each case we of course mean really repaying attention—the critical reader owes his opportunity so considerably and so gratefully to generalize.

II

We should have only to remount the current with a certain energy to come straight up against Tolstoy as the great illustrative masterhand on all this ground of the disconnection of method from matter—which encounter, however, would take us much too far, so that we must for the present but hang off from it with the remark that of all great painters of the social picture it was given that epic genius most to serve admirably as a rash adventurer and a "caution", and execrably, pestilentially, as a model. In this strange union of relations he stands alone: from no other great projector of the human image and the human idea is so much truth to be extracted under an equal leakage of its value. All the proportions in him are so much the largest that the drop of attention to our nearer cases might by its violence leave little of that principle alive; which fact need not disguise from us, none the less, that as Mr. H. G. Wells and Mr. Arnold Bennett, to return to them briefly again, derive, by multiplied if diluted transmissions, from the great Russian (from whose all but equal companion Turgénieff we recognize no derivatives at all), so, observing the distances, we may profitably detect an unexhausted influence in our minor, our still considerably less rounded vessels. Highly attaching as indeed the game might be, of inquiring as to the centre of the interest or the sense of the whole in *The Passionate Friends*, or in *The Old Wives' Tale*, after

having sought those luxuries in vain not only through the general
length and breadth of *War and Peace*, but within the quite respectable
confines of any one of the units of effect there clustered: this as preparing us to address a like friendly challenge to Mr. Cannan's *Round
the Corner*, say, or to Mr. Lawrence's *Sons and Lovers*—should we wish
to be *very* friendly to Mr. Lawrence—or to Mr. Hugh Walpole's
Duchess of Wrexe, or even to Mr. Compton Mackenzie's *Sinister Street*
and *Carnival*, discernibly, we hasten to add, though certain betrayals
of a controlling idea and a pointed intention do comparatively gleam
out of the two fictions last named. *The Old Wives' Tale* is the history
of two sisters, daughters of a prosperous draper in a Staffordshire town,
who, separating early in life, through the flight of one of them to
Paris with an ill-chosen husband and the confirmed and prolonged
local pitch of the career of the other, are re-united late in life by the
return of the fugitive after much Parisian experience and by her pacified
acceptance of the conditions of her birthplace. The divided current
flows together again and the chronicle closes with the simple drying
up determined by the death of the sisters. That is all; the canvas is
covered, ever so closely and vividly covered, by the exhibition of innumerable small facts and aspects, at which we assist with the most
comfortable sense of their substantial truth. The sisters, and more
particularly the less adventurous, are at home in their author's mind,
they sit and move at their ease in the square chamber of his attention,
to a degree beyond which the production of that ideal harmony between creature and creator could scarcely go, and all by an art of demonstration so familiar and so "quiet" that the truth and the poetry, to
use Goethe's distinction, melt utterly together and we see no difference
between the subject of the show and the showman's feeling, let alone
the showman's manner, about it. This felt identity of the elements—
because we at least consciously feel—becomes in the novel we refer
to, and not less in *Clayhanger*, which our words equally describe, a
source for us of abject confidence, confidence truly *so* abject in the
solidity of every appearance that it may be said to represent our whole
relation to the work and completely to exhaust our reaction upon it.
Clayhanger, of the two fictions even the more densely loaded with all
the evidence in what we should call the case presented did we but learn
meanwhile for what case, or for a case of what, to take it, inscribes
the annals, the private more particularly of a provincial printer in a
considerable way of business, beginning with his early boyhood and
going on to the complications of his maturity—these not exhausted

with our present possession of the record, inasmuch as by the author's announcement there is more of the catalogue to come. This most monumental of Mr. Arnold Bennett's recitals, taking it with its supplement of *Hilda Lessways*, already before us, is so describable through its being a monument exactly not to an idea, a pursued and captured meaning, or in short *to* anything whatever, but just simply *of* the quarried and gathered material it happens to contain, the stones and bricks and rubble and cement and promiscuous constituents of every sort that have been heaped in it and thanks to which it quite massively piles itself up. Our perusal and our enjoyment are our watching of the growth of the pile and of the capacity, industry, energy with which the operation is directed. A huge and in its way a varied aggregation, the mere number of its pieces, the great dump of its material, together with the fact that here and there in the miscellany, as with the value of bits of marble or porphyry, fine elements shine out, it keeps us standing and waiting to the end—and largely just because it keeps us wondering. We surely wonder more what it may all propose to mean than any equal appearance of preparation to relieve us of that strain, any so founded and grounded a postponement of the disclosure of a sense in store, has for a long time called upon us to do in a like connection. A great thing it is assuredly that *while* we wait and wonder we are amused—were it not for that, truly, our situation would be thankless enough; we may ask ourselves, as has already been noted, why on such ambiguous terms we should consent to be, and why the practice doesn't at a given moment break down; and our answer brings us back to that many-fingered grasp of the orange that the author squeezes. This particular orange is of the largest and most rotund, and his trust in the consequent flow is of its nature communicative. Such is the case always, and most naturally, with that air in a person who has something, who at the very least has much to tell us: we *like* so to be affected by it, we meet it half way and lend ourselves, sinking in up to the chin. Up to the chin only indeed, beyond doubt; we even then feel our head emerge, for judgment and articulate question, and it is from that position that we remind ourselves how the real reward of our patience is still to come—the reward attending not at all the immediate sense of immersion, but reserved for the after-sense, which is a very different matter, whether in the form of a glow or of a chill.

If Mr. Bennett's rotundity then is of the handsomest size and his manipulation of it so firm, what are we to say of Mr. Wells's, who, a novelist very much as Lord Bacon was a philosopher, affects us as taking all knowledge for his province and as inspiring in us to the very highest degree the confidence enjoyed by himself—enjoyed, we feel, with a breadth with which it has been given no one of his fellow-craftsmen to enjoy anything. If confidence alone could lead utterly captive we should all be huddled in a bunch at Mr. Wells's heels—which is indeed where we *are* abjectly gathered so far as that force does operate. It is literally Mr. Wells's own mind, and the experience of his own mind, incessant and extraordinarily various, extraordinarily reflective, even with all sorts of conditions made, of whatever he may expose it to, that forms the reservoir tapped by him, that constitutes his provision of grounds of interest. It is, by our thinking, in his power to name to us, as a preliminary, more of these grounds than all his contemporaries put together, and even to exceed any competitor, without exception, in the way of suggesting that, thick as he may seem to lay them, they remain yet only contributive, are not in themselves fully expressive but are designed strictly to subserve it, that this extra-ordinary writer's spell resides. When full expression of some particular truth, seemed to lapse in this or that of his earlier novels (we speak not here of his shorter things, for the most part delightfully wanton and exempt), it was but by a hand's breadth, so that if we didn't inveterately quite know what he intended we yet always felt sufficiently that *he* knew. The particular intentions of such matters as *Kipps*, as *Tono-Bungay*, as *Ann Veronica*, so swarmed about us, in their blinding, bluffing vivacity, that the mere sum of them might have been taken for a sense over and above which it was graceless to inquire. The more this author learns and learns, or at any rate knows and knows, however, the greater is this impression of his holding it good enough for us, such as we are, that he shall but turn out his mind and its contents upon us by any free familiar gesture and as from a high window forever open —an entertainment as copious surely as any occasion should demand, at least till we have more intelligibly expressed our title to a better. Such things as *The New Machiavelli*, *Marriage*, *The Passionate Friends*, are so very much more attestations of the presence of material than attestations of an interest in the use of it that we ask ourselves again and again why so fondly neglected a state of leakage comes not to be fatal to *any* provision of quantity, or even to stores more specially selected for the ordeal than Mr. Wells's always strike us as being. Is not the pang of witnessed waste in fact great just in proportion as we are touched by our author's fine offhandedness as to the value of the stores, about which he can for the time make us believe what he will? so that, to take an example susceptible of brief statement, we wince at a certain quite peculiarly gratuitous sacrifice to the casual in *Marriage* very much as at seeing some fine and indispensable little part of a mechanism slip through profane fingers and lose itself. Who does not remember what ensues after a little upon the aviational descent of the hero of the fiction just named into the garden occupied, in company with her parents, by the young lady with whom he is to fall in love?—and this even though the whole opening scene so constituted, with all the comedy hares its function appears to be to start, remains with its back squarely turned, aesthetically speaking, to the quarter in which the picture develops. The point for our mortification is that by one of the first steps in this development, the first impression on him having been made, the hero accidentally meets the heroine, of a summer eventide, in a leafy lane which supplies them with the happiest occasion to pursue their acquaintance—or in other words supplies the author with the liveliest consciousness (as we at least feel it should have been) that just so the relation between the pair, its seed already sown and the fact of that bringing about all that is still to come, pushes aside whatever veil and steps forth into life. To show it step forth and affirm itself as a relation, what is this but the interesting function of the whole passage, on the performance of which what follows is to hang?—and yet who can say that when the ostensible sequence *is* presented, and our young lady, encountered again by her stirred swain, under cover of night, in a favouring wood, is at once encompassed by his arms and pressed to his lips and heart (for celebration thus of their third meeting) we do not assist at a well-nigh heartbreaking miscarriage of "effect"? We see effect, invoked in vain, simply stand off unconcerned; effect not having been at all consulted in advance she is not to be secured on such terms. And her presence would so have redounded—perfectly punctual creature as she is on a made appointment and a clear understanding— to the advantage of all concerned. The bearing of the young man's act is all in our having begun to conceive it as possible, begun even to desire it, in the light of what has preceded; therefore if the participants have *not* been shown us as on the way to it, nor the question of it made beautifully to tremble for us in the air, its happiest connections fail and we but stare at it mystified. The instance is undoubtedly trifling, but in the infinite complex of such things resides for a work of art the shy virtue, shy at least till wooed forth, of the whole susceptibility. The case of Mr. Wells might take us much further—such remarks as there would be to make, say, on such a question as the due understanding, on the part of *The Passionate Friends* (not as associated persons but as a composed picture), of what composition is specifically *about* and where, for treatment of this interest, it undertakes to find its centre: all of which, we are willing however to grant, falls away before the large assurance and incorrigible levity with which this adventurer carries his lapses—far more of an adventurer as he is than any other of the company. The composition, as we have called it, heaven saving the mark, is simply at any and every moment "about" Mr. Wells's general adventure; which is quite enough while it preserves, as we trust it will long continue to do, its present robust pitch.

We have already noted that *Round the Corner*, Mr. Gilbert Cannan's liveliest appeal to our attention, belongs to the order of *constatations* pure and simple; to the degree that *as* a document of that nature and of that rigour the book could perhaps not more completely affirm itself. When we have said that it puts on record the "tone", the manners, the general domestic proceedings and *train de vie* of an amiable clergyman's family established in one of the more sordid quarters of a big black northern city of the Liverpool or Manchester complexion we have advanced as far in the way of descriptive statement as the interesting work seems to warrant. For it *is* interesting, in spite of its leaving itself on our hands with a consistent indifference to any question of the charmed application springing from it all that places it in the forefront of its type. Again as under the effect of Mr. Bennett's major productions our sole inference is that things, the things disclosed, *go on and on, in any given case, in spite of everything*—with Mr. Cannan's one discernible care perhaps being for how extraordinarily much, in particular example here before him, they were able to go on in spite of. The conception, the presentation of this enormous inauspicious amount as bearing upon the collective career of the Folyats is, we think, as near as the author comes at any point to betraying an awareness of a subject. Yet again, though so little encouraged or "backed", a subject after a fashion makes itself, even as it has made itself in *The Old Wives' Tale* and in *Clayhanger*, in *Sons and Lovers*, where, as we have hinted, any assistance rendered us for a view of one *most* comfortably enjoys its absence, and in Mr. Hugh Walpole's newest novel, where we wander scarcely less with our hand in no guiding grasp, but where the author's good disposition, as we feel it, to provide us with what we lack if he only knew how, constitutes in itself such a pleading liberality. We seem to see him in this spirit lay again and again a flowered carpet for our steps. If we do not include

Mr. Compton Mackenzie to the same extent in our generalization it is really because we note a difference in him, a difference in favour of his care for the application. Preoccupations seem at work in *Sinister Street*, and withal in *Carnival*, the brush of which we in other quarters scarce even suspect and at some of which it will presently be of profit to glance. "I answer for it, you know", we seem at any rate to hear Mr. Gilbert Cannan say with an admirably genuine young pessimism, "I answer for it that they were really *like* that, odd or unpleasant or un-contributive, and therefore tiresome, as it may strike you"; and the charm of Mr. Cannan, so far as up or down the rank we so disengage a charm, is that we take him at his word. His guarantee, his straight communication, of his general truth is a value, and values are rare—the flood of fiction is apparently capable of running hundreds of miles without a single glint of one—and thus in default of satisfaction we get stopgaps and are thankful often under a genial touch to get even so much. The value indeed is crude, it would be quadrupled were it only wrought and shaped; yet it has still the rude dignity that it counts to us for experience or at least for what we call under our present pitch of sensibility force of impression. The experience, we feel, is ever something to conclude upon, while the impression is content to wait; to wait, say, in the spirit in which we must accept this younger bustle if we accept at all, the spirit of its serving as a rather presumptuous lesson to us in patience. While we wait, again, we are amused—not in the least, also to repeat, up to the notch of our conception of amuse-ment, which draws upon still other forms and sources; but none the less for the wonder, the intensity, the actuality, the probity of the vision. This is much as in *Clayhanger* and in *Hilda Lessways*, where independently of the effect, so considerably rendered, of the long lapse of time, always in this type of recital a source of amusement in itself, and certainly of the noblest, we get such an admirably substantial thing as the collective image of the Orgreaves, the local family in whose ample lap the amenities and the humanities so easily sit, for Mr. Ben-nett's evocation and his protagonist's recognition, and the manner of the presentation of whom, with the function and relation of the picture at large, strikes such a note of felicity, achieves such a simulation of sense, as the author should never again be excused for treating, that is for neglecting, as beyond his range. Here figures signally the interesting case of a compositional function absolutely performed by mere multi-plication, the flow of the facts: the Orgreaves, in *Clayhanger*, are there, by what we make out, but for "life", for general life only, and yet, with their office under any general or inferential meaning entirely un-marked, come doubtless as near squaring aesthetically with the famous formula of the "slice of life" as any example that could be adduced; happening moreover as they probably do to owe this distinction to their coincidence at once with reality and charm—a fact aesthetically curious and delightful. For we attribute the bold stroke they represent much more to Mr. Arnold Bennett's aesthetic instinct than to anything like a calculation of his bearings, and more to his thoroughly ac-quainted state, as we may again put it, than to all other causes together: which strikingly enough shows how much complexity of interest may be simulated by mere presentation of material, mere squeezing of the orange, when the material happens to be "handsome" or the orange to be sweet.

III

The orange of our persistent simile is in Mr. Hugh Walpole's hands very remarkably sweet—a quality we recognize in it even while re-duced to observing that the squeeze pure and simple, the fond, the lingering, the reiterated squeeze, constitutes as yet his main perception of method. He enjoys in a high degree the consciousness of saturation, and is on such serene and happy terms with it as almost make of critical interference, in so bright an air, an assault on personal felicity. Full of material is thus the author of *The Duchess of Wrexe*, and of a material which we should describe as the consciousness of youth were we not rather disposed to call it a peculiar strain of the extreme unconsciousness. Mr. Walpole offers us indeed a rare and interesting case—we see about the field none other like it; the case of a positive identity between the spirit, not to say the time of life or stage of experience, of the aspiring artist and the field itself of his vision. *The Duchess of Wrexe* reeks with youth and the love of youth and the confidence of youth—youth taking on with a charming exuberance the fondest costume or dis-guise, that of an adventurous and voracious felt interest, interest in life, in London, in society, in character, in Portland Place, in the Oxford Circus, in the afternoon tea-table, in the torrid weather, in fifty other immediate things as to which its passion and its curiosity are of the sincerest. The wonderful thing is that these latter forces operate, in their way, without yet being disengaged and hand-free—disengaged, that is, from their state of *being* young, with its billowy mufflings and other soft obstructions, the state of being present, being involved and aware, close "up against" the whole mass of possibilities, being in short intoxicated with the mixed liquors of suggestion. In the fumes of this acute situation Mr. Walpole's subject-matter is bathed; the situation being all the while so much more his own and that of a juvenility re-acting, in the presence of everything, "for all it is worth", than the devised and imagined one, however he may circle about some such cluster, that every cupful of his excited flow tastes three times as much of his temperamental freshness as it tastes of this, that or the other character or substance, above all of this, that or the other group of antecedents and references, supposed to be reflected in it. All of which does not mean, we hasten to add, that the author of *The Duchess of Wrexe* has not the gift of life; but only that he strikes us as having received it, straight from nature, with such a concussion as to have kept the boon at the stage of violence—so that, fairly pinned down by it, he is still embarrassed for passing it on. On the day he shall have worked free of this primitive predicament, the crude fact of the con-vulsion itself, there need be no doubt of his exhibiting matter into which method may learn how to bite. The tract meanwhile affects us as more or less virgin snow, and we look with interest and suspense for the imprint of a process.

If those remarks represent all the while, further, that the perform-ances we have glanced at, with others besides, lead our attention on, we hear ourselves the more naturally asked what it is then that we expect or want, confessing as we do that we have been in a manner interested, even though, from case to case, in a varying degree, and that Thackeray, Turgénieff, Balzac, Dickens, Anatole France, no matter who, can not do more than interest. Let us therefore concede to the last point that small mercies are better than none, that there are latent within the critic numberless liabilities to being "squared" (the extent to which he may on occasion betray his price!) and so great a preference for being pleased over not being, that you may again and again see him assist with avidity at the attempt of the slice of life to butter itself thick. Its explanation that it *is* a slice of life and pretends to be nothing else figures for us, say, while we watch, the jam super-added to the butter. For since the jam, on this system, descends upon our desert, in its form of manna, from quite another heaven than the heaven of method, the mere demonstration of its agreeable presence is alone sufficient to hint at our more than one chance of being super-naturally fed. The happy-go-lucky fashion of it is indeed not then, we grant, an objection so long as we do take in refreshment: the meal may be of the last informality and yet produce in the event no small sense of repletion. The slice of life devoured, the butter and the jam duly appreciated, we are ready, no doubt, on another day, to trust ourselves afresh to the desert. We break camp, that is, and face toward a further stretch of it, all in the faith that we shall be once more provided for. We take the risk, we enjoy more or less the assistance—more or less, we put it, for the vision of a possible arrest of the miracle or failure of our supply never wholly leaves us. The phenomenon is too uncanny, the happy-go-lucky, as we know it in general, never *has* been trustable to the end; the absence of the last true touch in the preparation of its viands becomes with each renewal of the adventure a more sensible fact. By the last true touch we mean of course the touch of the hand of selection; the principle of selection having been involved at the worst or the least, one would suppose, in any approach whatever to the loaf of life with the *arrière-pensée* of a slice. There being no question of a slice upon which the further question of where and how to cut it does not wait, the office of method, the idea of choice and comparison, have occupied the ground from the first. This makes clear, to a moment's reflection, that there can be no such thing as an amorphous slice, and that any waving aside of inquiry as to the sense and value of a chunk of matter has to reckon with the simple truth of its having been *born* of naught else but measured excision. Reasons have been the fairies waiting on its cradle, the possible presence of a bad fairy in the form of a bad reason to the contrary notwithstanding. It has thus had connections at the very first stage of its detachment that are at no later stage logically to be repudiated; let it lie as lumpish as it will—for adoption, we mean, of the ideal of the lump—it has been tainted from too far back with the hard liability to form, and thus carries in its very breast the hapless contradiction of its sturdy claim to have none. This claim has the inevitable challenge at once to meet. How can a slice of life be anything but illustrational of the loaf, and how can illustration not immediately bristle with every sign of the extracted and related state? The relation is at once to what the thing comes from and to what it waits upon—which last is our act of recognition. We accordingly appreciate it in proportion as it so accounts for itself; the quantity and the intensity of its reference are the measure of our knowledge of it. This is exactly why illustration breaks down when reference, otherwise application, runs short, and why before any assemblage of figures or aspects, otherwise of samples and specimens, the question of what these are, extensively, samples and specimens *of* declines not to beset us—why, otherwise again, we look ever for the supreme reference that shall avert the bankruptcy of sense.

Let us profess all readiness to repeat that we may still have had, on the merest "life" system, or that of the starkest crudity of the slice, all the entertainment that can come from watching a wayfarer engage with assurance in an alley that we know to have no issue—and from catching for the very sake of the face that he may show us on re-appearing at its mouth. The recitals of Mr. Arnold Bennett, Mr. Gilbert Cannan, Mr. D. H. Lawrence, fairly smell of the real, just as the *Fortitude* and *The Duchess* of Mr. Hugh Walpole smell of the roman-tic; we have sufficiently noted then that, once on the scent, we are capable of pushing ahead. How far it is at the same time from being all a matter of smell the terms in which we just above glanced at the weakness of the spell of the happy-go-lucky may here serve to indicate. There faces us all the while the fact that the act of consideration as an incident of the aesthetic pleasure, consideration confidently knowing us to *have* sooner or later to arrive at it, may be again and again post-poned, but can never hope not some time to fall due. Consideration is susceptible of many forms, some one or other of which no conscious aesthetic effort fails to cry out for; and the simplest description of the cry of the novel when sincere—for have we not heard such composi-tions bluff us, as it were, with false cries?—is as an appeal to us when we have read it once to read it yet again. *That* is the act of considera-tion; no other process of considering approaches this for directness, so that anything short of it is virtually not to consider at all. The word has sometimes another sense, that of the appeal to us *not*, for the world, to go back—this being of course consideration of a sort; the sort clearly that the truly flushed production should be the last to invoke. The effect of consideration, we need scarce remark, is to light for us in a work of art the hundred questions of how and why and whither, and the effect of these questions, once lighted, is enormously to thicken and complicate, even if towards final clarifications, what we have called the amused state produced in us by the work. The more our amusement multiplies its terms the more fond and the more rewarded consideration becomes; the fewer it leaves them, on the other hand, the less to be resisted for us is the impression of "bare ruined choirs where late the sweet birds sang". Birds that have appeared to sing, or whose silence we have not heeded, on a first perusal, prove on a second to have no note to contribute, and whether or no a second is enough to admonish us of those we miss, we mostly expect much from it in the way of emphasis of those we find. Then it is that notes of intention become more present or more absent; then it is that we take the measure of what we have already called our effective provision. The bravest providers and designers show at this point something still in store which only the second rummage was appointed to draw forth. To the variety of these ways of not letting our fondness fast is there not practically no limit?—and of the arts, the devices, the graces, the subtle secrets applicable to such an end what presumptuous critic shall pretend to draw the list? Let him for the moment content himself with saying that many of the most effective are mysteries, precisely, of method, or that when they are not most essentially and directly so it takes method, blest method, to extract their soul and to determine their action.

It is odd and delightful perhaps that at the very moment of our urging this truth we should happen to be regaled with a really supreme specimen of the part playable in a novel by the source of interest, the principle of provision attended to, for which we claim importance. Mr. Joseph Conrad's *Chance* is none the less a signal instance of provision, the most earnest and the most copious for its leaving ever so much to be said about the particular provision effected. It is none the less an extraordinary exhibition of method by the fact that the method is, we venture to say, without a precedent in any like work. It places Mr. Conrad absolutely alone as a votary of the way to do a thing that shall make it undergo most doing. The way to do it that shall make it undergo least is the line on which we are mostly now used to see prizes carried off; so that the author of *Chance* gathers up on this showing all sorts of comparative distinction. He gathers up at least two sorts—that of bravery in absolutely reversing the process most accredited, and that, quite separate, we make out, of performing the manœuvre under salvos of recognition. It is not in these days often given to a refinement of design to be recognized, but Mr. Conrad has made his achieve that miracle—save in so far indeed as the miracle has been one thing and the success another. The miracle is of the rarest, confounding all calculation and suggesting more reflections than we can begin to make place for here; but the sources of surprise surrounding it might be, were this possible, even greater and yet leave the fact itself in all independence, the fact that the whole undertaking was committed by its very first step either to be "art" exclusively or to be nothing. This is the prodigious rarity, since surely we have known for many a day no other such case of the whole clutch of eggs, and these withal of the freshest, in that one basket; to which it may be added that if we say for many a day this is not through our readiness positively to associate the sight with any very definite moment of the past. What concerns us is that the general effect of *Chance* is arrived at by a pursuance of means to the end in view contrasted with which every other current form of the chase can only affect us as cheap and futile; the carriage of the burden or amount of service required on these lines exceeding surely all other such displayed degrees of energy put together. Nothing could well interest us more than to see the exemplary value of attention, attention given by the author and asked of the reader attested in a case in which it has had almost unspeakable difficulties to struggle with—since so we are moved to qualify the particular difficulty Mr. Conrad has "elected" to face: the claim for method in itself, method in this very sense of attention applied, would be somehow less lighted if the difficulties struck us as less consciously, or call it even less wantonly, invoked. What they consist of we should have to diverge here a little to say, and should even then probably but lose ourselves in the dim question of why so special, eccentric and desperate a course, so deliberate a plunge into threatened frustration, should alone have seemed open. It has been the course, so far as three words may here serve, of his so multiplying his creators or, as we are now fond of saying, producers, as to make them almost more numerous and quite emphatically more material than the creatures and the production itself in whom and which we by the general law of fiction expect such agents to lose themselves. We take for granted by the general law of fiction a primary author, take him so much for granted that we forget him in proportion as he works upon us, and that he works upon us most in fact by making us forget him.

Mr. Conrad's first care on the other hand is expressly to posit or set up a reciter, a definite responsible intervening first person singular, possessed of infinite sources of references, who immediately proceeds to set up another, to the end that this other may conform again to the practice, and that even at that point the bridge over to the creature, or in other words to the situation or the subject, the thing "produced", shall, if the fancy takes it, once more and yet once more glory in a gap. It is easy to see how heroic the undertaking of an effective fusion becomes on these terms, fusion between what we are to know and that prodigy of our knowing which is ever half the very beauty of the atmosphere of authenticity; from the moment the reporters are thus multiplied from pitch to pitch the tone of each, especially as "rendered" by his precursor in the series, becomes for the prime poet of all an immense question—these circumferential tones having not only to be such individually separate notes, but to keep so clear of the others, the central, the numerous and various voices of the agents proper, those expressive of the action itself and in whom the objectivity resides. We usually escape the worst of this difficulty of a tone *about* the tone of our characters, our projected performers, by keeping it single, keeping it "down" and thereby comparatively impersonal or, as we may say, inscrutable; which is what a creative force, in its blest fatuity, likes to be. But the omniscience, remaining indeed nameless, though constantly active, which sets Marlow's omniscience in motion from the very first page, insisting on a reciprocity with it throughout, this original omniscience invites consideration of itself only in a degree less than that in which Marlow's own invites it; and Marlow's own is a prolonged hovering flight of the subjective over the outstretched ground of the case exposed. We make out this ground but through the shadow cast by the flight, clarify it though the real author visibly reminds himself again and again that he must—all the more that, as if by some tremendous forecast of future applied science, the upper aeroplane causes another, as we have said, to depend from it and that one still another; these dropping shadow after shadow, to the no small menace of intrinsic colour and form and whatever, upon the passive expanse. What shall we most call Mr. Conrad's method accordingly but his attempt to clarify *quand même*—ridden as he has been, we perceive at the end of fifty pages of *Chance*, by such a danger of steeping his matter in perfect eventual obscuration as we recall no other artist's consenting to with an equal grace. This grace, which presently comes over us as the sign of the whole business, is Mr. Conrad's gallantry itself, and the shortest account of the rest of the connection for our present purpose is that his gallantry is thus his success. It literally strikes us that his volume sets in motion more than anything else a drama in which his own system and his combined eccentricities of recital represent the protagonist in face of powers leagued against it, and of which the dénouement gives us the system fighting in triumph, though with its back desperately to the wall, and laying the powers piled up at its feet. This frankly has been *our* spectacle, our suspense and our thrill; with the one flaw on the roundness of it all the fact that the predicament was not imposed rather than invoked, was not the effect of a challenge from without, but that of a mystic impulse from within.

Of an exquisite refinement at all events are the critical questions opened up in the attempt, the question in particular of by what it exactly is that the experiment is crowned. Pronouncing it crowned and the case saved by sheer gallantry, as we did above, is perhaps to fall just short of the conclusion we might reach were we to push further. *Chance is* an example of objectivity, most precious of aims, not only menaced but definitely compromised; whereby we are in presence of something really of the strangest, a general and diffused lapse of authenticity which an inordinate number of common readers—since it always takes this and these to account encouragingly for "editions"—have not only condoned but have emphatically commended. They can have done this but through the bribe of some authenticity other in kind, no doubt, and seeming to them equally great if not greater, which gives back by the left hand what the right has, with however dissimulated a grace, taken away. What Mr. Conrad's left hand gives back then is simply Mr. Conrad himself. We asked above what would become, by such a form of practice, of indispensable "fusion" or, to call it by another name, of the fine process by which our impatient material, at a given moment, shakes off the humiliation of the handled, the fumbled state, puts its head in the air and, to its own beautiful illusory consciousness at least, simply runs its race. Such an amount of handling and fumbling and repointing has it, on the system of the multiplied "putter into marble", to shake off! And yet behold, the sense of discomfort, as the show here works out, *has* been conjured away. The fusion has taken place, or at any rate *a* fusion; only it has been transferred in wondrous fashion to an unexpected, and on the whole more limited plane of operation; it has succeeded in getting effected, so to speak, not on the ground but in the air, not between our writer's idea and his machinery, but between the different parts of his genius itself. His genius is what is left over from the other, the compromised and compromising quantities—the Marlows and their determinant inventors and interlocutors, the Powells, the Franklins, the Fynes, the tell-tale little dogs, the successive members of a cue from one to the other of which the sense and the interest of the subject have to be passed on together, in the manner of the buckets of water for the improvised extinction of a fire, before reaching our apprehension: all with whatever result, to this apprehension, of a quantity to be allowed for as spilt by the way. The residuum has accordingly the form not of such and such a number of images, discharged and ordered, but that rather of a wandering, circling, yearning imaginative *faculty*, encountered in its habit as it lives and diffusing itself as a presence or a tide, a noble sociability of vision. So we have as the force that fills the cup just the high-water mark of a beautiful and generous mind at play in conditions comparatively thankless—thoroughly, unweariedly, yet at the same time ever so elegantly at play, and doing more for itself than it succeeds in getting done for it. Than which nothing could be of a greater reward to critical curiosity were it not still for the wonder of wonder, a new page in the record altogether—the fact that these things are apparently what the common reader has seen and understood. Great then would seem to be after all the common reader!

IV

We must not fail of the point, however, that we have made these remarks not at all with an eye to the question of whether *Chance* has been well or ill inspired as to its particular choice of a way of really attending to itself among all the possible alternatives, but only on the ground of its having compared, selected and held on; since any alternative that might have been preferred and that should have been effectively adopted would point our moral as well—and this even if it is of profit none the less to note the most striking of Mr. Conrad's compositional consequences. There is one of these that has had most to do with making his pages differ in texture, and to our very first glance, from that straggle of ungoverned verbiage which leads us up and down those of his fellow fabulists in general on a vain hunt for some projected mass of truth, some solidity of substance, as to which the deluge of "dialogue", the flooding report of things said, or at least of words pretendedly spoken, shall have learned the art of being merely illustrational. What first springs from any form of real attention, no matter which, we on a comparison so made quickly perceive to be a practical challenge of the preposterous pretension of this most fatuous of the luxuries of looseness to acquit itself with authority of the structural and compositional office. Infinitely valid and vivid as illustration, it altogether depends for dignity and sense upon our state of possession of its historic preliminaries, its promoting conditions, its supporting ground; that is upon our waiting occupancy of the chamber it proposes to light and which, when no other souree of effect is more indicated, it doubtless quite inimitably fills with life. Then its relation to what encloses and confines and, in its sovereign interest, finely compresses it, offering it constituted aspects, surfaces, presences, faces and figures of the matter we are either generally or acutely concerned with to play over and hang upon, then this relation gives it all its value: it has flowered from the soil prepared and sheds back its richness into the field of cultivation. It is interesting, in a word, only when nothing else is equally so, carrying the vessel of the interest with least of a stumble or a sacrifice; but it is of the essence that the sounds so set in motion (it being as sound above all that they undertake to convey sense) should have something to proceed from, in their course, to address themselves to and be affected by, with all the sensibility of sounds. It is of the essence that they should live in a medium, and in a medium only, since it takes a medium to give them an identity, the intenser the better, and that the medium should subserve them by enjoying in a like degree the luxury of an existence. We need of course scarce expressly note that the play, as distinguished from the novel, lives exclusively on the spoken word—not on the report of the thing said but, directly and audibly, on that very thing; that it thrives by its law on the exercise under which the novel hopelessly collapses when the attempt is made disproportionately to impose it. There is no danger for the play of the cart before the horse, no disaster involved in it; that form being *all* horse and the interest itself mounted and astride, and not, as that of the novel, dependent in the first instance on wheels. The order in which the drama simply says things gives it all its form, while the story told and the picture painted, as the novel at the pass we have brought it to embraces them, reports of an infinite diversity of matters, gathers together and gives out again a hundred sorts, and finds its order and its structure, its unity and its beauty, in the alternation of parts and the adjustment of differences. It is no less apparent that the novel may be fundamentally *organized*—such things as *The Egoist* and *The Awkward Age* are there to prove it; but in this case it adheres unconfusedly to that logic and has nothing to say to any other. Were it not for a second exception, one at this season rather pertinent, *Chance* then, to return to it a moment, would be as happy an example as we might just now put our hand on of the automatic working of a scheme unfavourable to that treatment of the colloquy by endless dangling strings which makes the current "story" in general so figure to us a porcupine of extravagant yet abnormally relaxed bristles.

The exception we speak of would be Mrs. Wharton's *Custom of the Country*, in which, as in this lady's other fictions, we recognize the happy fact of an abuse of no one of the resources it enjoys at the ex-

pense of the others; the whole series offering as general an example of
dialogue flowering and not weeding, illustrational and not itself
starved of illustration, or starved of referability and association, which
is the same thing, as meets the eye in any glance that leaves Mr. Wells at
Mr. Wells's best-inspired hour out of our own account. The truth is,
however, that Mrs. Wharton is herself here out of our account, even as
we have easily recognized Mr. Galsworthy and Mr. Maurice Hewlett to
be; these three authors, with whatever differences between them, remaining essentially votaries of selection and intention and being embodi-
ments thereby, in each case, of some state over and above that simple state
of possession of much evidence, that confused conception of what the
"slice" of life must consist of, which forms the text of our remarks.
Mrs. Wharton, *her* conception of the "slice" so clarified and cultivated,
would herself of course form a text in quite another connection, as
Mr. Hewlett and Mr. Galsworthy would do each in his own, which
we abstain from specifying; but there are two or three grounds on
which the author of *Ethan Frome*, *The Valley of Decision* and *The House
of Mirth*, whom we brush by with reluctance, would point the moral
of the treasure of amusement sitting in the lap of method with a felicity
peculiarly her own. If one of these is that she too has clearly a saturation—which it would be ever so interesting to determine and appreciate
—we have it from her not in the crude state but in the extract, the
extract that makes all the difference for our sense of an artistic economy.
If the extract, as would appear, is the result of an artistic economy, as
the latter is its logical motive, so we find it associated in Mrs. Wharton
with such appeals to our interest, for instance, as the fact that, absolutely
sole among our students of this form, she suffers, she even encourages,
her expression to flower into some sharp image or figure of her thought
when that will make the thought more finely touch us. Her step,
without straying, encounters the living analogy, which she gathers,
in passing, without awkwardness of pause, and which the page then
carries on its breast as a trophy plucked by a happy adventurous dash,
a token of spirit and temper as well as a proof of vision. We note it as
one of the *kinds* of proof of vision that most fail us in that comparative
desert of the inselective where our imagination has itself to hunt out
or call down (often among strange witnessed flounderings or sand-
storms) such analogies as may mercifully "put" the thing. Mrs.
Wharton not only owes to her cultivated art of putting it the distinction
enjoyed when some ideal of expression has the *whole* of the case, the
case once made its concern, in charge, but might further act for us,

were we to follow up her exhibition, as lighting not a little that question
of "tone", the author's own intrinsic, as to which we have just seen
Mr. Conrad's late production rather tend to darken counsel. *The
Custom of the Country* is an eminent instance of the sort of tonic value
most opposed to that baffled relation between the subject-matter and
its emergence which we find constituted by the circumvallations of
Chance. Mrs. Wharton's reaction in presence of the aspects of life
hitherto, it would seem, mainly exposed to her is for the most part the
ironic—to which we gather that these particular aspects have so much
ministered that, were we to pursue the quest, we might recognize in
them precisely the saturation as to which we a moment ago reserved
our judgment. *The Custom of the Country* is at any rate consistently,
almost scientifically satiric, as indeed the satiric light was doubtless the
only one in which the elements engaged could at all be focussed together. But this happens directly to the profit of something that, as
we read, becomes more and more one with the principle of authority
at work; the light that gathers is a dry light, of great intensity, and the
effect, if not rather the very essence, of its dryness is a particular fine
asperity. The usual "creative" conditions and associations, as we have
elsewhere languished among them, are thanks to this ever so sensibly
altered; the general authoritative relation attested becomes clear—we
move in an air purged at a stroke of the old sentimental and romantic
values, the perversions with the maximum of waste of perversions,
and we shall not here attempt to state what this makes for in the way
of aesthetic refreshment and relief; the waste having kept us so dangling
on the dark aesthetic abyss. A shade of asperity may be in such fashion
a security against waste, and in the dearth of displayed securities we
should welcome it on that ground alone. It helps at any rate to constitute for the talent manifest in *The Custom* a rare identity, so far should
we have to go to seek another instance of the dry, or call it perhaps
even the hard, intellectual touch in the soft, or call it perhaps even the
humid, temperamental air; in other words of the masculine conclusion
tending so to crown the feminine observation.

If we mentioned Mr. Compton Mackenzie at the beginning of these
reflections only to leave him waiting for some further appreciation,
this is exactly because his case, to the most interesting effect, is no simple one, like two or three of our others, but on the contrary mystifying
enough almost to stand by itself. What would be this striking young
writer's state of acquaintance and possession, and should we find it,
on our recognition of it, to be all he is content to pitch forth, without

discriminations or determinants, without motives or lights? Do *Carnival* and *Sinister Street* proceed from the theory of the slice or from the conception of the extract, "the extract flasked and fine," the chemical process superceding the mechanical? Mr. Compton Mackenzie's literary aspect, though decidedly that of youth, or that of experience, a great deal of young experience, in its freshness, offers the attraction of a complexity defiant of the prompt conclusion, really charms us by giving us something to wonder about. We literally find it not easy to say if there may not lurk in *Carnival*, for example, a selective sense more apprehensible, to a push of inquiry, than its overflooded surface, a real invitation to wade and upon which everything within the author's ken appears poured out, would at first lead us to suspect. The question comes up in like fashion as to the distinctly more developed successor of that work, before which we in fact find questions multiply to a positive quickening of critical pleasure. We ask ourselves what *Sinister Street* may mean as a whole in spite of our sense of being brushed from the first by a hundred subordinate purposes, the succession and alternation of which seem to make after a fashion a plan, and which, though full of occasional design, yet fail to gather themselves for application or to converge to an idea. Any idea will serve, ever, that has held up its candle to composition—and it is perhaps because composition proposes itself under Mr. Compton Mackenzie's energy on a scale well-nigh of the most prodigious that we must wait to see whither it tends. The question of what he may here mean "on the whole," as we have just said, is doubtless admonished to stand back till we be possessed of the whole. The interesting volume is but a first, committed up to its eyes to continuity and with an announced sequel to follow. The recital exhibits at the point we have reached the intimate experience of a boy at school and in his holidays, the amplification of which is to come with his terms and their breaks at a university; and the record will probably form a more squared and extended picture of life equally conditioned by the extremity of youth than we shall know where else to look for. Youth clearly has been Mr. Mackenzie's saturation, as it has been Mr. Hugh Walpole's, but we see this not as a subject (youth in itself is no specific subject, any more than age is) but as matter for a subject and as requiring a motive to redeem it from the merely passive state of the slice. We are sure throughout both *Sinister Street* and *Carnival* of breathing the air of the extract, as we contentiously call it, only in certain of the rounded episodes strung on the loose cord as so many vivid beads, each of its chosen hue, and the series of which, even with differences of price between them, we take for a lively gage of performance to come. These episodes would be easy to cite; they are handsomely numerous and each strikes us as giving in its turn great salience to its motive; besides which each is in its turn "done" with an eminent sense and a remarkably straight hand for doing. They may well be cited together as both signally and finely symptomatic, for the literary gesture and the *bravura* breadth with which such frequent medallions as the adventure on the boy's part of the Catholic church at Bournemouth, as his experiment of the Benedictine house in Wiltshire, as his period of acquaintance with the aesthetic *cénacle* in London, as his relation with his chosen school friend under the intensity of boyish choosing, are ornamentally hung up, differ not so much in degree as in kind from any play of presentation that we mostly see elsewhere offered us. To which we might add other like matters that we lack space to enumerate, the scene, the aspect, the figure in motion tending always, under touches thick and strong, to emerge and flush, sound and strike, catch us in its truth. We have read "tales of school life" in which the boys more or less swarmed and sounded, but from which the masters have practically been quite absent, to the great weakening of any picture of the boyish consciousness, on which the magisterial fact is so heavily projected. If that is less true for some boys than for others, the "point" of Michael Fane is that for him it is truest. The types of masters have in *Sinister Street* both number and salience, rendered though they be mostly as grotesques—which effect we take as characterizing the particular turn of mind of the young observer and discoverer commemorated.

That he *is* a discoverer is of the essence of his interest, a successful and resourceful young discoverer, even as the poor ballet-girl in *Carnival* is a tragically baffled and helpless one; so that what each of the works proposes to itself is a recital of the things discovered. Those thus brought to our view in the boy's case are of much more interest, to our sense, than like matters in the other connection, thanks to his remarkable and living capacity; the heroine of *Carnival* is frankly too minute a vessel of experience for treatment on the scale on which the author has honoured her—she is done assuredly, but under multiplications of touch that become too much, in the narrow field, monotonies; and she leaves us asking almost as much what she exhibitionally means, what application resides in the accumulation of facts concerning her, as if she too were after all but a slice, or at the most but a slice *of* a slice, and her history but one of the aspects, on her author's part, of the condition of repleteness against the postulate of the entire adequacy of which we protest. So far as this record does affect us as an achieved "extract", to reiterate our term, that result abides in its not losing its centre, which is its fidelity to the one question of her dolefully embarrassed little measure of life. We know to that extent with some intensity what her producer would be at, yet an element of the arbitrary hangs for us about the particular illustration—illustrations leaving us ever but half appreciative till we catch that one bright light in which they give out all they contain. This light is of course always for the author to set somewhere. Is it set then so much as it should be in *Sinister Street*, and is our impression of the promise of this recital one with a dawning divination of the illustrative card that Mr. Mackenzie may still have up his sleeve and that our after sense shall recognize as the last thing left on the table? By no means, we can as yet easily say, for if a boy's experience has ever been given us for its face simply, for what it is worth in mere recovered intensity, it is so given us here. Of all the saturations it can in fact scarce have helped being the most sufficient in itself, for it is exactly, where it is best, from beginning to end the remembered and reported thing, that thing alone, that thing existent in the field of memory, though gaining value too from the applied intelligence, or in other words from the lively talent, of the memorizer. The memorizer helps, he contributes, he completes, and what we have admired in him is that in the case of each of the pearls fished up by his dive—though indeed these fruits of the rummage are not all pearls—his mind has had a further iridescence to confer. It is the fineness of the iridescence that on such an occasion matters, and this appeal to our interest is again and again on Mr. Compton Mackenzie's page of the happiest and the brightest. It is never more so than when we catch him, as we repeatedly do, in the act of positively caring for his expression as expression, positively providing for his phrase as a fondly foreseeing parent for a child, positively loving it in the light of what it may do for him—meeting revelations, that is, in what it may do, and appearing to recognize that the value of the offered thing, its whole relation to us, is created by the breath of language, that on such terms exclusively, for appropriation and enjoyment, we know it, and that any claimed independence of "form" on its part is the most abject of fallacies. Do these things mean that, moved by life, this interesting young novelist is even now uncontrollably on the way to style? We might cite had we space several symptoms, the very vividest, of that possibility; though such an appearance in the field of our general survey has against it presumptions enough to bring us surely back to our original contention—the scant degree in which that field has ever had to reckon with criticism.

INDEX

Numbers in italics refer to main articles on subject

343